PSYCHOLOGY

for AS Level

Mike Cardwell

Liz Clark

Claire Meldrum

COLLINS

Published by HarperCollins *Publishers* Limited
77–85 Fulham Palace Road
Hammersmith
London W6 8JB

www.**Collins**Education.com
On-line Support for Schools and Colleges

British Library Cataloguing in Publication Data
A catalogue record for this publication
is available from the British Library.

ISBN 000 322476 7

Commissioned by Emma Dunlop
Project managed by Hugh Hillyard-Parker
Edited by Rosamund Connelly, Carol Schaessens
Index compiled by Christine Boylan
Picture research and permissions by Rebecca Green
Illustrations by Vicky Squires, Squires Graphics, Cambridge
Typesetting by Hugh Hillyard-Parker
Text and cover design by Patricia Briggs
Cover artwork by Terry Bambrook
Printed and bound by Scotprint, Musselburgh

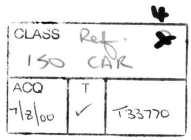
You might also like to visit:

www.**fire**and**water**.com
The book lover's website

Contents

Acknowledgements

Mike Cardwell would like to thank the three people who really matter – his wife, Denise, who makes him happy, and his children Chris and Alex, who continue to make him proud. Liz Clark would like to thank Charley for infinite support and patience that never cease to calm and restore balance when seemingly impossible deadlines loom. Also for the inspiration of a niece and nephew who are both considering psychology for their AS/A-level studies. Claire Meldrum would like to thank Stuart who, as always, showed tolerance and understanding of the obsessive preoccupation which seems to be the inevitable result of working on such a project. Thanks also go to colleagues and friends for their support and cheerful encouragement.

Our thanks also to the Collins staff, and particularly to Patricia Briggs for her helpful prompts and invaluable contributions, and to Pete Langley, who took over partway through the project. As cheerful but highly focused ringmaster, he has played a key role in bringing this book to completion and on schedule.

Last, but by no means least, we are, as ever, deeply indebted to Hugh Hillyard-Parker, who, along with Patricia, is responsible for the design of the book. He has remained serenely unflappable throughout, always offering constructive comments and soothing words whenever required.

Mike Cardwell, Liz Clark, Claire Meldrum
March 2000

Permissions

The Publisher, authors and editors would like to thank the organizations listed below for permission to reproduce material from their publications. Full bibliographic information for all sources is given in the 'References' section at the end of the book.

CHAPTER 1: HUMAN MEMORY
5   Fig. 1.1   Department of Psychology, Temple University, Philadelphia
6   Fig. 1.2   Academic Press Inc. (London) Ltd
7   In Focus   Department of Psychology, Temple University, Philadelphia
20   Activity 7   Academic Press Inc., Orlando
22   In Focus   Journal of Verbal Learning and Verbal Behaviour

CHAPTER 2: ATTACHMENTS IN DEVELOPMENT
35   Table 2.2   Child Development

CHAPTER 5: SOCIAL INFLUENCE
110   Fig. 5.1   Carnegie Press
121   Table 5.2   The American Psychological Association
126   Table 5.3   British Psychological Society

CHAPTER 6: QUANTITATIVE AND QUALITATIVE RESEARCH METHODS
138   Fig. 6.1   University of Nebraska Press
139   In Focus   American Psychological Association

CHAPTER 7: RESEARCH DESIGN AND IMPLEMENTATION, AND DATA ANALYSIS
155   Fig. 7.3   Holt, Rinehart & Winston
156   Fig. 7.4   Allyn & Bacon
157   Figs 7.5, 7.6 Blackwell Publishers
164   In Focus   Academic Press

CHAPTER 8: PREPARING FOR THE AS EXAMINATION
188ff. Sample   Assessment and Qualifications Alliance (AQA)
       questions

PHOTOGRAPHS
23   Getty Images
25   Rex Features Ltd (Mohammed Ali)
25   The Guardian/Garry Weaver (The Queen and Tony Blair)
51   Patacake Day Nursery, Cambridge
59   Andrew Brett Wallis/Telegraph Colour Library
67   Telegraph Colour Library
71   Bavaria-Bildagentur/Telegraph Colour Library (meditation photo)
71   Dennis Galante/Telegraph Colour Library (pills photo)
86   VCL/Spencer Powell/Telegraph Colour Library
99   Rex Features
110   Nils Jorgensen/Rex Features
119   Getty Images

Editor and author biographies

Mike Cardwell BSc, PGCE, MEd, is Senior Lecturer in Psychology at Bath Spa University College, where he teaches courses in social psychology, and Chief Examiner for the AQA (Specification A) AS- and A2-level psychology. Mike's other publications include *The Complete A–Z Psychology Handbook* (Hodder & Stoughton) and the *A-Level Revision Guide* (Longman). Mike is also an Editor of the journal *Psychology Review* and a regular contributor to student conferences. Although psychology takes up most of his time, he still avidly follows the fortunes of his home town football teams, Premier League Liverpool and Marine of the Unibond League.

Although a psychologist at heart and also by training, and someone who is passionate about education and good teaching, **Liz Clark** has worked in nurse education for the past 15 years. She is currently Head of Distance Learning at the Royal College of Nursing, where she is involved in developing and running a range of flexible-learning programmes. The experience of creating effective and highly accessible learning resources, that can be studied by distance-learning students with the minimum of teacher support, contributed to the original ideas and vision behind the first edition of this book. The publisher and editors believe that A-Level students deserve texts that intrigue, challenge and support, and above all that kindle their curiosity to find out more.

Claire Meldrum MA, MSc, PGCE, is a part time lecturer at City College, Norwich. She has nearly 20 years of psychology teaching experience on A-level, degree and 'Access to Higher Education' courses. She has also been an A level examiner for psychology, and is a member of the British Psychological Society, with particular interests in social and health psychology. Claire has published in the field of education, as well as having co-edited *Psychology for Nurses and Health Care Professionals* (1996). She has also contributed more recently to *Psychology and Social Care* (Messer & Jones 1999) and acts as consultant for the National Extension College. When time and weather allow, Claire enjoys gardening, the theatre and cinema.

Graham Davies, BA, MSc, PGCE, is a lecturer at Eastbourne College of Arts and Technology and from 1997–2000 was Principal Examiner for the AQA AS/A-level psychology module on Perspectives and Research Methods. He was previously the Principal Moderator for A-level psychology coursework and remains one of the team of Regional Coursework Advisers. He has written various journal articles and has been a speaker and workshop leader at a number of psychology conferences. He is an Honorary Life Member and former Chair of the Association for the Teaching of Psychology, for whom he edited the journal *Teaching Psychology* for some years. A keen mountain climber, he also thoroughly enjoys watching Wimbledon football club beat more fashionable opposition!

Cara Flanagan has published an array of A-level psychology books, such as the Letts *A-level Revision Guides*, as well as various teacher and student work packs, and articles for *Psychology Review*. Her most recent publications include *Early Socialisation* (1999), a book in the Routledge Modular Series of which she is an editor, and *Practicals for Psychology* (1998). Cara has recently been appointed Reviser for the new AS/A-level examinations, and is closely involved with the examining process. She also lectures part-time at Inverness College, living as she does in a remote part of the British Isles where she can see snow-covered mountains.

Simon Green, BSc, PhD, is Head of the School of Psychology at Birkbeck College, University of London. He was the Chief Examiner for AEB psychology between 1983 and 1986 and remains a Senior Examiner today. He is the author of *Principles of Biopsychology* and a contributor to several other psychology books. Simon has also written articles for a number of journals, including the *Psychology Review*. His main interest is finding better ways of managing stress.

Paul Humphreys is Senior Lecturer in Psychology at University College Worcester. His teaching and research interests include social relationships, sexualities, psychology and the media, and (ab)normality. He has been Chief Examiner for psychology at every pre-undergraduate level (O level 1983–88; AS level 1989–91; A level 1992–7) and is now Principal Examiner for the new A2 examination. Paul is the author of several books and in 1997 was conferred Honorary Life Membership of the Association for the Teaching of Psychology for his services to psychology.

Pamela Prentice BA, MEd, C.Psychol, AFBPsS, is Programme Manager for Humanities, including psychology, at Filton College, Bristol. She teaches A-level psychology and counselling up to HND level, and is an experienced AEB A-level examiner and OCN Moderator. She served five years on the committee for the ATP and two years on the BPS committee for the Division for

Teachers and Researchers in Psychology. Her background, prior to teaching, was as a Counselling Psychologist with the NHS. She has written a number of articles for *Psychology Review*. Pam's interests include Le Roc Jive dancing, bridge and general partying.

Jane Willson is Director of Studies for the A-level programme at City College, Norwich. She has many years' teaching experience in schools and FE and currently teaches psychology at A level and at degree level. She is a team leader for the AEB psychology A level and is a member of the ATP. She has written several other publications for A-level students and has also co-authored a book based on a research project about children's interaction with screen-based technology.

'Psychology, like all other sciences, can be misapplied. But, rightly used, psychology can make an immense contribution to human happiness.'

Rex and Margaret Knight (1959, p. 264)

In the four years since *Psychology for A Level* was first published, some major changes have occurred concerning the education of students over the age of 16 years. Among these changes are those related to the study of psychology beyond GCSE level. In September 2000, a new Advanced Subsidiary (AS level) psychology course will be introduced, with qualifications first awarded in August 2001. Students taking this course may use it (a) as a final qualification or (b) as 50 per cent of an Advanced Level qualification, which must be finished before an Advanced Level award can be made. The second part of the new Advanced Level award involves an A2 course of study. The first Advanced Level awards will be made in August 2002. More details about the AS specification (what used to be called a syllabus) are given later.

This book aims to provide a detailed coverage of all aspects of the new AS psychology course offered by the Assessment and Qualifications Alliance (AQA), Specification A.

The same editorial team who published *Psychology for A Level* (1996) has compiled this new textbook, *Psychology for AS Level*. According to its readers, one of the best features of *Psychology for A Level* was its accessibility, with material pitched at an appropriate level for students. We have maintained this reader-friendly approach in this new book. The contributing authors are all teachers and/or examiners of psychology, and consequently have a clear understanding of the needs of students. For most of you reading this book, psychology will be a completely new subject, and the terminology and issues may appear strange. In order to meet the needs of students taking this new examination, the book provides detailed descriptions and evaluations of the theories and research studies prescribed by the AS specification. Our aim is to make the study of psychology at AS level informative and fun, and to prepare you thoroughly for the examinations that you will take at the end of this part of your course.

Using the book

The book provides the usual features you would expect to find in any textbook. There is an **Index**, a comprehensive list of **References** and a **Glossary** that includes specification and examination terms. The additional features within each chapter that facilitate the use of the book and make it easier to relate to the requirements of the AQA specification include:

◆ A **Preview** at the start of each chapter and a **Chapter summary** at the end to enable you to check quickly the topics covered therein.

◆ **Activities**, within each chapter, designed to help you test your knowledge, apply psychological findings, carry out practical exercises and discuss ethical implications.

◆ **In Focus** boxes, used to highlight particularly important research studies or areas of special interest.

◆ **Diagrams**, **tables** and **pictures** to help make the psychological material even more accessible.

◆ A very special feature to be found at the end of each chapter is the **Exam summary** consisting of an exam-type question, carefully constructed to resemble the format and allocation of marks you will find in the examination itself. Furthermore, you will also find advice on how to answer the question, using the information in the chapter. These exam summaries have been written by the Chief Examiner.

◆ At the end of each chapter we have recommended **Further resources**. Where appropriate, website addresses, as well as book titles, have been given.

This book is designed specifically for the AQA, AS psychology course (Specification A) and therefore the contents of the book correspond very closely to the specification. Before you use this book as part of your study programme, it is worth spending some time looking at a detailed account of the specification and information about the examinations. These are provided by AQA (address given at end of this introduction). We shall provide only a brief outline here.

AQA (A) AS specification and examination

The AS-level specification is designed to be midway between the skills required for GCSE and the full A level (A2), and to take account of the target age (17+) of the majority of students who will be taking this exam. The AQA (A) AS-level course is organized into three modules, which mysteriously change their name to units when we deal with their assessment. Thus, you will be taught a *module* on Cognitive and Developmental Psychology, but examined on a *unit* of the same topics – simple really!

You will learn about the five core areas of psychology and about research methods. Each of these core areas is represented by a topic that will give you a good introduction to that area of psychology. The five core areas and their related topics are as follows:

◆ Cognitive Psychology – Human memory
◆ Developmental Psychology – Attachments
◆ Physiological Psychology – Stress
◆ Individual Differences – Abnormality
◆ Social Psychology – Social influence.

Each area also contains a 'critical issue', which represents either a key application of an area (e.g. eyewitness testimony in memory) or something that has special relevance to a particular topic area (e.g. ethical issues in social influence). The specific issues surrounding the assessment of these topics and critical issues are covered in Chapter 8, but it is worth emphasizing a few points here.

1 The five core areas above, together with Research Methods, are grouped together in three assessment units, each of which is worth one-third of the total marks:

Unit 1 – Cognitive and Developmental Psychology
Unit 2 – Physiological Psychology and Individual Differences
Unit 3 – Social Psychology and Research Methods.

2 All areas of this specification are compulsory – therefore, you must cover everything in this book. The specification entries are very carefully worded and questions will tend to reflect that wording. We have endeavoured to use the same wording as the specification, wherever possible, to make it easier for you to track your route through each topic. It is worth remembering that when questions are set, the question-setter will attempt to sample (eventually) all areas of the specification. Therefore, it is unwise to leave out any areas, even small ones, simply because they do not appeal to you.

3 There is some choice of questions in the examination, but there will not necessarily be a question on everything that appears in the AQA specification. There will, of course, be two questions on every area (i.e. Cognitive, Developmental, Physiological, etc.), so a good proportion of the specification will be covered in every examination.

4 The examination will test your knowledge and understanding (known as 'Assessment Objective 1' or simply AO1), and your analysis and evaluation (known as AO2) skills, together with your ability to design, conduct and report (in the Research Methods section, and known as AO3). In all but the Research Methods questions, you will find that AO1 questions are worth more (in terms of the total of marks available) than AO2 questions. As we stress in Chapter 8, AO2 questions are really quite different from AO1 questions and require you to engage with the subject material in the topic areas. We have attempted to show you how you might address each of these skills in the Exam summaries at the end of each chapter. Although these Exam summaries are comprehensive accounts of what is required in each area, they should not take the place of the subject specification that is published by AQA.

5 Several entries on the AQA specification are preceded by the words 'including' or 'e.g.'. Although the word 'including' indicates prescribed material on which questions may be asked, the use of 'e.g.' is merely illustrative of appropriate subject material. We have covered all prescribed material in this book, and have endeavoured, wherever appropriate, to cover all the examples mentioned in the specification as well.

Part of the joy of studying psychology is the thrill of finding out more about a particular topic. This book provides you with a comprehensive account of everything you need to succeed in the AS examination. However, you will find the further reading and websites at the end of every chapter a particularly valuable way of extending your own understanding of psychology and, specifically, the subject content of the AQA specification. Do, please, let us know, care of the Publisher, what you think of the book. Feedback from readers is enormously helpful and we shall pay close attention to it when we come to write the second edition of *Psychology for AS Level*.

Mike Cardwell, Liz Clark, Claire Meldrum

For details about specifications or any other documents concerning AS- or A-level psychology, contact: AQA Publications Department, Stag Hill House, Guildford, Surrey GU2 5XJ

Chapter 1

Human memory

Jane Willson

Preview

In this chapter we shall be looking at:

- short-term and long-term memory, including research into the nature and structure of memory, and models of memory

- explanations of forgetting in both short- and long-term memory, and research into the role of emotional factors

- memory research into eyewitness testimony, including reconstructive memory and face recognition.

Introduction

Philosophers have been interested in memory for over 2,000 years, but it is only in the last 50 years that psychologists have made a systematic study of the topic. Memory is studied within the branch of psychology known as *cognitive psychology*. This is a research field which focuses on the mental processes humans use to acquire, store, retrieve and use their knowledge about the world. Cognitive psychologists have investigated a wide range of topics including perception, attention, imagery, language, problem-solving, reasoning and decision-making. In this chapter, we are going to look at *memory*, which is central to *all* cognitive processes because we use it whenever we need to maintain information over time.

Imagine waking up one morning to find that you had completely lost your memory. You would not be able to remember your name, age or where you lived. You would not recognize friends and family, and you would not be able to understand programmes on the television or articles in the newspaper. You would not know what your plans for the day were and you would not be able to recall what you were thinking about just moments ago. You would, in fact, be virtually helpless without your memory. Psychologists have learned a great deal from the study of people who suffer from loss of memory (amnesia) after brain damage (see *In Focus,* 'The case of Clive Wearing', for a particularly profound case of amnesia).

Clive's case demonstrates that memory is crucial to our wellbeing and everyday functioning. It also demonstrates the enormous complexity of human memory. The fact that Clive continues to be able to talk, walk, play music, read and write in spite of huge impairments in his memory for personal history and general knowledge suggests that memory is not a unitary system. The case also raises a number of questions for cognitive psychologists. Why is it, for example, that Clive cannot recall a visit from his wife just two minutes later? It is possible that her visit never actually registers in his brain and so no memory trace is laid down. Another possibility is that the memory trace is laid down, but that it fades away very quickly. The third possibility is that the memory trace is laid down, but cannot be retrieved. The answer is not clear, but it is important to recognize that a normally functioning memory system must be capable of:

- registering information
- storing information over time
- retrieving information when required.

In the first section of this chapter we will be looking at these processes and also discussing some of the important theoretical explanations or *models* of memory.

Given the huge number of items that we put into our memories over the years, we are remarkably good at remembering things. However, as we know from experience, our memories can sometimes let us down. Cognitive psychologists have been interested in the mechanisms involved in *forgetting* and, in the second section, we shall be looking at the reasons why people sometimes fail to retrieve information.

Neisser (1976) has criticized much of the research on the psychology of memory, saying that it is overly theoretical and has little application in the real world. Partly in response to such criticisms, researchers are increasingly investigating practical aspects of memory. In the final section of this chapter, we will look at one such practical application, namely research into *eyewitness testimony* and into the related field of *memory for faces (face recognition).*

The case of Clive Wearing (based on Baddeley 1997)

Clive Wearing was a highly educated, talented musician and broadcaster who contracted a viral infection called encephalitis in 1985. Tragically, this disease left him with extensive brain damage, which has caused major memory disruption. He is still able to talk, read and write and has retained remarkably intact musical skills. He can still sight-read music and is able to play quite complex pieces on the piano and harpsichord. In all other respects, however, his memory is dramatically impaired.

His memory for past events in his life is hazy although he can recall certain key highlights with prompting. His visual memory is impaired and he is unable to recognize pictures of his old Cambridge college where he had spent four years of his life and which he had visited many times in subsequent years. He has identified the Queen and the Duke of Edinburgh in a photograph as people who had once sung in one of his choirs. His general knowledge is also reduced and he has no idea who wrote the play *Romeo and Juliet*. Nor can he recall anything about the composer Lassus, in spite of having written a book about him.

Even more disturbing is his apparent inability to lay down new memories. Clive is convinced that he has only just woken up and he keeps a diary in which he records this obsessive thought. There are pages of closely written text in which he gives the date and time followed by the statement: 'I have just regained consciousness.' or 'I'm conscious for the first time.' Whenever his wife visits, he greets her effusively as if he has not seen her for ages. If she leaves the room for a couple of minutes, the emotional greeting is repeated and this can happen time and time again.

It is now 15 years since the onset of the illness which caused Clive's memory loss and he is still trapped in an eternal present – he cannot use the past to anticipate the future. He is unable to enjoy books or television because he cannot follow the thread and he does not read newspapers because he has no context within which to embed the news stories. He cannot go out alone because he immediately becomes lost and he is unable to tell anyone who finds him where he is going or where he has come from. Clive himself has described his situation as 'Hell on earth. It's like being dead.'

Research into the nature and structure of memory

Several theories of memory are based on the assumption that there are three kinds of memory:

◆ sensory memory
◆ short-term memory
◆ long-term memory.

We shall consider each of these components in turn, but you should note that this distinction is no longer universally accepted by memory researchers. It is most associated with structural models such as the one proposed by Atkinson and Shiffrin (1968) which will be discussed on p. 6.

Sensory memory

Sensory memory is a storage system that holds information in a relatively unprocessed form for fractions of a second after the physical stimulus is no longer available. It has been suggested (e.g. Baddeley 1988) that one function of this kind of storage is to allow information from successive eye-fixations to last

for a long enough time to be integrated and so to give continuity to our visual environment. For example, if you move a lighted sparkler rapidly round in a sweeping arc, you will 'see' a circle of sparkling light. This is because the trace from the point of the sparkler is momentarily left behind. However, if you move the sparkler slowly, only a partial circle will be seen because the first part of the circumference will have faded by the time the sparkler gets back to its starting point. Similarly, if you watch a film, your conscious experience is of a continuous visual scene in which all of the action appears to be moving smoothly. In fact, the film is actually being presented as a rapid series of frozen images interspersed by fleeting moments of darkness. In order to make sense of it, your sensory store has to hold the information from one frame of film until the next is presented. These everyday examples seem to suggest that we are capable of storing visual images for very brief periods. It is assumed that we have separate sensory stores for all the senses, but it is the visual sensory store (*iconic memory*) which has attracted most research.

Sperling (1960) conducted a series of experiments in which he showed participants three rows of four letters for 50 milliseconds. He used a special viewing apparatus called a tachistoscope, but you can reproduce his study in a less sophisticated fashion in Activity 1.

Activity 1: Testing your visual store

Read all the instructions carefully before doing this test.

First cover up the grid of letters so that you cannot see them.

Sit in a darkened room with just a desk lamp for illumination. Once you have read these instructions, turn off the desk lamp and remove the cover from the grid. Turn the light on and, then, immediately off again. Try to recall as many letters from the grid as possible.

X	H	S	M
L	V	G	W
R	K	C	B

If you are typical of Sperling's participants, you will have recalled about four or five letters from the display. However, Sperling's participants reported the feeling that they had seen more than four or five letters, but were simply unable to recall any more. Sperling changed his experimental technique so that participants were asked only to recall one line of the display. The required line was cued by a tone, i.e. if participants heard a high-pitched tone, they were to recall the top line; a medium-pitched tone, the middle line; and a low-pitched tone, the bottom line. Under these circumstances, participants were able to recall approximately three out of the four letters. Since participants did not know in advance which line they would be required to recall, Sperling assumed that, for a fraction of a second, people had actually registered nine to ten items in the display, but that these faded from memory very quickly. Sperling's results have subsequently been confirmed in a number of similar studies (e.g. Cowan 1995), and the idea of a temporary visual store with a duration of approximately 200 to 400 milliseconds is widely accepted. The auditory store (*echoic memory*) has also been investigated (e.g. Darwin *et al.* 1972) and this appears to have a longer duration of two to three seconds. Sensory memory seems to play an important part in the memory system, but it is investigated in more depth by researchers in the field of *perception*. Memory researchers have focused their interest more on short- and long-term memory.

Short-term memory

Short-term memory (STM) is a system for storing information for brief periods of time. Some researchers (e.g. Atkinson and Shiffrin 1968) see STM simply as a temporary storage depot for incoming information, whereas others (e.g. Baddeley 1986, 1990; Gathercole 1992) prefer to use the term 'working memory' to indicate its dynamic, flexible aspects. We shall return to this difference of opinion when we consider various models of memory on p. 6. For the moment, we will look at specific topics related to the nature of STM:

◆ capacity

◆ duration

◆ encoding.

The capacity of short-term memory

Try Activity 2 before reading any further.

Activity 2: STM capacity

Try to work out the following problems using mental arithmetic. Do not write anything down.

(a) 5 x 7 =

(b) 53 x 7 =

(c) 53 x 78 =

You probably found problem (a) extremely easy, and problem (b) difficult, but possible. Problem (c), however, posed much more of a challenge because it stretched the limits of your STM by requiring you to carry too much information at once. It can feel quite frustrating as you struggle to hold on to relevant bits of information while manipulating others. This kind of exercise indicates that STM has a limited capacity, i.e. we can only hold a small number of items at any one time. One way of assessing STM capacity is by measuring *immediate digit span*. This technique usually involves reading out a list of random digits and requiring the participant to repeat them back in the correct order. The sequences usually begin with about three digits and steadily increase in length until it becomes impossible to recall them in serial order. Over a number of trials, the sequence length at which the participant is correct 50 per cent of the time is defined as their digit span. Most people have a digit span of 'seven, plus or minus two' (Miller 1956). Miller claimed that this finding holds good for lists of digits, letters, words or larger 'chunks' of information. According to Miller, *chunking* occurs when we combine individual letters or numbers into a larger meaningful unit.

For example, the digits 9 3 7 1 would represent four separate items to most people, but would form a chunk for you if they happened to be your bank PIN number.

There are some difficulties in using immediate digit span as a measure of STM capacity. One problem is that it is difficult to exclude the influence of long-term memory. For example, Bower and Winzenz (1969) found that digit strings that are repeated within a series of immediate-memory-span trials become progressively easier for participants to recall. This indicates that they are being stored in long-term memory. Another problem is that capacity seems to be influenced by various factors. For example, if participants read the digits *aloud* before attempting to recall them, performance is better than when they simply read them subvocally to themselves. Performance also improves if the numbers are grouped together rhythmically. Wickelgren (1964) found that grouping the items in sets of three is the most likely to improve digit span. This is probably why we tend to divide up telephone numbers into rhythmic groups rather than reciting the whole string of numbers in a monotone.

Some more recent researchers have found that *pronunciation time* may be a more important indicator of STM capacity than digit span. Schweikert and Boruff (1986) tested immediate span for a number of different types of stimulus, e.g. letters, colours, shapes and nonsense words. They found that people consistently remembered as many items as they were able to pronounce in approximately 1.5 seconds. Baddeley *et al.* (1975) found that participants, in a serial recall test, could remember more one-syllable words than five-syllable words. They concluded that long words were harder to recall because participants said the words to themselves under their breath and longer words take longer to articulate. Naveh-Benjamin and Ayres (1986) have tested immediate memory span for speakers of various world languages. They found, for example, that the digit span for native English speakers is considerably greater than for Arabic speakers. The only explanation for this finding is that Arabic numbers have more syllables and take longer to pronounce than English numbers.

Duration of short-term memory

However capacity is measured, it seems clear that STM is only able to hold a few items at any one time. It is also the case that, by its very nature, STM has a brief duration. The first attempts to measure the duration of STM were made independently by Brown (1958) and Peterson and Peterson (1959). They used a similar experimental method, which is now known as the Brown–Peterson technique. The technique involves presenting participants with consonant trigrams, which are sets of three unrelated consonants, e.g. CPW, NGV.

Note that such a sequence should be well within the normal memory span. Participants are then asked to count backwards in threes from a specified number in order to stop them thinking about the letters. After an interval ranging from between 3 and 18 seconds, the participants are asked to recall the original trigram. This procedure is then repeated several times. Typical results of Brown–Peterson experiments show rapid forgetting over a short interval and, after 18 seconds, the percentage of correctly recalled trigrams falls to 10 per cent. Sebrechts *et al.* (1989) briefly presented participants with lists of three common English nouns and then gave them an unexpected, serial recall test. Correct recall of the items fell to 1 per cent after only four seconds. Studies such as these demonstrate that information can vanish from STM in a matter of a few seconds if rehearsal is prevented, or if people are not making a conscious effort to retain it.

Encoding in short-term memory

A further question about the nature of STM concerns coding. When information arrives at the sensory registration stage, it is still in its raw form or original *modality*. For example, information presented visually is still in the visual modality. Psychologists have been interested in the question of what happens to such information when it reaches the STM. Does it stay in its original modality or is it recoded in some way? There are various ways in which we can encode stimulus inputs. Imagine looking at the word 'glove'. This could be stored as a *visual representation* so that you form a visual image of either the printed word itself or a pictorial image of an actual glove. You could form an *acoustic representation* by saying the written word aloud or under your breath – this has the effect of converting the written word into a verbal or speech code. Alternatively, you could form a *semantic representation*, which depends on your knowledge about the meaning of the word. You might, for example, think about the circumstances under which you need to wear gloves or about particular pairs of gloves that you have worn in the past.

It is not possible simply to ask people what codes they are using because memory processes are often unconscious. Much of the evidence about coding comes from studies into so-called *substitution errors*. These occur when people confuse one item for another. If, for example, they confuse letters, which *sound* alike, it indicates that acoustic coding is being used. If, however, letters that *look* similar are confused, it indicates that visual coding is being used. Conrad (1964) showed participants random sequences of six letters taken from the consonants B, C, F, M, N, P, S, T, V, and X. Six letters were shown in rapid succession on a screen and participants were required to write them down as they appeared. The rate of presentation was too fast for the participants to keep up so they had to rely on memory. Conrad carefully noted the errors and found that the significant majority involved the substitution of a similar sounding letter (e.g. 'B' for 'V' and 'S' for 'X'). In a similar study, Conrad demonstrated that participants found it more difficult to recall strings of acoustically similar letters (e.g. P, C, V, T, G, B, D) than strings of acoustically dissimilar letters (e.g. L, Z, K, F, X, H, W) even though they were presented visually. He concluded that such acoustic confusion provided evidence for acoustic coding in STM. Baddeley (1986) explored the effects of acoustic similarity using words rather than letters. He presented participants with sequences of five short words taken from a pool of words, which were acoustically similar (man, mad, mat, map, can, cat, cap). He compared their serial recall performance with that on sequences of short, acoustically dissimilar words (pen, day, few, sup, cow, pit, bar, hot) and sequences of short, semantically similar words (big, large, wide, high, great, tall, long, broad). Like Conrad, Baddeley found that words with similar sounds were much harder to recall than words that did not sound alike. Similarity of meaning had only a very slight detrimental effect on performance. Baddeley concluded that STM relies heavily on acoustic coding. Interestingly, he found that the effects of sound similarity disappeared when he tested participants' long-term memory. He extended the length of the word lists from five to ten and prevented participants from repeating the words by interrupting them after each presentation. The lists were presented four times and recall was tested after 20 minutes. Under these conditions, participants found recall of the semantically similar words much more difficult than recall of the acoustically similar words. Baddeley concluded that long-term memory makes use of semantic rather than acoustic coding.

It seems likely that acoustic coding is the preferred method of encoding in STM, but there are several studies which show that other modes of representation are also possible. An interesting study by Brandimonte *et al.* (1992) demonstrates not only that visual coding can be used in STM, but that, under certain circumstances, it is a superior method. They showed participants six line drawings of familiar objects like the ones shown in Fig. 1.1.

Once the participants had memorized the pictures, they were asked to form an image of each one in turn and to subtract a specified part of the drawing. They were then asked to name the resulting image, e.g. picture (a) is a wrapped sweet, but it becomes a fish when the right hand 'fin' is removed. Participants were able to name on average 2.7 of the six items. Another group of participants was given the same tasks to do except that they were prevented from articulating during the learning stage. While they were being shown the original pictures, they were asked to repeat the meaningless chant 'la-la-la-...'. This prevented them from converting the pictorial image into a verbal code as they would have done under normal circumstances. They were more successful when it came to identifying the subtracted image and were able to name 3.8 items correctly. This suggests that they were using visual coding and, therefore, found it easier to subtract a part from the visual image than the first set of participants who had coded the original stimulus in verbal form. There is also some evidence that items in STM can be coded in terms of their meaning, so it seems reasonable to conclude that acoustic coding is generally the preferred, rather than the exclusive, method of representation.

Long-term memory

Long-term memory (LTM) holds a vast quantity of information which can be stored for long periods of time. The information kept here is diverse and wide-ranging and includes all of our personal memories, our general knowledge and our beliefs about the world.

Figure 1.1
Stimuli used in the study by Brandimonte *et al.* (1992)

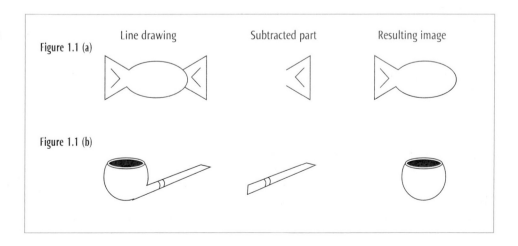

	Line drawing	Subtracted part	Resulting image
Figure 1.1 (a)			
Figure 1.1 (b)			

It also includes plans for the future and is the depository for all our knowledge about skills and expertise. LTM is not a passive store of information, but a dynamic system which constantly revises and modifies stored knowledge in the light of new information. LTM is a much larger, more complex memory system than STM and it is not so easy to characterize in terms of factors like capacity, duration and simple encoding:

◆ It is not possible to quantify the exact *capacity* of LTM, but most psychologists would agree that there is no upper limit – we are always capable of more learning.

◆ Similarly, the *duration* of the memory trace in LTM is considerably longer than in STM and can last anything from a few minutes to a lifetime.

◆ As far as *encoding* is concerned, there is some evidence (see, for example, Baddeley 1986, on p. 5) that the meaning of the stimulus is often the factor here, in other words, semantic coding is important. However, it is clear from our own experience that material can be represented in other ways as well. Our ability to recognize sounds such as police sirens and telephones ringing shows that we can store material in an acoustic form. We can also easily bring to mind pictorial images of people or places, which suggests some visual coding in LTM.

The huge capacity of LTM requires a highly organized structure, otherwise items would be difficult to retrieve. Research suggests that we often use semantic categories to help us organize material in our long-term memories and that visual imagery provides another method. You can find information on *organization* in LTM in the books recommended at the end of the chapter.

Models of memory

The multistore model of memory

A number of memory theorists have proposed that the memory system is divided into three stores, as outlined in the previous section. A typical theory of this type was proposed by Atkinson and Shiffrin (1968) and, because it quickly became the standard explanation of the memory system, it is often called the *modal model*. In this theory, they attempt to encompass all of memory and, in particular, focus on the distinction between short- and long-term memory. Their model arose from the *information-processing approach* which, in turn, derives from communication and computer science. According to this approach, memory is characterized as a flow of information through a system. The system is divided into a set of stages and information passes through each stage in a fixed sequence. There are capacity and duration limitations at each stage and transfer between stages may require recoding. Models based on information processing are represented in the form of flow charts like the one illustrated in Fig. 1.2.

Atkinson and Shiffrin proposed that external stimuli from the environment first enter sensory memory, where they can be registered for very brief periods of time before decaying or being passed on to the short-term store. STM contains only the small amount of information that is actually in active use at any one time. Verbal information is encoded at this stage in terms of its sounds. Atkinson and Shiffrin believed that memory traces in STM are fragile and can be lost within about 30 seconds unless they are repeated (rehearsed). Material that is rehearsed is passed on to the long-term store where it can remain for a lifetime, although loss is possible from this store through decay or interference.

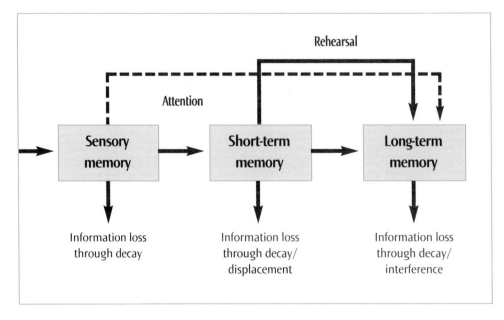

Figure 1.2
Summary of the Atkinson and Shiffrin (1968) modal model of memory

Coding in LTM is assumed to be in terms of meaning, i.e. semantic. In addition to describing the *structural features* of the memory system, Atkinson and Shiffrin also proposed various *control processes*, which are strategies used by individuals to manipulate the information flowing through the system. One of the most important of these is rehearsal, which allows information to be recycled within STM and passed on into LTM.

Evaluation of the multistore model

A crucial aspect of the multistore model is that there are distinct short-term and long-term stores. We have already looked at some of the experimental evidence which suggests that LTM and STM operate differently in terms of capacity and duration. There are several other studies which support the idea of two separate stores. See *In Focus* for a study which supported the idea of differential coding in the two stores.

Other evidence in support of the distinction between STM and LTM comes from case studies of people with brain damage which gives rise to memory impairment. Milner (1966) reported on a young man, referred to as HM, who was left with severe memory impairment after brain surgery. He was able to talk normally and to recall accurately events and people from his life before surgery, and his immediate digit span was within normal limits. He was, however, unable to retain any new information and could not lay down new memories in LTM. When told of the death of his favourite uncle, he reacted with considerable distress. Later, he frequently asked about his uncle and, on each occasion, reacted again with the level of grief appropriate to hearing the news for the first time. KF, a motorcycle accident victim investigated by Shallice and Warrington (1970), suffered from the reverse of this memory impairment. He had no difficulty in transferring new items into LTM but had a grossly impaired digit span. Cases such as these and that of Clive Wearing (see *In Focus* on p. 2) lend support to the Atkinson and Shiffrin model, in that they seem to point to a clear distinction between LTM and STM.

There does seem to be fairly strong support for a difference between LTM and STM in terms of duration, capacity, effects of brain damage and forgetting

---

in focus

Kintsch and Buschke (1969) on differential coding

Kintsch and Buschke (1969) presented participants with printed lists of 16 English words. One list comprised eight sets of synonyms, i.e. words which have a similar meaning, e.g. sad and unhappy. The other list comprised eight sets of homophones (or homonyms), i.e. words which sound the same but have different meanings, e.g. tax and tacks. Examples of two lists similar to those used by Kintsch and Buschke are shown in the box on the right.

After presentation of the first list, participants were given a probe word and asked to recall the word that came after this on the original list. For example, 'rug' would require the response 'mad'. Kintsch and Buschke argued that semantic confusion might occur between 'rug' and 'carpet' and so elicit the wrong response of 'warm'. They carefully noted the number of semantic confusions that occurred and found that words at the beginning of the list caused more semantic confusions than words at the end of the list. They concluded that words at the beginning of the list had been sufficiently rehearsed to pass into LTM and that these caused confusion because LTM codes semantically. Words at the end of the list were still circulating in STM where coding is acoustic and so no semantic confusion arose. These findings were confirmed when the test was repeated for List 2, i.e. the words which sound the same. Here, the pattern of errors was reversed – acoustic confusion occurred more at the end of the list than at the beginning. This suggests that items at the end of the list, which are still in STM, are coded in terms of their sound.

List 1 (synonyms)	List 2 (homophones)
angry	tacks
pleased	so
forest	buy
hot	owe
sofa	tied
ocean	flower
beautiful	fare
woods	sew
carpet	their
warm	tax
sea	flour
happy	by
rug	there
mad	oh
couch	tide
pretty	fair

mechanisms (see section on forgetting on p. 11). However, there are problems with the model of Atkinson and Shiffrin. The model is too simple and inflexible and fails to take account of factors such as the strategies people employ to remember things. It also places emphasis on the *amount* of information that can be processed rather than its nature. Some things are simply easier to remember than others, perhaps because they are more interesting, more distinctive, funnier, or whatever. The multistore model cannot account for this. It is also criticized for focusing on the structure of the memory system at the expense of adequately explaining the processes involved. For example, visual stimuli registering in sensory memory are thought to be changed to an acoustic code for access to STM. In order to translate the pattern of the letter 'M' into the sound 'em', the individual needs to access knowledge about letter shapes and sounds which is stored in LTM. This means that information from LTM must flow backwards through the system to the recoding stage prior to STM. This suggests that the flow of information through the system is interactive rather than strictly sequential as Atkinson and Shiffrin suggested. Their suggestion that rote rehearsal is the only means of transfer from STM into LTM has also been criticized. This criticism will be considered in more detail in the discussion of alternative models of memory, such as the levels of processing approach on p. 10. Similarly, another model – the working memory model of Baddeley and Hitch (1974) – casts doubt on the assumption of Atkinson and Shiffrin that STM is a unitary store with a severely limited capacity.

The working memory model

One of the criticisms of the multistore model is that it is too simplistic and assumes that STM and LTM act as unitary stores. It seems much more likely that both memory systems are divided into separate components which have different functions. The first people to explore the notion of a multicomponent, short-term store were Baddeley and Hitch (1974). They conducted a study in which participants were given digit strings to rehearse while, at the same time, carrying out verbal reasoning tasks similar to those in Activity 3. Try Activity 3 before reading any further.

Imagine trying to do these reasoning tasks and simultaneously rehearsing a string of digits – you probably think that this would be very difficult, if not impossible. Baddeley and Hitch reported that their participants were rather alarmed at the prospect of trying to do both tasks at once. In order not to overload the participants, the investigators first gave only two digits to recall. However, they found no detrimental effects on performance at either task and so increased the number of digits to six. Even with six digits to recall

Activity 3: Verbal reasoning task
Read the following set of statements and then decide for each one, as quickly and accurately as you can, whether it is true or false.

1	B is followed by A	BA
2	A does not follow B	BA
3	A is not preceded by B	BA
4	A is not followed by B	BA
5	B follows A	AB
6	B is preceded by A	BA
7	A does not precede B	BA
8	B is not preceded by A	BA
9	B is followed by A	AB
10	A follows B	AB

(and note that this is very close to normal digit span), there was no effect on *accuracy* of performance on the two tasks, although there was a very slight slowing on the reasoning task. This finding is not compatible with the Atkinson and Shiffrin view of a unitary short-term store. Instead, it suggests that STM, or *working memory* as Baddeley and Hitch prefer to call it, consists of several different components which can work independently of one another.

Baddeley and Hitch concluded on the basis of this and other studies, that STM is a flexible and complex system which consists of a central control mechanism assisted by a number of *slave systems*. The model has been modified slightly in the light of experimental studies (e.g. Baddeley 1986) and is shown in simple form in Fig. 1.3.

The *central executive* is the most important component in the model and is responsible for monitoring and coordinating the operation of the slave systems. It is flexible in that it can process information from any modality and also has some storage capacity, although this is very limited. It seems to play a major role in attention, planning and in synthesizing information, not only from the slave systems but also from LTM.

The *phonological loop* stores a limited number of sounds for brief periods and can be thought of as an inner ear. It is now thought to be made up of two components (Gathercole and Baddeley 1993). One component is the phonological store, which allows acoustically coded items to be stored for a brief period. The other component is the *articulatory control system*, which allows subvocal repetition of the items stored in the phonological store.

The *visuo-spatial scratch pad* stores visual and spatial information and can be thought of as an inner eye. Like the phonological loop, it has limited capacity, but the limits of the two systems are independent. In

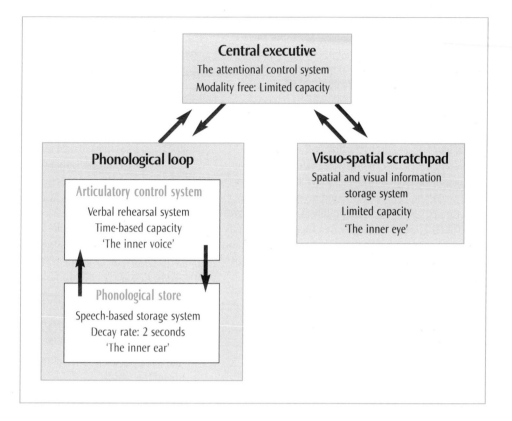

Figure 1.3
The working
memory model
Source: Cohen
et al. (1993)

other words, it is possible, for example, to rehearse a set of digits in the phonological loop while simultaneously making decisions about the spatial layout of a set of letters in the visuo-spatial scratchpad. A good example of the operation of working memory is given in Activity 4.

Evaluation of the working memory model

The working memory model appears to have a number of advantages over the simplistic formulation of the Atkinson and Shiffrin concept of STM. It effectively accounts for our ability to store information briefly, while, at the same time, actively processing the material. There is a considerable body of empirical research which seems to support the existence of the two slave systems. For example, Baddeley *et al.* (1975) conducted a series of studies which investigated the word-length effect. They found that memory span for visually presented one-syllable words was significantly greater than for polysyllabic words. This suggested that the phonological loop was only able to hold a limited number of syllables. However, subsequent studies demonstrated that articulation time, rather than number of syllables, was the limiting factor. They compared span performance on two-syllable words such as 'cricket' and 'bishop', which are spoken quickly, with performance on two-syllable words such as 'harpoon' and 'Friday', which take longer to say. Recall was consistently better for the words which can be articulated more quickly. If participants are prevented from rehearsing the words subvocally by

Activity 4: Operating your working memory

Baddeley (1997) has suggested that you can get a good feel for the operation of working memory by the following task. Try to work out how many windows there are in your home.

If you are like most people, you will have formed a mental image of your home and counted the windows either by imagining the outside of the house or by walking through the house room by room. The image will be set up and manipulated in your visuo-spatial scratch pad and the tally of windows will be held in the phonological loop as you count them subvocally. The whole operation will be supervised by the central executive, which will allocate the tasks and recognize when the final total has been reached.

having to repeat an irrelevant sound such as 'la-la-la...' (articulatory suppression), the word-length effect disappears. It is assumed that the articulatory suppression task fills the phonological loop and, therefore, takes away the advantage of rehearsal. Based on the results of these studies, Baddeley and colleagues concluded that memory span is dependent on time rather than the number of items, and that people can remember as much as they are able to say in approximately 1.5 seconds.

The visuo-spatial store has not been investigated in the same depth as the phonological store, but there is experimental evidence which supports its existence. For example, Baddeley *et al.* (1973) gave participants a simple tracking task which involved holding a pointer in contact with a moving spot of light. At the same time, participants were asked to perform an imagery task. Participants were required to imagine the block capital letter 'F' and then, starting at the bottom left-hand corner, were to classify each angle as a 'yes' if it included the bottom or top line of the letter and as a 'no' if it did not. Participants found it very difficult to track the spot of light and accurately classify the angles in the letter imagery task. However, they were perfectly capable of carrying out the tracking task in conjunction with a verbal task. This suggests that the tracking and letter imagery tasks were competing for the limited resources of the visuo-spatial scratchpad, whereas the tracking task and the verbal task were making use of the separate components of the visuo-spatial scratchpad and the phonological loop respectively.

This model has proved influential and is still being developed and expanded. The main weakness, however, is that the component we know least about (the central executive) is the most important. It has a limited capacity, but no one has been able to quantify it experimentally. Richardson (1984) argues that there are problems in specifying the precise functioning of the central executive. He believes that the terminology is vague and can be used to explain any kind of results. In other words, it can give rise to a circular argument, i.e. if we give participants an articulatory suppression task and this affects performance, we assume the phonological loop is normally utilized in the task, but if performance is not affected, we assume the central executive is normally utilized in the task. Hence, it is difficult to falsify the model.

Levels of processing

The working memory model has been much more effective than the multistore model in explaining the active nature of short-term memory processing. It allows for different types of processing depending on the nature of incoming information, but it does not consider the effects of differential processing on long-term retention of information. An important approach which looked specifically at this aspect was put forward by Craik and Lockhart (1972). They rejected the idea of separate memory structures put forward by Atkinson and Shiffrin and believed, instead, that stimulus inputs go through a variety of *processing operations*. According to them, processing varies in terms of depth, 'Trace persistence is a function of depth of analysis, with deeper levels of analysis associated with more elaborate, longer lasting, and stronger traces' (p. 675). The first

stages of processing are shallow and involve recognizing the stimulus in terms of its physical appearance, e.g. the shape of the letters a word is written in. The deepest level of processing involves coding the input in terms of its meaning. Rehearsing material simply by rote repetition, as in the Atkinson and Shiffrin model, is called *maintenance rehearsal* and is regarded as shallow processing. It is distinguished from *elaborative rehearsal* in which links are made to semantic associations. The assumption of the model is that *shallow processing* will give rise to weak, short-term retention, whereas *deep processing* will ensure strong, lasting retention.

This central assumption has been tested in numerous studies. For example, Hyde and Jenkins (1973) presented auditorily lists of 24 words and asked different groups of participants to perform one of the following so-called orienting tasks:

◆ rating the words for pleasantness

◆ estimating the frequency with which each word is used in the English language

◆ detecting the occurrence of the letters 'e' and 'g' in any of the words

◆ deciding the part of speech appropriate to each word (e.g. noun, adjective)

◆ deciding whether the words fitted into a particular sentence frame.

Half the participants were told in advance that they would be expected to recall the words (*intentional* learning group) and the other half were not (*incidental* learning group). After testing all the participants for recall of the original word list, Hyde and Jenkins found that there were minimal differences in the number of items correctly recalled between the intentional learning groups and the incidental learning groups. This finding is predicted by Craik and Lockhart because they believe that retention is simply a byproduct of processing and so *intention* to learn is unnecessary for learning to occur. In addition, it was found that recall was significantly better for words which had been analysed semantically (i.e. rated for pleasantness or for frequency) than words which had been rated more superficially (i.e. detecting 'e' and 'g'). This is also in line with the theory because semantic analysis is assumed to be a deeper level of processing than structural analysis.

Evaluation of levels of processing

The levels of processing approach was influential when it was first formulated, and researchers in the field welcomed its emphasis on mental processes rather than on rigid structures. However, it soon became clear that the model was too simplistic and that it was descriptive rather than explanatory. A major problem is *circularity*, i.e. there is no independent definition of depth. The model predicts that deep processing will lead to better retention – researchers then conclude that, because retention is better after certain orienting tasks, they must, by definition, involve deep processing. Think back to the Hyde and Jenkins study, for example. The orienting task that gave rise to the lowest level of recall was the sentence frame task. Hyde and Jenkins assumed that the poor recall reflected shallow processing and yet, on the face of it, judgements about sentence frames would appear to require semantic analysis and, thus, deep processing.

Other researchers have questioned the idea that depth of processing alone is responsible for retention. Tyler *et al.* (1979), for example, gave participants two sets of anagrams to solve. Some were easy like DOCTRO and others were more difficult such as OCDRTO. In a subsequent, unexpected, recall task, participants remembered more of the difficult than the easy anagrams, in spite of processing levels being the same. Tyler and colleagues suggested that retention was influenced by the amount of processing *effort* rather than depth.

Craik and Lockhart themselves (1986) have since suggested that factors such as *elaboration* and *distinctiveness* are also important in determining the rate of retention; this idea has been supported by research. For example, Hunt and Elliott (1980) found that people recalled words with distinctive sequences of tall and short letters better than words with less distinctive arrangements of letters. Palmere *et al.* (1983) made up a 32-paragraph description of a fictitious African nation. Eight paragraphs consisted of a sentence containing a main idea, followed by three sentences each providing an example of the main theme; eight paragraphs consisted of one main sentence followed by two supplementary sentences; eight paragraphs consisted of one main sentence followed by a single supplementary sentence; and the remaining eight paragraphs consisted of a single main sentence with no supplementary information. Recall of the main ideas varied as a function of the amount of elaboration. Significantly more main ideas were recalled from the elaborated paragraphs than from the single-sentence paragraphs. This kind of evidence suggests that the effects of processing on retention are not as simple as first proposed by the levels of processing model.

Summary: Short- and long-term memory

In this section, we have considered the differences between various types of memory. Early structural models such as that of Atkinson and Shiffrin emphasized the distinction between the different memory structures of sensory, short-term and long-term memory. There is a considerable body of evidence which appears to support the distinction between STM and LTM. In particular, they appear to differ in terms of capacity, duration, effects of brain damage and forgetting mechanisms. Multistore models have been influential and have stimulated considerable research, but they are too simplistic to explain the whole memory system.

Baddeley and Hitch attempted to explain the function of STM and proposed a working memory model in which a central executive mechanism directs and coordinates slave systems. Such a model explains how we can manipulate information within the STM. It is a promising model and is still being developed, but it does not provide a complete account.

An alternative approach, which rejects the concept of separate memory stores, was proposed by Craik and Lockhart. They believed that retention depends on the depth of processing afforded the incoming stimulus. This model was welcomed at first, but it has been criticized for circularity and lack of explanatory power. Memory continues to be an active research field in psychology, but there is not yet a single theory which is able to account for this hugely complex processing system.

Forgetting

To understand how the memory system works, it is important to look at some of the reasons why we lose information – in other words, how we forget. We will look at some psychological explanations of forgetting:

♦ *displacement* – items currently in STM are pushed out to make room for incoming new items

♦ *decay theory* – the memory trace fades away with time so that it is no longer available

♦ *interference theory* – memory traces are disrupted or obscured by other incoming information.

♦ *retrieval failure* – items stored in LTM cannot be accessed because suitable retrieval cues are not available.

Forgetting in short-term memory

Displacement

We have already considered the view that the capacity of STM is limited to approximately seven items (e.g. Miller 1956). If this were the case, a possible mechanism for forgetting from STM could be *displacement*. In other words, material currently circulating in STM which has been insufficiently processed to pass on to LTM, will be pushed out or displaced by new, incoming information. Waugh and Norman (1965) used the *serial probe technique* to investigate this idea. This technique involves the presentation of a set of digits followed by the repetition of one of those digits (the probe). Participants then have to recall the digit which followed the probe in the original list. Waugh and Norman found that recall was good if the probe came towards the end of the 16 digit list, but poor for items at the beginning of the list. This is consistent with the notion of displacement because digits at the end of the list would still be available in STM, whereas digits at the beginning of the list would seem to have been displaced by the ones that came later. However, this may not be the only explanation. Shallice (1967) found that a faster rate of presentation of the digits produced better recall, which suggests that time may be an important factor in forgetting. With the faster presentation rate, earlier digits had less time to disappear from memory. In practice, it has been difficult to isolate the effects of displacement from decay.

Decay

According to *decay theory*, information is forgotten because of the passage of time rather than because of the displacement of the memory trace. It is thought that some kind of structural change occurs in the brain when a memory is laid down. Hebb (1949) believed that, as a result of excitation of the nerve cells, a brief memory trace is laid down. At this stage of the process, which corresponds to STM, the trace is very fragile and likely to be disrupted. With repeated neural activity (e.g. brought about by rehearsal), a permanent structural change is effected and the trace is no longer susceptible to decay. This means that, according to Hebb, trace decay can *only* account for forgetting in STM.

Studies based on the Brown/Peterson technique discussed on p. 4 seem to provide support for the decay theory of forgetting in STM. You will recall that forgetting of consonant trigrams was rapid when rehearsal was prevented. This finding was initially interpreted as evidence that the memory trace for the trigram becomes increasingly faded and decayed as

time elapses. However, it is notable that participants generally have little trouble recalling the trigrams on the first couple of trials. Problems seem to set in only as the number of trials increases, suggesting that later trigrams may be interfering with earlier ones. Try Activity 5 now before reading any further.

You probably found that the first triplet of words was accurately recalled, but that it was harder to recall the subsequent triplets. However, you should have noticed that recall improved again when you got to column 5. This seems to be because items from a *new* category give you the opportunity to start afresh and avoid confusion with earlier items. This effect is known as *release from proactive inhibition* and has been demonstrated by Wickens (1970) in a series of studies. He has shown this effect not only with changes of semantic categories, but also with changes from digits to letters, large to small items and dark to light backgrounds. This kind of evidence suggests that the Brown–Peterson findings can be explained in terms of interference rather than decay.

It is difficult to test decay theory without introducing confounding factors, but Reitman (1974) proposed a technique which she hoped would be as pure a measure as possible. She decided that participants should be given a task that intervened between learning and recall, preventing rehearsal but offering no opportunity for new learning. She showed participants lists of five words for 2 seconds and then, for a further 15 seconds, asked them to listen out for a faint tone presented over earphones. She reasoned that this tone-detection task would require effort and attention, but not involve any new learning. Under these conditions, recall of the five words declined by about 24 per cent over the 15-second period. She concluded that this decline in performance could be explained by decay. However, it is of course impossible to guarantee that no new information entered STM during the 15-second delay.

Activity 5: Interference or decay?

Cover up the lists of words with a piece of paper and uncover them, from left to right, as you progress through the exercise. Under each list of words you will find a number. Count backwards in threes from this number for 10 seconds and then, without looking back, try to write down the three words. Carry on until you have completed all 8 lists.

banana	apple	cherry	apricot	dog	cat	sheep	daisy
peach	grape	lemon	melon	goat	cow	horse	rose
plum	orange	pear	lime	pig	fox	mouse	tulip
327	519	128	385	729	610	486	923

It is clear that STM is a fragile store from which information can be easily and quickly lost. The precise mechanism of forgetting is unclear, but it seems likely that interference, displacement and decay all have a role to play.

Forgetting in long-term memory

Decay

We have already seen that memories transferred to the long-term store are relatively stable and long lasting. It is, however, only too obvious from our own experience that we often fail to remember things. Trace decay was discussed above as a method of forgetting in STM, but some psychologists have also argued that material can be lost from LTM in the form of decay through disuse. The idea here is that knowledge or skills which have not been used for a long time will eventually fade away. However, skills that require motor memory, such as riding a bicycle or swimming, do not seem to be forgotten, even after long periods without practice. For example, Fleischman and Parker (1962) found that people trained to fly using a simulator lost none of their skills over a 9- to 24-month period. This lack of forgetting does not, however, seem to be true of all skills. McKenna and Glendon (1985) studied 215 shop and office workers who had volunteered to learn the skills of cardiac resuscitation. Various measures of performance were tested over a three-month to three-year period after completion of training. Performance dropped sharply on all measures after only three months, and declined to extremely low levels after three years. Baddeley (1999) suggests that flying a plane or riding a bike involves a continuous skill where each action provides the cue for the next action. Such skills appear to require little maintenance to be retained. Skills such as resuscitation, however, are much more complex and require accurate knowledge as well as motor skill. According to Baddeley, these need frequent refreshing if they are to be maintained. There is evidence to suggest that certain verbal memories are remarkably resistant to long-term decay. Bahrick and Phelps (1987), in a long-term study of American college graduates, found that they showed rapid forgetting of Spanish vocabulary over the first three or four years after graduation, but then showed remarkably little further decline over the following 30 to 50 years. All these findings suggest that, even where time plays a part in forgetting, it cannot be the only factor.

Interference

There are problems in separating out the effects of time and interference, but Baddeley and Hitch (1977) conducted a study in which they attempted to avoid these difficulties. They asked rugby players to recall the names of teams they had played against during the previous season. Because of illness, other commitments, etc., some of the players had been unable to play in all the fixtures. This meant that, for some players 'two games back' meant two weeks ago, whereas for others 'two games back' meant four or five weeks ago. In other words, over the same period of time, some players had taken part in more games than others. This allowed Baddeley and Hitch to find out whether forgetting depended on elapsed time or the number of intervening games. The findings clearly showed that the mere passage of time was not the factor which determined how well team names could be recalled. The critical factor was the number of games played during that time period. In other words, forgetting appeared to be due to interference rather than trace decay.

If interference is the major cause of forgetting in LTM, it should be the case that people will remember material over a time period, provided no interfering material intervenes. It is clearly difficult to create a situation where human participants are immobilized after learning, with no opportunity for the occurrence of any intervening new learning. Instead, researchers have turned their attention to looking at the effects of different types of interfering material on recall. A classic study was conducted by McGeoch and McDonald (1931) who asked participants to learn and relearn lists of adjectives and then compared their performance on recall tests after various interpolated tasks. Forgetting was least when participants simply had to rest during the interval between learning and recall. Forgetting rates increased when participants were required to learn unrelated material such as nonsense syllables in the interval. Rates were even higher when other adjectives were learned in the interval, and were at their highest when the adjectives to be learned were similar in meaning to the original list. This study demonstrates that forgetting increases as a function of the similarity of the interfering material.

A distinction has been made between two types of interference:

◆ *Retroactive interference* occurs when new information interferes with old information. For example, if you move house and change telephone number, you will soon find that the new number supersedes the old.

◆ *Proactive interference* occurs when an old memory trace disrupts new information. You may, for example, suddenly find yourself dialling your old number even though you have not used it for months.

Retroactive interference was widely studied up until the 1960s, but has attracted less attention since then. Such studies typically made use of the technique of paired-associates, in which a word is associated with one word on list A (e.g. apple – fish) and with a completely different word on list B (e.g. apple – shoe). Participants are required to learn list A and then to learn list B. When given the stimulus 'apple' and asked to recall its paired associate from list A, participants frequently suffer from retroactive interference – in other words, they recall the paired associate from list B. Slamecka (1960) conducted a study in which he gave participants sentences to learn by heart. He presented the sentence for two, four or eight trials and followed presentation either by a rest period or by an interlude in which four or eight trials of another sentence were presented. Learning increased as a function of the number of initial learning trials, but forgetting occurred as a result of retroactive interference from the second learning task.

The classic study on *proactive interference* was conducted by Underwood (1957). He noted that students who had learned a list of nonsense syllables showed a greater rate of forgetting after 24 hours than would be expected. Given that these students had not been required to learn any more nonsense syllables in the intervening period, Underwood decided that retroactive interference was not causing the forgetting. Instead, he realized that this group of students had taken part in a number of his earlier memory experiments and so concluded that the interference causing their forgetting was proactive. He confirmed this suspicion by gathering data about the number of previous studies completed by the students and found that, the more lists of nonsense syllables, they had learned earlier, the more likely they were to forget a new list over a 24-hour period.

Evaluation of interference theory

There seems to be little doubt that interference between memory traces can cause forgetting. Recall can be impaired both from prior learning (proactive interference) and from later learning (retroactive interference) and, in both cases, the greater the similarity of the interfering material, the greater the interference. However, much of the evidence for interference theory has come from artificial laboratory experiments which have little relevance to everyday situations. There is also experimental evidence which demonstrates that interference cannot be a complete explanation of forgetting. Tulving (1966) gave lists of words to participants and then tested their free recall. One group was given one presentation of the words followed by a single recall test and then re-presented with the list and tested again. A second group was given the list of words and then tested on three separate occasions without any further presentation of the list. A striking finding was that participants in this group recalled, on average, about 50 per cent of

the words on each of the three tests, but that the words differed on each trial. Tulving concluded that all the words were still available in memory but not always readily accessible. This finding is difficult to reconcile with interference theory. How could a word that had been lost through interference on trial one, suddenly become available again on trial three? Studies such as this made psychologists think that forgetting can occur as a result of problems at the retrieval stage.

Retrieval failure

According to retrieval failure theory, forgetting occurs because the correct retrieval cues are not available. We are all familiar with the feeling that we know something, but just cannot bring it to mind – the name of an actor in an old film on TV, for example. Brown (1991) has reviewed 25 years of research into the so-called 'tip-of-the-tongue' phenomenon, and reported that people can generally correctly recall the first letter of the target name or word between 50 and 70 per cent of the time. They also seem to be fairly accurate at identifying the correct number of syllables in the word. One area of interest within the field of tip-of-the-tongue research is the effect of so-called 'interlopers'. Imagine that you are doing a crossword and searching for a word that means 'a South American beaver-like rodent' and a friend says that it is something like 'coyote'. Will this help or hinder you in finding the correct word, 'coypu'? Perfect and Hanley (1992) have not found a clear-cut answer and suggest that it depends on factors such as the distinctiveness of the target word and its similarity to the interloper.

Much of the research into retrieval cues has been conducted by Tulving. For example, Tulving and Osler (1968) presented participants with lists of words, each of which was paired with a weakly associated cue word, e.g. city – dirty. Participants were then tested either for free recall or were cued with the associated word, i.e. given the word 'dirty'. Cued recall consistently produced better performance than free recall. To counteract the argument that any semantically associated word might have elicited the target, Tulving and Osler gave some participants weak, semantic associates which had not been the original cue words, e.g. 'busy'. Such cues did not facilitate recall, so Tulving and Osler (1968, p. 593) concluded that 'Specific retrieval cues facilitate recall if and only if the information about them is stored at the same time as the information about the membership of the word in a given list'. While Tulving has continued to stress the importance of cues at the memory encoding stage, he later (1983) acknowledged that cues not present at the time of learning can be helpful under certain circumstances.

Context-dependent and state-dependent learning

How we encode material at the time of learning is clearly important. Psychologists have also been interested in the effects of the learning environment on recall. Godden and Baddeley (1975) presented deep-sea divers with lists of words to learn. They either learnt them on the beach or under 15 feet of water. Recall was then tested in either the same or the opposite environment. Findings showed clearly that recall was significantly better if tested in the same environment. This kind of finding obviously has practical applications and raises the question of whether students will perform better in exams if they are tested in their original classrooms. In general, it has been found that environmental differences need to be substantial before any significant difference in recall performance can be demonstrated. It has also been shown that simply imagining the original environmental setting can be helpful. Smith (1979) gave participants a list of 80 words to learn while sitting in a distinctive basement room. The following day, he tested some participants in the same basement room and others in a fifth-floor room with completely different furnishings and atmosphere. Average recall for the basement group was 18 items, but for those in the fifth-floor room, recall averaged 12 items. A third group was tested in the upstairs room, but first instructed to imagine themselves back in the basement room. These students recalled an average of 17 items.

We have looked at the role of the external environment in context-dependent learning. There is also some evidence that the internal environment, i.e. physiological state or mood might also have some effect. Goodwin *et al.* (1969) found that heavy drinkers who learn things in a drunken state are more likely to recall them in a similar state. Eich (1980) has shown this effect with a range of other drugs including marijuana.

Research into the role of emotional factors in forgetting

Psychologists have often ignored the role of emotion in human cognitive processes, but it seems likely that the way we feel has an impact on the way we remember things. There is some evidence that memory is better for material that is congruent with a person's current mood. For example, depressed people tend to recall more unhappy memories than non-depressed people. Clark and Teasdale (1982) investigated people whose depression fluctuated through the 24 hour cycle, and found that they were consistently less likely to recall happy memories during their sad phases than during their relatively neutral phases. Studies have also been conducted on non-depressed individuals by manipulating their mood, e.g. by asking them to think about happy or sad events from their lives. In a review of 29 such studies, Blaney (1986) found strong evidence for mood congruence in recall tests. There is less conclusive evidence for mood dependence, i.e. the idea that your recall when you are in a particular mood depends on your mood when you first learned the material. However, in a meta-analysis (review of the results) of research studies into mood dependence, Ucros (1989) found a moderately strong relationship between mood at the learning and retrieval stage. She also found that mood dependence was more likely if the stimulus material was about real life, rather than artificially constructed material, and that adults were more likely to demonstrate mood dependence than children.

Flashbulb memories

One particular type of memory which seems to be influenced by emotion has been called *a flashbulb memory*. This is a particularly vivid, detailed and long-lasting memory of an event which is usually highly significant and emotional and is often somewhat unexpected. It can be a personal event or something which provokes worldwide interest, e.g. the assassination of President Kennedy or the death of Princess Diana. According to Brown and Kulik (1977), who first described this type of memory, the event must be surprising and have real consequences for the person's life. They believed that such an emotional event triggers a neural mechanism which causes the details of the scene to be imprinted on the memory. They believed that this is a special type of memory because of the detail and accuracy with which the event is remembered and the fact that the structural form of the memory is always so similar. They found that six kinds of information were most likely to be recalled about the moment when the news of the event was first heard. People remember:

◆ where they were

◆ what they were doing

◆ the person who gave them the news

◆ what they felt about it

◆ what others felt about it

◆ what happened in the immediate aftermath.

Not all psychologists agree that flashbulb memories are special. Neisser (1982), for example, believes that the enduring nature of such memories results from frequent rehearsal and reworking after the event, rather than from neural activity at the time. As far as the uniformity of the memories is concerned, Neisser believes that it simply reflects normal narrative convention. In other words, when we recount important events, we do so by using conventional storytelling techniques. Neisser also argued that flashbulb memories are subject to the same types of inaccuracy and forgetting as any memories. McCloskey *et al.* (1988) tested participants' memories for the explosion of the American space shuttle 'Challenger'. Recall was tested after a few days and then, again, after nine months. It was found that there was significant forgetting over time and that recall was often inaccurate. Weaver (1993) found that American college students had no more vivid memories about the decision of President Bush to bomb Iraq than they had of a trivial event, such as meeting a friend. Conway (1995) has criticized such studies by pointing out that such an event (i.e. the bombing of Iraq) did not meet the criteria for a flashbulb memory. He believes that it was neither unexpected nor likely to have immediate consequences for the students concerned. In his own study (Conway *et al.* 1994), it was found that British undergraduate students had vivid and accurate memories about the unexpected resignation of Margaret Thatcher as Prime Minister, even after 11 months.

It is still unclear whether flashbulb memories represent a particular type of memory or whether they are substantially similar to most memories for events.

Repression

A very different view of forgetting was proposed by Freud (1915–18), who believed that certain memories become inaccessible as a result of *repression*. According to Freud, this is an unconscious process that ensures that threatening or anxiety-provoking memories are kept from conscious awareness. Freud formulated his ideas on repression in the course of treating patients with neurotic disorders and he gave examples in his case studies. It has proved difficult to demonstrate the existence of repression in the laboratory, although a number of attempts have been made.

Levinger and Clark (1961) asked participants to generate associated words to a series of words presented by the researchers. Some of these words were emotionally neutral (e.g. tree, window) and others were emotionally arousing (e.g. angry, quarrel). When asked to recall the associated words, participants showed a significant tendency to recall the neutral associations rather than the emotional ones. This appears to offer support for the idea of repression since it looks as though anxiety-provoking responses had been repressed. However, a more complicated picture has since emerged from other studies. For example, Bradley and Baddeley (1990) gave participants a similar association task and then tested half of them immediately after the study and the remaining half after an interval of 28 days. Just like Levinger and Clark, they found that recall was poor for

the emotional associations when tested immediately, but that emotional associations were significantly better remembered than neutral associations after a 28-day delay. Holmes (1990), in a review of studies, concluded that there is no convincing experimental support for the concept of repression.

There is some evidence that events associated with pain are forgotten more easily than events associated with pleasure. Robinson *et al.* (1980), in a study on the effectiveness of three different types of painkillers, asked women to rate the pain they had experienced during childbirth. They rated the pain at the time of the birth, after 24 hours, after five days and, again, after three months. Although the levels of pain experienced varied depending on the type of analgesic used, all three groups of women demonstrated that the memory of the pain faded considerably over time. However, it could be argued that the pain of childbirth is not typical. Hunter *et al.* (1979), for example, found no decline in pain ratings over time when patients were asked to assess painful procedures such as sampling cerebro-spinal fluid.

Recently, research interest has focused on repressed memories associated with child sexual abuse. This is a controversial area because memories of abuse 'recovered' in psychotherapy can lead to great distress and, in some cases, prosecutions years after the alleged events. The controversy revolves around the issue of whether these *recovered memories* are genuine. The main problem with establishing the validity of the claims is that there is usually no independent, objective corroborative evidence. There is sadly no doubt that cases of child abuse do occur, and it may well be the case that memories of the abuse are repressed. Williams (1992), for example, found that 38 per cent of a group of African-American women who were known to have suffered abuse some years before, reported repressed memories of the abuse. However, it also seems clear that some of these so-called repressed memories are false memories. Loftus (1997) has conducted an extensive review of studies which indicate that even psychologically healthy individuals can be made to alter their memory for events on the basis of false suggestions. As Baddeley (1999, p. 143) has written about reports of recovered memories: 'It is important to exercise great caution in interpreting such reports, particularly when they become part of a legal process which is likely to be costly both financially and emotionally to patients and their families.'

Summary: Forgetting

In this section, we have looked at various ways in which we might forget and have considered how forgetting mechanisms might differ in STM and LTM.

Displacement, trace decay and interference theories are all based on the assumption that material becomes lost and is no longer available for retrieval. It seems likely that all of these factors have a role to play in forgetting, but it has sometimes proved difficult to disentangle their effects in the laboratory.

While it seems likely that some material is irretrievably lost from memory, it is often the case that we have a memory 'on the tip of the tongue'. Some psychologists, notably Tulving, believe that forgetting occurs as a result of retrieval failure. In other words, the material is available in the memory store but not immediately accessible. According to this idea, we need cues to help us retrieve material, and these cues are most likely to be helpful if they were encoded at the time of original learning. The context in which we learn things and our physiological state may also affect the accuracy of recall.

Emotional factors may also be important in determining what is remembered. Events that are particularly salient for us may be remembered as flashbulb memories. These are thought to be qualitatively different from other memories in terms of their vividness and accuracy over long periods. However, it is not universally accepted that flashbulb memories are genuinely unique.

Repression is an explanation of forgetting first put forward by Freud. According to this view, unpleasant memories are pushed from conscious awareness. It is difficult to demonstrate the existence of repression in laboratory experiments. A real-life situation where repressed memories are thought to occur is in the area of child abuse. While there is some evidence to suggest that traumatic childhood experiences may be repressed, it is possible that some so-called recovered memories of abuse are induced during therapy.

CRITICAL ISSUE: Eyewitness testimony

In 1978, Neisser wrote a paper called 'Memory; what are the important questions?' in which he criticized contemporary psychologists for concentrating almost exclusively on theoretical concepts and ignoring practical issues about memory. It is certainly true that much of the research up to the late 1970s was laboratory-based and often involved memory for unconnected lists of digits, words and nonsense syllables. One exception to this is the work of Bartlett (1932), but his ideas had little influence at the time. Since Neisser's challenge, there has been a growing interest in practical, applied aspects of memory, and the research field on everyday memory is considerable. One particular area of interest is eyewitness testimony. Try Activity 6 before reading any further.

Activity 6: Real-life details

Without looking anything up, do the following tasks.

1 Draw a picture of a 10p coin.
2 Write down the address and telephone number of your GP's surgery.

You may be surprised how difficult it is to remember exactly what a 10p coin looks like without having one in front of you. If you compare your drawing with a real coin, you will probably find a number of inaccuracies. In real life, if you think about it, you do not need to remember every detail as long as you are able to recognize coins so that you can use them appropriately.

Similarly, unless you are unfortunate enough to have to visit your GP regularly, you will probably not have the surgery phone number and address readily available in your head. However, you can easily look the number up and you know where the surgery is and how to get there, even if you do not know the precise address. In other words, there are many areas of everyday memory where it is unnecessary to have exact recall. However, in certain instances, such as taking exams or giving testimony about a crime, accuracy is extremely important. Inaccurate eyewitness testimony can have very serious consequences leading to wrongful convictions and, in some cases in the US, to the death penalty (Loftus and Ketcham 1991). For example, Rattner (1988) reviewed 205 cases of wrongful arrest and found that, in 52 per cent of cases, this was due to mistaken eyewitness testimony. Psychologists have been interested in investigating some of the reasons why eyewitness testimony can be unreliable and some of the ways that accuracy might be improved.

Reconstructive memory

One possible reason that people recall events inaccurately is that memory is distorted or reconstructed by the individual's prior knowledge and expectations. The pioneering work on *reconstructive memory* was carried out by Bartlett (1932). Bartlett argued that we do not record memories passively, as we might if we were taking a photo. He believed that we need to make what he called *effort after meaning*, in order to make more sense of the event. So, instead of storing an exact replica of the initial stimulus, we weave it with elements of our existing knowledge and experience to form a reconstructed memory representation. Bartlett carried out a number of experiments to investigate how people recall things such as stories, pictures or faces. In one of his best-known studies, Bartlett read English participants a folk tale derived from Red Indian culture called 'The war of the ghosts'. This was an unusual story for people from a Western culture to understand because it contained unfamiliar supernatural concepts and an odd causal structure. After an interval, participants were asked to recall as much of the story as possible. Bartlett found that their accounts were distorted in several ways that, generally, made them more consistent with a Western world-view. Specifically, he found the following differences:

◆ *Rationalizations* – People included new material or added justifications for the action which were not in the original.

◆ *Omissions* – Certain elements were left out, particularly those elements which were hardest for Westerners to understand.

◆ *Changes of order* – Events were sometimes reordered to make the story more coherent.

◆ *Alterations in importance* – Certain themes were given more prominence than in the original story.

◆ *Distortions of emotions* – People incorporated their own feelings and attitudes towards the story.

Bartlett also presented line drawings like the one in Fig. 1.4 and then asked his participants to draw them from memory.

Although not asked to do so, participants spontaneously gave a label to the drawing, e.g. they variously named picture (b) a pickaxe, turf-cutter, shovel, or similar, and their subsequent reproduction reflected this label so that the final drawing was a distortion of the original.

Bartlett (1932, pp. 19–20) wrote at the time: '...for the presented visual pattern seemed at once to 'fit into' or 'match' some preformed scheme or setting. I shall call this fundamental process of connecting a given pattern with some setting or scheme: effort after meaning.' So, according to Bartlett, we store memories in terms of our past experience or *schemas*.

Schemas

Schemas are knowledge packages which are built up through experience of the world and which can aid the interpretation of new information. Imagine, for example, that you are going for a meal in a restaurant. Through past experience, you will already be familiar with the kinds of things you would expect to see in a restaurant (e.g. tables, chairs, waiters, menus, other customers) – in other words, you will have a restaurant schema. This means that you do not have to waste attentional resources on mundane, expected features of the place, but can direct your attention to choosing food from the menu.

Bartlett's ideas were regarded as rather vague and his studies were seen to lack experimental rigour by his contemporaries. It is certainly true that his experiments were poorly designed in some ways and that his instructions to participants were rather vague. Gauld and Stephenson (1967), in semi-replications of Bartlett's story studies, found that errors were significantly reduced where participants were given explicit instructions that highlighted the importance of accurate recall. However, in the 1970s, there was a revival of interest in the idea of schemas, and more elaborate formulations were put forward (e.g. the script theory of Schank and Abelson 1977). Cohen (1993) has suggested five ways in which schemas might affect memory:

◆ *Selection and storage* – Those inputs from the environment which are not compatible within a currently activated schema are likely to be ignored.

◆ *Abstraction* – Schemas would allow the central meaning of the input to be stored without the necessity of storing precise details. For example, we remember the gist of a conversation, rather than the exact wording.

◆ *Interpretation and integration* – Schemas provide past knowledge to interpret current situations. Schema-based knowledge can help us to infer what is not actually seen because we fill in missing information to form an integrated memory, i.e. to make sense of what we have seen.

◆ *Normalization* – Memories of events are distorted to fit in with prior expectations. We might, for

Figure 1.4
Figures used by Bartlett to study memory for drawings
Source: Bartlett (1932)

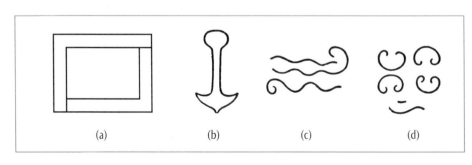

(a)   (b)   (c)   (d)

example, report that a bank robber wore a mask, whereas he had actually worn dark glasses. Our 'memory' has been distorted by a schema based on information drawn from films or TV depictions of bank raids.

◆ *Retrieval* – Schemas may aid retrieval by providing the basis for a correct guess. If we cannot recall precisely what we had for breakfast last Tuesday, our schema for weekday breakfast supplies 'cereal' and this has a good chance of being correct.

This means that schemas are usually useful to us because they make our experiences more predictable and use our attentional resources efficiently. However, as Bartlett suggested, they can lead to distortions of memory in certain circumstances.

Schemas and memory errors

Brewer and Treyens (1981), for example, investigated the effects of schemas on visual memory by asking their 30 participants, one at a time, to wait in a room for 35 seconds. The room was designed to look like an office and contained 61 objects. Some objects were compatible with an office schema, such as a desk, calendar or typewriter (this was 1981!), but a few items were included which were incompatible such as a skull, a brick and a pair of pliers. In a subsequent, unexpected, recall test, participants were most likely to recall typical office items, i.e. items with high schema expectancy. They were less successful at recalling the incompatible items like the brick, but eight participants recalled the really bizarre item – the skull. Most of the errors in recall were *substitutions,* i.e. participants tended to recall falsely the presence of objects such as books, pens and a telephone, which would have high schema expectancy, but which were not actually present on this occasion. Other errors involved *wrong placement* of items, e.g. a note pad was 'remembered' as being on the desk (where it might be in an office schema) instead of being on the seat of a chair (as it was in reality). These findings suggest that participants were using schemas to ensure rapid encoding of the visual information available to them during their 35-second wait. At the retrieval stage, recall was influenced by the schema so that typical items were recalled, even if they were not actually present. The finding that the particularly bizarre item was frequently recalled is not so easy to accommodate within schema theory. However, a modified version of schema theory, proposed by Graesser and Nakamura (1982) accounts for this apparent anomaly. According to this so-called *schema-plus-tag theory*, we store a memory for a specific event with the general schema for that event and we attach to the schema a tag or marker to indicate any particularly unexpected or remarkable

aspects. For example, try thinking back to a psychology class a couple of weeks ago. Because you have psychology classes every week and are presumably in similar classrooms with the same teacher and the same group of students every time, you will find it difficult to recall exact details of one particular class – in other words you are likely to rely heavily on your schema for such classes. If, however, a student collapsed in the class and had to be rushed to hospital, you would remember that particular class because it would be stored with a tag to record that extraordinary event. The Brewer and Treyens experiment showed that people can sometimes falsely remember objects that did not exist. List (1986) has shown that schemas can also affect recall of events. She asked people to rate various events in terms of their probability in a shop-lifting scenario. She then compiled a video showing eight different shoplifting acts, each of which incorporated some of the events rated as high-probability and some of the events rated as low-probability. She showed this video to a new set of people and, one week later, tested their recall. She found that they were more likely to recall high- rather than low-probability events and that, if they made inclusion errors of events which had not actually occurred in the video, they were more likely to be high-probability events.

Evaluation of research on reconstructive memory

Bartlett has been criticized for his choice of material in his studies of reconstructive memory. He used folk tales, which he assumed would be less meaningful to people of other cultures, but he had no objective measure of meaningfulness. Later studies have provided support for some of Bartlett's ideas by using more rigorous methods. Bransford and Johnson (1972), for example, constructed some prose passages which would be difficult to understand in the absence of context. They then compared recall performance between a group of participants who had been supplied with contextual information and a group who had not received this additional information. You can try one of their studies for yourself in Activity 7 on p. 20. Do this now before reading on.

You probably found the task in Activity 7 quite difficult because the passage was hard to understand – in other words, you lacked an appropriate schema and so could not relate the passage to stored information. However, if you now turn to look at Fig. 1.6 (on p. 22), then read the passage again, it will probably fall into place. Bransford and Johnson found that recall was significantly better for the group given the picture than for the group which simply read the passage.

Activity 7: Out of context

Read the following passage at normal reading speed once. Then cover it up and write down as many points from the passage as you can remember.

'If the balloons popped, the sound wouldn't be able to carry since then everything would be too far away from the correct floor. A closed window would also prevent the sound from carrying, since most buildings tend to be well insulated. Since the whole operation depends on the steady flow of electricity, a break in the middle of the wire would also cause problems. Of course, the fellow could shout but the human voice is not loud enough to carry that far. An additional problem is that the string could break on the instrument. Then there would be no accompaniment to the message. It is clear that the best situation would involve less distance. Then there would be fewer potential problems. With face to face contact, the least number of things could go wrong.'

Source: adapted from Bransford and Johnson (1972)

In another study on the constructive nature of memory, Bransford and Johnson (1973) asked participants to read an ambiguous passage which could be interpreted in one of two ways:

◆ viewing a peace march from the fortieth floor of a tall building

◆ a description of a trip to an inhabited planet in outer space.

Bransford and Johnson found that recall depended on the context provided. For example, participants who thought the passage was about a trip into space were more likely to recall a sentence about the atmosphere not requiring the wearing of special clothing than the group who thought the passage was about viewing a peace march.

There seems little doubt that we do use stored knowledge and past experience to make sense of new information and that memories for events can be distorted because of this. This may well account for some instances of inaccurate eyewitness testimony. However, schema theories have been criticized on several counts (Cohen 1993):

◆ It is not clear at what stage selection, abstraction, integration and normalization occur.

◆ The concept of a schema is too vague to be useful.

◆ Schema theory overemphasizes the fallibility of memory and ignores the fact that quite complex events can sometimes be remembered accurately and in detail.

◆ Schema theory does not explain how schemas are acquired in the first place.

◆ There is no adequate explanation of how the correct schema is activated to interpret new information.

Loftus' research into eyewitness testimony

We have already seen that schemas, i.e. prior knowledge, can affect the way we remember events. Elizabeth Loftus, one of the leading researchers in the field of eyewitness testimony, has been primarily interested in the effects on memory of information provided *after* the event. She and her colleagues have carried out many studies which show that memory for events can be changed or supplemented by later information. They have used the *experimental method* and the controlled environment of the laboratory, but employed stimulus material that mimics real-life situations. In a typical experiment, participants are first shown a film or series of slides depicting an event such as a car accident. In the interval between viewing the slides and being tested for recall, participants are provided with information which either conflicts or is consistent with the original witnessed event. For example, Loftus (1975) showed 150 participants a film depicting a car accident. After the showing, participants were divided into two groups and each group was asked ten questions about what they had seen. The first group was asked questions which were entirely consistent with the original film, e.g. 'How fast was the white sports car going when it passed the 'Stop' sign?'. The second group was given the same questions with the exception of one – 'How fast was the white sports car going when it passed the barn when travelling along the country road.' This question was misleading because there was no barn in the film. After one week, the participants were all asked a further ten questions and, for both groups, the final question was: 'Did you see a barn?' Loftus found that only 2.7 per cent of the participants in the first group gave the incorrect answer 'Yes', whereas 17.3 per cent of the second group (i.e. those given the misleading question) answered 'Yes'. Loftus concluded that, for these people, the nonexistent barn had been added to the original memory representation of the event at the question stage, so that it is now recalled as being part of the original event (see *In Focus*, 'Loftus' experiments on misled memory', for details of a further experiment).

It seems that eyewitnesses can be misled by false postevent information, even when that information is discredited. Lindsay (1990) showed a sequence of slides in which a maintenance man was seen stealing money

Loftus' experiments on misled memory

Loftus *et al.* (1978) showed a sequence of 30 coloured slides to 195 participants who were divided into two groups. The slides showed a sequence of events leading up to a car accident and one of the slides depicted a red Datsun car stopping at a road junction. For one group, this slide depicted a 'Stop' sign at the junction, whereas, for the other group, the slide depicted a 'Yield' sign ('Give Way' is the English equivalent). After the slide presentation, both groups were given a set of 20 questions to answer. For half the participants in each group, this set included the question 'Did another car pass the red Datsun while it was stopped at the 'Stop' sign?' and, for the other half, the set included the question 'Did another car pass the red Datsun while it was stopped at the 'Yield' sign?'. This means that half the participants received a misleading question and half received a question that was consistent with what they had actually seen. After a short interval of 20 minutes, participants were given a recognition test, i.e. they were given 15 pairs of slides to look at and had to pick from each pair the slide which had been included in the first presentation. One of the pairs consisted of one slide showing the Datsun stopped at the 'Yield' sign and the other slide showing the Datsun stopped at the 'Stop' sign (see Fig. 1.5).

 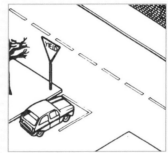

Figure 1.5
The red Datsun at a Stop sign (left) and at a Yield sign (right)
Source: Loftus *et al.* (1978)

Seventy-five per cent of the participants who had received consistent questions picked the correct slide, but only 41 per cent of the group who had been given the misleading question were correct. A second phase of the experiment delayed the presentation of questions and the subsequent recognition test for a week after the initial presentation of the slides.

Under these conditions, accuracy for the misled group dropped to 20 per cent. Such findings suggested to Loftus and her colleagues that the correct information had been deleted from the memory and replaced by the fictitious information. This conclusion was reinforced by Loftus and Loftus (1980) in a later, similar experiment. This time, they offered monetary rewards to participants for selecting the correct slides. They found that accuracy did not increase with the amount of money offered – participants in the misled group still had a strong tendency to select the incorrect slide regardless of the reward.

and a calculator from an office. Participants were then given a written account to read, but were told, in advance, that any references to the theft would be inaccurate. In spite of these warnings, a subsequent recall test showed that memory for the incident was considerably distorted by this postevent information.

In another series of experiments, Loftus has shown that the precise wording of questions to eyewitnesses can be a crucial factor in prompting false memories. Loftus and Palmer (1974) showed participants a film of a car accident and then asked them: 'How fast were the cars going when they hit each other?' All participants were asked the same type of question except that the word 'hit' was variously replaced with 'smashed', 'collided', 'bumped', or 'contacted'. It was found that the word used affected speed estimation – 'smashed' produced the highest estimate (40.8 mph) and 'contacted' produced the lowest estimate. A week later, when people were asked if they had seen any broken

glass, those in the 'smashed' group were consistently more likely to answer (wrongly) 'Yes'.

In a similar study, in which film footage of a car accident was shown, participants were asked either 'Did you see *a* broken headlight?' or 'Did you see *the* broken headlight?'. People who had seen a version of the film in which there really was a broken headlight were equally likely to answer 'Yes' to either of the questions. However, people who had seen a version with no broken headlight were more than twice as likely to recall one when asked about 'the' rather than 'a' broken headlight.

Of course, in real life, events which might have to be recalled later in a court of law, often take place unexpectedly and in an atmosphere of tension. It is difficult to reproduce such conditions in the laboratory for various practical and ethical reasons. However, Loftus (1979) tried to achieve this effect in a study carried out at the University of Michigan (see *In Focus*, 'The weapon focus').

Figure 1.6
Visual
source for
Activity 7

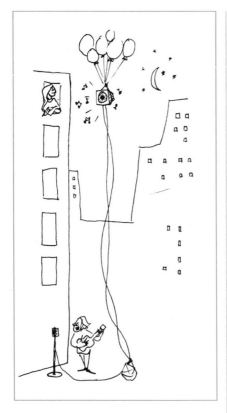

Loftus' conclusions about the effects of fear and anxiety have been supported by other laboratory studies, but were called into question by a study carried out by Christianson and Hubinette (1993). They questioned 110 witnesses who had, between them, witnessed a total of 22 genuine, as opposed to staged, bank robberies. Some of these witnesses had been onlookers who happened to be in the banks at the time, whereas others were bank employees who had been directly threatened in the robberies. Victims were more accurate in their recall and remembered more details than people who had been bystanders. This superior recall continued to be evident, even after a 15-month interval. Christianson and Hubinette concluded that people are good at remembering highly stressful events if they occur in real life rather than in the artificial surroundings of the laboratory.

Most of the studies we have considered so far stress the malleability of recall for events. However, it is important to note that witnesses are not always susceptible to misleading postevent information. People are generally not misled by information if it is blatantly incorrect. Loftus (1979) showed participants a set of slides which depicted the theft of a large, red purse from a handbag. In an immediate recall test, 98 per cent of the participants correctly remembered the colour of the purse. They were then asked to read an account of the incident allegedly written by a professor of psychology (this was designed to lend weight to the accuracy of the account). One of these accounts contained errors relating to unimportant items in the slide sequence, e.g. the wrong colour was given for items which were not central to the action. The other account contained, in addition to these minor errors, the more glaring statement that the purse was brown. In a second recall test, all but two of the participants resisted this blatantly wrong information and again correctly recalled that the purse was red. This suggests that memory for information which is particularly noticeable and salient at the time is less subject to distortion than memory for peripheral details. In other words, people can ignore new information under certain circumstances and so maintain their original memory representation intact.

in focus

'The weapon focus'

Loftus (1979) asked volunteers to participate in an experiment and invited them to come individually to the University experimental laboratory. When each participant arrived, he or she was asked to wait in a room outside the laboratory for a few moments. During this wait, some participants were allowed to overhear a low-key discussion in the laboratory about an equipment failure. A person then emerged from the laboratory holding a pen and with grease on his hands. He uttered a single comment and then walked past the participant and out of the room. Other participants overheard a heated and hostile exchange between people in the laboratory. After the sound of breaking glass and crashing chairs, a man emerged from the laboratory holding a paper-knife covered in blood. This man, too, made a single statement before leaving the room. Participants were then given 50 photos and asked to identify the person who had come out of the laboratory. People who had witnessed the man holding the pen, accurately identified the person 49 per cent of the time, whereas those who had witnessed the man with the blood-stained letter-opener were successful only 33 per cent of the time. This finding has come to be known as 'the weapon focus', whereby the witness concentrates on the weapon (in this case, the blood-stained paper knife) and this distracts attention from the appearance of the perpetrator. Loftus concluded that the fear or anxiety induced by the sight of a weapon narrows the focus of attention and gives rise to very accurate recall of the central details of the scene, but diminishes accurate recall of peripheral details.

Evaluation of Loftus' research

Loftus and her colleagues have made an important contribution to our understanding of the fallibility of eyewitness testimony. It seems clear from her research that memory for events can be fundamentally altered in the light of misleading postevent information. However, her studies have been criticized for artificiality. It is obviously difficult to reproduce in the laboratory the kind of events which arise spontaneously in real life, and it is quite possible that eyewitnesses remember real events rather differently from staged events, as Christianson and Hubinette's theory suggested.

It is also possible that participants in experiments are less accurate than real-life witnesses because they know inaccuracies will not lead to serious consequences. Foster *et al.* (1994) tested this possibility in a study where participants were shown a video of a bank robbery and subsequently asked to identify the robber in an identity parade. One group of participants were led to believe that the robbery was a real event and that their responses would influence the trial, while the second group assumed that it was a simulation. Identification of the robber was more accurate for the first group, suggesting that consequentiality is an important factor for witnesses.

It has also been suggested that the method of testing witnesses' recall could be a factor in explaining some of Loftus' findings. For example, she often used forced-choice tests (e.g. picking one of two slides), but this may give a false picture. Koriat and Goldsmith (1996) have shown that witness accuracy can be dramatically increased if tests do not rely on forced-choice format and if witnesses are allowed to give no answer if they feel unsure. It also seems to be the case that witnesses are able to produce far more accurate memories for events if they are given the appropriate

Accounts from eyewitnesses are often fallible and incomplete

cues. The Cognitive Interview technique, for example (see *In Focus* on p. 24), seems to elicit memories that are more accurate and richer in details than other types of questioning.

Loftus has been criticized not just for her experimental methods but also for her explanation of the effects of postevent information. She believes that in the light of misleading information, the original memory is deleted and replaced by the new, false memory. Other researchers have disputed this and believe that the original memory trace is still available, even though it has been obscured by new information. Bekerian and Bowers (1983) replicated the study by Loftus *et al.* (1978) in which a car is shown stopping at either a 'Stop' or a 'Yield' sign. In the recognition phase of the study, the participants were presented with the pairs of slides in chronological order, i.e. the order in which they were first shown (unlike the Loftus *et al.* study where presentation was random). Under these circumstances, recall of the misled participants was almost exactly as accurate as of the control group. Bekerian and Bowers concluded that the original memory representation had not been lost for these participants. Looking at the slides in the correct sequence provided enough cues to reactivate the original memory in spite of the postevent misleading information. However, other researchers have failed to replicate this result, so it remains unclear whether the original memory trace is destroyed or obscured.

The interviewees in the study by Geiselman and colleagues (see *In Focus*) were undergraduate students who watched video tapes and so the study could be criticized for artificiality. However, Fisher *et al.* (1989) later trained a group of detectives in Florida in the use of the Cognitive Interview and then assessed their performance when interviewing genuine witnesses to crimes. When their performance was compared to pretraining levels, it was found that the information gain was as much as 47 per cent.

There have since been a number of studies which have investigated the effectiveness of the Cognitive Interview. Bekerian and Dennett (1993) have reviewed 27 such studies and found in all cases that the cognitive approach has provided more accurate information than other interview procedures.

Memory for faces (face recognition)

We have so far considered the accuracy of memory for events, but eyewitnesses are often called upon to describe some of the people involved in those events. Descriptions might include things like build, hairstyle, clothes, voice, face and the context in which the person was seen. Factors such as clothes, hairstyle and context are likely to change and so might seem like less helpful cues for memory. For example, you are less likely to

in focus

The Cognitive Interview

In view of the finding that accounts from eyewitnesses are often fallible and incomplete, psychologists have attempted to develop memory retrieval techniques aimed at eliciting more accurate information. One example is the Cognitive Interview Schedule devised by Geiselman *et al.* (1985) and designed to be used by police investigators. The interview technique is based on four instructions:

◆ To *recreate the context* of the original incident – This does not involve revisiting the scene of the crime, but trying to recall an image of the setting including details such as the weather, the lighting, distinctive smells, any people nearby or what you were feeling at the time.

◆ To *report every detail* – You are required to report back any information about the event you can remember, even if it does not seem to you to have a bearing on the crime.

◆ To *recall the event in different orders* – You are encouraged to describe the events in reverse order, or to start with an aspect of the scene which seems most memorable and work backwards or forwards from that point.

◆ To *change perspectives* – You are asked to attempt to describe the incident from the perspective of other people who were present at the time.

Geiselman and colleagues tested the effectiveness of the Cognitive Interview Schedule by comparing it with standard police interviewing techniques. They showed police training videos of violent crimes to a group of 89 students. About 48 hours later, the students were interviewed individually by American law enforcement officers (detectives, CIA investigators and private investigators). The interviewers had either been trained in standard police interviewing techniques or in the new Cognitive Interview Schedule. Each interview was taped and analysed for accuracy of recall. Results were recorded as:

◆ the number of correct items recalled

◆ the number of errors – this category was subdivided into incorrect items (number of items incorrectly recalled, i.e. the assailant was wearing a brown coat instead of a black one) and *confabulated* items (number of items described, but not actually shown on the video).

Average number of items recalled in Standard and Cognitive Interviews (based on Geiselman 1988)

	Cognitive	Standard
Correct items	41.15	29.4
Incorrect items	7.3	6.1
Confabulated items	0.7	0.4

As you can see, people recalled considerably more items in the cognitive than in the standard interview although error rates were very similar.

recognize your doctor at the swimming baths, or your newsagent in a different shop. Young and Bruce (1991) have called this the *Little Red Riding Hood effect*. However, it seems that people often take too much account of external factors which are subject to change at the expense of paying attention to more stable factors like facial features. Buckhout (1974) set up a bag-snatching incident on a college campus that was observed by 52 student witnesses. They were then asked to pick out the 'thief' in each of two identity parades organized by Buckhout. The real 'thief' appeared in the first parade, while someone who looked similar appeared in the second. Ten witnesses felt unable to pick out anyone from either parade, while seven picked the right man in the first line-up, but changed their mind in favour of the similar man in the second parade. Twenty-eight witnesses selected a completely 'innocent' man from at least one of the line-ups and only seven people picked the correct culprit from the first parade and stuck to this choice, even after seeing the second parade. Buckhout concluded that recognition was unreliable, partly because of the surprise element (none of the students had expected to witness a 'crime'), but partly because of the changes in context (a bare room instead of the college campus) and appearance (changes to clothes, hair, etc.). It seems that, in brief glimpses, the face of the other person is not the main focus of attention.

Factors affecting face recognition

Familiarity

Look at the faces in Fig. 1.7. You will almost certainly have found no difficulty in recognizing all of them very quickly and will not be surprised that we find face recognition easy if the face is familiar. The effect of *familiarity* may be a factor in explaining our ability to recognize faces of people from our own race better than faces of people from other races (e.g. Buckhout and Regan 1988). It is possible to make recognition errors with well-known faces, but usually only if they are distorted in some way or appear in a totally unexpected context. However, we need to maintain exposure to the faces otherwise face recognition accuracy will decline. Bahrick (1984) tested the face recognition accuracy of college lecturers for their students. Lecturers taught the students three to five times per week over a term of 10 weeks. They were subsequently given face recognition tasks in which they had to pick out each of the students' faces from an array of five photos (on each presentation, four of the photos were of students whom the lecturers had not taught). After a delay of 11 days, recognition was reasonably good (69 per cent), but correct identifications dropped to 48 per cent after a year and were no better than chance after a delay of eight years. It seems that recognition for familiar faces fades once exposure ceases. However, in the case of teachers, there is probably also an interference effect because of the ever-changing groups of students they meet over the years.

One factor that seems to be important about familiar faces is that, because we are frequently exposed to them, we have had the opportunity to view them from a variety of angles. Ellis and Shepherd (1992) have shown that face recognition is better for faces that have been seen in a variety of poses. This may be a factor which accounts for some of the discrepancies between laboratory recognition tests and real-life situations.

Many laboratory tests of face recognition are based on people's memory for faces seen in a series of photographs rather than for faces seen in real life. Bahrick (1984) asked students to study photos of 20 target faces for a period of 5 seconds each with a view to picking them out in a subsequent recognition test. The target faces were then presented amongst a set of distractor faces (i.e. ones which had not been in the original presentation). Even though the students had been given instructions to pay close attention to the photos and were expecting to be tested, only 29 per cent of the responses were correct. However, when Bahrick asked students to pick out the photos of other students whom they had met in class at least 40 times over the previous ten-week term, recognition rates rose to 38 per cent (note that, in this case, students had not been given instructions to study the faces and were not expecting a recognition test). This suggests that faces that are seen only briefly in the two-dimensional form of a photograph are less easy to recognize than people encountered in everyday life.

Distinctiveness

Distinctiveness seems to be another factor which facilitates face recognition. Valentine and Bruce (1986) showed participants a set of photos of familiar and unfamiliar faces. Participants were required to rate each face in terms of how they thought it would stand out in a crowd. Valentine and Bruce used these ratings to sort the photos into two groups: typical and distinctive. A different group of participants were then shown the original set of photos (i.e. typical and distinctive), that were presented one at a time in random order. The participants' task was to respond as quickly as possible to each photo by saying whether the face was familiar or not. Responses were considerably faster for the distinctive faces. Political cartoonists make use of distinctiveness as a way of making their cartoon creations instantly recognizable. Rhodes *et al.* (1987) used computer graphics to exaggerate the features on drawings of faces. They found that the computer-generated versions were easier for people to recognize than the originals.

Stereotyping

Yarmey (1993) found, in a study with 240 students, a readiness to link facial features to underlying personality characteristics. The students were shown videos depicting 30 unknown, White males aged between 25 and 30 years and asked to select the young men who best fitted certain roles (the roles broadly fitted two *stereotypes* which Yarmey called 'good guys' and 'bad guys'), e.g. clergyman, doctor, mass murderer, armed robber. It was found that there was considerable

Figure 1.7
Some familiar faces

agreement amongst the students about which young men fitted which stereotypical role. As Yarmey points out, this has important legal implications, for example in terms of the reliability of juries. Although there is no evidence that facial features really are related to personality, it seems that people are prepared to make judgements about criminality based on the facial characteristics of suspects.

Recall of faces

We have looked so far at our ability to recognize faces and seen that several factors can influence accuracy. It seems that it is much easier for us to recognize faces than to recall them. This could partly be due to the fact that we find it difficult to describe faces in words. Try writing down a description of your face that would allow someone who had never seen you before to recognize you. You will almost certainly find this a difficult, if not impossible task. Imagine how much more difficult it would be to describe a face that you had seen only fleetingly at the scene of a crime. We are rarely called upon to describe faces but, if we were witnesses to a crime, we might be required by the police to provide an accurate description of the perpetrator. The photofit system, whereby a composite face is constructed from a large collection of features (e.g. noses, eyes, mouths, eyebrows) was devised in an attempt to overcome some of the difficulties of verbal description. However, research evidence suggests that this technique leads to poor recognition. Christie and Ellis (1981) found, for example, that target faces were better recognized from verbal descriptions than from photofit reconstructions. Davis *et al.* (1978) found that most people have difficulty in producing a likeness of a face even when the face is right in front of them. They also found that, when asked to match a photofit picture with an appropriate original face, participants performed at little better than chance level. Baddeley (1999) has suggested that performance is bad because photofit relies on breaking the face down into individual features, whereas we actually perceive faces in terms of holistic patterns. Cohen (1996) suggests that better rates of accuracy can be achieved by using systems based on computer graphics such as E-fit (Electronic Facial Identification Technique). In this system, instead of selecting features in isolation from one another, witnesses can build up more holistic images.

Summary: Eyewitness testimony

In this section, we have looked at an important application of memory research – namely eyewitness testimony. Although it is possible, under certain circumstances, for people to recall events vividly and in accurate detail, eyewitness testimony can be unreliable. The consequences of inaccurate testimony can be extremely serious leading to wrongful conviction and even, in the worst cases, wrongful execution. It is, therefore, important for psychologists to investigate the reasons for inaccurate recall and to suggest ways in which it might be improved.

One possible reason that people recall events inaccurately is that memories are distorted or reconstructed. Research into reconstructive memory was first carried out by Bartlett. He believed that we store memories in terms of our past experience (schemas) and that these influence our memory for events. Bartlett's own research has been criticized as being too vague, but subsequent researchers have supported his idea about the importance of schemas.

Elizabeth Loftus has been one of the leading researchers in the field of eyewitness testimony. She has been particularly interested in the effect on recall of information provided after the event. She has conducted numerous studies which seem to suggest that eyewitness testimony can be very malleable and subject to distortion. Her work has been extremely influential, but has been subject to the criticism that it is too artificial and fails to reflect the factors that influence real-life recall.

A particular area of interest within the field of eyewitness testimony is our ability to recognize faces. It appears that we often pay more attention to changing factors about a person, such as their clothing and the context in which we see them, than to facial characteristics, but we are quite skilled at recognizing familiar faces and ones which have particularly distinctive features. Recognition is more difficult for faces of other racial groups and for faces seen fleetingly or from only one orientation. However, recognition of faces is considerably better than recall.

Chapter summary

◆ In this chapter, we have considered several aspects of memory research. We store vast amounts of information in our memories and, most of the time, are extremely good at retrieving that information. Psychologists have been interested in investigating how memories are stored and whether there are separate stores for different types of information.

◆ The **multistore model** of memory first proposed by **Atkinson and Shiffrin** in 1968 distinguishes between **short-term** and **long-term memory.** These two stores are thought to differ in terms of their **capacity, encoding** and **duration.**

◆ The multistore model was the first information-processing model of memory and was very influential. However, it was criticized for being too simplistic and inflexible. **Baddeley and Hitch** (1974), for example, believed that STM operated more like a **working memory** and proposed that it consisted of a flexible and complex system of components under the control of a central executive. This model has been influential and has been supported in many experimental studies. Its major weakness, however, is the lack of evidence about the precise role and functioning of the central executive.

◆ The **levels of processing model** of **Craik and Lockhart** (1972) is rather different. Instead of proposing separate stores, Craik and Lockhart believed that the crucial factor in laying down new memories is the amount and depth of processing they receive. This model has received experimental support, but is criticized because it is descriptive rather than explanatory.

◆ Although we are generally good at retrieving information stored in memory, we do sometimes forget. Psychologists have proposed many reasons why we forget. **Decay** and **displacement** seem to be the main forgetting mechanisms in STM, whereas **retrieval failure** and **interference** account for much of the forgetting from LTM. Cognitive theories often fail to take account of **emotional factors**, but it seems likely that we forget some things because they are too painful to recall. **Freud** called this kind of forgetting **repression**. More modern research in this area has focused on recovered memory and the controversy over 'false memory'. **Flashbulb memories** have been a particular area of interest. These are memories for important events in our lives which appear to be remembered with enormous clarity and accuracy. However, some psychologists such as Neisser reject the idea that flashbulb memories are special in any way and believe that

they are subject to the same kinds of distortion and forgetting as other memories for events.

◆ One important application of memory research is **eyewitness testimony**. People are often able to recall events accurately and in detail, but eyewitness testimony can be fallible. Given the potentially serious consequences of inaccurate testimony, psychologists have sought to understand the reasons why people remember inaccurately and tried to find ways of improving their recall. One important factor seems to be that we have a tendency to distort or reconstruct memories. **Bartlett** introduced the concept of **reconstructive** memory to explain how we store memories in terms of our past knowledge and experience (schemas) and that these influence us when we come to recall the memory. Bartlett's own research has been criticized for lack of experimental rigour, but the concept of schemas continues to be important.

◆ Elizabeth **Loftus** has probably been one of the most influential researchers in the field of eyewitness testimony. She has been particularly concerned with the effects of misleading information provided after the event. Her studies have shown that testimony can be distorted by postevent information and by leading questions. This obviously has serious implications for the legal system. However, psychologists have also developed a practical method of gaining more accurate eyewitness testimony: the Cognitive Interview Schedule.

◆ As well as recalling a sequence of events, eyewitnesses are sometimes required to **recognize faces**. Various factors affect accuracy in face recognition, but we find it easier to recognize familiar faces and those which are distinctive. Reading a face holistically is also easier than recalling it feature by feature.

Exam summary

The AQA examination will test your understanding of the following areas:

◆ research into the nature (encoding, capacity and duration) and structure of short-term (pp. 3–5) and long-term memory (pp. 5–6)

◆ Atkinson and Shiffrin's multistore model of memory (pp. 6–8)

◆ alternative models of memory – working memory (p. 8–10) and levels of processing (pp. 10–11)

◆ explanations of forgetting in short-term memory (pp. 11–13)

◆ explanations of forgetting in long-term memory (pp. 13–15)

◆ research into the role of motivational factors in forgetting: flashbulb memory (pp. 15–16) and repression (p. 16).

◆ research into eyewitness testimony: reconstructive memory (pp. 17–20), Loftus' research into EWT (pp. 20–3), face recognition (pp. 23–6).

Exam question

The following question is typical of one drawn from the material above, and should take 30 minutes to answer:

(a) Explain what is meant by 'flashbulb memories' and 'repression' as they apply to memory. *(3 + 3 marks)*

(b) Describe one research study that has investigated the role of repression in forgetting. *(6 marks)*

(c) Describe one study that has investigated the phenomenon of flashbulb memory. *(6 marks)*

(d) 'On the basis of research investigations into the effect of emotional factors in memory, it seems inevitable that the accuracy of our memory for emotion arousing events will suffer.'

To what extent is this conclusion appropriate? *(12 marks)*

Suggested answer structure

(a) This question has two 'parts' ('flashbulb memories' and 'repression') which should be treated independently. You are asked to *explain* these terms, rather than simply define them. This might include a *description*: flashbulb memories are those memories that accompany a particularly significant emotionally arousing event, and repression refers to the expulsion from the conscious mind of thoughts and memories that might provoke anxiety. An *explanation* might also involve the psychological processes that would explain how these influences on our memory of an event operate. Flashbulb memories are covered on pp. 15–16, and repression on p. 16.

(b) Research studies of repression have typically been of two types; one based on naturalistic observation and the other on experimental manipulations. Naturalistic studies such as that carried out by Robinson *et al.* (1980) (see p. 16) have enabled researchers to gather valuable insights concerning the role of repression in everyday life (e.g. forgetting the pain of childbirth). Experimental manipulations include the study carried out by Levinger and Clark (1961) on the repression of word associations, and the subsequent extensions and developments of this study (see also p. 16). Note that this question does not *specify* which study must be described, so other relevant studies you may know about would also be relevant. You may, for example, have read about how memories can be affected by conditions of extreme emotion (as demonstrated in the investigation of holocaust survivors). Note that you are not being asked to offer any evaluation of this study, merely describe it. Note also that the question only asks for *one* study (not two, or three ...).

(c) Recent research has been carried out by Brown and Kulik (1977) who asked people to recall the circumstances of how they heard the news of President Kennedy's death, and a series of 10 other dramatic events (see p. 15). McCloskey *et al.* (1988) also carried out a study of people's flashbulb memories of the Challenger Space Shuttle disaster (p. 16). The same advice concerning the need for just *one* study and no need for evaluation applies here as well.

(d) The AQA specification requires candidates to study 'research into the role of emotional factors in forgetting'. The previous parts of this question asked for explanations and research studies relating to repression and flashbulb memories. Here you are being given the opportunity to assess whether emotion-arousing events affect the accuracy of memory (i.e. review strengths and weaknesses of the quotation). This assessment may take the form of an evaluation of the research itself (e.g. problems of verification in natural studies and real-life relevance of laboratory manipulations) or perhaps an examination of the claims in the quotation itself. For example, the fact that some laboratory studies of repression report poor memory for emotionally arousing events may be interpreted more as a reluctance to report unpleasant experiences, rather than a failure of memory. Some research on flashbulb memories for significant and emotional events (pp. 15–16) also challenge the claims in the quotation. You may, of course, offer support for the quotation's claims. For example, studies of heavy drinkers (e.g. Goodwin *et al.*, p. 15) demonstrate the effect of mood on memory and Loftus' study on 'weapons focus' (p. 22) concluded that anxiety impaired accurate recall.

Further resources

Baddeley, A.D. (1999) *Essentials of Human Memory*, Hove: Psychology Press.

An excellent, up-to-date book on memory, covering a wide area of topics.

Henderson, J. (1999) *Memory and Forgetting*, London and New York: Routledge.

A very readable book aimed at A-level students. It provides extra detail for those interested in finding out more about the topics covered in this chapter.

Websites

www.vuw.ac.nz/psyc/fitzMemory/contents.html

This partly interactive site looks at issues around recovered memories.

www.vuw.ac.nz/psyc/hudson_police/title.html

This looks at the reliability of police officers' memories. The site includes information on accuracy, confabulation training, stress and pressure.

Chapter 2

Attachments in development

Cara Flanagan

Preview

In this chapter we shall be looking at:

◆ the development and variety of attachments: including individual and cross-cultural variations, and a consideration of how such attachments form (e.g. learning theory and Bowlby's theory of attachment)

◆ separation, deprivation and privation: the effects of short- and long-term separation/deprivation from one's attachment figure, and the consequences of having formed no attachments at all (privation)

◆ the critical issue of day care and how it may affect a child's cognitive and social development.

Introduction

When you become 'attached to' someone, it means you have formed a special bond or relationship with that person, and they with you. Relationships and attachments are important throughout people's lives, but they have a special importance during infancy.

In the first section of this chapter we will consider in what way attachments are especially important for infants. We will also look at the sequence of the development of attachments, and at individual and cross-cultural variations. We will then consider why an infant becomes attached to one person rather than another.

If attachments are so important, then this would lead you to expect that a loss of attachments would have negative consequences for individuals. In the second section of this chapter we will consider the short- and long-term effects of separation. Furthermore, we will consider whether there is a difference between *loss* of attachment (deprivation) and *lack* of attachment (privation).

Does this psychological research have any relevance to 'real life'? It most definitely has. People are very concerned about the effects of separation when parents go out to work and their children are placed in day care. Does this harm the cognitive and social development of their children? The final section of this chapter considers this critical issue and the application of research on the development of attachments.

The development and variety of attachments

What is attachment? Attachment is a strong emotional tie that develops over time between an infant and their primary caregiver(s). It is a reciprocal tie because each partner is attached to the other. Maurer and Maurer (1989) suggested that attachments 'are welded in the heat of interactions'. In other words, attachments depend on interaction between two people rather than simply being together. Maccoby (1980) identified four characteristic effects of this tie:

◆ seeking proximity, especially at times of stress

◆ distress on separation

◆ pleasure when reunited

◆ general orientation of behaviour towards the primary caregiver.

The development of attachments

We will begin by considering how attachments develop and why attachments form, as well as looking at stages in the development of attachment.

Why do infants form attachments?

Infants are physically helpless and need adults to feed, care for, and protect them; without such assistance they cannot survive. (Psychologists generally use the term 'infant' to refer to children of less than 2 years; the term 'child' is used to refer to anyone between the age of 2 and adolescence.) Therefore, it is likely that infants are born with an innate tendency to form an attachment in order to increase their chances of survival. The term 'innate' refers to any behaviour that is inherited. Since attachment is a reciprocal process, it is also likely that adults are innately 'programmed' to become attached to their infants – otherwise they would not respond to their infant, and the attachment bond would not develop.

It is also likely that attachment has a long-term benefit in addition to the short-term benefit of ensuring food and safety. In the long term, it may be of fundamental importance for emotional relationships (see *In Focus*, 'Imprinting in non-human animals'). Similar claims have been made for the process of attachment in humans. The infant's first relationship acts as a template for later relationships; it gives them a model of how to behave. Bowlby (1981) called this the *internal working model*, a mental model of the world that enables individuals to predict, control and manipulate their environment. Individuals have many such models or *schema*. Some are concerned with the environment or world in general, and others are 'organismal' and tell us about ourselves and our relationship with the world. One such organismal model is concerned with the relationship between oneself and one's primary caregiver, and Bowlby suggested that this model provides a basis for all other relationships.

There is also evidence that imprinting in humans, like imprinting in birds, affects later sexual relationships. The 'Westermarck effect', named after Westermarck (1891), describes the fact that if children spend considerable time together before the age of 6, they *avoid* subsequently forming sexual relationships with these individuals, a kind of reverse imprinting. This would clearly be useful in avoiding incest. Incest is nonadaptive because the offspring of such unions have a greater chance of developing recessive genetic disorders. There is evidence to support the Westermarck effect. For instance, Shepher (1971) found that not one of the 3,000 Israeli marriage records he studied was between individuals who had been raised together on the same Kibbutz, a kind of communal farming community found in Israel.

Stages in the development of attachment

What is the sequence of events leading up to the development of attachment? This question was answered in a classic study conducted by Schaffer and Emerson (1964) (see *In Focus*, 'Research into the developments of attachment'). Schaffer and Emerson concluded that there were certain identifiable stages or phases in infant development, as outlined in Table 2.1.

---

in focus

Imprinting in non-human animals

To some extent our views about attachment are derived from research using non-human animals. Konrad Lorenz (1952) studied the behaviour of birds, who are *precocial* animals because they are mobile from the moment of hatching. They are likely to *imprint* on the first moving object they see at that moment, and this imprint has important short- and long-term effects.

In the short term, the young follow their mother-figure, which is important for food and safety. Lorenz (1937) demonstrated this with a clutch of gosling eggs, which were divided into two groups. One group was left with their natural mother, the other eggs were kept in an incubator. When the latter group hatched, the first living (moving) thing they saw was Lorenz and they soon started following him around. Lorenz marked the two groups to distinguish them and placed them together with their mother. The goslings quickly divided themselves up, one following their natural mother and Lorenz's brood following him.

One important long-term effect of imprinting may be on the choice of partner for mating. If an individual mates with a member of another species, they may produce offspring, but the offspring are invariably sterile, as is the case with mules (the product of a horse and a donkey). Therefore, it is important to be able to identify a member of your own species. Immelman (1972) demonstrated the role of imprinting in an experiment where Zebra finches were reared by Bengalese finches, and vice versa. The finches preferred to mate with their foster species even when given a free choice. This is called *sexual imprinting,* whereas the tie between a parent and offspring is called *filial imprinting.*

Lorenz suggested that imprinting should take place during a special window, or critical period, in development. He claimed that if the young did not imprint at this time, they would never form these bonds with a mother figure. Subsequent research has shown that the concept of a sensitive period better describes the fact that young animals are especially sensitive to acquiring certain responses at set times during development, but these responses may be learned at any time (Sluckin 1965).

Table 2.1	Phases in the development of attachment	
0 to 2 months	Preattachments (indiscriminate social responsiveness)	At this stage, infants produce similar responses to all objects, whether they are animate or inanimate. Towards the end of this period, infants are beginning to show a greater preference for social stimuli, such as a smiling face, and to be more content when they are with people.
2 to 7 months	Attachment-in-the-making (recognition of familiar people)	Infants become more social. They prefer human company and can distinguish between familiar and unfamiliar people. However, they are still relatively easily comforted by anyone, and do not yet show anxiety with strangers. The most distinctive feature of this stage is their general sociability (enjoyment of being with people).
Around 7 months to 24 months	Specific or clear-cut attachments (separation protest and stranger anxiety)	Infants begin to show a distinctly different sort of protest when one particular person puts them down (*separation protest*). Equally, they show especial joy at reunion with that person and are most comforted by this person. They are said to have formed a *specific attachment*. Around the same time, the infant begins to display *stranger anxiety*, an uneasiness with strangers.
Around 8 months onwards	Multiple attachments	Very soon after the main attachment is formed, infants also develop a wider circle of attachments depending on how many consistent relationships they have. The quality of these attachments is a matter of some debate. Some psychologists believe that there remains one special attachment figure (referred to as 'monotropy'). Other psychologists have suggested that all attachments are equivalent though qualitatively different.

Source: based on Schaffer and Emerson (1964), Bowlby (1969) and Schaffer (1998)

More recent research suggests that some aspects of this *stage account* are not entirely accurate. Very young infants appear to be far more social than was once thought. They recognize their caregivers at an earlier age and interact far more with other people. For example, Bushnell *et al.* (1989) found that infants, who were less than 24 hours old, look longer at their mother than at another woman. Camras *et al.* (1991) found that, by about 3 months, infants are beginning to smile more at familiar than unfamiliar people, suggesting that they are actually relatively discriminating in their social interactions, even at that early age.

As regards the appearance of separation anxiety, there appears to be close agreement, according to a recent review of research evidence by Schaffer (1998). This may be explained in terms of general mental or *cognitive* development. Around the same age that the first specific attachments form (at about 7 months), there are other aspects of development that are also changing. Perhaps, most importantly is the infants' sense of object permanence – the knowledge that things that are out of sight actually still exist. It was Piaget (1954) who introduced this concept that

younger infants lose interest in things which disappear (you can demonstrate this yourself if you try to play the game of peek-a-boo with a very young infant – they are simply not interested). Once infants have acquired a sense of object permanence, they also are aware that when their caregiver leaves the room, the caregiver continues to exist. They continue to watch for the caregiver's return rather than instantly turning their attention to something else.

We should also consider physical development. It is no accident that the time when specific attachments develop in human infants is also the time when they become mobile. It is interesting to note that Ainsworth (1967) reported that Ugandan babies expressed stranger anxiety at the slightly earlier age of 6 months *and* that their motor development was more advanced.

Therefore, we can conclude that there is support for the view that a certain kind of attachment appears around this age of 7 months – the kind of attachment where an infant expresses separation anxiety. However, other evidence is less supportive of the stage theory. Infants are much more social at an earlier age than was once thought.

Research into the development of attachments: Schaffer and Emerson

Schaffer and Emerson (1964) set out to provide descriptive data about attachment. Specifically, they aimed to explore the age of onset and the intensity of attachments, and the objects of attachment, and to search for any individual differences. They studied 60 infants from a mainly working-class area of Glasgow. The infants were observed every four weeks until they were 1 year old and then again at 18 months. At the start of the investigation the youngest participant was 5 weeks and the oldest 23 weeks.

Observations were conducted in the children's homes. Schaffer and Emerson used two measures to determine the strength of attachment. One was 'separation anxiety' – the distress shown by the infants when separated from their main caregiver. Schaffer and Emerson asked the mothers about situations where separation protest was shown, and to whom these protests were directed. This meant that they could rate the intensity of attachment at each monthly visit. They asked the mothers to consider seven everyday situations: the infant was left alone in a room, left with other people, left in the pram outside the house, left in the pram outside the shops, left in the cot at night, put down after being held by an adult, or passed by while sitting in a cot or chair.

The second measure of attachment was *stranger anxiety*. Very young infants show no anxiety when they are left with a stranger but, at a certain age, this starts. Schaffer and Emerson regarded this as another sign of the onset of attachment. Schaffer and Emerson measured stranger anxiety by starting every visit by approaching the infant and noting at what point the infant started to whimper, thus displaying anxiety.

Schaffer and Emerson's findings were:

1 *Age of onset* – Half of the children showed their first specific attachment between 6 to 8 months. Fear of strangers occurred about a month later in all the children.

2 *Intensity* – This peaked in the first month after attachment behaviour first appeared. However, there were large individual differences. Schaffer and Emerson observed that intensely attached infants had mothers who responded quickly to their demands (high responsiveness) and who offered the child the most interaction. Infants who were weakly attached had mothers who failed to interact.

3 *Objects of attachment* – Soon after one main attachment was formed, the infants also became attached to other people. By 18 months, very few (13 per cent) were attached to only one person. One-third of the infants had five or more attachments, such as their father, grandparent or older sibling. In 65 per cent of the children, the first specific attachment was to the mother, and in a further 30 per cent, the mother was the first joint object of attachment. Fathers were rarely the first sole object of attachment (3 per cent), but 27 per cent of them were the joint first object.

4 *Time spent with infant* – In 39 per cent of the cases, the person who usually fed, bathed and changed the child was *not* the child's primary attachment object. In other words, many of the mothers were not the people who performed these tasks, yet the mother did tend to be the main attachment object.

The important conclusions are that specific attachments were first formed around the age of 7 months, and that there were soon multiple attachments. Attachments seemed to be formed to individuals who were prepared to play, be responsive and interact socially with the child, rather than just spending time with the infant.

Activity 1: Investigating separation anxiety

Consider how you might investigate separation anxiety in infants. How would you determine:

1 how strong their response is
2 whom they are most attached to?

Variety of attachments: individual differences

We will now move from the development of attachments to consider *individual differences*, i.e. the ways that attachment varies from one individual to another, and from one culture to another.

Assessing secure and insecure attachment

Probably the most widely researched individual difference is in terms of how securely attached children are to their caregiver(s). We have already seen how Schaffer and Emerson assessed the intensity of attachment (see *In Focus* on p. 32). Mary Ainsworth developed another, more rigorous, method of measuring attachment in a procedure called the *Strange Situation* (see *In Focus* below).

The importance of the Strange Situation as a research tool is that it enables us to assess whether or not children are securely attached. Ainsworth and Bell (1970) classified children as belonging to one of three groups: *secure* (also known as type B), and two types of insecure attachment, *avoidant* (type A), and *ambivalent* (type C). In American samples, the proportion of children in each of these three groups is approximately 70 per cent, 15 per cent and 15 per cent respectively.

in focus

The Strange Situation (Ainsworth and Bell 1970)

The Strange Situation is a method of assessing how securely, or insecurely, an infant is attached to its caretaker. In terms of the kind of method used, it can best be described as a structured observation. It takes place in a laboratory with a set arrangement of attractive toys and furniture. The infants have to be mobile and the assessment is typically made with infants between 12 and 18 months of age. The procedure aims to record the *organization* of attachment behaviour, rather than to measure the *amount* of attachment.

In the Strange Situation the following sequence of events takes place. All the sessions, except the first one, take three minutes.

1 The mother and child are introduced to the room.

2 The mother and child are left alone and the child can investigate the toys.

3 A stranger enters the room and talks with the mother. The stranger gradually approaches the infant with a toy.

4 The mother leaves the child alone with the stranger, and the stranger interacts with the child.

5 The mother returns to greet and comfort the child.

6 The mother leaves the child with the stranger.

7 The stranger tries to engage the child.

8 The mother returns.

There is a detailed coding scheme to assign children to one of the three categories of attachment. In broad terms, *securely attached* infants (type B) tend to explore the unfamiliar room; they are subdued when the mother leaves and greet her positively when she returns. In contrast, *avoidant* infants (type A) do not orientate to the mother while investigating the toys and room, they do not seem concerned by her absence, and they show little interest in her when she returns. The *ambivalent* infants (type C) often show intense distress particularly when the mother is absent, but they reject the mother by pushing her away, often this occurs when the mother returns. Main and Cassidy (1988) have subsequently identified a further group of children, referred to as *disorganized* (type D). These children show inconsistent behaviour, confusion and indecision. They also tend to freeze or show stereotyped behaviours such as rocking.

In summary, attachment is assessed in terms of four aspects of the infant's behaviour:

◆ separation anxiety – This is the unease the child shows when left by their caregiver.

◆ the infants' willingness to explore – It is assumed that a more securely attached child will explore more widely.

◆ stranger anxiety – Security of attachment is assumed to be related to *greater* stranger anxiety.

◆ reunion behaviour – Insecurely attached children often greet their caregiver's return by ignoring them or behaving ambivalently.

In general, studies have found that for a particular child the Strange Situation classification (SSC) is usually the same at different ages (i.e. it is reliable or consistent). When differences occur, these are often associated with changes in the form of care, such as changes in family structure (Melhuish 1993). Two studies have even found similar types of attachment at 1 year and 6 years (Main and Cassidy 1988), and a study conducted in Germany found 78 per cent of the children were classified in the same way at these two ages (Wartner *et al.* 1994).

Any form of measurement (such as a ruler) should be *reliable*. It should also be *valid*, meaning that it should be measuring something that is real. One way to assess validity is in terms of *ecological validity*, i.e. the extent to which a laboratory finding (such as the Strange Situation) can be generalized to the real world. Research has found that the classification of attachment from the Strange Situation is related to children's reactions when they are separated in more natural circumstances, such as when a child is left with a babysitter (e.g. Smith and Noble 1987). The issue of validity will be considered further in our evaluation of the Strange Situation procedure.

Other investigations have reported that the security of attachment predicts children's later abilities. Secure infants appear more cooperative with their mother at 2 years (Matas *et al.* 1978). In addition, infants rated as secure in their second year have later been found to be rated by their nursery school teachers as being more popular, having more initiative, being higher in self-esteem, being less aggressive and being social leaders. Secure children were also rated as more popular by other children (Sroufe 1983). The children in Sroufe's study were also observed again at 11 years. The secure infants were rated as higher in social competence, self-confidence and self-esteem (Elicker *et al.* 1992). Thus, these and similar studies support the claim that the Strange Situation is measuring a psychologically important characteristic.

What causes the different attachment types?

Originally, Ainsworth and Bell supposed that secure attachments were the result of mothers being responsive to children's needs. Their study claimed to show a relationship between maternal responsiveness and the three types of attachment. However, there were flaws in this study. For example, the individuals who rated maternal responsiveness in the Strange Situation were aware of how these observations were related to attachment type. As a result, their scoring of behaviour may have been biased (because the raters should have been unaware of the meaning of their ratings). More recently, a better-controlled study by Isabella *et al.* (1989) has claimed to find the relation between responsiveness and attachment as predicted by Ainsworth. Mothers and

infants who tended to be responsive to each other at 1 month, and at later ages, were more likely at 12 months to have a secure relationship. Those who had a more one-sided pattern of interaction tended to have insecure relationships. If you recall, Schaffer and Emerson (1964) produced similar findings. Ainsworth *et al.* (1974) called this the *caregiving sensitivity hypothesis*, that attachment depends on the warm and loving responsiveness of the caregiver.

An alternative hypothesis, the *temperament hypothesis*, has been put forward by Kagan (1982). He suggested that certain innate personality or temperamental characteristics might account for behaviour in the Strange Situation rather than it being the result of the caregiver's responsiveness. It may be that some children are innately more vulnerable to stress, so each child will respond differently according to their innate temperament: children who behave in an avoidant way are difficult to upset, whereas ambivalent infants are easy to stress. Secure infants are somewhere between these two.

Research has found that newborns who are less able to attend to people and objects are more likely to develop insecure attachments at later ages (Waters 1978), and that newborns who showed signs of behavioural instability (e.g. tremors or shaking) were less likely to become securely attached to their mother than were newborns who did not (Belsky and Rovine 1987). Thus, there is a possibility that infant temperament contributes to the form of attachment.

An evaluation of the Strange Situation

The Strange Situation has produced evidence that certain children are secure or insecure, either as a result of their caregiver's responsiveness or of their innate responsiveness. However, there is one main objection to the evidence from the Strange Situation.

It is assumed in the Strange Situation that the behaviour being tested is in some way a characteristic of the child. It may only be a characteristic of the *relationship* being tested. Research has shown that children can have different attachment classifications with different parents. For example, they may be classified as having a secure attachment to their mother and an avoidant relationship with their father (Lamb 1977). This suggests that the attachment classification is not simply a matter of a child's character. If it were, then the child should have the same relationship with both mother and father. This causes problems when we claim to correlate early attachment type with later behaviour. We may in fact be correlating one early *relationship* type with later behaviour, which is all right if that relationship was the most significant influence on that child's emotional development. This is the problem with drawing conclusions from correlational evidence – we cannot be certain that A (attachment relationship) causes B (later behaviour). There may well be several intervening variables, such as other early emotional experiences of the infant. Or it may be that some children are simply good at forming relationships, which could explain why they have formed a secure early relationship with their caregiver and also why they tend to do well later in life.

Cross-cultural variations in secure and insecure attachments

In the same way that there are differences in attachment behaviour from one individual to another, there are also variations from one culture to another. Across the world and across history there have been many different forms of child-rearing and these may be related to differences in attachment, especially secure and insecure attachment (see *In Focus* for a description of some variations in child-rearing).

Researchers in many different countries have used the Strange Situation to investigate secure and insecure attachment. The results of 32 such studies undertaken in eight different countries have been summarized by Van IJzendoorn and Kroonenberg (1988), as shown in Table 2.2. Bee (1999) points out that the most striking finding is that there is considerable consistency across cultures, and concludes that it is likely that the same caregiver–infant interactions contribute to secure and insecure attachments in all cultures. In addition, cross-cultural studies have found a relationship between secure attachment and later adjustment. For example, in a study of Israeli infants, Sagi (1990) found that securely attached infants were later rated as having better social skills. This further supports the view that secure attachment is important in all cultures for healthy psychological development and that the concept of an internal working model may be a universal explanation.

in focus **Cultural differences in child-rearing**

Japanese child-rearing appears to place greater value on developing close family relationships; young infants are rarely separated from their mothers and the mothers are highly responsive to their needs (Miyake *et al.* 1985). In addition, greater prominence is given to allowing children to develop their own group identity and the ability to solve problems within a group. Some of the American styles of child-rearing seem harsh and inappropriate to Japanese parents – the fostering of independence, coupled with adults acting as arbiters in disputes, does not correspond with the practice in Japan. These different patterns of child-rearing are associated with different outcomes in terms of attachment processes (shown in Table 2.2, with American children showing a much higher percentage of *avoidant* attachment, i.e. demonstrating independence). However, it is important to remember that these are not experimental studies, so we cannot be sure that this is a causal relationship. The differences in attachment relationships between cultures could be caused, for the sake of argument, by genetic differences between cultures, rather than by differences in child-rearing practices.

Table 2.2 Cross-cultural differences in secure and insecure attachment, using the Strange Situation

Country	Number of studies	Percentage of each attachment type (to the nearest whole number)		
		Secure	Avoidant	Resistant
West Germany	3	57	35	8
Great Britain	1	75	22	3
Netherlands	4	67	26	7
Sweden	1	74	22	4
Israel	2	64	7	29
Japan	2	68	5	27
China	1	50	25	25
United States	18	65	21	14
Overall average		65	21	14

Source: Van IJzendoorn and Kroonenberg (1988, pp. 150–1)

Problems with cross-cultural use of the Strange Situation

One problem lies in the assumption that anxiety on separation means the same thing in all cultures. The Strange Situation measurement assumes that separation anxiety indicates secure attachment. However, in other cultures, the reason infants become anxious in the Strange Situation may *not* be due to secure or insecure attachment. Consider the comments by Miyake *et al.* (1985) about Japanese children (see *In Focus*). In Japan, infants very rarely leave their mother. Therefore, the Strange Situation is an unusual and particularly stressful event for them. Their excessive distress is likely to be due to the unusualness of the situation, rather than because of insecure attachment. Grossman *et al.* (1985), working in Germany, found a higher proportion of avoidant children (i.e. showing independence), and it was suggested that this may be a result of the greater value placed on this characteristic by parents in this culture. The same problems may arise in considering the behaviour of children in different social classes, or those who experience different forms of childcare in America and Britain. This leads us to conclude that the Strange Situation may be a culturally specific way of assessing security of attachment.

Another problem relates to the concept of 'culture'. One of Van IJzendoorn and Kroonenberg's key findings was that the variation of attachment *within* cultures was one and a half times greater than the variation *between* cultures. This suggests that it is wrong to think of one culture as consisting of the same or similar practices. In reality, all cultures consist of many subcultures, each with different child-rearing styles. To make generalizations about a culture is to oversimplify the relationship between parenting and attachment styles.

Multiple attachments

Bowlby (1953, 1988) claimed that infants need one special attachment relationship, which is qualitatively different from all others, in order to develop their internal working model. He used the term *monotropy,* which means 'turning towards one person', to describe this unique bond. There is considerable debate about whether this *primary bond* is universally true. In some cultures, children have equivalent relationships with many caregivers, and still develop into psychologically healthy adults. Thomas (1998) questions whether the tendency to form a single main attachment is actually good for healthy psychological development. It might be more desirable to have a network of attachments to sustain the needs of a growing infant who has a variety of demands for social and emotional interactions. Thomas claims that in Caribbean cultures, multiple attachments are the rule. Even in Western European culture, infants do form several attachments and these are all beneficial, probably precisely because of their qualitative differences. For example, fathers' style of play is more often physically stimulating and unpredictable, whereas mothers are more likely to hold their infants, soothe them, attend to their needs and read them stories (Parke 1981).

On the other hand, in Schaffer and Emerson's study (1964), it was found that even though infants do form multiple attachments, they appear usually to have one primary attachment. Ainsworth (1967) studied members of the Ganda tribe of Uganda, where the pattern of childcare involved multiple carers, and concluded that the infants nevertheless formed one primary attachment. Tronick *et al.* (1992) studied a pygmy tribe, the Efe from Zaire, who live in extended family groups. Infants and children were looked after by whoever was closest to hand. They were breastfed by different women, but usually slept with their own mother. Tronick and colleagues found that by the age of 6 months, the infants still showed a preference for their mothers, a single primary attachment.

A study by Fox (1977) looked at life in Kibbutzim, where children spend most of their time with nurses called *metapelets,* but see their mothers for a few hours a day after work. When the children were placed in the Strange Situation, they protested equally when either mother or metapelet left, but were more comforted by their mothers at reunion. This would again suggest that, despite having multiple carers, the infants still had one special relationship. However, we should note that the metapelets changed fairly frequently, and also had to divide their attention among many children and had less interest in any one individual, which would explain why the children were usually less attached to their metapelet.

Bowlby's (1969) view was that this one special relationship was uniquely important for emotional development, whereas Lamb (1981) argued the opposite case, that different attachments simply serve different purposes, rather than being in a hierarchy. For example, as we have seen, fathers tend to be more playful, while mothers might be good for quieter activities.

Explanations of attachment

Why do infants become attached to one person rather than another? What is the purpose of attachment? We have already considered some answers to these questions. For instance, it appears that a child becomes attached to a responsive caregiver or to someone who protects them. Here, we will focus on two explanations for who and why: *learning theory* and *Bowlby's* approach. Learning theory takes the view that attachment is a learned process (nurture), whereas Bowlby argued that attachment is an inherited behaviour (nature). These are examples of the *nature–nurture debate.*

Learning theory

Learning theory is the view put forward by behaviourists at the beginning of the twentieth century to explain how all behaviour is acquired, using the principles of conditioning:

- *Classical conditioning* – Dogs salivate when they feed. Salivation is an unconditioned response (UR) to an unconditioned stimulus (food – the US). The stimulus (US) and response (UR) are innately linked. If a bell is rung every time food appears, the animal comes to associate bell and food so that the bell alone will produce the UR. The bell was a neutral stimulus (NS), but is now a conditioned stimulus (CS) and the salivation is now a conditioned response (CR). Thus the animal has learned a new stimulus–response link.

- *Operant conditioning* – An animal is placed in a cage where food will be delivered if it presses a lever. At first the animal presses the lever accidentally and is rewarded by receiving food. This increases the probability that the behaviour (lever pressing) will be repeated. The food or *reward* is *reinforcing*. If the lever press results in an electric shock this will decrease the probability of the response being repeated. The shock acts as a *punishment*.

We can explain attachment in terms of the principles of classical conditioning. An infant is born with reflex responses. The stimulus of food produces a sense of pleasure – an unconditioned stimulus and an unconditioned response respectively. The person providing the food (usually the mother) becomes associated with this pleasure and therefore becomes a conditioned stimulus. The food-giver then becomes a source of pleasure, independent of whether or not food is supplied. This, according to learning theory, is the basis of the attachment bond.

Activity 2: Formation of attachment

Try to express the formation of attachment between an infant and their caregiver using the terminology of classical conditioning: NS, US, UR, CS, and CR.

In the 1950s, Dollard and Miller (1950) proposed a further adaptation of learning theory, based in part on operant conditioning, but with the inclusion of a mental state. They suggested that the human infant, when hungry, feels uncomfortable and enters a *drive state*. The drive motivates the baby to find some way to lessen the discomfort of being hungry. Of course, in early infancy the baby can do little more than howl and it is up to other people to feed it. Being fed satisfies the infant's hunger and makes it feel comfortable again. This results in *drive reduction*, which is rewarding, and the child learns that food is a reward or primary reinforcer. The person who supplies the food, the mother, is associated with the food and becomes a secondary reinforcer. From then on, the infant seeks to be with this person because she is now a source of reward. The infant has thus become attached.

Evaluation of learning theory as an explanation of attachment

Clearly, learning theory predicts that an infant's attachment will be to the person who gives greatest pleasure or drive reduction, probably the person who feeds them. Schaffer and Emerson (1964) found that this was not always true. In their study, fewer than half of the infants had a primary attachment to the person who usually fed, bathed and changed them. Another piece of evidence against the role of reinforcement came from classic research by Harlow (Harlow and Zimmerman 1959, Harlow and Harlow 1962) on the behaviour of rhesus monkeys (see *In Focus*, 'The formation of love in infant monkeys'). This, again, showed that feeding was not the main source of reinforcement and, therefore, not the sole basis for attachment. However, Harlow did find that *contact comfort* was a key source of reinforcement, but this was still not sufficient for healthy development. We should, of course, be cautious about making any generalizations about human behaviour on the basis of research with rhesus monkeys.

Behaviourism is often criticized for being *reductionist*. This means it 'reduces' the complexities of human behaviour to over-simple ideas such as stimulus, response and reinforcement. It then uses these concepts as building blocks to explain complex human behaviours such as attachment. It may be that these concepts are too simple to explain a complex behaviour such as attachment.

Bowlby's theory of attachment

Schaffer and Emerson (1964) claimed that Harlow's evidence was important in relieving the 'stranglehold' that behaviourism had on psychological research relating to attachment. The other reason for a movement away from learning theory was John Bowlby's (1969) theory, which suggested that attachment could be understood within the framework of evolutionary theory. Features of Bowlby's theory are outlined below.

Darwin's theory of evolution proposed that all psychological and physical characteristics are naturally *selected*. A characteristic is selected because it helps those individuals who possess that characteristic to

The formation of love in infant monkeys

The first, and perhaps most famous, study to show that attachment is not based on the supply of food was conducted by Harlow and Zimmerman (1959) on infant monkeys. The infant monkeys were placed in a cage with two wire-mesh cylinders, each with a face – so they looked a little like another animal. On one cylinder the baby monkey could obtain milk from a teat, while the other cylinder was covered with terry cloth towelling (giving contact comfort). If food was the cause of attachment, then one would expect the monkeys to cling to the bare cylinder which supplied the milk. In fact, the monkeys spent most of their time on the cloth-covered cylinder and would jump on to this cylinder when frightened (for instance by a noisy mechanical toy, as illustrated in Fig. 2.1). They also used the cloth-covered cylinder as a secure base for exploration. The study indicated that simply supplying food is not sufficient for the formation of attachment.

However, the cloth-covered 'mother' did not provide sufficient 'love' to enable healthy psychological development. In later life, the monkeys were either indifferent or abusive to other monkeys and had difficulty with mating and parenting. This shows that contact comfort is preferable to food comfort, but in itself is not sufficient for healthy development. Presumably, infants need a responsive carer.

In another experiment, Harlow and Harlow (1962) compared monkeys raised in total isolation with those raised with a cloth 'mother'. When placed with other monkeys, the isolated ones remained withdrawn and extremely fearful. In comparison, monkeys raised with a cloth 'mother' were much more able to engage in social activity. This shows that contact comfort had some value for subsequent social development.

In another experiment, four young monkeys were raised on their own without any 'mothers'. They spent the first few months huddled together, but gradually developed more independence and finally appeared to have suffered no ill effects. This suggests that the infant–infant affectional bond can be just as effective as the mother–infant bond.

This work, which would now be considered unethical, was crucial in demonstrating that neither feeding nor physical contact could explain attachment and healthy development.

Figure 2.1 The infant monkey clings to the cloth-covered 'mother' when frightened

survive and reproduce. This means that any characteristic of a currently living organism is likely to have some survival value, otherwise it would not have been selected. It is important to realize that this notion of selection is a passive one – no one is doing the selecting – it is selective pressure. The essential principle is that any behaviour that increases an individual's chances of survival and reproduction is desirable and *adaptive* because it helps the organism to adapt to its environment.

Bowlby argued that attachment is one such behaviour. It is easy to see why attachment would be adaptive in terms of survival. It helps to ensure warmth,

protection and food for young animals. It also gives young animals the opportunity to be around adults and to learn how to fend for themselves through imitation. Bowlby further suggested that attachment acts as a 'secure base' for exploration, which promotes cognitive development.

Attachment is also adaptive from the parents' point of view. Any parent who does not have a strong desire to be attached to their offspring decreases the likelihood of their young surviving, and that may be the end of their genetic line.

Infants are born 'programmed' to become attached and adults are also 'programmed' to form this kind of relationship with their infants. *Social releasers* are necessary to ensure an interaction takes place. These are social behaviours that elicit a caregiving reaction from another, such as smiling, crying, cooing and simply looking appealing. Bowlby suggested that these behaviours are innate in infants (and all animals), and that the responses are innate in caregivers. They are critical in the process of forming attachments.

Activity 3: Social releasers

Draw up a list of ten social releasers used by infants or individuals of any age. (A social releaser would be anything that encourages a caregiver reaction from another.) For each of these, state whether you think the behaviour or characteristic is innate and what response it might elicit from a caregiver.

Do you think the caregiver's responses are innate? To what extent will people differ in their responses, and why?

The concept of a *critical period* is a feature of biological characteristics. If development does not take place during a set developmental period, then it may not take place at all. For instance, in the development of the human embryo the arms begin to develop between Day 24 and 26. Any interference with development at this critical stage will permanently affect the limbs' development. If attachment is innate and therefore biological, we would expect there to be a critical period for its development. Bowlby suggested that if a child does not form an attachment before the age of $2\frac{1}{2}$ years, then it would not be possible thereafter. We will consider the evidence for this in the section on deprivation and privation.

Bowlby also suggested that if attachments were not formed by the age of $2\frac{1}{2}$, then the child would suffer permanent emotional damage, especially in terms of being able to form lasting relationships. The means by which this is achieved is called the *internal working model*, as already described. Bretherton and Waters (1985) suggest that secure children have developed a positive working model of themselves, based on their feelings of security derived from having a sensitive, emotionally responsive and supportive primary caregiver. In contrast, avoidant children are assumed to have a primary caregiver who is rejecting, resulting in their having a working model of themselves as unacceptable and unworthy. Ambivalent children have a primary caregiver who is inconsistent and consequently, the children tend to have a negative self-image and exaggerate their emotional responses as a way to obtain attention. This hypothesis provides one

possible explanation of the fact that early patterns of attachment are related to later child characteristics.

The claim about the working model is not without controversy. It could be that negative family characteristics explain why early attachments are insecure and also directly influence later relationships. So, the negative family characteristics are the cause of both.

Summary of Bowlby's theory

Why do infants become attached to one person rather than another? Bowlby would argue that the primary caregiver is the one who is most responsive and available and who enters into mutual interactions.

What is the purpose of attachment? Bowlby's theory suggests that attachment is an adaptive process that maximizes the survival of the infant and helps perpetuate the genetic line of the parent. Infants are born with an innate tendency to elicit social responses from caregivers. Caregivers also have an innate predisposition to respond to the infant's social releasers and to form a bond. This happens during a critical period, and the primary attachment relationship may result in an internal working model for future relationships.

Evaluation of Bowlby's theory

There are many flaws with the theory. For example, it does not explain *why* some children are able to cope with poor attachment experiences while others suffer long-term consequences, as we will see in the next section.

Another issue relates to Bowlby's argument that early attachment forms a template for future relationships. This would lead us to expect children to form similar sorts of relationships with all people because they are always working from the same template. However, the correlations among a child's various relationships are actually quite low. For example, parent–child relationships are not always positively correlated with child–peer relationships (Howes *et al.* 1994).

Even if there are positive correlations, there is an alternative explanation to that of the internal working model – namely that some infants may simply be better than others at forming relationships, as we saw when considering the temperament hypothesis (Kagan 1982). Children who are appealing to their parents are also likely to be appealing to other people.

One final point we should note is regarding the evolutionary argument, which is a *post-hoc* (after the fact) assumption rather than proven fact. In other words, we are making the judgement by looking backwards and arguing that a specific behaviour must be adaptive because it persists. We cannot *know* this is true, but are assuming it is likely. It could be that the value of the behaviour is simply neutral rather than positive.

Despite these criticisms, Bowlby's theory continues to have an enormous impact on psychology and the emotional care of young children.

Section summary

Attachment is a reciprocal and intense emotional tie with another person. The development of attachment can be described in terms of a series of stages or phases. The stage of specific attachments is marked by the appearance of separation and stranger anxiety, and can be explained in terms of cognitive development generally. Soon afterwards, other attachments appear.

Attachment behaviour varies from one individual to another, in terms of secure and insecure attachment. This is measured using the Strange Situation, which has been shown to be reliable, but the validity is questionable. Secure attachment may be explained in terms of caregiver sensitivity or the child's innate temperament, or it may be a feature of the relationship and not, therefore, a personality characteristic at all.

There is evidence to show that there is considerable cross-cultural consistency in attachment behaviour in the Strange Situation. The relationship between early attachment and later adjustment also appears to be universal. However, children in other cultures may feel anxious in the Strange Situation for reasons other than insecure attachment, which would suggest that the Strange Situation measurement may not be universally valid. With respect to the question of multiple attachments, it is not clear whether the variety of relationships that an infant has are equivalent, or whether one primary attachment is essential for emotional development (monotropy).

Attachment can be explained in terms of learning theory (nurture) or Bowlby's theory (nature). Classical and operant conditioning suggest that infants will become attached to the person who feeds them, either by becoming a conditioned stimulus (association) or secondary reinforcer (drive reduction). However, research doesn't support this reductionist view. Bowlby argued that attachment behaviour is innately adaptive. According to Bowlby, social releasers are important during a critical period of development and later relationships are based on the internal working model. However, Bowlby's theory cannot explain all individual differences, nor the fact that individuals tend to form different kinds of relationship later in life.

Separation, deprivation and privation

If attachment is critical to healthy psychological development, then Bowlby's theory would predict that any disruption to this process will result in the opposite effect – unhealthy psychological development. One way of determining the validity of Bowlby's theory is to consider the effects of separation. The concept of *separation* refers simply to being separated from a caregiver. *Deprivation,* on the other hand, implies that the separation has entailed some bond disruption – separation plus the disruption or loss of attachments. Finally, *privation* refers to the situation where no attachments have ever been formed.

Short-term effects of separation

Separation protest

Robertson and Bowlby (1952) described the immediate response to separation as the 'protest–despair–detachment' (PDD) model (see *In Focus*).

The extent of the distress varies according to the initial security of attachment (as discussed earlier), as well as individual temperamental differences and also experience. If children are frequently left and then reunited with their caregiver, they may be better at coping, as long as they have learned that being left is reliably followed by reunion.

It also is important to remember that the caregiver may also experience separation anxiety, and that the same phases of distress are manifested throughout life when coping with loss – for example, when coping with the death of a loved one (Kübler-Ross 1969).

If infant–caregiver separation continues for a prolonged period, the result is likely to be severe *anaclitic depression* in the infant. This term was first used by Spitz (1945) to describe the severe and progressive depression found in institutionalized infants, resulting from prolonged separation from their mothers. The term 'anaclitic' means 'arising from emotional dependency on another'. Spitz and Wolf (1946) studied 100 apparently normal children who became seriously depressed after staying in hospital. They observed that the children generally recovered well if the separation lasted less than three months. Longer separations were rarely associated with complete recovery.

Subsequent research has found similar reactions in other primates. Hogg *et al.* (1994) examined the effects of a 24-week separation on three infant gorillas that had been living with their mothers. During separation, the

Protest–despair–detachment model

Robertson and Bowlby (1952) observed that there are three progressive reactions to separation: *protest*, *despair* and *detachment*. The children in the study, aged between 1 and 4 years, were placed by their parents in residential nurseries (often because their mother was entering hospital) or were themselves hospitalized.

The initial *protest* involved crying, grizzling and calling the name of the mother, with the child appearing distraught and panic-stricken. These behaviours lasted from several hours to about one week.

Protest reactions typically gave way to *despair*, where the child became apathetic, uninterested in their surroundings, cried occasionally, and had a continuing need for their mother.

This, in turn, was followed by *detachment* as the child cried less and became more alert and interested. The detachment at first sight appeared to indicate recovery, but this seems to have been at the cost of suppression of feelings for the mother. When the mother returned, the child responded to her with a lack of interest, and was often angry and rejecting.

infants' behaviour initially showed threat responses and increased locomotion, both of which are characteristic behaviours of the protest stage of anaclitic depression. Upon reunion, the infants did not immediately engage in attachment behaviours with their mothers and spent more time in contact with each other.

Criticisms of the protest–despair–detachment model

Barrett (1997) examined films made by Robertson and Bowlby of children who were separated from their caregivers, and claimed that the children's initial response to separation could be better described as a determined effort to cope rather than to protest. This led Barrett to suggest a more complex account of the effects of separation that was related to individual differences. For example, a securely attached child may show little initial protest and cope relatively well, whereas an ambivalent or avoidant child would be plunged more immediately into protest and despair and become quite disorientated.

This version has the advantage of acknowledging the active role of the child and the interactive nature of the relationship. It has the disadvantage of possibly being overly complex and leading to an underestimation of the effects of separation.

Separation through hospitalization

Most of us assume that unless it is absolutely necessary, young children should not be separated from their mothers when, for instance, one of them has to go into hospital. Today, this is such a prevailing assumption that it is easy to forget that 30 years ago, attitudes were very different. Parental hospital visits were restricted and children were often placed in unfamiliar day nurseries when their mother went into hospital. There

was little concern about the effects of these separations, and little was done to help the children adjust to their new surroundings.

Psychological research played a major part in changing this. An important study by Robertson and Robertson (1971) showed that, given appropriate preparation and care, children could adjust to separation from their mother. The Robertsons were successful in minimizing the distress of children whom they cared for on separate occasions in their own home. They prepared each child for the separation – the child visited the Robertsons' home beforehand, and during the separation, the Robertsons talked to the child about the child's mother. In comparison, the Robertsons also studied a cheerful and affectionate 18-month-old boy who was taken into residential care for nine days. He became progressively more withdrawn and despairing, despite receiving excellent physical care. On return home he was sullen, rejected his mother, and there were severe behaviour problems throughout his childhood, including the fact that he repeatedly ran away from home.

Prior to this research, psychologists, doctors and nurses felt that all that was required to maintain psychological health was to provide good physical care. The Robertsons demonstrated that substitute emotional care was vital in preventing bond-disruption and preventing emotional maladjustment.

Activity 4: Your own experiences of separation

Think of your own experiences of separation from the people whom you love – either when you were younger or more recently. How did you respond and what did you feel? What things helped you to feel better?

Long-term effects of separation

Concerns about the long-term effects of separation were given an impetus by Bowlby's report in 1944 that delinquency was associated with young children's separation from their mother (see *In Focus*). He suggested that the separation was the cause of the delinquency.

Bowlby's maternal deprivation hypothesis

Bowlby developed the idea that if an infant was unable to develop a 'warm, intimate, and continuous relationship with his mother (or permanent mother-substitute)' (Bowlby 1953, p.13), then the child would have difficulty forming relationships with other people and be at risk of behavioural disorders. (Note that the use of the term 'maternal' was used to describe mothering from a mother *or* any mother-substitute). This became known as the *maternal deprivation hypothesis*. One source of evidence was his own research, but there were a number of other studies conducted around the time of the Second World War that indicated a key role for separation. For example, Spitz and Wolf's (1946) study mentioned earlier, and that of the Robertsons (Robertson and Robertson 1971), both indicated that separation may lead to subsequent emotional maladjustment.

Evaluation of the maternal deprivation hypothesis

There are various issues to be considered. First, much of the evidence used to support the idea came from studies of children in institutions where they were deprived *in many ways*. Therefore, it may not be *maternal* deprivation, but other forms of deprivation (e.g. physical deprivation) which affected subsequent development.

Second, not all research has found that separations lead to maladjustment. A later study by Bowlby *et al.* (1956) found no such ill effects. A group of children with tuberculosis was studied. They were under the age of 4 when they were first hospitalized. The nursing regimes tended to be strict and the care impersonal, but many of the children were visited weekly by their families (i.e. bond disruption was minimized). Information was obtained about these children when they were between 7 and 14 years old. They were assessed by psychologists and their teachers were also interviewed. When the children who had TB were compared with a control group of children who had not been in hospital, it was found that there were no differences in terms of delinquency or problems in forming social relationships. Therefore, it would appear that separation does not inevitably have harmful effects, as long as bond disruption is minimized.

Michael Rutter (1981) identified some further problems with the maternal deprivation hypothesis in a

---

in focus — Bowlby's 44 thieves study

Bowlby (1944) conducted research with 88 clients from the child guidance clinic where he worked as a psychiatrist. Forty-four of the children had been referred to the clinic because of stealing (the 'thieves'). Bowlby identified some of these children as 'affectionless psychopaths' because they appeared to have little sense of social responsibility and showed no guilt for their crimes. Other children referred to the clinic had not committed any crimes; they were emotionally maladjusted, but did not display antisocial behaviour. None of these children were diagnosed as affectionless psychopaths. This group acted as a control.

Bowlby interviewed the children and their families and was able to build up a record of their early life experiences. He found that a large number (86 per cent) of those thieves diagnosed as 'affectionless psychopaths' had experienced 'early and prolonged separations from their mothers', whereas very few of the non-psychopathic thieves or the other children had experienced such separations.

This appears to suggest that early separations may well be related to later emotional maladjustment. However, there have been a number of criticisms made about the methodology:

◆ The data on separation were collected retrospectively and may not be reliable.

◆ Some of the children had actually been separated for rather short periods and it is difficult to see how this might be the cause of such a serious condition.

◆ There are other methodological problems, such as the lack of true control groups and problematic sampling.

◆ The evidence is *correlational*, which means that we can only say that separation and affectionless psychopathy are linked, not that one caused the other.

classic book entitled *Maternal Deprivation Revisited*. Rutter supported Bowlby's hypothesis in general, but felt refinements were needed. He claimed that:

◆ Bowlby confused 'cause and effect' with an 'association'. The fact that early separation and later maladjustment are linked does *not* mean that one caused the other. Rutter suggested that instead, it could be that some families are 'at risk' because of, for example, poor living conditions or unsettled interpersonal relationships. These factors might lead to both early separation and later maladjustment. See *In Focus* below for a discussion of research supporting this hypothesis.

◆ Bowlby did not distinguish between different kinds of deprivation. An infant or child can be *deprived* of a caregiver's presence, meaning that the child had formed attachment bonds, but these were now disrupted; or the child can suffer from *privation*, which is the lack of ever having any attachments.

Before moving on to consider privation as distinct from deprivation, there is one final point to make. Bowlby's maternal deprivation hypothesis was developed in the early 1950s. He later went on to formulate the more positive 'attachment theory'. This theory, which you read about in the last section, focused on the benefits of attachment rather than the consequences of deprivation. The earlier maternal deprivation hypothesis, however, had an enormous impact on the way we treat children.

Privation

Bowlby may have been wrong about the effects of deprivation, but privation may be a different matter. There have been two main lines of evidence regarding privation:

◆ a set of case histories, collected over the last 50 years, of children raised in extreme isolation

◆ longitudinal studies of children in institutional care.

The case-history approach

Case histories of children who have been raised in isolated and deprived circumstances demonstrate two things: (a) some children never recover from their early privation, and (b) other children show remarkable recovery. See *In Focus*, 'Three cases of isolation', for three such case histories. Why did Genie fail to recover while the other children seemed to be more resilient? It may be due to the length of time in isolation. Genie was 13, which may be beyond the age of recovery, whereas the others were much younger. It may be because of the actual experiences in isolation. The Czech twins had each other, although Genie's mother claimed to have had a relationship with her daughter even though Genie was locked up (Rymer 1993). It may be related to some unique characteristic of the individual – Genie's father had locked her up because he thought she was retarded. It may be related to subsequent care – the Czech twins

---

in focus

The effects of discord versus separation

Rutter (1981) suggested that antisocial disorders are linked with broken homes, *not* because of the separation involved, but rather because of discord and disharmony. It is likely that affectionless psychopathy is due *not* to breaking of relationships, but because of the *initial* failure to form bonds. He tested this in his own research in The Isle of Wight study (Rutter 1976). Over 2,000 boys, aged between 9 and 12, and their families, were interviewed. Some children had experienced separation as a result of the physical illness or death of their mother; others had experienced separation due to psychiatric illness or discord within the family. In the latter case, the boys were four times more likely to become delinquent than when separation was due to illness. This supports Rutter's hypothesis that it is family discord, rather than separation on its own, that causes delinquency and emotional maladjustment.

More recent research by Cockett and Tripp (1994) also supported this finding. They compared the experiences of 152 children living in a variety of different families, including *reordered families*, i.e. those where parents had divorced and remarried, often with stepsiblings. Cockett and Tripp found that the children from reordered families were more likely to have encountered health problems, experienced friendship difficulties and suffered from low self-esteem. Those children living in intact families, where there was marital *discord*, did less well than children whose parents rarely argued, but they were better off than those from reordered families. The conclusion is that reordering is worst, followed by discord alone, but discord was still found to be a significant factor. It is worth noting, however, that the reordered families were also more likely to be receiving social security benefits, had moved house more often, and were less likely to own their own car. Therefore, the problems associated with reordering might have been due to a variety of factors other than parental divorce and remarriage.

were cared for by a pair of loving sisters, whereas there is uncertainty about the quality of the foster care Genie received because there were continuing wrangles about who should look after her, and she was later fostered by a family where she was abused.

These questions highlight some of the problems with the case-history approach. The evidence is also retrospective, so we cannot be sure about the actual conditions the children endured; nor is it possible to make generalizations about human behaviour on the basis of individuals who may have unique characteristics. Nevertheless, we might cautiously conclude from these case histories that recovery from privation does seem possible when good emotional care is offered at a sufficiently young age.

Studies of institutionalization

Another way to study privation is to consider the effects of institutionalization, in situations where infants have never had the opportunity to form any attachments. Bowlby's early view was that a 'bad' home (i.e. psychologically impoverished) was preferable to an institution because institutions 'convert a physically neglected but psychologically well-provided child into a physically well-provided but emotionally starved one' (Bowlby *et al.* 1952). One early study showed that children living in orphanages did improve dramatically

in terms of intellectual development when they were given greater emotional attention. Skodak and Skeels (1949) compared the development of one group of orphans raised in a home for children who were mentally retarded (where the women there gave them attention) with another group who remained in an institution. After one and a half years, the IQs of the control group fell from an average of 87 to 61 points, whereas the average IQs rose from 64 to 92 points in the group who were transferred to the home. Skeels (1966) assessed the children 20 years later and claimed that the effects were still apparent.

Barbara Tizard and co-workers conducted a larger-scale study over a period of almost 20 years (see *In Focus* on p. 45). The conclusions were again that recovery is possible given the right circumstances and the 'right' individual. Some children are more resilient than others. Clarke and Clarke (1979) put forward a transactional model to explain this. It may be that the adopted children in Tizard's studies got on well within their families because the families made special efforts to love them, whereas they did not experience this outside the home and thus were unable to form relationships as easily or well. This would suggest that the children's ability to form relationships *was* affected by their early privation, and reminds us of the reciprocal nature of relationships. Children who have

Three cases of isolation

The first case outlined is that of Isabelle. She had been kept in isolation in a darkened room with her mother who was deaf and without speech (Mason 1942, Davis 1947). Isabelle had not been given an adequate diet and had severe rickets. During her isolation, she communicated with her mother using gestures. The mother escaped from the isolation when Isabelle was about 6 years old. On her admission to hospital, Isabelle behaved like a wild animal and only made croaking sounds. After one week in the hospital, she started to make speech sounds and seemed to pass rapidly through the normal stages of speech. After 18 months, she had a vocabulary of over 2,000 words, could read and write, and could compose imaginative stories.

The second case involves Czechoslovakian, male, identical twins whose mother died after giving birth (Koluchová 1976). The children went to a children's home for 11 months, then spent six months with their aunt, and next went to stay with their father and stepmother. The father was of low intelligence and the stepmother was exceptionally cruel. The boys were never allowed out of the house and were kept in either a small, unheated closet or in a cellar. When discovered at 7 years, the children could hardly walk, had acute rickets, were very fearful and their spontaneous speech was very poor. After placement in a hospital and then a foster home, excellent gains were made. The children are now adults, and appear well adjusted and cognitively able (Clarke, personal communication).

Genie, the third case, was found when she was 13 years old (Curtiss 1977). Her history was one of isolation, severe neglect and physical restraint; she was kept strapped to a child's potty in an attic. Her father punished her if she made any sound. On discovery, her appearance was of a 6- or 7-year-old child. She was described by Curtiss as 'unsocialized, primitive, and hardly human'; she made virtually no sounds and was hardly able to walk. Genie never achieved good social adjustment or language despite intervention and being placed with a foster family.

suffered early privation may cope as long as the other partner is willing to make special efforts, but when they are with others who are not making special efforts, their early experiences may cause difficulties. The reason this is called a 'transactional model' is that it identifies an *interaction*. The effects of privation are not straightforward, but interact with other factors so that sometimes there are no effects from privation, whereas in other situations these effects are apparent.

One of the consequences of psychological research into the effects of institutionalization has been to reduce greatly the extent to which children are placed in such care. As a result, it has not been possible to replicate such studies until recently, when a natural opportunity for further study presented itself. In Romania, many children were placed in orphanages from birth and experienced considerable deprivation. Rutter *et al.* (1998) studied 111 Romanian orphans

adopted in the UK before the age of 2. On arrival, these children were physically undersized, but by the age of 4 they had caught up spectacularly to age-related milestones. However, age at adoption was negatively correlated with attainment of developmental milestones. In other words, the later the children were adopted, the slower their progress. This suggests that the longer children experience emotional deprivation, the longer it will take for them to recover.

The picture portrayed so far appears to suggest that early privation is not irreversible unless the same (privated) circumstances are prolonged. However, another finding from Harlow's research concerned the extent to which deprived (or privated) infants were able to become good parents. You may recall that the monkeys who were raised with the cloth 'mother' went on to be abusive and uncaring parents. Quinton *et al.* (1985) conducted a study that sheds light on this

Tizard and Hodges' study of the effects of institutional care

The focus of this longitudinal study by Barbara Tizard and colleagues was on 65 children who had been placed in an institution when they were less than 4 months old. There was an explicit policy in the institution against caregivers forming attachments with the children and, before the age of 4, the children had had an average of 50 different caregivers. This would suggest that the children (and the caregivers) were unlikely to have formed any specific attachments.

By the age of 4, 24 of the institutionalized children had been adopted, 15 had returned to their natural homes, and the rest remained in the institution. The children were assessed at ages 4, 8 and 16 (Tizard and Rees 1975, Tizard and Hodges 1978, Hodges and Tizard 1989). In the final analysis, it was found that the adopted children generally had close attachments to their parents and good family relationships, whereas this was less true for the children who had been restored to their homes, suggesting that Bowlby was wrong in thinking that 'bad' homes were preferable. However, the latter group had often returned to the same difficult circumstances that had precipitated the need for care in the first place, and to parents who may have felt ambivalent about them. In contrast, adopted children went to homes where the parents had very much wanted a child.

The conclusion was that the two ex-institution groups, adopted and restored, differed *within* their family relationships. However, there were similarities in the behaviour of the two groups *outside* the family, when interacting with other adults and peers. Both groups were more likely to seek adult attention and approval than the control children, and were less successful in peer relationships. Therefore, we can conclude that the early detrimental effects of institutionalization were seen to be improved by subsequent attachments, *but* there were also lasting effects.

Two points to consider in relation to this study are:

◆ There were considerable individual differences within each group – suggesting that there are numerous factors at work, not simply attachment experiences.

◆ Not all children were followed through the whole study (only 42 were left at the end) – those who 'dropped out' may have biased the final sample. For example, Hodges and Tizard reported that adopted children who remained in the study had fewer adjustment problems at age 4, whereas the restored children who remained in the study had earlier shown more adjustment problems than those who dropped out.

question with respect to human behaviour. They compared the behaviour of 89 women who had been raised in residential children's homes with a matched group of women raised in 'normal' homes. The women were observed interacting with their own children, and it was found that they were less sensitive, less supportive and less warm than the group of non-institutionalized women. Importantly, Quinton and his co-workers found that those institutionalized women who had had positive school experiences in childhood and favourable psychosocial circumstances in adulthood functioned as well as the comparison group. Once again, this illustrates the fact that continuing poor experiences are associated with poor recovery, but that recovery is possible when a child has improved care during childhood.

Evaluation of institutional studies

We might consider the fact that institutionalized children, like isolated children, did not experience total privation. They may have received peer support which, as we have seen in Harlow's research with monkeys, may compensate for a lack of adult attachments. Another study showed that the same is true for humans. Freud and Dann (1951) studied six war orphans whose parents had been murdered in a concentration camp when they were only a few months old. The infants had had very limited contact with anyone other than each other. When they were freed from the camp, the children had not yet developed speech properly, were underweight, and expressed hostility towards adults. However, they were greatly attached to each other. At the age of about 3, they were brought to England where they were well cared for in a hostel called 'Bulldogs Bank'. These children went on to show good recovery and formed attachments with the women caring for them. Their early peer support presumably helped them to recover. They were also relatively young.

The other issue to consider is that institutional care can involve more than emotional deprivation. Certainly the Romanian orphans spent great lengths of time in their cots with no intellectual stimulation and received very poor physical care. Therefore, again, we may be confusing deprivation from physical care and the lack of attachments. On the other hand, a classic study by Widdowson (1951) does suggest that it *is* emotional care that is paramount. He studied a group of apparently malnourished orphanage children. Despite being given dietary supplements, they remained underdeveloped. However, when a new supervisor arrived who gave them better emotional care, they began to improve. Many of the studies of children reared in isolation or in institutions, mentioned in this chapter, have found significant physical

underdevelopment. It is possible that the hormones produced by stress affect growth as well as physical health to produce what is called 'deprivation dwarfism'.

Reactive attachment disorder

Some children who experience early disruptions in the attachment process *do* appear to be *unable* to recover. These are children who are diagnosed with *reactive attachment disorder*. The symptoms are: lack of ability to give and receive affection, cruelty to others especially pets, abnormalities in eye contact and speech patterns, lying and stealing, lack of long-term friends, and extreme control problems (Parker and Forrest 1993). It is suggested that the cause of the disorder is a lack of primary attachments due to early maternal rejection and separation. For example, one typical case history described a young boy whose mother had not wanted him and offered him for adoption. This was followed by a series of foster homes until he was finally adopted at age 18 months. However, he appeared unable to accept the affection that his adopted parents tried to give him and, as an older child, engaged in lying, stealing, sending death threats and going into wild rages (Flanagan 1996).

Maternal rejection can occur even when the mother remains present, as in the case of *primary rejectors* (Jones *et al.* 1987). These tend to be middle-class women who have had an unwanted child, a difficult pregnancy, and/or experienced early separation from their infant due to problems at the time of birth. The mothers may well have good relationships with other children and are able to offer a good standard of physical care. Rejection starts from the time of birth and the mother–infant relationship never recovers. Gradually, the guilt and lack of empathy that the mother feels turns into anger and later, as the child grows up, a period of stress or naughtiness may result in excessive punishment and abuse.

However, it is possible that the reason for the initial breakdown between caregiver and child was some aspect of the child's temperament, and this has continued to affect other attempts to form relationships.

Activity 5: Managing children's separation anxiety

Imagine that you are a psychologist and have been asked to give advice to a hospital or unit where sick children are being cared for. The senior manager wants to know what they should do to improve the child's experiences while staying in hospital, particularly with regard to separation from parents. What three pieces of advice would you give them, based on psychological research?

Section summary

The findings about the short-term effects of separations are reasonably clear. If young children are not given adequate support (in terms of the provision of substitute emotional care), then there follows protest, despair and detachment. Prolonged separation leads to anaclitic depression. These problems may be avoided if it is possible to prevent bond-disruption during short-term separations.

The longer-term effects are less clear, but suggest that separations in themselves do not necessarily lead to later psychological problems. Early research by Bowlby and others led to the formulation of the maternal deprivation hypothesis, but this has since been criticized by Rutter. First, he suggested that Bowlby misinterpreted correlational evidence; it might, instead, be discord that causes both separation and subsequent maladjustment. Second, Rutter suggested that deprivation and privation should be distinguished. Studies of isolated and institutionalized children suggest that recovery from privation is possible when good emotional care is offered at a young enough age. However, apparently privated children (i.e. children who have experienced privation) may have formed attachments with peers, or they may have experienced more than emotional deprivation (for example, physical deprivation as well). There are some children with reactive attachment disorder for whom recovery appears unlikely.

CRITICAL ISSUE: Day care

Some of the research in this chapter may seem rather dated. This is because psychology has moved on from the issue of how deprivation and privation affect children, to focus on how we can improve situations where children are experiencing separation, deprivation and privation. The care of adopted children is one area of concern and another relevant issue is the consideration of the effects of day care.

We almost take it for granted today that local communities should be equipped with good preschool day-care facilities. However, psychologists have not always promoted this idea. One of the major issues raised by Bowlby's (1953) maternal deprivation hypothesis was the potentially *detrimental* effect of day care. If separations from the child's main caregiver, especially before the age of $2\frac{1}{2}$, are harmful, then shouldn't we stop mothers (or primary caregivers) going out to work? Although Bowlby did not suggest that women should stay at home to look after their children, this was the message taken from his work (Holmes 1993). Bowlby's arguments could alternatively be interpreted as favouring *improved* day care where the child's emotional needs were placed foremost.

We will consider the potential effects of day care on both cognitive and social development, and then we can consider how day care could be improved to avoid possible negative effects.

Effects of day care on cognitive development

Cognitive development concerns the growth of the child's thinking abilities. There are several factors that would lead us to expect that separation (i.e. disruption of attachment bonds) might cause delays in cognitive development:

◆ Stimulation is important for cognitive development. A study by Dennis (1973) of children in a Lebanese orphanage showed that if children had little opportunity for play or social contact, then after a year their scores on a development test were half those expected for their age. It is possible that children in day care receive less stimulation. This was one of the findings from studies of childminding (see *In Focus*, 'Childminding', on p. 48), which may be equally true of some day-care centres.

◆ A secure base for exploration is important for cognitive development. Bowlby's theory of attachment proposed that a key purpose of attachment is the provision of a secure base. Children who are insecure are less able to explore their world confidently and this may hinder their cognitive development. This is supported by research.

Activity 6: Your experience of day care

Before you started school, were you cared for at home (a) by your mother or father, (b) by a childminder, or (c) at a nursery? What did you feel about the experience?

◆ List the advantages and disadvantages you think this may have had.

◆ List all the people you remember feeling attached to as a preschool child.

◆ Who were you most closely attached to as a child?

You might like to ask others about their early experiences using the same questions, and compare the answers.

Childminding

Mayall and Petrie (1983) studied a group of London children aged under 2 and their mothers and childminders. The study found that the quality of care provided by childminders varied considerably. Some children did well, but other children were 'failing to thrive'. In the case of the children who weren't doing well, there were two possible explanations. Some of them came from homes where there was ongoing conflict and the children's problems could be explained in terms of this discord. The other explanation lies in the childcare environment. Mayall and Petrie found that some children often spent the day in an understimulated environment, lacking love and attention.

An earlier study by Bryant et al. (1980) examined the quality of care provided by childminders for nearly 100 children. Again, they found that a significant number of the children were not doing well, and some were actually disturbed. They also explained this in terms of the childcare environment, suggesting that many minders appeared to feel that they did not have to form emotional bonds with the children, nor did they have to stimulate them. In fact, to the contrary, minders rewarded quiet behaviour, thereby encouraging passivity and understimulation. Bryant et al. concluded that 'minding is thought to be a good form of care because it approximates more closely to being at home, but this may be a government-sponsored myth because childminding is a cheap form of care'. Childminding can work extremely well, but it seems that the aims of the childminder may not always foster attachment and cognitive development.

Cognitive and social effects of day care

Andersson (1992) conducted a study of the effects of day care in Sweden. A sample of over 100 children was studied from both lower- and middle-class homes, including one- and two-parent families. The children were assessed at ages 8 and 13 in terms of their cognitive and socio-emotional competence. This was determined by teacher assessments and IQ data. Andersson found that school performance was highest in those children who entered day care before the age of 1. School performance was lowest for those who did not have any day care. This suggests that day care is not harmful in terms of social and cognitive development, and may even be beneficial.

However, we should consider the fact that Andersson found that those children who entered day care before the age of 1 also came from higher socio-economic status homes. So the reason they did better at school may not be because of the day-care experience, but rather because they came from more affluent homes (probably with better-educated parents). Nevertheless, the day-care experience could have been detrimental and it wasn't.

It is also significant that this study was conducted in Sweden. A similar study looking at children in Texas (reported by Andersson) found the opposite – those children who were in day care from a very young age later had poorer peer relationships and emotional health. The different results may be due to the different infant care practices in both cultures. In Sweden, a substantial part of the infant's first year is spent with one or both parents due to a special parental leave system for both mothers and fathers. This means that infants may be able to form stronger attachments at home before they start day care, and therefore the separation as a result of day care will have less effect (because they are more securely attached). In Texas, parents may have less time to form secure relationships before their infants start day care and this may mean that home–infant attachments are less secure. Therefore, the infants fare less well in the day-care environment.

In addition, day care in Sweden is given a great deal of financial support from the government and may, therefore, be of a generally higher quality than in the US. In Sweden, day care has very low staff/child ratios and carers are highly trained. Texas, on the other hand, is a state with very low standard requirements. This suggests that it is quality of care that should concern us, rather than the question of whether or not day care is a good thing.

For example, Hazen and Durrett (1982) found that securely attached young children were more independent explorers of their environment and were also more innovative in their approach to problem-solving.

These two reasons can explain how cognitive development may be affected by day care. However, research has not found ill effects. For example, a classic study by Kagan *et al.* (1980) assessed a group of 33 children in a day-care centre in Boston, USA. The children attended the Treemont Centre full time from the age of $3\frac{1}{2}$ months, and were compared with a matched control group cared for at home by their mothers. Each member of staff at the school had special responsibility for a small group of children, thus ensuring close emotional contact. In the following two years, the children were assessed in terms of their attachments and cognitive achievements, as well as general sociability. Kagan and his colleagues found no consistently large differences between the two groups of children. There was, however, large variability among the children, but it was not related to the form of care, suggesting that day care had no detrimental effects.

More recently, Andersson (1992) considered the long-term effects of day care (see *In Focus,* 'Cognitive and social effects of day care'). The advantage of this study was the length of the follow-up period, which was 13 years. Again, the findings showed no ill effects from day care and, in fact, those children who entered day care before the age of 1 year showed the highest scores for cognitive as well as socio-emotional development. Burchinal *et al.* (1989) also found that the IQ of children entering school, after having spent time in day care, was usually higher than that of children who had been at home with their mothers.

How can this be? One suggestion is that women who go out to work may provide better *quality* care when they are at home, because they are more contented in themselves. For example, Brown and Harris (1978) found that women who don't work and who have several young children to care for are more likely to become seriously depressed. Williams (1987) argued that work increases a woman's sense of achievement, sense of personal worth and self-esteem. Shaffer (1993) reported that children of working mothers tend to be more confident in social settings

Children are not harmed by working moms

A study evaluating the development and health of more than 6,000 youngsters suggests that children of women who work outside the home suffer no permanent harm because of their mother's absence (Harvey 1999).

'I found there was no difference between children whose mothers were employed versus children whose mothers were not employed during the first three years,' said Elizabeth Harvey, a psychologist at the University of Massachusetts. 'Being employed is not going to harm the children.'

Harvey's study, published in the March 1999 issue of the journal *Developmental Psychology,* came to a different conclusion than some earlier studies of the same group of children. The new work examined the children at a later age, 12 years old. This suggests that problems detected in children of working mothers at ages 3 and 4 may have gone away by the time the children were 12.

In the study, Harvey used data from the National Longitudinal Survey of Youth, an in-depth interview study of 12,000 young people between the ages of 14 and 22 that started in 1979. Harvey concentrated on children born to the women in the study after 1980. The children were assessed every other year from 1986 to 1994. There were more than 6,000 children of all races in Harvey's study, and most were evaluated more than once. The youngest child assessed was 3, the oldest 12.

Harvey used standard psychological tests to evaluate children's language development, academic achievement, self-esteem and behaviour problems. Some of the results were based on reports of the parents. In comparison with children of mothers who did not work, Harvey said she found no statistically significant difference for any of the outcome measures.

Fundamentally, said Harvey, the study suggests issues exist in raising children that are more important than outside employment of the mother. These include the quality of the parent–child relationship and the quality of the child's day-care arrangement, she said. 'The message should be that being at home during the early years, or being employed during those years, are both good choices', Harvey said. 'Both can result in healthy, well-developed children.'

Source: adapted from the *Beloit Daily News,* 1 March 1999

and less stereotyped than those who have remained in their mother's care. It might be that going out to work enables some women to be *better* mothers. At the very least, working mothers shouldn't feel guilty (see *In Focus*, 'Children are not harmed by working mums').

Enrichment programmes

We should also consider the fact that some parents may, for one reason or another, be less able to cater sufficiently for their children's intellectual needs. It has been argued that some children start school at a disadvantage because they lack the intellectual stimulation enjoyed by other children. Such disadvantages inevitably only get worse and perpetuate a cycle of failure. For this reason, various intervention programmes have been set up, such as the massive Operation Headstart in the US in the 1960s. This programme was designed to reverse the effects of what was seen as social disadvantage by providing intensive preschool education for certain children. In the first year of the programme (1965), over half a million children were involved. When children in the preschool programme entered school, they showed more advanced cognitive and social behaviour than children who were not involved in the programme. These apparent gains appeared to be short-lived, but later research found continuing positive effects. For example, Lazar and Darlington (1982) reported that the Headstart children were less likely to be placed in special classes, were more likely to go to college and, in terms of social benefits, were less likely to need welfare assistance or become delinquent.

In terms of day care, the important point for us is that Headstart showed that day care was certainly not detrimental and may well have been beneficial. The lack of large-scale success may be due to the variety of other factors that influence children's scholastic success. The Headstart effects have been found to be stronger when the preschool programme had been followed up with later interventions.

Effects of day care on social development

Secure attachment is claimed to be of prime importance for emotional and social development. Therefore, if separation harms attachment, we would expect to see differences in terms of social and emotional development in those children placed in day care. Clarke-Stewart *et al.* (1994) investigated the relationship between time spent in day care and quality of attachment in over 500 children. They found that 15-month-old children who experienced 'high-intensity' childcare (30 hours or more a week from age 3 months) were equally distressed when separated from their mothers in the Strange Situation as 'low-intensity' children (less than 10 hours a

week). This suggests that attachment was not affected by the experiences of separation.

A recent study conducted by the National Institute of Child Health and Human Development (NICHD) Early Child Care Research Network (1997) sheds more light on this. They examined over 1,000 infants and their mothers at age 6 months and again at 15 months. The mothers were interviewed and the infants were observed at home and, where possible, in day care. The findings showed that those infants with extensive day-care experience did not differ from infants without day care in terms of the distress they exhibited during separations from mother in the Strange Situation. This suggests that the day-care experience had no immediate effects on attachment. Also, the study did not find any differences in terms of the age of the infants when they first started day care, the amount of day care, or the type of care. However, they did find effects in relation to maternal sensitivity and responsiveness. Infants were less likely to be secure when low maternal sensitivity or responsiveness was combined with poor quality childcare, more than minimal amounts of childcare, or more than one care arrangement. In other words, a build-up of negative factors did create problems.

Interaction effects

Egeland and Hiester (1995) found an interesting interaction effect. This study looked at about 70 children, about half of whom entered day care before the age of 1, and the rest remained at home with their mothers. All the children came from impoverished backgrounds. Security of attachment was assessed in the Strange Situation around the age of 1, and then the children were assessed again at the age of $3\frac{1}{2}$ years in a structured observation session. Day care appeared to have a negative effect for secure children, but had a positive influence for insecure children. We might be able to

Activity 7: Your views on day care

Do people think that a woman's place is in the home and that working mothers are not a good thing? Undertake your own survey which includes questions such as: Do you believe mothers should stay at home to look after their children? In what way do children suffer if they are placed in day care? What kinds of childcare arrangements do you think are best for the social, cognitive and emotional development of a child?

It might be a good idea to record your responses by age group (say under 20, 20 to 39, and over 40) and gender. Are there differences in attitudes in different groups of people?

explain this in terms of the fact that insecurely attached children *needed* compensatory education, and therefore benefited from day care, whereas the securely attached children did not require this extra attention. However, later reports on socio-emotional development found no differences between the two groups. These findings again suggest that what appears to matter is not the day-care experience itself, but the *conditions* under which it may be positively beneficial.

Ways of improving the quality of day care

Schaffer (1998) suggests that, given necessary safeguards, care outside the home may be positively beneficial as a supplement to home experiences, especially for some children. But what are these safeguards? Schaffer lists the two main ones as *consistency* and *quality*.

Consistency of care

We considered the issue of consistency in the context of Fox's study of metapelets on Kibbutzim (see p. 36). The same issue was also mentioned in relation to the institutionalized children in Tizard and Hodges' study (see *In Focus* on p. 45), where the children had had an average of 50 different caregivers before the age of 4.

It was suggested that the reason why the children may have been less securely attached to the metapelets and to the caregivers in the institution was because each metapelet looked after several children and they also changed fairly frequently. These factors make it difficult for the children to establish attachment bonds with such individuals, and are also likely to affect the feelings of the caregiver for the child. If you know that you are going to have a continuing and lasting relationship with a child (as a parent does), then you are more likely to devote the appropriate kind of resources. On the other hand, if a relationship is likely to endure for only a brief time, the adult may make less

commitment, perhaps because of their own fear of being hurt when the relationship ends.

The NICHD study found that low child-to-staff ratios were related to more sensitive and positive interactions with the caregiver. They found that even an infant-to-caregiver ratio as low as three-to-one can overwhelm a caregiver.

The question of consistency, according to Schaffer, is an organizational matter. A day-care centre needs to find some way of ensuring minimal turnover of staff, and to arrange that each child is assigned to one specific individual who is more or less constantly available and feels responsible for that child. It may also be important to establish consistent routines and physical environments.

Quality of care

It is probably more difficult to define quality, although Schaffer suggests that it can be expressed in terms of:

◆ The amount of verbal interaction between caregiver and child, which should ideally be one-to-one as far as possible – Tizard (1979) found evidence that, irrespective of social class, the conversations between mother and child were more complex than between nursery teacher and child. Teachers had fewer exchanges and elicited less from the children, which may be due to the teacher's inevitably divided attention and less intimate relationship with the child.

◆ Having sufficient stimulation, such as suitable toys, books and other play things.

◆ Giving sensitive emotional care. The NICHD study found that about 23 per cent of infant care providers gave 'highly' sensitive infant care, while 50 per cent of them provided only 'moderately' sensitive care, and 20 per cent were 'emotionally detached' from the infants under their care.

Research has found no evidence that either cognitive or social development is impaired in children who experience day care, while some children positively benefit.

Howes and Hamilton (1992) also found that secure attachments only occurred with 50 per cent of caregivers, as opposed to 70 per cent of mothers. The lower rate of attachment probably reflects the lower quality and closeness of the caregiver relationship. This is probably due to the fact that day-care assistants are less committed to the child, less attached and engage in less intense interactions, which highlights the importance of both the consistency and quality of care.

However, Scarr (1997) found that quality of childcare doesn't have short- or long-term effects. Her study assessed a group of 141 children under the age of 5, and then four years later, and obtained ratings of their social competence and academic achievement. The children's progress was more closely related to parental characteristics rather than to the quality of childcare.

Teaching day care providers

One study (Howes *et al.* 1998) considered the value of a programme designed to improve the quality of caregiver interactions. A number of caregivers were involved in in-service training to increase their sensitivity. Six months after training, Howes *et al.* found that the children (aged around 2 years old) became more secure and the caregivers were rated as more sensitive after training. There was a control group of caregivers who received no training. The attachment of the children in their care and their own sensitivity remained unchanged. The results of this study suggest that a modest intervention programme directed at improving caregiving practices can improve the attachment security of the children in day care.

The effects of separation on parents

One issue that is frequently overlooked is the reciprocal nature of the separation. Parents may themselves suffer when separated from their children, and this may affect their ability to give quality care when they are with their children. For many parents, work is an economic necessity. In addition, parents are often made to feel guilty about leaving children in day-care facilities. It might be helpful to provide more interlinking between home and day care – for example, by providing such services in the workplace.

Summary: Day care

One interpretation of attachment theory is that day care may be damaging because of the separation from the child's primary caregiver. An alternative way to interpret attachment theory is to suggest that when children are separated, the key factor is that they continue to receive sensitive caregiving. This would lead us to recommend attention to the quality of day care.

Some day-care experiences may lack stimulation and attachment opportunities, but, in general, cognitive development doesn't appear to suffer as a result of day care, and some children even benefit, possibly because they lack certain opportunities at home.

Children in day care appear to be as securely attached to their primary caregivers as those who are at home full-time, although children who are insecurely attached appear to benefit more from day care. This highlights the fact that one cannot simply say that day care is good or bad. The effects are related to other circumstances in the child's life and in some situations, day care may be positively beneficial.

The focus, therefore, is on improving the day-care experience through greater consistency and quality, in terms of lower staff turnover, lower staff–infant ratios, and increased responsiveness towards the child. It may be possible to teach caregivers important skills.

Schaffer (1998) concludes that what has been seen as an 'evil necessity' should be recognized as presenting opportunities for advancement.

Chapter summary

◆ Schaffer and Emerson have described the **development of attachment** as a sequence from asocial behaviour through to the first specific attachments and separation anxiety, which appear around the age of 7 months. Multiple attachments appear soon afterwards.

◆ **Individual differences** in attachment include secure and insecure attachment as assessed in **Ainsworth's** Strange Situation. These differences may be due to the caregiver's responsiveness or the child's innate temperament, or may be a feature of different relationships rather than individuals.

◆ There are **cross-cultural variations** and similarities in child-rearing methods and attachment behaviour. However, the Strange Situation may not be universally valid. Multiple attachments are found in some cultures and subcultures, and it is not clear if monotropy is still the rule.

◆ **Explanations of attachment** include **learning theory** (nurture) and **Bowlby's theory** (nature). Learning theory predicts that attachments will form with the person who feeds you. Bowlby argued that attachments are adaptive and form the basis of all later relationships, through the internal working model. There are criticisms of both theories.

◆ The **short-term effects** of **deprivation/separation** have been described in terms of protest–despair–detachment model and anaclitic depression. If bond-disruption is avoided, the ill effects can be overcome.

◆ The **long-term effects** of **deprivation/separation** may include affectionless psychopathy, as suggested by **Bowlby's maternal deprivation hypothesis**. However, Rutter has suggested that discord, rather than separation, may be the cause of maladjustment, and that deprivation may not have long-lasting effects, whereas privation will.

◆ Studies of **privation** have considered the lives of isolated children, children in institutions (such as in **Tizard and Hodges'** study of **institutionalization**), and reactive attachment disorder. It appears that

children are generally able to recover from privation when good emotional care is offered at a young enough age. However, it is difficult to assess the extent of an individual's emotional privation as they may, for example, have formed relationships with peers.

◆ The debate has moved on from whether separation is good or bad, to consider how we can improve a child's separation experience.

◆ This can be considered in the context of the critical issue: **day care**. Research has found no evidence that either **cognitive** or **social development** is impaired in children who experience day care, while some children positively benefit. The reason it is not good for all children may be due to a lack of consistency in caring and reduced quality of caregiver interactions. It may be possible to improve these.

Exam summary

The AQA examination will test your understanding of the following areas:

◆ the development of attachments (pp. 29–32)

◆ research into individual differences in attachment, and the notion of secure and insecure attachments (pp. 32–5)

◆ cross-cultural variations in attachment (pp. 35–6)

◆ explanations of attachment (pp. 36–40)

◆ research into the short-term (pp. 40–1) and long-term (pp. 41–3) effects of deprivation/separation

◆ research into privation and its effects (pp. 42–6)

◆ day care and its effects on cognitive and social development (pp. 47–52).

Example question

The question below is typical of one drawn from the material above, and should take you 30 minutes to answer:

(a) Explain what is meant by the terms *deprivation* and *privation*. *(3 + 3 marks)*

(b) Describe one study that has explored the effects of deprivation and one that has explored the effects of privation. *(6 + 6 marks)*

(c) 'Mother love in infancy is vital for our long-term wellbeing.'

To what extent has psychological research supported the importance of early attachments for later development? *(12 marks)*

Suggested answer structure

(a) Full marks for each of these terms requires accurate and detailed explanations. The terms are *defined* on p. 40, but an *explanation* requires more than this. You may, for example, illustrate your definition by explaining that deprivation may be a result of bond-disruption, such as might happen after traumatic separation from the attachment figure. Privation, on the other hand, may occur as a result of institutionalized care.

(b) It is often difficult to distinguish deprivation from privation in research studies because we may not know much about the early experiences of the children involved. This question requires a *description* of two studies. When describing studies, it is worth trying to illustrate the main aims, methods, results and conclusions of the study (what researchers call an *abstract*). Examples of appropriate research related to deprivation would be Bowlby's study of juvenile thieves (p. 42) and Rutter's Isle of Wight study (p. 43). Examples of research related to privation would include one of the case studies of privation detailed on p. 44, and Tizard and Hodges' study of the effects of institutional care (p. 45).

(c) This last part of the question calls for a much more discursive and evaluative response. The quotation suggests that 'mother love' is vital for our long-term wellbeing. You may choose to engage with that through discussion of the importance of *multiple attachments* (p. 36), particularly the importance of the father. The quotation also claims that this love is vital for our 'long-term wellbeing'. Cross-cultural research (p. 35) has not always supported the importance of early stimulation for later development. Alternatively, you may explore research that has shown how security of early attachment predicts children's later abilities (p. 34). Remember that this part of the question constitutes the AO2 part of the assessment (see Chapter 8) and so requires more than simply *describing* studies that might have some relevance in the context of this question.

Further resources

Flanagan, C. (1999) *Early Socialisation: Sociability and Attachment,* London: Routledge.

> *A short book written specifically for A-level students which covers lots of evidence and evaluation.*

Schaffer, H.R. (1998) *Making Decisions about Children,* Oxford: Blackwell.

> *A comprehensive and up-to-date review of research and issues related to attachment and separation.*

Smith, P.K., Cowie, H. and Blades, M. (1998) *Understanding Children's Development* (3rd edn), Oxford: Blackwell.

> *The latest edition of this standard developmental text includes a range of relevant research studies reported in detail.*

Chapter 3

Stress

Simon Green

Preview

In this chapter we shall be looking at:

◆ stress as a bodily response, including the physiological systems underlying the stress-response and the links between stress and physical illness, including the effects of stress on the immune system

◆ the sources of stress, such as life changes and workplace stressors, and individual differences in reactions to stress, including factors such as personality, culture, and gender

◆ methods of coping with stress, covering physical and psychological approaches, and the central role of 'control'.

Introduction

The term *stress*, as we use it today, was first used by the American physiologist Walter Cannon in 1914. However, it was the experimental work of Hans Selye in the 1930s which really introduced the topic into the scientific and psychological world. Selye was actually working on the effects of various hormones in rats. The animals had to be injected daily, and after some months they developed gastric (stomach) ulcers and greatly enlarged adrenal glands. At first, he thought it was the effect of the hormones, but when he ran control animals injected with harmless saline, they too showed the same symptoms. He concluded that it was the stress of the daily injection procedure that was causing the tissue damage, and confirmed it by demonstrating that other stressors, such as exposure to extreme changes in temperature, forced exercise or surgical procedures, led to the same effects. On the basis of these studies, Selye proposed that in animals and humans, the body responds to a range of psychological and physical stressors with the same pattern of physiological activation, which he called the *General Adaptation Syndrome* (Selye 1956), and that this activation can in some circumstances lead to harmful changes in the body.

This was the beginning of the modern study of stress. Stress is now a common topic of conversation.

It is believed to account for high levels of anxiety and depression, for increased vulnerability to colds and flu, and for heart attacks and strokes (damage to the brain's blood supply). Every week in papers and magazines there are articles on how to cope with the high levels of modern-day stress, and thousands of professional and amateur psychologists make a living out of stress and its consequences.

In this chapter we shall look at the background to modern stress research, and evaluate the evidence for links between stress and psychological and physical disorders. We shall see that some common assumptions about the effects of stress are well-founded, but that some are not supported by experimental evidence. We shall also see how successful methods of coping with stress have to take into account the causes of stress and the physiological mechanisms of the stress-response.

Definitions

Before we look at the bodily responses involved in stress, we have to be clear about what we mean by stress. Originally Selye borrowed the term from engineering – the idea of materials undergoing physical tension. In his model, the response of the body is the *stress-response*; any stimulus producing the stress-response is a *stressor*. This approach is now seen as too rigid, as we can see by briefly reviewing three different definitions of stress:

◆ the response definition

◆ the stimulus definition

◆ the transactional model.

The response definition of stress

This is Selye's approach, and means that any stimulus which produces the stress-response is by definition a stressor. A friend of mine is phobic about staplers, and shows an intense stress-response if he has to handle one (especially blue ones). To him they are an effective stressor, but does this mean that in general we classify staplers as stressors? Of course not. We need to acknowledge the important role of individual differences.

The stimulus definition of stress

This approach argues that we can agree that certain events, such as examinations, are stressful, and so any reaction they produce in people can be called a stress-response. Unfortunately, again, there are individual differences. For example, not everyone finds examinations stressful, and although we can agree that major life events such as a death in the family are stressful, we would disagree on how stressful less significant events are.

The transactional model of stress

This is the most popular approach to studying stress today. It argues that the key to defining the degree of stress experienced by an individual lies in their perception of themselves and their world. It is close to Selye's original model, in that anything that produces the body's stress-response is by definition a stressor, but develops it by saying that it is not the stimulus itself but our *perception* of it that is critical.

The second crucial aspect to the transactional approach is the role of coping abilities, i.e. our systems for handling the problems and situations that life throws at us. These could be the learning and revision we have done for an exam, our savings when the mobile-phone bill comes in, or our psychological make-up in the face of divorce or the death of a relative or friend. Again, as Fig. 3.1 shows, it is not simply our actual coping abilities, but how we *perceive* them that is critical. Some people are pessimistic about exam preparation, although, annoyingly, everyone else knows that they always prepare well and do brilliantly. That doesn't matter; if they see themselves as underprepared, that is what they have to deal with, however unrealistic it may be.

In the transactional model, a state of stress exists when there is a mismatch between the demands we perceive the world is making on us and our perceived coping strategies.

Some people overestimate the demands of exams, and underestimate their preparations. They will be highly stressed, even though, objectively, they shouldn't

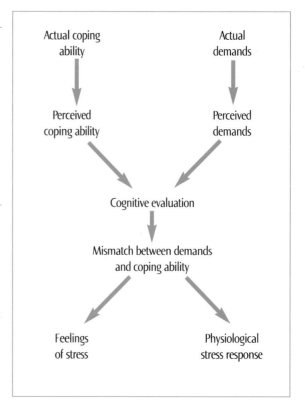

Figure 3.1
Simplified view of the transactional model of stress

be, and will do extremely well. Others, through underestimating the demands of the examination and overestimating their preparations, will do badly, but at least won't be stressed while they fail. The key features are the perception and evaluation of demands and coping abilities, so the important development over Selye's original ideas is the introduction of a central *cognitive* element. This allows us to emphasize and explain the role of individual differences in the perception of and reactions to stressful situations. It also means that we can use cognitive strategies to help people cope with stress, as we shall see later.

Stress as a bodily response

An important feature of the transactional model of stress is that a perceived mismatch between demands and coping abilities leads to activation of the body's stress-response. This was first described by Selye, and stands today largely unchanged.

Before considering Sely's General Adaptation Syndrome, however, we need to look at some physiology.

Physiology of the stress-response

Our bodily stress-response primarily involves two systems: the autonomic nervous system, and one centred on the pituitary gland. The two systems come together in their actions on the adrenal gland.

We have two adrenal glands, lying just above the kidneys. Each adrenal gland is made up of two distinct

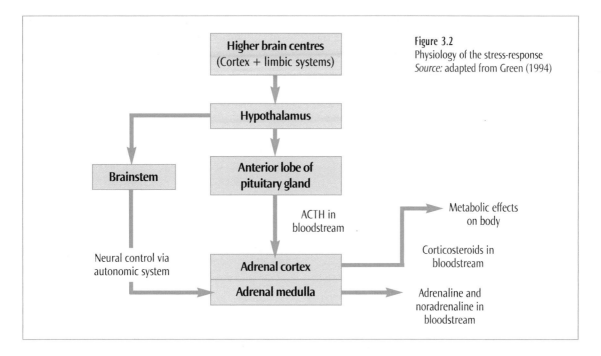

Figure 3.2
Physiology of the stress-response
Source: adapted from Green (1994)

sections, the *adrenal cortex* and the *adrenal medulla*. These two sections release different sets of hormones into the bloodstream (see Fig. 3.2) and are controlled by the two systems mentioned above.

Adrenal cortex

This is under the control of the *pituitary gland*. This gland lies in the skull cavity just below the surface of the brain, to which it is attached by a stalk (the *infundibulum* – see Fig. 3.3). The pituitary has been called the master gland of the body, as it releases a number of hormones into the bloodstream which in turn control many vital body functions. One of these hormones is *ACTH (adrenocorticotrophic hormone)*, which travels to the adrenal cortex and stimulates the release of hormones called *corticosteroids*. There are a large number of corticosteroids, divided into two groups called glucocorticoids and mineralocorticoids.

Corticosteroids, as we shall see later, have a wide range of effects on various processes in the body.

The pituitary is directly connected by the infundibulum to that part of the brain known as the *hypothalamus*. The reason for the connection is that neurons in the hypothalamus actually control the secretion of pituitary hormones such as ACTH. Damage or stimulation of areas of the hypothalamus can directly alter levels of pituitary hormones in the bloodstream, showing that the hypothalamic-pituitary connection allows hormonal or endocrine activity to be influenced by brain systems.

Adrenal medulla

The control of this part of the adrenal gland is very different. The *autonomic nervous system (ANS)* is a network of neurons running from centres in the lower parts of the brain (the brainstem) out to the organs of the body such as the heart, digestive system, the circulatory (blood) system, and various glands including the adrenal medulla. The role of the ANS is to

Figure 3.3
The functioning of the pituitary gland

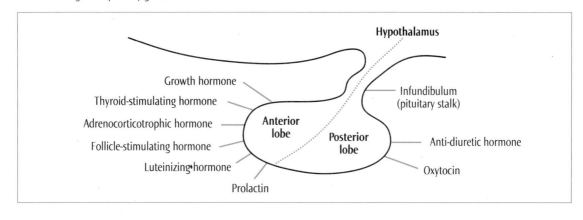

maintain the normal functioning of these systems in response to demands made on the body. When you run, you need more energy and oxygen supplied to the muscles, so our energy reserves (fats and carbohydrates) have to be 'mobilized' into sugars and fatty acids in the bloodstream, and our heart rate and blood pressure have to increase. All this is carried out by the ANS without our conscious control.

To help it carry out its functions, the ANS has two subdivisions, the sympathetic and the parasympathetic. Each has neural pathways running to the internal organs of the body. When *sympathetic activation* dominates, we see a pattern of bodily arousal: heart rate and blood pressure increase; fats and carbohydrates are mobilized; activity in the digestive tract slows down – a pattern known as *sympathetic arousal. Parasympathetic* dominance leads to the opposite picture, with heart rate and blood pressure returning to normal and digestion speeding up – a pattern of calm and bodily relaxation.

The adrenal medulla is controlled by the ANS, and sympathetic activation stimulates it to release the hormones *adrenaline* and *noradrenaline* into the bloodstream (in the USA these are called *epinephrine* and *norepinephrine*). Adrenaline is well known as an arousal hormone, and noradrenaline has similar effects. Together they reinforce the pattern of sympathetic activation, stimulating heart rate and blood pressure and further mobilizing energy reserves.

Activating the body's stress-response

Selye identified activation of these two systems – the hypothalamic-pituitary axis and the ANS-adrenal medulla – as the main components of the body's response to stressors, and also began the debate as to why they should be activated under these conditions.

The key to this is to understand that the two systems, when aroused, prepare the body for energy expenditure. Corticosteroids, adrenaline, and noradrenaline mobilize energy reserves and sustain blood flow and heart rate to get oxygen to the muscles. They do this under normal circumstances to supply our daily energy needs, but in stressful situations we also have to consider the role of higher brain centres.

Normally the hypothalamus and the ANS chug along perfectly well without our conscious

involvement, making sure that the body's physiological systems function within normal limits. There is a rare developmental abnormality that leads to the birth of a baby without higher brain centres such as the cerebral cortex; these children can survive despite such drastic loss as the hypothalamus, and the ANS can regulate their internal physiological processes even in the absence of the higher centres. However, we do need the higher centres when things happen in the world around us to which we have to respond quickly.

To our ancestors, the appearance of a sabre-toothed tiger on the horizon was a signal to run for their lives. Alternatively, if they were hunting, the appearance of a suitable target was a signal to chase. Either way, the reaction was due to higher brain centres in the cortex and limbic system perceiving and evaluating the situation as either threatening or attractive. But to run in any direction needs energy. So, to make sure the energy was available, the higher centres would communicate with the hypothalamus and the ANS, and would stimulate a pattern of bodily arousal; ACTH would be released from the pituitary, leading to the secretion of corticosteroids from the adrenal cortex, and sympathetic ANS arousal would lead to the secretion of adrenaline and noradrenaline from the adrenal medulla. When the emergency was over, the systems would return to their normal level of functioning.

Cannon (1914) had called this pattern of bodily arousal the 'flight or fight' response. Selye's experimental studies showed that it was also central to the stress-response he observed in his rats, and later proposed that these two systems were activated by any physical or psychological stressor. He proposed a model, the General Adaptation Syndrome, which besides serving to explain the short-term effects of exposure to stressors, also accounted for stress-related illnesses such as gastric ulcers.

The General Adaptation Syndrome

The General Adaptation Syndrome (GAS) (Selye 1956) has three stages (see Fig. 3.4). In the first *alarm* stage, the presence of a stressful event is registered; this can be a threat from outside or a physical stressor, such as

Figure 3.4
The three stages of Selye's General Adaptation Syndrome

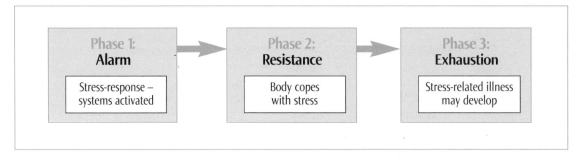

Phase 1: **Alarm**	Phase 2: **Resistance**	Phase 3: **Exhaustion**
Stress-response – systems activated	Body copes with stress	Stress-related illness may develop

injury or illness affecting the body. The hypothalamic-pituitary system secretes a surge of ACTH which, in turn, releases corticosteroids from the adrenal cortex, while sympathetic ANS activation leads to increased adrenaline and noradrenaline secretion from the adrenal medulla. The body is prepared for energy expenditure, i.e. to respond to the perceived threat.

In the second stage of *resistance*, the body's stress-response is fully activated and apparently coping with the stressor, and from the outside things seem to be back under control. However, if the stressor is long-lasting or chronic, the body enters the third stage of GAS, the stage of *exhaustion*. It is at this point that stress-related conditions such as raised blood pressure, ulcers, depression and anxiety may develop. However, before looking in more detail at why chronic stress can be harmful, there is an evolutionary issue to consider.

The evolution – or not – of the stress-response

The body systems underpinning stress-response are also responsible for providing energy resources whenever we need them. This can be under normal circumstances of physical activity (running up the stairs), or fleeing from predators (not too common in our society), or chasing mates (also not too common in our society). The most intense activation is when potential threats (severe stressors) are perceived, as survival is our most basic instinct.

For our ancestors, threats were external – e.g. large predators, other people – and the adaptive response very physical – flight or fight. Our body's arousal systems allowed them to react effectively, providing the energy for muscular and therefore physical activity. Such threats were usually short-lasting, and, depending on the outcome, the arousal systems would return to normal baseline functioning (if you escaped or won), or

shut down completely (if you lost). This was a highly effective mechanism for keeping people alive.

It was a mechanism with a long evolutionary history. All animals more complex than jellyfish need to respond to threats, to expend energy in reacting to danger. In fact, the systems are so effective that there has been little change in their basic organization from more primitive mammals, such as shrews, up to and including humans. Unfortunately, humans, unlike other animals, have also evolved socially and culturally.

Although some sociobiologists like to argue the opposite, we do live in a world very different from that of our Neanderthal ancestors. In the industrialized world, we have created a technologically advanced society, with complex family, social and economic structures. The threats to us are unlikely to be large predators (physical threat and violence, while still too common, are not part of most people's daily experience). The daily stressors can still be physical – longer working hours leading to fatigue, for instance – but these are dominated now by psychological stress. We have become an introverted and self-aware society, worrying about relationships, careers, the future of the environment, even how we look, and whether we are happy or not. We sit in traffic jams late for work or feel pressured to succeed in examinations.

These anxieties are *internally generated* by our thoughts and feelings, but can still lead to that sense of fear and foreboding which is probably not so different to our Neanderthal ancestor seeing the tiger on the horizon. And certainly our stress-response systems can't tell the difference. Worrying over the credit card bill is just as effective at activating the stress-response as preparing to run from the tiger.

Unfortunately, the reaction to the credit card bill does not usually involve running as fast as you can and climbing a tree. Our stress-response is geared to providing the energy resources needed for physical action, but our contemporary stressors do not require immediate physical activity. In addition, there is usually

Nowadays daily stressors are psychological, rather than physical

Activity 1: Your responses to different stressors

Think back to the last time you were stressed because you were in frightening circumstances (perhaps walking home through an unlit lane late at night). How did you feel?

Now think of the last time you were stressed because you were stuck in a traffic jam, or perhaps battling to meet an assignment deadline. Were there any similarities in the way you felt in each of these situations. Did you deal with each of these in different ways?

no immediate coping reaction possible; our stressors are long lasting, or chronic, as anxieties over relationships and careers do not disappear overnight. We have, in evolutionary terms, primitive stress-response systems increasingly unsuited to the world we now live in.

The worst-case scenario is that we have highly aroused stress-response systems providing energy with nowhere to go. If the stressor is chronic, this arousal is sustained for long periods, and it is in these circumstances that the damaging effects of stress occur.

Stress and physical illness

The last phase of Selye's GAS is the stage of exhaustion. In Selye's time, it was thought that the constant outpouring of stress hormones eventually depleted our stores, so that a literal state of 'exhaustion' occurred. It was this that led to stress-related illness. Nowadays, the view has changed to one in which it is the hormones themselves that are seen as responsible for the negative effects of stressful situations. The two main reasons for this change in view are, first, that hormone supplies are rarely exhausted – even under the most severe pressure – and, second, that we now know far more about the widespread effects of these hormones on the body.

Stress-related activation of the hypothalamic-pituitary axis and the sympathetic branch of the ANS leads to the increased secretion of corticosteroids, adrenaline and noradrenaline. Heart rate and blood pressure increase and energy reserves are mobilized in the form of fatty acids and glucose in the bloodstream. We will look at some of the possible harmful effects of this energy mobilization in a moment, but another important feature of the body's stress-response is that, besides activating some systems, it shuts down others. Blood supply is prioritized, increasing to heart and skeletal muscles and the brain, decreasing to systems of no immediate use such as the digestive tract (another sometimes embarrassing effect is the apparent loss of control of the bladder and increased diarrhoea when under stress. In evolutionary terms, this is seen as adaptive – lose a pound or so of urine or faeces, and you run faster...).

Our immune system is also inhibited in stressful situations. This is an immensely complicated system of cells and chemicals that protects the body from infection by viruses and bacteria, and helps in repairing tissue damage (see *In Focus*, 'The immune system and stress'). During stress, however, everything is geared to escape, so protection and tissue repair can wait until the emergency is over.

So the picture is one in which the body's systems are totally directed to survival in the face of threat. As long as the threat is short lived, this is an excellent survival strategy. However, if the threat is long lasting, the combination of maximum activation of the stress-response arousal pathways and the shutting down of nonessential systems can lead to problems.

Psychosomatic illness

'Psyche' means 'the mind' and 'soma' refers to 'the body'. 'Psychosomatic' is a rather old-fashioned term for the influence of the mind on the body, i.e. explaining physical symptoms not through physical damage or infection, but through psychological processes such as fear and anxiety. It is used in particular to describe stress-related physical illnesses, which include:

◆ hypertension

◆ cardiac disease

◆ migraine

◆ asthma

◆ gastric ulcers

◆ eczema.

It is important to remember that all of these conditions can have other causes besides chronic stress. Heart disease and hypertension may have a genetic component, and are certainly linked to diet. Often, it may be a case of stress interacting with these other factors to make the situation worse.

It is also important to remember that while chronic stress may not lead to obvious illness in the sense that you have a heart attack, catch flu, or develop stomach ulcers, it can damage the body, making these conditions more likely to happen. There are many stages of deterioration between a healthy heart and blood supply (together called the *cardiovascular* system) and an actual heart attack or stroke.

How does stress damage the body?

We can divide the possible ways in which stress can damage the body into some simple categories:

◆ direct mechanical effects

◆ energy mobilization

◆ suppression of the immune system

◆ other effects.

Direct mechanical effects

The body's stress-response increases heart rate, pumping blood around the body at faster speeds and at a higher pressure. At particular points in the cardiovascular system, notably where blood vessels branch, this increased mechanical pressure can simply

The immune system and stress

Our main defence against infection by foreign agents is the immune system. This is an immensely complicated network of cells and chemicals throughout the body that functions to seek out and destroy invading particles. Any agent that stimulates an *immune response* is called an *antigen*. Familiar antigens are bacteria, viruses, fungi (such as moulds and yeasts) and protozoa (single celled organisms like the amoeba that live in water and can cause infections such as dysentery). Sometimes, normally harmless particles, such as dust and pollen, cause an overreaction of the immune system, and this is the basis of *allergies*. The immune system provides three different mechanisms of immunity:

◆ nonspecific immunity

◆ cell-based immunity

◆ antibody-based immunity.

Key players in our immune system are the white blood cells made in the bone marrow and circulating in the bloodstream. The two types of white blood cell are *lymphocytes* and *phagocytes*. Phagocytes are cells which simply surround and ingest foreign particles wherever they encounter them, and so are responsible for *nonspecific immunity*. Phagocytes come in two forms: *monocytes* are found attached to particular tissues throughout the body, while *macrophages* circulate in the bloodstream.

Lymphocytes can also be divided into two classes. T cells mature in the thymus gland and are responsible for cell-based immunity, while B cell lymphocytes mature in the bone marrow and are responsible for antibody-based immunity. To help them perform their functions, T cells come in different forms:

◆ *Killer T cells* seek out and destroy cells recognized as foreign (e.g. in transplanted tissues) and cells infected with antigens such as viruses and bacteria.

◆ *Memory T cells* have a biochemical system that 'remembers' the chemical characteristics of infectious agents; if that antigen is encountered again, the immune response is faster and more effective. Catching mumps and measles as a child leads to memory T cell formation and resistance to those infections for some years.

◆ *Helper T cells* respond to infections by stimulating increased production and growth of both T and B type lymphocytes. This component of the immune system is the one mainly targeted by the AIDS virus.

While T cell-based immunity attacks antigens which are in body cells, B cells are involved in destroying invading agents while they are still in the bloodstream and before they enter the body's tissues. They do this by producing large proteins called *antibodies,* which attach themselves to the virus or bacteria, slow them down, and make it easier for them to be destroyed by other immune cells such as the phagocytes.

Antibodies (a class of proteins called *immunoglobulins*) are specific to a particular virus or bacteria. Vaccination in childhood uses small amounts of inactive infectious agents (e.g. measles, mumps, polio) to stimulate the immune system to produce specific antibodies and memory T cells to provide protection for years to come against a particular infectious agent. A current controversial idea is that in some children, this early challenge to the immune system produces an overreactive response which can result in allergic conditions such as asthma and eczema later in life.

The immune system is very complicated and stress-response hormones can affect it directly. For instance, high levels of corticosteroids can shrink the thymus gland, preventing the growth of T cells. The immune system is also more sensitive to stress than was thought. Short-lasting life events, such as brief marital strife, can cause suppression (see main text), while long-term life stress causes parallel long-term reductions in immune function (Willis *et al.* 1987). On the other hand, exercise, diet and social support can improve immune function, and as a self-regulating system, it will also recover from suppression if the stressful situation is resolved (Sapolsky 1994).

wear away the blood-vessel lining. Like any hydraulic system, increased pressure leads to increased damage and a shorter life. The scarring of the vessels acts as a collection point for fatty acids and glucose circulating in the bloodstream as part of our energy mobilization; this leads to the formation of clumps, or *plaques*, slowly blocking the blood vessel. This is the process of *atherosclerosis*.

Energy mobilization

As mentioned earlier, our contemporary problem is one of chronic energy mobilization as part of the stress-response which then has nowhere to go, as physical activity is rarely the coping response to psychological stress. The core of mobilization is the effect of corticosteroids, adrenaline and noradrenaline in releasing stored carbohydrates and fats from their storage cells into the bloodstream in the form of glucose and free fatty acids. They can then be transported to the muscles and brain cells which need them as an energy source.

If they are not burnt up in energy expenditure, the body's systems will try to restore balance by reabsorbing excess levels back into storage cells when the current emergency passes. If the stress is chronic, reabsorption cannot cope, so high levels of glucose and free fatty acids remain in the bloodstream, where they contribute to the furring up of the cardiovascular system. This can lead to raised blood pressure (*hypertension*) and atherosclerosis (as outlined above). Plaques blocking the tiny blood vessels of the brain are the cause of strokes, while raised blood pressure can produce a brain haemorrhage (breaking of a blood vessel and bleeding into brain tissue).

Suppression of the immune system

Short-term stress involves suppression of the immune system (*immunosuppression*) as part of the need to divert all resources into coping with the emergency. The main players in this effect are the corticosteroids released from the adrenal cortex, which directly reduce immune function. They stop the production, for instance, of lymphocytes (white blood cells which destroy infectious agents), leading to shrinkage of the thymus gland, one of the main lymphocyte production sites. Incidentally, this characteristic makes corticosteroids valuable treatments for a range of *autoimmune disorders*. These are diseases where the body's immune systems begin to attack its own structures, and include some cancers and arthritic conditions. Steroid creams also reduce inflammation, as inflammation is caused by the action of immune cells fighting off infectious agents. However, long-term use of corticosteroids still suppresses overall immune function, and is used only as a treatment of fairly last resort.

Short-term suppression of the immune system is not dangerous, but chronic suppression leaves the body vulnerable to infection and disease. The best current example is AIDS, which also involves long-term immunosuppression and leaves the sufferer vulnerable to a host of possible illnesses. So we would expect chronic stress to lead to more frequent illnesses and infections. We shall look at the experimental evidence in the next section.

Other effects

The stress hormones, such as corticosteroids, adrenaline, and noradrenaline, have many complex effects on the body. Apart from energy mobilization and immunosuppression, they also affect many hormones released by the pituitary gland. Earlier in the chapter, we referred to the role of the pituitary as a master gland, secreting many hormones which in turn control a variety of bodily functions. Secretion of many of these hormones is disrupted by the stress-response, leading to various problems.

The pituitary controls sexual and reproductive functions. In males, testosterone production declines during the stress-response, leading to problems with erections and sexual desire. In females, menstrual cycles can be disrupted and sexual desire reduced. Pituitary release of growth hormone is inhibited, potentially affecting growth and repair of bone structure; there is a rare condition known as *stress dwarfism*, in which children suffering extreme chronic stress through deprivation or abuse fail to grow normally.

Another aspect of the body's stress-response is a loss of pain sensitivity (stress-induced analgesia). During emergencies, the release of brain neurotransmitters called *enkephalins* and *endorphins* is increased. These control our pain sensitivity, and it makes sense for this to be reduced during emergencies so we are not diverted from coping with the situation. There are many examples of people suffering severe injury during battle but only realizing it when the conflict has subsided.

Research evidence

The picture outlined above of the effects of stress on the body has developed through studies of various kinds. Probably the most common method has been the correlation of scores on life-event scales with illness (the use of life-event scales is discussed in the next section). A problem with the correlational approach is that cause–effect relationships cannot be identified. However, if enough studies point in the same direction, then we can be reasonably sure that a relationship exists.

Scores on life-event scales correlate with levels of depression, anxiety and physical illness. These correlations are usually significant, even if not dramatically high, and a causal link between life stress and health is widely accepted. For instance, significant life change (sometimes referred to as *psychosocial change*) has been shown to predict the onset of upper respiratory tract (throat) infections, with an impressively consistent four-day delay between the event and the infection (Evans and Edgerton 1991, Evans *et al.* 1993). More convincing, perhaps, are studies which directly measure effects of stressors on our physiological systems (see *In Focus*, 'Cohen *et al.* (1993)' and 'Kiecolt-Glaser').

The picture that emerges is one where stress increases the release of stress hormones and, by the mechanisms outlined earlier, these directly suppress immune function. This does not necessarily lead to illness; to go down with colds and flu, you need to be exposed to the virus as well, but the stressed individual is left more vulnerable to infection and disease.

Stress increases heart rate and blood pressure, and increases the chances of cardiovascular disease (damage to the heart and blood vessels), especially atherosclerosis. This is shown most dramatically in controlled studies with monkeys (discussed in more detail later; see p. 77). Psychosocial stressors, such as isolation, lead to chronic (long-lasting) increases in heart rate, and eventually to atherosclerosis (Watson *et al.* 1998).

It also turns out that some monkeys have sympathetic nervous systems (see p. 58) that are particularly responsive to stressors (*hyperreactive*). As the sympathetic system is responsible for increasing heart rate and for releasing adrenaline from the adrenal medulla, this would make them particularly vulnerable to stress-induced cardiovascular disease. Similar findings have been reported in humans (Rozanski *et al.* 1999).

Summary: Stress as a bodily response

The scientific study of stress began with the work of Selye in the 1930s. Today stress is defined as a gap between the perceived demands on you and your perceived coping responses. Stress leads to activation of the body's stress-response. The main components are release of corticosteroids from the adrenal cortex, and sympathetic arousal, leading to increased secretion of adrenaline and noradrenaline from the adrenal medulla.

Selye's General Adaptation Syndrome – with its phases of activation of the stress-response, resistance, and exhaustion – described how chronic stress could lead to illness. The release of stress hormones and increases in heart rate and blood pressure affect the cardiovascular system (heart and blood vessels) through direct mechanical effects and through raised levels of fats and glucose in the bloodstream. Stress hormones also suppress the immune system and have a range of other effects on the body.

Research evidence shows that in humans and animals, stress can lead to vulnerability to infections and directly to illnesses such as atherosclerosis.

Cohen *et al.* (1993)

Cohen *et al.*'s (1993) study used 154 men and 266 women volunteers. The level of stress in their lives was measured in three ways:

◆ a life-event scale covering the previous year

◆ a perceived stress scale, assessing the individual's own perception of the level of stress in their lives

◆ a negative affect (emotion) scale, measuring levels of, for instance, anxiety, fear, depression and irritation.

The experimenters combined scores on the three scales to produce a Psychological Stress Index for each person.

They then exposed the volunteers to nasal drops containing respiratory viruses and used blood measures and clinical observation for the following six days to see whether respiratory tract infections (colds) developed. They found a difference between groups with low scores on the Stress Index and those with high scores, with highly stressed participants developing significantly more clinical colds.

This study clearly shows that stress increases vulnerability to infectious diseases using direct measures to isolate cause–effect relationships.

in
focus **Kiecolt-Glaser**

Janice Kiecolt-Glaser has pioneered the study of immune function in people exposed to high levels of stress. Previously, it was largely psychological or physical ill health that was measured, i.e. actual depression, respiratory tract infection or heart disease. However, not all people exposed to high levels of stress developed disorders (hence the relatively low correlations between these in life-event studies). Kiecolt-Glaser reasoned that although they may not show obvious illness, many people may have lowered immune function (*immunosuppression*) caused by stress, which would leave them vulnerable to illness.

Her group devised ways of measuring the activity of the immune system from blood samples (these days it can also be assessed from salivary samples). They then compared immune function in control groups with groups accepted to be under chronic stress, and found significant immunosuppression in these high-risk groups (Kiecolt-Glaser *et al.* 1984, 1987):

◆ unhappily married women

◆ recently separated women, especially if they were unhappy about the separation

◆ long-term carers for Alzheimer patients

◆ medical students taking examinations.

Other researchers have reported similar findings for the recently bereaved (Antoni 1987), and recently, Kiecolt-Glaser's group have found reductions in immune function in couples even after short episodes of marital conflict (Kiecolt-Glaser *et al.* 1998). They also found significant increases in release of stress hormones, and interestingly, changes in these stress indicators were greater and longer-lasting in women.

Sources of stress

Remembering from the start of this chapter that the common definition of stress views it as rooted in the demands that we perceive, we can describe many sources of stress. We make demands on ourselves: am I happy enough, rich enough, do I look okay, will I meet this deadline? Other people make demands on us: get this job done, make me happier, earn more money, be my friend. We get stuck in traffic jams, break down on the motorway; friends and relations have accidents, become ill, sometimes die; we all have accidents and illnesses. Whether these situations are stressful depends on our coping abilities, but some of them are almost certain to be.

As we saw in the last section, experimental approaches to the study of stress need to define and, if possible, *quantify* the stress in people's lives, so that reliable links can be made to physical and psychological disorders. The problem is that the sources of stress are so varied that many approaches have been developed. We shall look at some of the most popular ones.

Research into sources of stress

The Social Readjustment Rating Scale (SRRS)

This scale, developed by Thomas Holmes and Richard Rahe (1967), is known more popularly as the Holmes–Rahe Life Events Rating Scale. Together with some later variations, the Holmes–Rahe has been the most widely used of all methods for assessing life stress.

The context is that things happen in life to which we have to make psychological adjustments. The more we have to adjust, the more stressful the event is. Holmes and Rahe made a list, based on their experience as clinicians, of major life events. They then asked hundreds of men and women, representing a variety of ages and backgrounds, to rate the events in terms of the amount of readjustment they would require, i.e. their psychological impact. Death of a spouse came out top, and was given an arbitrary value of 100. Other events were given ratings relative to their ranking, so that redundancy, for instance, came out as 47, a house move as 20, and holidays as 13.

Once the scale was constructed, it was simply a matter of asking participants to check off any of the 43 life events they had experienced over a given period, usually two years, but sometimes one. The experimenter then totalled their score and used it as an index of the life stress in that person's life. Using *retrospective* (asking people with possible stress-related illnesses to look back at the previous two years) and *prospective* (assessing life stress and then observing participants over the following months) studies,

Holmes and Rahe proposed that a score of 150 or more increased the chances of stress-related health breakdown by 30 per cent, while a score of over 300 increased the odds by 50 per cent.

Evaluation of the SRRS

Many studies have been done on the link between life events and health breakdown using the SRRS. Although significant correlations are often found, they tend to be relatively small (the highest at about 0.30), suggesting a relationship between stress and health, but not a strong one. However, it also became clear that there were problems with the scale:

◆ The scale values for different events are arbitrary and will certainly vary from person to person. Some people violently dislike holidays or Christmas, and would have them near the top rather than at the bottom. Others might find marital separation a relief from a highly dysfunctional marriage. The stress of taking out a large mortgage depends on your income. Each of us could devise a personal rating scale, as the stress of an event depends upon the individual's perception of it.

◆ The relationship between SRRS score and health is only correlational, and tells us nothing about causality. Depression or chronic physical illness may lead to life problems rather than being caused by them.

◆ Health outcomes can include anything from psychological disorders, through heart disease and diabetes, to accidents and injuries. To be really useful, the model relating life change to health should be more specific as to how particular events lead to particular outcomes. As we saw in the last section, the stress-response has many effects on the body, but it should still be possible to predict that some life events may lead to psychological problems, and others to physical problems.

◆ Some life events are positive. People getting married probably see it as a positive change, while 'change in financial state' can clearly be positive or negative. The SRRS does not distinguish positive from negative, as the model assumes that any life change is stressful, without supporting evidence.

◆ Self-report of life events can be surprisingly unreliable. Raphael *et al.* (1991) had participants fill out a life-events scale for the previous year, and then repeated the exercise every month for another year. As time passed, the agreement on life events between the later reports and the first declined significantly.

◆ Retrospective studies are most common and involve people with illnesses possibly related to stress. Asking them to review the previous year could involve their attributional style. They may see illnesses such as heart disease and cancer as medical problems, attributing them to family history, for instance, rather than to life events, which they may then underreport. Alternatively, they may habitually associate illness with psychological stressors and so overreport the significance of life events. You cannot assume they will be objective.

However, despite these criticisms, the SRRS was a major step in stress research:

◆ It was the first detailed attempt to quantify levels of stress in people's lives.

◆ Its use confirmed that life events could lead to health breakdown.

Other life-events scales

In the years following the introduction of the SRRS, refinements were made to life-event scales to try and overcome the criticisms outlined above. A popular version is the Life Experiences Survey (LES) (Sarason *et al.* 1978). Based very much on the SRRS, the LES has 57 items, but these can be rated in terms of their positive or negative impact on a seven-point scale (highly negative, −3, through neutral, 0, to highly positive, +3). This allows for individual differences in the perception of events to be taken into account. There are also specialized sections which can be used for particular subgroups, such as students. The LES produces scores for positive change, negative change and total change. As you might expect, health problems correlate more highly with negative life-change scores, than with positive or total change.

One general problem with the life-event approach is that it concentrates on events which are by their nature unusual. In any given study, 10 to 30 per cent of participants may experience none of the scale items, although they are not all free of stress. This is because incidents we would not count as major events can themselves be a source of considerable stress. These are everyday occurrences: worrying about friendships, losing the car keys, concerns over appearance (weight, hair loss, skin condition), keeping up with college courses, minor health problems. For most people, these have more daily impact than SRRS-style items.

To assess these very real sources of stress, Lazarus and his group (Kanner *et al.* 1981) devised the Hassles Scale. The original form had 117 items, although versions can be constructed for subgroups, such as students (e.g. unfriendly classmates, boring teachers). As they thought that positive events in life could reduce the impact of daily hassles, the group also introduced an Uplifts Scale, with 135 items which cheer people up; items include getting on well with your partner and feeling healthy.

Keep a diary over the next week. Make a note of all the hassles (completing the diary may be one) that you have experienced each day. Next to that, make a list of all the uplifts that you experienced in that same day. Independently of these lists, give yourself a rating (perhaps between 1 and 10) for how you feel (i.e. your general sense of psychological wellbeing) and any health problems experienced that day.

At the end of the week, plot these on a graph. Is there any relationship between the degree of hassles or uplifts on a particular day, and the sense of perceived wellbeing? Did you experience more health problems when you had experienced more hassles? Can you think of any other explanations for a possible relationship between these variables?

Research shows that scores on the Hassles scale can correlate with levels of depression, anxiety, and health problems. DeLongis *et al.* (1982) compared Hassles scores with Life Events, and found that although both correlated significantly with health status, the association for Hassles scores was greater. Uplift scores had no statistical relationship with health outcomes.

In the final section of this chapter, on stress management, we shall see that various factors can help protect us against the negative effects of stress. Recent variations of the life-event approach to stress include some assessment of these factors along with the life-event scale. For example, Moos and Swindle (1990) propose eight areas of common life stressors:

- illness and other medical problems
- home and local environment (items such as safety and traffic)
- family finance
- relationship with partner
- children
- extended family
- work (discussed in the next section)
- relationships outside the family.

These areas are assessed using their Life Stressors and Social Resources Inventory (LISRES), which also incorporates measures of factors which may help cope with life stressors. These include social support networks and financial state.

Research using scales of major life events and daily hassles supports the idea that there are many sources of stress in life, and that they can affect physical and psychological health. Correlations are not huge, but are often significant. This means that in a general sense, the stress in each of our lives can potentially affect our health and how we operate from day to day. There are also situations where stress-related problems can have more direct effects, and this brings us to the area of applied stress research.

Applied stress research: stress in the workplace

Through its effects on psychological and physical health, stress can affect performance at work, whether you are an office worker, an MP, teacher, police officer or social worker. All jobs involve a certain amount of stress, but there is a growing interest in work conditions that increase stress. Private and public companies have an interest in maintaining productivity and performance, which are both affected by stress-related illness. In fact, the study of workplace stress is an area of occupational psychology and is one of the fastest growing fields of psychology.

Sources of stress in the workplace depend on the type of work or enterprise you are looking at. An assembly-line worker in a car factory has different problems from a middle-rank manager in a City bank. There are, however, some sources of stress which apply to most workers:

- *Relations with co-workers* – These can be with those on the same level, with those working under you, or with your superiors.

- *Physical environment* – Space, temperature, lighting and arrangement of an office (open plan or separate rooms) can all affect the individual.

- *Career progression* – Do you have one, or are you stuck forever on the same grade?

- *Workload* – We seem to be moving to a macho culture in which long hours at work are seen as a mark of esteem, to the cost of both the individual and social structures. This is directly related to the next point.

- *Home–work interface* – In an era where people seem to be working longer and longer hours, and with more women in the workplace, there is increasing conflict between work and home responsibilities.

- *Job insecurity* – With a move away from 'jobs for life', long-term security can be hard to find. Constant job change can be exciting and invigorating, but it can also be stressful.

- *Lack of control* – In many organizations, workload and work pattern are decided by other people. As we shall see later, loss of control is a major source of stress.

◆ *Role ambiguity* – A major factor contributing to work-related stress is a lack of clarity about the requirements of one's work role. This sometimes results from having no clear (or contradictory) guidelines or standards of performance.

These sources of stress are highly significant to the individual concerned, but they also affect the organization. Stress can lead to physical and psychological consequences, which, in turn, affect productivity, through decreased motivation at work and time off with health problems. In the USA, and increasingly in companies over here, occupational psychologists are brought in to identify sources of stress in the workplace and to advise on methods of reducing them. By assessing the organizational structure and interviewing employees at all levels of the hierarchy, they try to pinpoint key problems and to produce solutions. These can involve changes in methods of communication, in the physical arrangement of workplaces, the introduction of different work schedules or management structures, etc.

Sweden was one of the first countries to take stress in the workplace seriously and pioneered the systematic collection of evidence to find out how it might affect health and productivity. In one of the earliest studies, Johansson *et al.* (1978) investigated employees in a Swedish sawmill. Raw timber (trees) came in at one end and prepared planking came out of the other. One type of employee was seen as especially vulnerable; this was a small group of highly skilled 'finishers', who as their name implies, finished off the wood as the last stage of processing the timber. The rate at which they worked determined the overall productivity of the sawmill, and everyone's wages depended on productivity (this is known as 'piecework'). In addition, and despite being skilled work, the job was repetitive and machine-paced, in that the wood came along on moving belts. Because of the need to concentrate, they also worked largely in isolation.

The workplace is a major source of stress

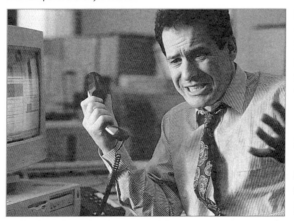

The investigators recorded levels of stress hormones (adrenaline and noradrenaline) at various intervals during work days and on rest days, and looked at patterns of sickness and absenteeism. The results were clear. This high-risk group had raised levels of stress hormones on work days, a higher incidence of stress-related health problems, and took more days off work than a control group of cleaners. Conclusions to the study were that their work environment contained sources of high stress:

◆ responsibility for the wage rates of the whole factory

◆ highly skilled but monotonous and repetitive work

◆ machine-paced work (i.e. lack of control)

◆ working in social isolation.

Suggestions for change included moving to a salary structure (set weekly wage) rather than piece rates, allowing workers to rotate jobs in the sawmill to provide variety and social contact, and allowing more control over the assembly line.

In theory, any organization could be studied in the same way. Of course, some situations simply have stress built in and it would be naive to expect all workplace stress to be eliminated, but most organizations could introduce relatively minor changes which would still help their employees.

Individual responses to stress

One of the enduring beliefs about stress is that it is bad for you, and the evidence in previous sections should have convinced you that our stress-response can have damaging effects. However, frustratingly, correlations between health problems and scores on life-stress or hassles scales, for instance, are never very high, even if they are significant. In every study, participants experiencing apparently similar levels of stress can show very different outcomes: some show psychological or physical disorders, while others sail along with few obvious effects.

In fact, the question of individual differences in vulnerability to stress is as interesting as the effects of stress itself. Of course, some of these differences are rooted in physiology. There is clear evidence for variable patterns of stress-response between individuals, with some having highly reactive hormonal and ANS systems, and others having more stable systems. But the main interest has been in psychological factors influencing our response to stressors.

Personality and Type A Behaviour

In the early 1960s, Friedman and Rosenman (1974) studied the behaviour of patients suffering from coronary heart disease (CHD), and proposed that a particular behaviour pattern was associated with increased vulnerability to this stress-related illness. This behaviour pattern is characterized by constant time-pressure, doing several tasks at once, being intensely competitive in work and social situations, and being easily frustrated by the efforts of others (Table 3.1). This has become known as the *Type A behaviour pattern*.

Since their original work, many studies have looked at the relationship between Type A behaviour and CHD. Some of these have been retrospective (looking at the previous behaviour of patients with CHD) and some prospective (measuring Type A behaviour using questionnaires and then following participants' health outcomes over months or years). Significant correlations have been found, but these are never very high, and many negative findings have been reported. Even the value of the Type A concept has been questioned (Evans 1990).

To try to make some sense of this, the behaviour pattern has been more closely analysed, and it turns out that a critical personality variable is hostility. When high levels of hostility are combined with high levels of Type A behaviour, correlations with CHD are significantly increased (Matthews and Haynes 1986). Particularly vulnerable are individuals who repress high levels of hostility rather than expressing it (although that may be better for the rest of us, of course). In fact, some of the most successful interventions to help people characterized as Type A have focused on the element of hostility (see *In Focus*).

Despite the fact that Type A behaviour seems to be a risk for stress-related illness, many Type A individuals survive quite happily with their pressured and competitive lives. In the last section of this chapter, which looks at stress-management techniques, we will see that one of the key factors in managing stress is a strong sense of commitment and control. There is no reason why Type A people should not also show high levels of commitment and control; in fact, they would be expected to. They are high achievers and so must be very committed, and they like to do everything themselves, as they do not believe anyone else can do it as well, i.e. have a strong sense of control.

So, along with factors which make them vulnerable, such as haste, time pressure and doing too many things as once, the Type A person may also score highly on protective factors such as control and commitment. There are also other less specific elements which have been shown to protect against stress, such as physical exercise and social support, which may additionally help the Type A person avoid the negative effects of stress.

Gender

Although sources of stress may vary between males and females, especially if the female takes most responsibility for home and children, there is no evidence that the levels of stress each experience are any different. There is some evidence that physiological reactions to stressors (the stress-response) may distinguish the two groups.

Frankenhaeuser *et al.* (1976) measured levels of the stress hormone adrenaline in boys and girls taking an examination. The boys showed a much more rapid increase in hormone levels, which took longer to return to normal after the examination. The girls' increase was slower and smaller, and returned to baseline quicker. Interestingly, performance in the examination was roughly the same for the two groups and so were levels of reported (subjective) anxiety and stress.

Similar results were reported by Stoney *et al.* (1990), who found that women showed smaller rises in blood pressure due to stressful tasks than did men. Possible explanations for these findings might be that:

◆ the hypothalamic-pituitary and ANS stress pathways are more reactive in men than in women

◆ men and women vary in their attitude to the test, and this psychological difference influences the stress-response: for instance, men may be more competitive and 'aroused' during the test, leading to more sustained physiological arousal.

On the whole, men show more stress-related physiological arousal than women across a range of psychological and physical stressors (Vogele *et al.* 1997), even though both genders report similar levels of subjective stress. This means that men should be more vulnerable to stress-induced illness, but as we shall see, other factors influence our responses to stress and our vulnerability to illness. Physical exercise and social support are important 'buffers' against stress-induced illness, and you can argue that these vary between the genders. Men tend to take more physical exercise, while women make more use of social support

Table 3.1	Type A behaviour pattern

Time pressure
◆ working against the clock
◆ doing several things at once
◆ irritation and impatience with others
◆ unhappy doing nothing

Competitive
◆ always plays to win at games and at work
◆ achievements measured as material productivity

Anger
◆ self-critical
◆ hostile to the outside world
◆ anger often directed inwards

in
focus

Coping with Type A Behaviour

The original work of Friedman and Rosenman on the Type A behaviour pattern (described in the main text) emphasized urgency, competitiveness and time pressure as the crucial elements. When a series of studies failed to show high correlations between Type A scores and coronary heart disease (CHD), original data from Friedman and Rosenman's work were reanalysed for other possible factors. It appeared that a key element in producing significant correlations between Type A behaviour and CHD was a high level of hostility and aggression.

Controlling for other risk factors, such as age, weight or smoking, studies of a variety of populations (e.g. employees of power companies, medical students, lawyers) have confirmed the link between hostility and CHD, atherosclerosis and early death (Williams 1989). It also appears that hostility openly expressed is less damaging than hostility repressed.

Other experimental studies have demonstrated that the physiological arousal associated with hostility and aggression is particularly apparent in situations involving other people. With cognitive stressors, such as doing mental arithmetic, hostile people show no more arousal than nonhostile people; but when being repeatedly interrupted during a task by a confederate of the experimenter, or being given misleading instructions for an insoluble task, stress-response measures, such as blood pressure rises, are far greater in hostile participants.

Type A behaviour can be modified. The most effective way is through *multidimensional approaches*. These combine general advice on health-related behaviours and heart disease (especially diet and smoking), with nonspecific relaxation techniques, such as progressive muscle relaxation or meditation. The third element is cognitive therapy, to help people understand why their behaviour puts them at risk and to help them to modify it. Such programmes have been shown to reduce CHD and death rates in participants who had already survived a heart attack (Friedman *et al.* 1986).

If the participant has high levels of aggression and hostility, which substantially increase health risks, these are often addressed directly through psychotherapy or *anger-management programmes*. These are cognitive–behavioural techniques in which the person is first encouraged to analyse situations where they become angry. This gives them insight into the causes of confrontations. Then they are trained in relaxation procedures to cope with the arousal produced by provocations, and at the same time encouraged to develop cognitive coping strategies (e.g. 'I don't need to take this personally') through role-play. Given that anger and hostility are potent risk factors for stress-related illness, such directed therapies are becoming increasingly popular.

networks, so predictions as to who should show more vulnerability to stress are very difficult. One simple conclusion reached by Frankenhaeuser is that women on average live longer because they show less stress-related physiological arousal than men.

Activity 3: Gender differences in coping with stress

It is commonly believed that males and females deal with stress in different ways. Men tend to work it out with physical exercise, whilst women make more extensive use of social support networks. Is this still the case?

Try asking your nonpsychology peers how they tend to deal with stressful events. Are there gender differences that support this belief?

Culture

Stress is found in all communities, but the sources can vary a great deal depending on the sort of society you are looking at. In the developed West, we do not worry so much about finding food and water day by day, while people in the Third World spend less time worrying about which primary school to choose or why they haven't been promoted. However, all of these different sources of stress conform to the basic idea that stress exists when the perceived demands on you outweigh your perceived coping resources.

Great variation is also found in coping strategies. Several studies have looked at different ethnic groups in Western societies and how they cope with common stressors. For instance, social support is an important protective factor against stress, and there are clear ethnic variations in how it is used. Kim and McKenry (1998) looked at social support networks in a range of ethnic groups in America. They found that African-Americans, Asian-Americans, and Hispanics all used parents and children for social support more than did Caucasian (White) Americans. African-Americans were more likely to be members of religious organizations, while Asian-Americans and Caucasians took more part in recreational groups. Such cultural variations in social networks have clear implications for coping with stress.

For instance, compared to White Americans, African-American and Asian-American carers for Alzheimer (dementia) patients report more belief in filial (children's) duty to parents, use faith and religion as part of their coping strategy, and report lower levels of depression and stress related to caring (Connell and Gibson 1997). It would be valid to link their lower levels of stress to the cultural differences in attitudes to social and family life, and their religious networks.

One of the difficulties in assessing cultural variations in relation to stress and responses to stress is that cultures vary along many other dimensions which can affect health. Heart disease, hypertension, and depression, for instance, can be affected by your genetic inheritance, diet and general lifestyle, and social organization. To isolate effects of stress is therefore virtually impossible. As an example, Weg (1983) studied the Abkarsian people of Georgia (formerly part of the USSR), who have a high percentage of individuals living beyond 100 (400 per 100,000, compared to 3 per 100,000 in the UK). Factors which emerged as important were:

◆ genetic inheritance
◆ high levels of social support
◆ physically active lifestyles of work and recreation
◆ diet high in fruit and vegetables, low in meat
◆ no alcohol or smoking
◆ low reported stress levels.

It is impossible to decide which one of these factors is most important. Regardless of which culture you study, health outcomes are a complicated mixture of inheritance, lifestyle, social networks and stress. Sources of stress and methods of coping will vary between cultures, but stress-related problems will still depend on available coping strategies versus the demands being made on the individual.

Summary: Sources of stress

There are many sources of stress, and various methods have been used to assess them. Life-event scales use questionnaires to quantify the degree of life change people experience. Despite some major problems, such as individual differences, life-event scales have remained popular for measuring common life stressors, while other scales, such as the Hassles scale, assess everyday minor stressors. Research findings show that life-event scores correlate with levels of psychological and physical disorders. More focused approaches look at stress, for instance, in the workplace and can identify specific sources of stress in organizations.

Reactions to stress are influenced by a number of factors, such as Type A behaviour which can make people more vulnerable to stress-related illness. Gender is also important, as females tend to have lower stress-related physical arousal, which may leave them less vulnerable to illness. Cultures also vary in the range of stressors experienced and in the types of coping strategies available. Use of social support, in particular, distinguishes different cultures and ethnic groups.

CRITICAL ISSUE: Stress management

The public perceives stress as one of the most prevalent 'diseases' of the last 20 years. It is also seen as fundamental to the way we live; as the pace of life increases, so, inevitably, does the stress of keeping up. In parallel with the increase in research into the negative effects of stress, such as psychological and physical disorders, so an industry has grown up devoted to methods of managing stress. These are by now many and varied, but can be divided into four major categories:

◆ *physical approaches* – the use of drugs and biofeedback to target directly the stress-response systems themselves

◆ *general psychological approaches* – the use of techniques of relaxation, meditation and hypnosis to reduce the bodily arousal associated with stress

◆ *specific psychological approaches* – for example, cognitive and behavioural training to help people control specific stressors in their lives

◆ *aspects of lifestyle* – e.g. exercise and social support.

Physical approaches

Drugs

The most commonly used drugs to combat stress are the *benzodiazepine* (BZ) anti-anxiety agents and *beta-blockers*. BZs, such as librium (chlordiazepoxide) and valium (diazepam), are the most prescribed drugs for psychological disorders and can be very effective against states of stress and anxiety. They appear to act by reducing activity of the brain neurotransmitter *serotonin*. Beta-blockers, such as inderal, do not enter the brain, but directly reduce activity in pathways of the sympathetic nervous system around the body. As sympathetic arousal is a key feature of stressful states, they can be very effective against symptoms such as raised heart rate and blood pressure. (They have also been used when bodily arousal can reduce performance in groups such as musicians and snooker players.)

There are important problems with the use of drugs:

◆ Long-term use of BZs especially can lead to psychological and physical dependency. They should only be prescribed for short periods of a week or so, to help cope with short-term stress.

◆ All drugs have side effects; BZs can cause drowsiness and affect memory.

◆ Drugs treat symptoms, not causes. Many stressors are essentially psychological, so drugs, while helping in the short term, may prevent the real cause of stress being addressed. They are best used to manage acute (short-lived) stressors, such as the initial shock of a bereavement, or examinations

(although see side effects, above), especially if psychological coping techniques are introduced at the same time.

Biofeedback

This technique involves recording the activity of the physiological systems of the body's stress-response, such as heart rate, blood pressure or tension in the neck muscles, that can lead to stress-induced headaches. Recording is usually via electrodes on the skin to a hand-held monitor that the patient holds.

The patient is encouraged to try various strategies to reduce the physiological readings. These can be muscle relaxation or meditation, or even altering their posture. The aim is to find a strategy to reduce, for instance, blood pressure consistently, and then to transfer the strategy to the world outside the laboratory and to practise it regularly.

This approach can be very successful for some individuals, but it is often found to be no more effective than muscle relaxation procedures without biofeedback (Masters *et al.* 1987). This is a critical issue because biofeedback is expensive in terms of equipment and time. There is, however, some evidence that it is more effective in children, who treat it as a game and are also more optimistic about its effects (Attanasio *et al.* 1985).

General psychological approaches

Progressive muscle relaxation

Although we all think we know how to relax, effective relaxation has, in practice, to be learnt. Rather than simply thinking about nice things, progressive muscle relaxation is, strange as it may sound, an active approach to reducing bodily arousal. A standard procedure would be to train clients consciously to clench and unclench muscles, to get them used to the sensations of tension and relaxation. Whole-body relaxation would begin with the muscles of the toes, tensing and then relaxing them, and then working up through the legs, body and head (facial muscles). Eventually, the client understands the sensations well enough to use progressive muscle relaxation in real life as a method to

Different approaches to stress management

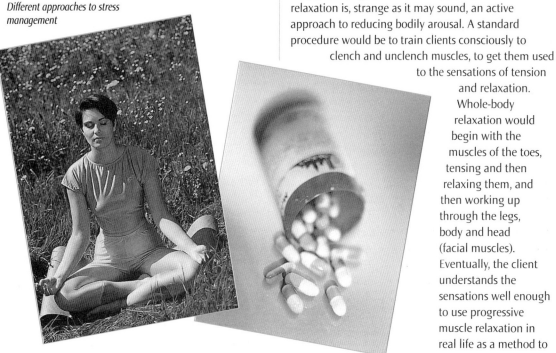

reduce bodily arousal. During relaxation, stress-response mechanisms are inactive, heart rate and blood pressure fall, and the picture is one of parasympathetic dominance (see p. 58). If practised regularly, such relaxation techniques are effective in reducing stress, but are not effective in all situations:

◆ They take time and space – If you are stuck in a traffic jam or in the middle of an examination, full progressive relaxation is inconvenient, if not impossible. However, the training also involves cognitive strategies to help relaxation, such as imagining yourself in pleasant, unarousing surroundings, taking deep breaths, and consciously telling yourself to relax. Relaxation of some muscle groups is usually possible. Taking two minutes to run through a learnt procedure like this can pay dividends in most stressful situations.

◆ Relaxation techniques address bodily or physiological arousal by reducing activation of stress-response systems – This is undoubtedly beneficial, but long-lasting severe stressors need more than nonspecific relaxation; their source has to be identified and targeted, usually via cognitive and behavioural strategies. Relaxation can still remain as an important component of stress management, but long-term adjustment requires more focused intervention as well.

Meditation

Meditation is similar to progressive muscle relaxation in that the aim is to reduce bodily arousal and to achieve a state of transcendental calm. This is achieved through sitting quietly and repeating your mantra – a single sound or word – while you breathe deeply and regularly. The aim is to empty your mind of distracting and arousing thoughts. Like muscle relaxation, it can be used to combat stressful situations with a state of calm which prevents activation of the stress-response systems (Lichstein 1988). With your mantra readily available it may be more 'portable', but otherwise has the same problem of not addressing the source of long-term stressors. With practice, though, it gives the individual confidence in coping with short-term stress,

Activity 4: Practising relaxation techniques

If you find this or any other chapter difficult to take in, it may be due to the fact that you are stressed and finding it difficult to concentrate. Take a few minutes to practise the relaxation techniques outlined above. Study is always easier when we are relaxed, so a few minutes invested in this way will pay dividends later on.

and can be an important accessory to other methods of stress management.

Hypnosis

There is currently a controversy in psychology as to whether the hypnotic trance is a special state of consciousness. What is not in doubt is that some individuals are more suggestive than others, and for these people, the hypnotic state is one of complete relaxation; in fact, the hypnotist uses relaxation techniques to ease the client into the hypnotic state.

It is doubtful whether hypnotically induced relaxation is more effective against stress than muscle relaxation and meditation. Some people can, after training, achieve self-hypnosis and use it in stressful situations in the same way others would use relaxation and meditation, and this perhaps is the key issue. If an individual learns a general technique to reduce bodily arousal and to limit the stress-response, then research suggests that it doesn't make much difference which one they use (Tapp 1985); what is important is that they believe in the one they adopt and learn to use it effectively.

These general psychological techniques are used to reduce the physiological arousal associated with stress, and can do so very effectively. With severe long-term stressors, such as a poor marriage or problems at work, they do not provide a solution but only temporary respite. For this type of problem, strategies have to address the cognitive element of the stress-response using specific psychological techniques.

Specific psychological approaches

At the beginning of this chapter we discussed the definition of stress. The trigger in stressful situations, according to the definition, is the perceived gap between the demands being made on you and the coping responses you have available. So, a straightforward approach to stress management would be either to reduce the perceived demands or to improve your coping abilities, or, preferably, both. Cognitive–behavioural approaches aim to do this by encouraging the client to perceive and evaluate stressful situations accurately (often we overestimate the demands being made on us), and to improve coping skills and techniques by training and practice.

Meichenbaum's Stress-Inoculation Training

Meichenbaum's (Meichenbaum and Cameron 1983) approach has three phases:

◆ *Conceptualization* – This is the main cognitive element. The client is encouraged to relive stressful situations and to analyse various features. What was actually stressful about it? How did they attempt to cope? Why wasn't it successful? If many situations are stressful, do they have elements in common, such as the presence of strangers or the knowledge that performance is being assessed, as in examinations and tests? These discussions can be individual or in groups, where the sharing of experience can help achieve a greater understanding of the nature of stress and the client's reactions to it. Clients reach a more realistic understanding of the demands being made on them.

◆ *Skills training and practice* – Once the key elements of the stressful situations have been identified, clients can be taught specific and nonspecific strategies for coping with them. The relaxation techniques described earlier help them to cope with the initial arousing effects of stress. Training in particular skills then helps reduce the particular demands. For instance, if examinations are the problem, knowing the syllabus in detail and developing simple strategies of learning, revising, and time allocation can reduce stress. Relaxation techniques can be used in the examination room to keep arousal under control. Mock examinations can be taken to practise stress management.

As another example, many people find social interactions stressful. Surprisingly perhaps, social skills such as body posture, eye contact and conversational give-and-take can be taught relatively easily and practised in the therapeutic setting. Again, general relaxation techniques help to limit stress-induced arousal.

◆ *Real-life application* – The final stage is for the client to go out into the real world and to put the training to the test. Contact with the therapist is maintained, and follow-up sessions and further training are provided if necessary. The reinforcement of successful coping with examinations or social interactions then becomes self-sustaining.

Evaluation of Meichenbaum's approach

◆ Meichenbaum's programme is directed at both ends of the stress problem: sources of stress and coping strategies. By reviewing the coping methods they have used in the past, clients can gain a clearer understanding of their strengths and weaknesses. The acquisition of new skills and techniques reduces the gap between demands and coping resources, and gives clients more confidence in their ability to handle previously stressful situations.

◆ The combination of cognitive (thinking about situations in the past and using cognitive strategies as part of a general relaxation technique) and behavioural (training in new skills) therapies, in theory, makes stress-inoculation training a powerful

method of stress management. However, few controlled studies of its effectiveness have been carried out, although Meichenbaum has reported encouraging results (Meichenbaum and Turk 1982).

◆ It takes time and application – and money. Clients have to go through a rigorous programme over a long period, requiring high levels of motivation and commitment. It is not a quick and easy fix.

◆ There is evidence that the way we cope with life's stressors can reflect basic aspects of our personality, possibly innate or acquired during early experience. Examples include locus of control, discussed later in this section. Any technique aimed at improving stress management may be acting against habits which are well established, even if they are not very effective. Changing cognitions and behaviour will always be difficult.

Hardiness

According to Kobasa (Kobasa and Maddi 1977), the concept of 'hardiness' is central to understanding why some people are vulnerable to stress and some resistant. Hardiness includes a range of personality factors which, if present, provide defences against the negative effects of stress. These factors are:

◆ *Control* – This is the belief that you have control over what happens in your life, rather than attributing control to outside influences. It is similar to locus of control, discussed later, and attributional style, the tendency to attribute causes to either yourself (*dispositional* attribution) or to external factors over which you have no control (*situational* attribution).

◆ *Commitment* – This is a sense of involvement in the world around you, including people as well as jobs and careers. The world is seen as something to engage with, rather than to stand apart from. It includes a strong sense of purpose in your activities.

◆ *Challenge* – Life changes are seen as challenges to be overcome, or as opportunities, rather than as threats and stressors. Life is not about comfort and security, but change and growth.

Kobasa has presented evidence that people who have high scores on scales measuring hardiness are significantly less likely to suffer stress-related physical and psychological disorders than those with low hardiness scores. In theory, their positive approach means that life events are not seen as stressful, but as challenges and opportunities which they can overcome. This leads to less activation of the stress-response and its negative consequences.

Her studies of personality and stress have identified other factors involved in coping with stress and have implications for stress management.

Kobasa *et al.* (1985), using previous work suggesting that physical exercise and social support also protected against stress-related illness, rated participants on the presence or absence of the three factors: hardiness, social support and regular exercise. They then followed the participants and assessed the severity of any subsequent psychological (depression and anxiety) or physical illnesses (this was what we call a prospective design).

Results showed clearly that participants with no protective factors had higher scores on severity of illness scales than any other group. In addition, the presence of one, two, or all three protective factors was associated with steadily decreasing illness scores, implying that the factors acted additively in improving resistance to stress. Of the three, hardiness seemed to have the greatest impact.

Kobasa's belief that hardiness is an important element in stress management led her to propose ways in which it could be improved. As with stress-inoculation training, the procedure has three aspects, the first two of which are quite similar to the first stage of stress-inoculation training:

◆ *Focusing* – The client is trained and encouraged to spot signs of stress, such as muscle tension, increases in heart rate and anxiety. This allows them to recognize stressful situations and therefore to identify sources of stress.

◆ *Reliving stressful encounters* – The client analyses recent stressful situations in terms of how they were actually resolved, ways in which they could have turned out better, and ways in which they could have turned out worse. This gives them insight into their current coping strategies and how they are probably more effective than they imagine.

◆ *Self-improvement* – Central to hardiness is the belief that you can cope with life's challenges. Often, however, we are faced with stressors which cannot be easily managed. In this case, it is important to recognize and to take on challenges that we *can* cope with. In this way we confirm that we still have control over some events in our lives, and it this sense of personal control and effectiveness that is basic to stress management.

Evaluation of Kobasa's concept of hardiness

◆ The concept of hardiness itself has been criticized. The relative importance of the three factors (control, commitment, challenge) is unclear, although there is evidence for the role of control and commitment in reducing responses to stressors. As we shall see, the importance of control in stress management cannot be exaggerated, and the concept of hardiness overlaps substantially with issues of personal control and may not be very different from it.

◆ Kobasa's studies usually involve White middle-class businessmen, and results cannot reliably be generalized to women or to different classes and cultures.

◆ There are few systematic studies of the effectiveness of hardiness training. As with stress-inoculation training, it is lengthy and requires commitment and motivation, and would never be a rapid solution to stress management problems. It also has the problem of addressing basic aspects of personality and learnt habits of coping. These are notoriously difficult to modify.

Kobasa's work does draw attention to two other factors important in coping with stress: exercise and social support.

Exercise

Earlier in this chapter, we reviewed the physiological mechanisms of the stress-response, and the role of these systems in mobilizing energy reserves and increasing heart rate and blood pressure. Many of the damaging effects of stress are linked to energy mobilization in situations where physical action is not appropriate or possible, leading to high levels of glucose and free fatty acids floating around in the bloodstream. These can then contribute to furring up of the arteries (atherosclerosis).

If the stress is short-lived, our physiological systems will restore normal blood levels by storing away excess glucose and fats. If stress is long-lasting (chronic), then the constant energy mobilization overwhelms our body's capacity to cope, and disease can result.

Physical exercise is an obvious and effective way of removing excess glucose and fats; they are mobilized to provide for physical activity and blood levels fall as they are burnt up by the muscles. So, we would predict that regular physical exercise should have beneficial effects on stress-related arousal, and this is exactly what we find.

Correlational studies, where levels of fitness and exercise are recorded, along with frequency of stress-related disorders, such as depression and high blood pressure, show consistently that exercise is associated with lower levels of depression and a lower incidence of hypertension (raised blood pressure) (Holmes 1993). But causality is a problem; perhaps depression leads to people taking less exercise, rather than vice versa?

Luckily, many studies have used prospective designs. Jennings *et al.* (1986), for instance, had participants undergo physical training programmes. Separate groups followed programmes of either less than their normal physical activity, the same level as normal, above-normal levels, or far-greater-than-normal levels. Results showed clearly that regular exercise at above-normal or far-above-normal levels produced significant reductions in heart rate and blood pressure.

There is no doubt that exercise is an effective way of keeping the cardiovascular system in shape and counteracting the negative effects of stress. It also has been shown to have positive effects on mood and general wellbeing, so the benefits are psychological as well as physical.

Social support

Although it is easy to make the assumption that a wide network of friends and relations must make life less stressful, it is more difficult to provide convincing experimental evidence. The extensive work of Brown and Harris (1978), demonstrating that loneliness and social isolation were factors in causing depression in women with young children, can be related to the idea that social support protects against the psychological effects of stress.

Most studies are correlational, assessing levels of social support through questionnaires and correlating these scores with levels of stress-induced disorder. Evidence consistently shows a significant association. For instance, in the workplace, job-related stress is reduced in organizations with high levels of support from co-workers (Constable and Russell 1986). More direct studies have demonstrated lower levels of cardiovascular activity (heart rate and blood pressure) during difficult tasks when a friendly companion is present (Kamarck *et al.* 1998), indicating less stress-induced arousal. Even recovery from heart disease is faster when the patient has high levels of social support (Kulik and Mahler 1989).

The most convincing findings are from studies of monkeys. Some species, such as the cynomolgus monkey, are highly social animals with complex networks of relationships. If they are kept in isolation, heart rates and blood pressure immediately increase, while chronic (long-lasting) isolation leads to atherosclerosis and heart disease. When isolated animals are returned to the colony, they increase their rate of affiliative (friendly) behaviours over pre-isolation levels, as though compensating for the lack of social contact (Watson *et al.* 1998).

The correlational work with people and the experimental work with monkeys suggest strongly that social support helps protect us against the damaging effects of stress. It is also clear that the level of social support varies; for instance, men seem to have larger networks, but women seem to use them more effectively (Ratcliffe-Crain and Baum 1990), and this has been related to the more severe effects of bereavement stress in men than women (Stroebe *et al.* 1999). The value of social support also helps explain the upsurge in unofficial support groups in particular areas,

such as Alcoholics Anonymous, groups for parents who have lost children, or sufferers from particular chronic illnesses, such as cystic fibrosis or cancer.

There are various categories of social support:

◆ *Emotional support* – This can provide comfort and reassurance, and, by raising the person's sense of self-esteem and self-worth, help them feel able to cope with the situation.

◆ *Practical support* – Friends and support groups can help in practical ways, for instance by lending money or helping sort out affairs after bereavement.

◆ *Advice* – Friends, and especially special interest support groups, can be a source of information and advice, commenting on possible coping strategies and suggesting others. Often, people you know will have met the particular situation before and you can learn from their experience.

The mechanisms underlying the protective effects of social support are unclear. Although talking with other people can help the cognitive evaluation of stress-induced demands and give reassurance that friends are around who will help with coping, the work with monkeys shows strongly that isolation is very stressful, and that the simple physical closeness of others reduces physiological arousal directly. One could speculate that with humans, we have a combination of help at the cognitive and practical level, along with a more primitive need to be close to other people. The evidence suggests that hugging children is both reassuring and stress-reducing.

Control

The concept of control is central to stress and stress management. When there is a gap between perceived demands and perceived coping resources, we define it as 'state of stress', but it is also a situation of being out of control. The Meichenbaum and Kobasa approaches to stress management both directly address ways of increasing the sense of being in control. Analyses of how people try to impose control reveals that several different types of control exist:

◆ *Informational* – Your train stops unexpectedly on the way to an important meeting. Informational control is finding out what the problem is and how long the delay will be.

◆ *Decisional* – Before you travel, there are alternatives: car, train, bus. Even if the decision turns out badly, you have control at that stage.

◆ *Behavioural* – Is there direct action you can take? If the train stops in a station, and you know the problem is serious, are there alternative forms of transport you can take, such as buses or taxis?

◆ *Cognitive* – This refers to the use of cognitive relaxation techniques (as described earlier) to reduce directly the stress-induced arousal. Think about the meeting itself – is it absolutely critical that you be there? Will the world stop turning if you are late?

◆ *Retrospective* – This means thinking about the stressful situation after it is resolved. How did you cope, was it effective, what would you do differently next time, e.g. leave more time, not travel by train? Explaining how things happened and how they could be avoided in the future, is an important aspect of control.

Put so straightforwardly, stress management looks simple. Unfortunately, in real life it can be hard to act so rationally, especially when it goes against aspects of the personality.

The concept of *locus of control* (Rotter 1966) refers to individual differences in how we see the world and our ability to control what happens to us. There are two extremes:

◆ *Internal locus of control* – This refers to people who attribute events that happen to them to sources within themselves; they are responsible. This can be misplaced, as some events are clearly out of our control; the train breaks down, but a strong internal locus of control would lead to the assumption that the situation was a result of your choice of travelling by train. On the positive side, a strong internal locus of control goes along with the belief that you can control much of your life and succeed in difficult or stressful situations. People with a strong internal locus tend to cope well with stressful situations, showing less physiological arousal.

◆ *External locus of control* – The person with an external locus of control attributes events in their lives to outside agencies and factors. They have a sense that 'things happen to them' and are largely uncontrollable. Luck or fate are important factors. As you would expect, people who sense they have little control over life events confront stressful

situations with a more passive or fatalistic attitude, where a more active strategy is usually better for stress management. They suffer more stress-related illness and are less active in coping (Kamen and Seligman 1989).

Most people are not at the extremes, but can often be characterized as more internal or more external. Locus of control questionnaires are common in stress research, as locus of control relates to how we cope and how we react to stress, and one of the aims of stress-management training is to internalize the sense of control. However, as a fundamental part of personality, locus of control is hard to modify. It emerges during development, probably as a mixture of inherited factors and early social experience.

Many experimental studies have looked at levels of control and reactions to stress. The work of Seligman on learned helplessness is probably the best known (see *In Focus*), showing that animals and people can in some circumstances learn that coping is impossible in some situations, and that this learning can transfer to other circumstances. Other work shows that even the illusion of active coping can reduce stress. Rats given repeated and uncontrollable footshocks develop gastric (stomach) ulcers; give them a lever to press, and even though pressing has *no* effect on the number of shocks, they develop far fewer ulcers (Sapolsky 1994). A similar effect is seen in people exposed to uncontrollable loud noises. The group given a button to press, which had no effect on the frequency of noises, still showed a smaller activation of the stress-response than the group simply exposed to the noise (Glass and Singer 1972).

This can be seen in everyday life. People are far more stressed by air travel than by car travel, even though statistically you are much safer in the air. However, you have no control when you fly, whereas the car is under your control.

Summary: Stress management

There are many approaches to stress management, divided into four major categories:

◆ physical, using drugs and biofeedback

◆ general psychological, using muscle relaxation, meditation, and hypnosis

◆ specific psychological, using cognitive–behavioural techniques

◆ aspects of lifestyle, such as exercise and social support.

General approaches are used to reduce stress-related arousal, while specific training uses cognitive and behavioural methods to modify cognitive strategies of

---

Activity 5: Taking control

Think about a recent stressful event you have experienced. Using each of the different types of control listed (informational, decisional, etc.), write down how you dealt with the event, and how you might have imposed a greater degree of control over the event in order to minimise the degree of stress experienced.

in focus

Stress in monkeys and rats

In 1958 Brady *et al.* conducted their 'executive monkey' study. Monkeys received electric footshocks at 20-second intervals for periods of six hours at a time, with six hours rest in between. Shocks were not signalled. Monkeys were run in pairs with one in each pair – the executive – able to press a lever to postpone shocks for 20 seconds. The other monkey could not press the lever but received any footshocks (a 'yoked' animal). Not all shocks can be avoided on this schedule, and after many sessions executives began to die of gastric ulceration. Brady concluded that the shocks themselves were not severely stressful, as the yoked monkeys showed less ulceration, but the stress of trying to avoid the shocks was the critical element. Note that this study ran for days; over short periods, trying to exercise control through bar-pressing is associated with *reductions* in stress responses (see main text).

Weiss (1972) repeated Brady *et al.*'s study with rats. He found that giving feedback on successful shock avoidance (by sounding a tone) reduced ulceration in executives to below that of yoked controls; the feedback tells the animal it has avoided shocks and increases its sense of 'control' over the situation. The yoked animal cannot respond and so lacks any control at all over what is going on. The lack of control and the stress of the footshocks leads to more ulceration in this group.

Another important factor was the animal's natural level of activity. In both studies, active animals ulcerated more than less active animals, and such *individual differences* are also found in humans. It is well established that reactivity of our stress-response systems varies not just between genders (see main text), but also between individuals, so that one person may show substantial arousal to a mild stimulus, while another may show no response at all. Physical activity is undoubtedly important in reducing the negative effects of stress (see main text), but people or animals who are naturally more active are not automatically more healthy, as their activity may include this type of hyperreactive stress-response system. Although they may be burning up energy faster, they are also mobilizing reserves faster because of their energetic stress response.

In another set of studies Seligman (1975) showed that rats given inescapable footshocks failed to learn to escape from avoidable footshocks on a later test. He called this learned helplessness. It can also be demonstrated in humans (Hiroto and Seligman 1975). Using loud noise as a stressor, they found that participants exposed to uncontrollable loud bursts of noise performed poorly on a later task in which the noise was controllable; they had learnt from the earlier experience that they could not control the noise, so did not try. Seligman suggests that the experience of life as uncontrollable is stressful and an important factor in the development of psychological depression.

These studies show the importance of control and feedback on successful coping in reducing levels of stress, and fits in well with the role of these factors in human responses to stress discussed in the main text. It is also important to note that the severely stressful nature of these studies makes them unethical, and they could not be performed today.

stress management. Evidence shows that physical exercise and social support can be effective in reducing the impact of life stressors.

We can use various types of control to help in managing stress, and improving this sense of being in control is an important part of cognitive approaches. People vary in their locus of control, the extent to which they see themselves at the mercy of events in their lives. The challenge for stress-management programmes is to improve this fundamental aspect of personality.

Chapter summary

◆ A state of stress exists when there is a mismatch between the perceived demands (**stressors**) on us and our perceived coping strategies. Stressors lead to activation of the bodily stress-response. This involves the autonomic nervous system (ANS) and the hypothalamus-pituitary gland link, both acting on the adrenal gland to release different sets of hormones which control many vital bodily functions.

◆ **Selye's General Adaptation Syndrome** (GAS) has three stages: activation of stress-response, resistance (apparent coping with stressors), and exhaustion (through long-term or chronic stress), when stress-related conditions may develop.

◆ The **relationship between stress and physical illness** may stem from a primitive 'flight or fight' stress-response system which produces more energy resources than we require to combat our contemporary stressors. Increased heart rate affects the **cardiovascular** system, wearing away blood vessel linings. Corticosteroids, adrenaline and noradrenaline release stored carbohydrates and fats into the bloodstream, which, if not expended or reabsorbed, remain in the bloodstream leading to hypertension and atherosclerosis (blocking of blood vessels). Stress hormones also supress the **immune system**, which can, especially if long-term or chronic (**immunosuppression**), leave the body vulnerable to infection and disease.

◆ Research into sources of stress has produced several life-event scales, the most widely used being Holmes and Rahe's Social Readjustment Rating Scale (SRRS). This scores major life events and life changes according to their psychological impact, proposing that higher scores on the SRRS increase the chances of stress-related health breakdown. Other scales, such as the Hassles scale, deal with minor, everyday stressors, which correlate significantly with health status.

◆ Research into **workplace stressors** includes studies of workplace relationships, the physical environment, **work overload** and **role ambiguity**. Workplace stress not only significantly affects individuals, but also affects organizations and productivity.

◆ **Individual differences** have been shown to relate to vulnerability to stress. **Friedman and Rosenman's** (1974) Type A behaviour pattern showed some correlations with increased vulnerability to stress-related illness, but Type A people may also score highly on protective factors such as control and commitment.

◆ Research into **gender** differences reveals that men show more stress-related physiological arousal than women, and that sources of stress may vary between genders. However, both genders report similar levels of subjective stress.

◆ Social support is an important protective factor against stress, and there appear to be clear cultural and ethnic variations in how it is used. However, **cultures** vary along many dimensions which affect health, such as genetic inheritance, lifestyle and diet, and in the range of stressors experienced, so assessing cultural variations to stress can be difficult.

◆ **Physical approaches** to **managing the negative effects of stress** include **drugs**, such as benzodiazepine (BZ) and beta-blockers. However, although drugs can be effective in reducing states and symptoms of stress, they can lead to dependency, have side effects and may prevent the real causes of stress being detected. **Biofeedback** involves recording the body's physiological systems, e.g. blood pressure, and then finding strategies to reduce the readings.

◆ General **psychological approaches**, such as relaxation, meditation and hypnosis, are used to reduce the bodily arousal associated with stress. Specific psychological approaches, such as **Michenbaum's Stress-Inoculation** Training uses cognitive–behavioural techniques to encourage clients to relive, analyse and evaluate stressful situations more accurately. They are then taught specific and non-specific strategies for coping, which should become self-sustaining.

◆ **Kobasa's** concept of **hardiness** centres on personality factors which provide defences against the negative effects of stress. These include: belief that we have control over our lives, commitment to engaging in the world around us, and seeing life changes as challenges rather than threats or stressors. Kobasa proposed increasing hardiness by focusing on recognizing signs of stress, reliving stressful encounters, and self-improvement, especially by taking on challenges that we can cope with.

◆ Physical exercise, to keep the cardiovascular system in shape, and using social support networks effectively are both also thought to help protect against the damaging effects of stress.

◆ The concept of **control** is central to stress and stress management. The gap between perceived demands and perceived coping resources is a state of stress, but also a situation of being 'out of control'. Several different types of control exist, such as informational, decisional and behavioural. Improving the sense of being in control is an important part of cognitive approaches.

◆ Internal locus of control refers to people who attribute events that happen to them to sources within themselves. They generally cope well with stressful situations, showing less physical arousal. External locus of control refers to people who

attribute events in their lives to outside forces. They generally suffer more stress-related illness and cope less well.

◆ There are **strengths and weaknesses in stress-control methods**. The difficulties include: trying to change fundamental aspects of personality; the time, commitment and money needed to follow these methods through; the few controlled studies of their effectiveness and the generalization of results across gender and cultures.

Exam summary

The AQA examination will test your knowledge of the following areas:

◆ the body's response to stressors (pp. 56–8)

◆ Selye's General Adaptation Syndrome (pp. 58–9)

◆ research into the relationship between stress and illness – cardiovascular disorders and effects on the immune system (pp. 60–3)

◆ research into the sources of stress including the effects of life events (pp. 64–6) and workplace stressors (pp. 66–7)

◆ individual differences in modifying the effects of stress – personality (pp. 67–9), gender (pp. 68–9) and cultural differences (pp. 69–70)

◆ stress management techniques – physical (p. 71) and psychological (pp. 71–5) approaches

◆ strengths and weaknesses of these techniques

◆ the role of control in the perception of stress (pp. 75–7).

Example question

The question below should take you 30 minutes to answer:

(a) Describe two ways in which the body responds to stressors. *(3 + 3 marks)*

(b) Explain the role of personality and gender in modifying the effects of stress. *(6 + 6 marks)*

(c) 'Lack of control is a major source of perceived stress.'

To what extent is control an important determinant of our experience of stress? *(12 marks)*

Suggested answer structure

(a) The hypothalamic-pituitary axis and the ANS-adrenal medulla link (the main components of the

body's response to stressors) are explained on pp. 56–8. Note that 3 marks are given for each of the two ways and the amount written for each of these should reflect that.

(b) This question asks for an explanation of both personality *and* gender in the modification of our reaction to stress. Friedman and Rosenman's 'Type A behaviour pattern' is probably the best-known example of how personality influences how we deal with stress. An account of this can be found on pp. 67–9.

Research into gender differences in stress reaction has found that males and females differ in levels of the stress hormone adrenaline during stressful situations, and females show smaller rises in blood pressure in response to stressful tasks than do men (p. 68). Possible explanations for this difference can be found on pp. 68–9.

(c) This last part of the question calls for a much more discursive and evaluative response. The quotation suggests that a sense of control is an important determinant of our experience of stress. An account of the role of control can be found on pp. 75–7. There are a number of different ways that people can exert control over a situation (informational, decisional, behavioural, etc.). The question, however, asks for more than a straight description of these. To reinforce the importance of control, you might write about the nature of learned helplessness (*In Focus* , p. 77) and comment on research that has explored the relationship between control and stress (e.g. Sapolsky 1994, Glass and Singer 1972, p. 76). Underlying this analysis is the suggestion that people differ in their locus of control, which influences how they see the world and which affects their ability to control what happens to them (p. 76).

Further resources

Sapolsky, R.M. (1994) *Why Zebras Don't Get Ulcers*, New York: Freeman.

> *A very readable account of stress, stress-related diseases, and coping. Sapolsky has a catchy style, not academic, but with excellent detail and memorable examples to put across the ideas.*

Sarafino, E.P. (1999) *Health Psychology* (3rd edn), New York: Wiley.

> *Comprehensive textbook covering the physiology and psychology of stress, stress-related disorders, and coping strategies.*

Websites

www.about.com/

> *A searchable site that covers (among other things) a wide range of sites about stress and stress management.*

www.mentalhealth.net/

> *A starting point for searching the web for topics related to stress, stress management and other areas of mental health.*

Chapter 4

Abnormality

Pamela Prentice

Preview

In this chapter we shall be looking at:

◆ defining psychological abnormality and the limitations associated with attempts to define psychological abnormality

◆ biological and psychological models of abnormality, including the assumptions made by different models in terms of the possible causes of abnormality and implications for treatment

◆ critical issue: eating disorders – anorexia nervosa and bulimia nervosa.

Introduction

This chapter will consider a range of definitions and models of psychological abnormality in relation to what are often called 'mental disorders', examples being: phobias; clinical depression; eating disorders and schizophrenia. Definitions of psychological abnormality refer to the different ways in which abnormality has traditionally been defined. Whilst most of these definitions have practical value, this chapter will consider their limitations in terms of operational or ethical difficulties and cultural relativism.

A model of abnormality offers a complete and coherent explanation for the origins of abnormal behaviour and psychological functioning according to its own perspective, or orientation. Each model, in the light of its orientation, leads to quite different ideas about treatment methods for mental disorders, or psychological problems. This chapter will outline and consider the biological model of abnormality, along with a number of psychological models of abnormality. The critical issue for consideration in this chapter is eating disorders. The clinical characteristics of anorexia nervosa and bulimia nervosa will be outlined. This will be followed by biological and psychological explanations for these disorders, along with research on which these explanations are based.

Defining psychological abnormality

The term *psychological abnormality* here refers to behaviours and psychological functioning which is considered to be different from the 'normal', and in the main refers to what are generally called 'mental disorders'.

There are a number of definitions of abnormality and in this section four definitions will be discussed, along with their limitations (including cultural relativism). These are:

◆ statistical infrequency

◆ deviation from social norms

◆ deviation from ideal mental health

◆ a failure to function adequately.

Statistical infrequency

According to this definition, any behaviour that is statistically infrequent is regarded as abnormal. It is assumed that most people do not stray very far from the 'norm' or average. A physical example of this would be, for instance, height or foot size. Shoe manufacturers will take this into account when deciding how many of each shoe size to produce. A given population of adult females placed into a normal distribution pattern would show that most adult females would take a shoe size of between 3 and 9. Therefore, manufacturers would produce very few adult female shoes below or above these sizes and people requiring these would probably need to find a specialist or have their shoes made to measure. In terms of psychological attributes,

Figure 4.1
The normal distribution
pattern of IQ scores

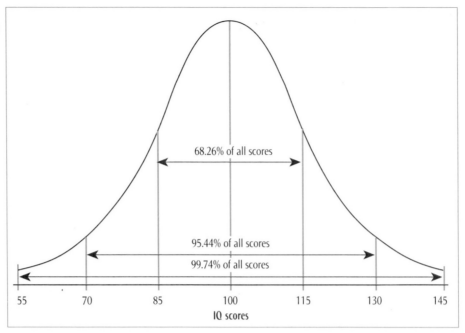

68.26% of all scores

95.44% of all scores

99.74% of all scores

| 55 | 70 | 85 | 100 | 115 | 130 | 145 |

IQ scores

it is assumed that personality traits and behaviour can also be placed into a normal distribution pattern. This method is used to assess mental retardation and mental genius, on the assumption that intelligence can be measured by IQ tests, whose scores are plotted against a normal distribution pattern. You are probably already familiar with a 'normal distribution pattern' from your learning in the 'research design and statistics' element of your AS in psychology. However, see Fig. 4.1 for an example in relation to IQ. The main problem with statistical definitions of IQ is that a deviation of a very high IQ tends to be regarded positively and not as 'abnormal', whereas a deviation of a very low IQ tends to be viewed negatively and is more likely to be regarded as 'abnormal'. As Davison and Neale (1997) point out, many behaviours that are statistically infrequent, such as great athletic ability, are not generally regarded as abnormal.

Mental health

When considering psychological abnormality in terms of mental health, problems such as depression and anxiety are 'normal' human conditions in a statistical sense, in that most people suffer from these from time to time and in relation to specific events in their lives. However, to become 'clinically depressed' or suffer from a severe anxiety disorder such that it is diagnosed as a 'mental disorder' is not quite so 'normal' in a statistical sense across the whole population. Taking the population of people diagnosed with a mental disorder, however, depression and anxiety disorders are the most frequently diagnosed. It seems, therefore, that statistical frequency or infrequency is relative to the population under consideration.

Statistical infrequency may be a useful definition of abnormality in general terms, but it falls short when applied to mental disorders. It is only possible to determine mental-disorder statistics for those who have been diagnosed by a clinician. This may not necessarily reflect the true prevalence of any given mental disorder because many people suffer from mental disorders but do not seek professional help.

Gender issues

Females are more likely than males to consult their doctor for anxiety problems, whereas males are more likely to bottle up their anxiety, or try to deal with it in physical ways, such as vigorous sporting activity. Bennett (1995) believes that the socialization of men in industrialized societies has created masculine stereotypes that alienate men from seeking help for psychological problems because they are taught from an early age to distance themselves from their emotions. Therefore, statistical data may be more a reflection of male and female socialization than a true reflection of real differences between males and females for any given mental disorder.

Cultural issues

Similar issues have been considered with regard to specific cultural, or ethnic groups. For example, mental disorders appear to be statistically infrequent in some ethnic groups, but this may simply reflect their reluctance to seek professional help, owing to their cultural beliefs. Cohen (1988) describes how in India, mentally ill people are cursed and looked down on. Rack (1982) points out that in China, mental illness also carries a great stigma and that the Chinese are therefore careful to diagnose only those whose behaviour is indisputably psychotic (i.e. where thinking and emotion are so impaired that the individual is out of contact with reality). Depression, a frequently diagnosed disorder in our own culture, appears to be absent in Asian cultures, and a general explanation for this has been that Asian people tend to live within extended families with ready access to social support. However, Rack (1982) points out that depression is equally common among Asians, but that Asians consult their doctor for physical problems only and rarely with 'emotional' distress. They might seek help for the physical symptoms or side-effects of depression, such as tiredness, sleep disturbances and appetite problems, but would probably not mention their mood state. They do not see this as the responsibility of the doctor and instead sort it out within the family. Therefore, statistical infrequency merely reflects the statistical likelihood of seeking professional help, rather than an indication of whether a particular mental disorder is present or absent in a particular culture. A further example of this is found with Puerto Ricans, who generally react to stressful situations with severe heart palpitations, fainting and seizures, but this is regarded as quite a normal reaction in their culture, according to Guarnaccia *et al.* (1990).

It may, in fact, be inappropriate to identify mental disorders as examples of abnormality if we wish to define abnormality in terms of statistical infrequency. A large-scale survey undertaken across 48 states in the USA and reported by Kessler *et al.* (1994) underlines this argument. The survey found that 48 per cent of the people in their survey had suffered from at least one psychological disorder at some point in their lives.

Deviation from social norms

Society sets up rules for behaviour based on a set of moral standards. These become established as *social norms* and if anyone violates these moral standards then they are regarded as deviant or 'abnormal'. Szasz (1972) wrote extensively on this issue, suggesting that 'madness' is manufactured solely in order to label those people in society who do not conform to the rules of society or to conventional standards of morality.

Historical issues

Two examples will serve to illustrate how beliefs about 'abnormality' and social norms of morally acceptable behaviour change over time:

◆ Until as recently as the early years of the twentieth century, unmarried women in the UK who became pregnant were sometimes interned in mental institutions and in many cases the babies were taken away for adoption. Some of these women were in their early teens when they became pregnant and remained in mental institutions for the rest of their lives.

◆ The second example is that of homosexuality, long regarded as a deviation from social norms. In the UK, homosexual acts were regarded as criminal offences, even among consenting adults, until the 1960s, and The American Psychiatric Association classified homosexuality as a mental disorder until 1973.

Cultural issues

A diagnosis of insanity has been used in Russia as a way of detaining political dissidents. In Japan, a diagnosis of insanity has been used as a threat to ensure a strong work ethic. According to Cohen (1988), because of Japan's drive for industrial success, 'loony-bins' are required for those who are unwilling to conform to the demands of industry. Therefore, in order to instil the appropriate terror, the 'bins' must be sufficiently unattractive. Conditions in Japanese mental hospitals are similar to the old Victorian asylums in the UK, being overcrowded, dirty and often brutal in their discipline. Between 1955 and 1990 the number of inpatients in mental hospitals in Japan increased from 100,000 to around 400,000. Mental illness in Japan is regarded as shameful and ex-patients are not allowed to work as cooks or bakers, to enter public baths, or to hold a driving licence.

In present-day Western culture, the term *mental disorder* is not generally used to define 'deviant' behaviour, either political or sexual. There have been criminal cases (e.g. murder or sexual crimes) where the perpetrator has pleaded the insanity defence, but this is not a matter of course (see *In Focus* for a recent example of invoking the insanity defence). There are types of behaviour that are generally regarded as

The insanity defence

Lorena Bobbitt pleaded temporary insanity and was acquitted in January 1994 of the charge of maliciously wounding her husband. In June 1993 she had taken a kitchen knife and cut off his penis whilst he slept. She claimed that she had suffered many years of abuse by John Bobbitt and that after one episode of abuse she suffered a brief psychotic episode in which she was compelled to commit the act.

unacceptable, such as rape and mass murder, where it is difficult to accept that such violation of others could possibly be normal. In such cases, there is a tendency to regard the perpetrators of the crimes as abnormal and their extreme antisocial behaviour as inherent in their personality. Otherwise, if they, as people, were regarded as 'normal' and merely their behaviour as 'abnormal' then the inference is that anyone could be a potential rapist or mass murderer, which is too unsettling a notion for most people to contemplate. There are those who believe that DNA markers will eventually be identified for antisocial behaviour (see *In Focus*), yet studies in social psychology have shown that, in certain circumstances, so-called 'normal' people can behave in violent and antisocial ways. A prime example of this is football hooliganism.

In Britain it has been suggested that there is a culture bias in mental health because diagnostic statistics for mental disorders show significant differences between ethnic or cultural groups. For instance, Cochrane (1977) reported that Black (African-Caribbean) immigrants are between two to seven times more likely to be diagnosed with schizophrenia than Whites. In contrast, Cochrane (1983) reported that rates of hospital admission for schizophrenia among South Asians (from India, Pakistan, Bangladesh, Hong Kong) are comparable to Whites. An immediate explanation for these differences is that diagnostic figures merely reflect high or low rates for a particular disorder in the population of the country of origin. However, this cannot explain the high figures for schizophrenia diagnosis among African-Caribbeans in Britain because, as Cochrane (1983) points out, this has not been found to the same extent anywhere else in the world. How, then, can these differential diagnoses be explained?

Fernando (1988) claims that stereotyped ideas about race are inherent in British psychiatry. For example, there are stereotypes of Black violence and the belief that Blacks cannot 'use' help and are therefore not suitable for open hospitals. Research has shown that the compulsory detaining of African-Caribbean patients in secure hospitals is higher than for any other group (e.g. Ineichen *et al.* 1984, McGovern and Cope 1987). Cochrane and Sashidharan (1995) identified a culture

'blindness' in diagnosis, suggesting that it is a common assumption that the behaviours of the White population are normative and that any deviation from this by another ethnic group reveals some racial or cultural pathology.

Expected versus unexpected behaviour

We tend to make judgements about whether behaviours that deviate from the norm are merely 'eccentric' or whether they are abnormal in a pathological sense. Running across a rugby pitch in the nude, or being buried alive for 30 days may be regarded as strange, or idiosyncratic, but we would not necessarily assume that the person is mentally disturbed. However, if someone is walking down the street talking out loud to an invisible person, or if someone insists that Martians have taken over their brain, then we would be more likely to suspect a mental disorder. Thus, only particular kinds of 'abnormal' behaviour tend to be regarded as pathological. Even in this sense we should take into account 'cultural relativity'. For example, walking around nude in public may be considered normal in some cultures and talking to an invisible person is considered normal in certain African and Indian cultures following a bereavement, where people believe it is possible to remain in contact briefly with a lost loved one.

On a day-to-day basis 'deviation from social norms' can be a useful way of detecting when others may need help. We constantly distinguish between normal and abnormal behaviour according to what is expected in a given situation, according to the social norms of the time. Much of our behaviour is context-specific and out of context it may seem bizarre. For example, what would you think if you were walking through the park and someone sitting on a bench suddenly jumped up and started singing and dancing? You would probably think that this person was rather odd. But if you then saw a film crew you would contextualize the scene, assume the person was an actor and perhaps stay around to watch. At a practical, everyday level, deviation from social norms can be a useful way to identify mental problems. We learn what to expect

The genetic defence for psychopathic murderers

There is a current suggestion that sociopaths and psychopaths may have a genetic defect, and that this is the cause of their antisocial and often violent behaviour. This could be viewed as a mitigating circumstance for the apparently cold-blooded murderer or rapist. A number of defence lawyers in the USA have recently put forward the genetic argument in defence of their client. They have provided phenotype data (family trees) showing an ancestry of violent criminals, suggesting that the accused was not exercising free will, but acted as a result of a genetic defect. So far this defence has not resulted in acquittal.

from individuals on a day-to-day basis and if their behaviour deviates drastically from this, then we become alarmed on their behalf. This may be vital to the receipt of suitable help because, for example, people with clinical depression are often unable to motivate themselves to seek assistance, and people suffering from schizophrenia are characterized by a lack of insight regarding their problem. An important point to note here is the shift in emphasis from the *person* to the *behaviour* that is being regarded as abnormal.

Activity 1: Explaining unexpected behaviour

Refer to the example of 'singing and dancing' behaviour in the text. Drawing on your own experience, provide examples of unexpected behaviours and how you interpreted or explained them.

Deviation from ideal mental health

The notion of 'ideal mental health' was first put forward by Jahoda in 1958 and turns the traditional notion of abnormality on its head, by looking at positives, rather than negatives – the notion of mental 'health' rather than mental 'illness'. Jahoda identified six major criteria relating to ideal mental health; if these are deviated from, or are in deficit, then the person would be vulnerable to a psychological problem or mental disorder. The six criteria are examined here in detail.

1   Positive attitudes towards the self

This means to have a *positive self-concept* and a *sense of identity*. Jahoda (1958) suggested that a mentally healthy attitude towards the self included self-respect, self-confidence, self-reliance and self-acceptance; the person has learnt to live with themselves, accepting both their limitations and possibilities. What is important here, is to view oneself realistically and objectively. Unfortunately, many people develop a negative self-concept or low self-esteem because of the way they have been treated by others and perhaps made to feel small and unimportant. The humanistic model of abnormality explains the origins of low self-esteem (see p. 97). In relation to a sense of identity, Jahoda claimed that to be mentally healthy, a person must know who they are and not feel any basic doubts about their inner identity. She drew upon the work of Erikson (1963) who suggested that a sense of identity is the accrued confidence to maintain inner sameness and continuity, in contrast to someone who is unsure of their identity and consequently shies away from forming intimate relationships.

2   Self-actualization of one's potential

This emanates from the work of Abraham Maslow (1954), who suggested that we all have potential in certain directions (for example, intellectual, artistic, athletic) and that we constantly strive to fulfil this potential. Mental health problems occur when we are prevented from fulfilling our true potential. Unfortunately, in reality, very few people achieve their full potential in life, which may be because of their own particular environment or through some failing within themselves. It would seem, then, that if *self-actualization* is a criterion for ideal mental health, then most of us would be mentally unhealthy and would fit the criteria for abnormality. There is an additional problem with this view. Seeking to fulfil one's own potential as a prime goal in life may be acceptable in some cultures but not in other cultures. For example, in some cultures, elders in the family plan the person's future out for them. This planning might include such things as arranged marriages, which are common in Asian cultures. It may, therefore, be regarded as 'abnormal' to pursue one's own goals if they are in conflict with those of one's culture. The pursuit of self-actualization, or personal happiness is, perhaps, a privilege for those living in an industrialized society which is affluent and where one is freed from the need to pursue the basic necessities for survival.

3   Resistance to stress

This is what Jahoda (1958) calls 'integration', or the *ability to tolerate anxiety without disintegration*. The mentally healthy person has, therefore, developed good coping strategies for dealing with stressful situations. Indeed, it does seem that those people who are more vulnerable to stress and anxiety are more likely to develop psychological problems, and a great deal of research has been undertaken to identify effective coping strategies to reduce stress. It should be noted, however, that some people actually work more efficiently in moderately stressful situations and that an optimum level of anxiety increases performance. For example, many actors will say that they give their best performances when they experience a certain amount of anxiety.

4   Personal autonomy

This means that the person is reliant on their own inner resources and can remain relatively stable even in the face of hard knocks, frustrations and deprivations. This is because, according to Maslow (1954), autonomous people are not dependent upon other people. They are self-contained and dependent upon their own potentialities and resources. Jahoda (1958) describes personal autonomy as an *ability to make our own decisions on the basis of what is right for ourselves,* rather than to satisfy others. However, as already mentioned in relation to self-actualization, in many cultures there is an overwhelming sense of duty to others and it would not be regarded as 'normal' to put one's own wishes before those of others.

5   Accurate perception of reality

This means *seeing oneself and the world around one in realistic terms*, rather than either through 'rose-tinted glasses' or in an overly pessimistic manner. Indeed, if someone continually distorts reality, then they are not really living in the real world and their views and behaviours are bound to appear abnormal to others. If someone only ever sees the best in people then this may endear them to others, but it also leaves them vulnerable to those who may take advantage. Conversely, someone who is overly morbid and pessimistic is a likely candidate to develop a depressive disorder and would not endear themselves to others very easily. However, psychologists who support Existentialist and Phenomenologist ideas would challenge the notion of an objective reality, believing that we create our own reality. Perceptions of reality differ over time (remember people once thought the world was flat) and also differ between cultures. For example, seeing or hearing someone who has died would be considered normal in some cultures, but regarded as psychotic hallucinations in other cultures.

6   Adapting to the environment

This means *being flexible rather than rigid, being able to adapt and adjust to change*. Someone who is fixed in old ways of thinking and behaving may appear abnormal to younger people and to those who have been able to adjust to a changing environment.

If you think you can communicate with the dead, does this mean you're abnormal?

However, it would be jumping to conclusions to suggest that they were mentally unhealthy as a consequence. Trying to adapt to the environment can even, in some cases, be a potential cause of psychological problems, especially in affluent industrialized societies, where not being able to afford the latest luxury or technological equipment can itself cause some people to become depressed.

Sex-role stereotyping

Mental health statistics indicate that certain mental disorders are diagnosed more frequently in men, while others are diagnosed more frequently in women (e.g. eating disorders being diagnosed predominantly in women and antisocial personality disorder predominantly in men). The view that this can be explained through biological differences has been challenged by those who claim that these differences merely reflect stereotyped judgements among mental health professionals. Broverman *et al.* (1981) suggest that a double standard of mental health exists within the health profession. She points out that certain behavioural characteristics are thought to be pathological in members of one sex, but not in the opposite sex. Men and women are trained from birth to fulfil different social roles. Therefore, if health consists of good adjustment to one's environment, then healthy adjustment for a woman or man will be accepting the behavioural norms for their sex. Broverman and colleagues maintain that one of the dangers of mental health professionals adopting the 'adjustment' notion of health is that they actively reinforce and perpetuate sex-role stereotypes.

Evaluating the 'ideal mental health' concept

In conclusion, meeting all six criteria would be appear to be quite a tall order for anyone, and as such most people are likely to fall short of 'ideal mental health'. One of the problems with setting up a notion of ideal mental health is that some people regard themselves as having mental problems when they would not meet the criteria for diagnosis, whilst others regard themselves as psychologically healthy when perhaps they are not. Shedler *et al.* (1993) compared people's self-reports of mental health using questionnaires, with clinicians ratings of those same people. These were then grouped into three categories of genuinely distressed, genuinely healthy and 'illusory mental health' (regarded as mentally healthy on the self-report, but mentally unhealthy in the opinion of the clinicians). The 'genuinely healthy' and 'illusory healthy' groups were then given stressful tasks, during which their heart rate and blood pressure were measured. They were then asked to report how stressed they believed themselves to be whilst undertaking the task. The 'illusory healthy' group were found to be more physically distressed but reported themselves to be less distressed than the 'genuinely healthy' group. Shedler and colleagues concluded that some people are psychologically defensive and will deny having mental problems.

The concept of 'ideal mental health' may be useful in providing some basic, possible explanations for why someone may be suffering from a psychological problem or mental disorder. However, setting up criteria whereby most people are likely to fall short of 'ideal mental health' may not be a very useful way of addressing abnormality, because setting up standards that most people are unable to meet is more likely to create anxiety.

Activity 2 provides a few examples of the types of questions people are asked to answer in order to provide a measure of how close they are to 'ideal mental health'.

Activity 2: You and 'ideal mental health'

Do you fit the criteria for 'ideal mental health'? Answer the following questions with YES or NO and find out.

1   Do you feel anxious in social situations?

2   Are you often confused about who you really are and what you want from life?

3   Do you often feel that other people, or circumstances, prevent you from achieving what you want in life?

4   Do you often feel under stress in your work or studies?

These are a few examples from a longer list of questions.

If the person answered 'no' to most of the questions, then, according to this theory, they are likely to be in 'ideal mental health'. However, remember this is merely a theory, so please don't conclude that you have a psychological problem if you answered 'yes' to any of these questions. Remember, there are limitations to the concept of 'ideal mental health'. In fact, many people find it difficult to answers these kinds of questions with a simple ' yes' or 'no'; for many, a more accurate answer is 'sometimes'.

Failure to function adequately

People with clinical depression or anxiety often experience considerable suffering and distress and a general dysfunction in their everyday activities, such as being unable to go to work. But these are not true definitions of 'abnormality'. They are more a way of determining the extent of a person's problems and the

likelihood that they might need professional help. A student experiencing anxiety and distress about a forthcoming exam may behave uncharacteristically and indeed inadequately, but this would not necessarily be regarded as abnormal behaviour. Conversely, sociopaths might exhibit behaviour, such as violence and aggression, but be unlikely to experience personal suffering, distress, or any general dysfunction, because of their amoral attitudes. Comer (1997) points out that psychological abnormality is not necessarily indicated by dysfunction alone. For example, some people protest against social injustice by depriving themselves of necessities, such as food. It is when abnormal behaviour interferes with daily functioning, such that people lose the ability to work or the motivation to care for themselves properly, that the behaviour becomes pathological. Perhaps using the criterion of 'failure to function adequately' as a definition of abnormality is the most humane way of addressing psychological problems and mental disorders. In this way it is left to the person, or others close to them, to decide if they need or wish to seek help. This philosophy avoids unnecessary labelling, which was criticized by many psychologists in the 1960s.

Labelling

Goffman (1968) maintained that labelling someone as mentally ill gave them a stigma that might stick long after the person had recovered from the problem. Scheff (1966) suggested that once labelled, a person was likely to accept the diagnosis and behave accordingly, because he or she would be rewarded for adopting the role and punished for trying to escape from it. To some extent, however, there is an inevitability about labelling. First, when people are absent from work, employers expect an explanation and this usually entails labelling the problem. Second, people suffering from mental problems, as with physical problems, are usually confused and concerned about their condition, as are their families, and they naturally seek to label the problem. Without a professional label, people invent their own, often letting their imagination run wild and creating unwarranted fears. Despite this, psychologists, in the main, disagree with labelling someone as 'abnormal' or as having a mental disorder, because they think it forces people into categories, whilst ignoring individual differences and therefore overlooking important information. Many psychologists also regard the labelling of a set of symptoms as unnecessary for psychological treatment.

Enforced detaining in mental institutions

The 'failure to function adequately' view of abnormality carries certain implications. If someone's behaviour appears strange or 'abnormal' to others, then providing they are not harming themselves or others, and providing their behaviour is not dysfunctional, such as preventing them from carrying on their daily lives, then no intervention is required. This is in sharp contrast to times prior to the Mental Health Act 1983, when people could be detained in mental institutions against their will on the authority of a health professional, guardian or spouse. This was the case for a husband who wished to have his wife detained, but the laws did not work in the opposite direction, i.e. if a wife wished to have her husband detained. Detaining someone in a mental hospital without their consent is still possible in the UK under Sectioning laws (see *In Focus*), but this is restricted to a short period, after which the person's consent is required. People cannot any longer be detained indefinitely against their will, other than in a psychiatric prison. Indeed, with recent moves within the NHS towards care in the community and the closing of mental hospitals, the situation has reversed. In-hospital care is now largely restricted to psychiatric wards within general hospitals and demand far exceeds current provision, which means that mentally ill people may not always get the treatment they need.

A 'failure to function adequately' does, however, mean that someone with a psychological problem that does not fit the criteria for a serious mental disorder should still be given appropriate professional help if their problem is causing a dysfunction in their daily living. Unfortunately though, for people with less severe psychological problems, but fitting the criteria of a failure to function adequately, NHS provision is not always available and there are generally long waiting lists for treatment. It is thus now more politically expedient than ever for mental health professionals to leave people alone unless there is a severe dysfunction.

Cultural issues

The 'failure to function adequately' criterion could explain why statistics show a higher incidence of psychological problems among people from minority ethnic groups. As Fernando (1988) points out, being a member of a minority ethnic group could be stressful owing to the exploitation, deprivation and harassment often experienced and, as Cochrane and Sashidharan (1995) point out, racism and prejudice have a significant impact upon psychological wellbeing. They also explain that migration from Third World to First World countries means that the first generation of migrants is likely to be exposed to economic uncertainty, substandard housing and harsh working conditions. These have mental health implications for new immigrants, but their problems may mistakenly be attributed to ethnicity.

---

 in focus

Sectioning laws

Patients can be admitted to a psychiatric hospital without giving their consent under sectioning laws included in the Mental Health Act 1983 for England and Wales.

Section 2 of the Act allows for 28-day compulsory admission and detention for assessment, which may be followed by medical treatment. Section 2 may be implemented when it is thought:

(a) that the patient suffers from a mental disorder that requires assessment and treatment, and

(b) that detention is necessary for the patient's own health or safety or the protection of others.

To invoke Section 2, application must be made by the patient's nearest relative, or an approved social worker, together with the medical recommendations of two doctors.

Section 3 is a compulsory treatment order for up to six months, which may be renewed for a further six months and subsequently for 12 months at a time. The grounds for a treatment order are that:

(a) medical treatment in hospital is appropriate owing to the nature or degree of mental illness or mental impairment, or psychopathic disorder

(b) such treatment is likely to alleviate or prevent deterioration of the condition

(c) treatment is necessary for the health and safety of the patient or the protection of others and it cannot be provided unless the person is detained.

To invoke Section 3, an application is made by an approved social worker and is based on two medical recommendations. A Section 3 cannot normally be imposed if the nearest relative objects.

Section 4 can be invoked in an emergency. A detention order for 72 hours would be invoked by one doctor and an approved social worker. This is then usually converted into a Section 2 order.

Social class issues

In relation to social class, research has indicated that the higher prevalence of severe mental disorders in socially disadvantaged groups is largely due to their exposure to more *stressful life experiences*, compared with those in more advantaged social groups. The first large-scale survey to support this hypothesis was the Midtown Manhattan Study (Srole *et al.* 1961, and Langner and Michael 1962). The study found the lowest levels of psychiatric impairment in the upper classes, slightly more in the middle classes and the highest levels in the lower classes. These findings were supported in a British study (Cochrane and Stopes-Roe 1980), which also found that lower social status was associated with higher risk of psychological problems.

A major study by Brown and Harris (1978) found a high incidence of depression among working-class housewives in Camberwell, London. The main vulnerability factors they identified were long-term periods of adverse circumstances, together with the cumulative effect of short-term life events, combined with factors such as lack of paid employment. In addition, the middle and upper classes have more 'positive' life experiences to offset the 'negative' and those in the lower classes have less control over their environment. Cochrane (1995a) points out that people living in high-rise flats are more prone to psychological problems than those in 'traditional' accommodation. An explanation for this may be that people who have been rehoused in tower blocks report a drop in the quality of relationships with neighbours, which may be an important factor in mental health, because neighbours are a potential source of social support. However, Cochrane points out that neighbours can also be a source of irritation and even fear. Halpern (1995) claims that if a neighbourhood becomes labelled as a dumping ground for 'problem families', then people who were not originally a 'problem' themselves may develop adverse reactions which may affect their mental health.

The *'social drift' hypothesis* offers another explanation for the higher incidence of serious mental disorder in lower socio-economic groups. This explanation is that the early onset of a major mental disorder, such as schizophrenia, might reduce the chances of establishing a career and the person may then subsequently 'drift' down the socio-economic scale. This indicates that social class is largely a consequence of, rather than a contributory factor in, mental disorder. Support for this is found in cases where the initial onset of schizophrenia has occurred later in life. It has been noted that many such individuals had previously established a good career. Cochrane (1983) points out that the higher incidence of schizophrenia in poor areas could reflect the number of people who move to those areas after the onset of their illness, because it is all they can afford, rather than that they had lived there all their lives.

Gender issues

Other studies have examined reasons why certain psychological problems appear to be more prevalent in men or women. Howell (1981) points out that women's experience in this culture predisposes them to depression and therefore clinicians are diagnosing a *situation* rather than a *person*. Cochrane (1995b) explains that depression can be related to the long-term effects of child abuse and also to gender role socialization, which produces increased female vulnerability. He points out the adverse effects on women of power relationships and sex discrimination. Despite the vast amount of evidence relating women's depression to sociocultural factors, clinicians continue to ignore environmental circumstances and convey the message that the problem lies in the person's illness (Johnstone 1989). Johnstone believes this also applies to men. Unemployed men have a high rate of psychiatric breakdown. Johnstone explains that by labelling the problem as a mental disorder, not only does the person have the stigma of a psychiatric label, but the problem is seen only in individual terms, rather than in the wider political and social context. Bennett (1995) believes that the socialization of men in industrialized societies has created masculine stereotypes that alienate men from seeking help for psychological problems.

Summary: Defining psychological abnormality

Although the concept of 'abnormal' as distinct from 'normal' behaviour may be useful as a general guide for identifying whether someone may require professional assistance, its use is limited because it is difficult to determine what is 'normal', other than at a statistical level. When considering mental disorders, the *statistical definition* falls down because studies show that most people suffer from psychological problems at some time or other in their life and, therefore, psychological problems are statistically 'normal'.

What is considered *deviation from social norms* changes over time and differs between cultures. Therefore, this remains a subjective measurement of abnormality. This approach has also been used as a means of social control.

The concept of *'ideal mental health'* is at a first glance quite appealing, but unfortunately the criteria are so demanding that almost everyone is bound to fall into the category of mental 'ill' health.

A *failure to function adequately* as a definition of abnormality offers the most humane definition because it leaves power with the individual, rather than the professionals. According to this definition, a person's behaviour may appear strange to others, but if they are functioning adequately and causing no harm to others, then there is no necessity to seek professional assistance. This avoids labelling and perhaps unnecessary intervention. On the other hand, if someone is not functioning adequately, this criterion should ensure that they receive help, even if the problem, as defined in mental disorder terms, is not regarded as very serious.

With each of these definitions there are issues surrounding culture, gender and social class, which have important consequences for an understanding of how abnormality is viewed and dealt with.

Models of abnormality

Models of abnormality are conceptual models, each offering different explanations for the origins of mental disorders. Psychiatrists usually adopt the medical model (mental disorder as an 'illness'), whilst psychologists tend to reject the concept of 'mental illness' in favour of models such as the psychodynamic, behavioural, cognitive or humanistic. The adoption of a particular conceptual model is very important because it will influence the type of research that is conducted and also the methods of treatment adopted.

Medical model

Basic assumptions

The medical model has dominated the field of mental health for the past 200 years. It is a biological approach, which regards abnormality of mental functioning as an 'illness' or 'disease'. This is because mental disorders are thought to be related to the physical structure and functioning of the brain. Some mental disorders are thought to have an *organic basis*, such as a brain tumour, or poisoning due to alcohol or drug abuse, resulting in anatomical deterioration. Syphilis, for example, was identified in the nineteenth century as the cause of deterioration in specific regions of the brain resulting in symptoms of a mental illness known as *general paresis*. The symptoms of this disorder were:

◆ delusions of grandeur, such as believing that one is God

◆ delusions of persecution, believing that everyone is plotting against one

◆ other bizarre behaviours, which now come under the general heading of *psychosis*.

Unfortunately, little can be done to arrest mental deterioration caused by disease or brain damage. Disorders where a clear organic cause has not been identified have been traditionally referred to as *functional disorders*.

Biochemical theory

During the twentieth century, the medical profession has increasingly advanced its biological understanding of mental disorders to include the role played by biochemicals. Functional disorders are now also thought to be physical in origin, symptoms occurring as a consequence of biochemical changes in the brain resulting in a dysfunction of neurotransmitters. Why these chemical changes take place is not yet clear, but they may be due to infections, life stress or a genetic defect.

Genetic research

Important new genetic research has highlighted the possibility that some people may be genetically at risk of developing a mental disorder, but so far the only strong evidence relates to conditions such as schizophrenia and manic-depression. Since no preventative measures to arrest the onset of these psychoses have yet been developed, the publicity surrounding such research may unfortunately serve to create further anxiety in relatives of a diagnosed person. Moreover, by focusing attention and research funding on genetics, attention is distracted from environmental influences, which are thought to play a significant role in mental disorders.

Advances in genetic research raise ethical and practical concerns about the consequences of trying to engineer a better society by genetic means (see *In Focus*, 'Genetic engineering').

The concept of no blame

A diagnosis of mental 'illness' implies that the person is in no way responsible for the abnormality of functioning and as such is not to blame. The concept of 'no blame' is generally thought to be more humane and likely to elicit a much more sympathetic response from others. However, antipsychiatrists, such as Szasz (1972), pointed out that, even more than physical illness, mental illness is something that people fear – largely because it is something they do not understand.

in focus

Genetic engineering

Genetic research has posed ethical considerations. One of these is the potential danger of genetic engineering, through enforced sterilization of those who may carry defective genes. This has already been proposed in some regions of China. The major ethical issue here, aside from human rights, is that a potential genotype defect will not necessarily manifest itself in the phenotype (observable characteristics of an individual). The phenotype is thought to be a product of the interaction between the genotype and environmental experience.

In general, people do not know how to respond to someone diagnosed as mentally ill. There may also be fears that the person's behaviour might be unpredictable and potentially dangerous. Therefore, sympathy is more likely to give way to avoidance of the person, which in turn leads to the person feeling shunned.

Implications for treatment

Since mental problems are viewed as physical illnesses, then physical treatments are regarded as the most appropriate. The main treatment, assuming that chemical imbalance is at the root of the problem, is to treat with drugs – known as *chemotherapy*. Drugs for mental disorders range from minor tranquillizers (for anxiety disorders), to antidepressants (for depressive disorders), through to major tranquillizers (for severe psychotic disorders), such as schizophrenia. These drugs have been found to be effective in relieving the symptoms of mental disorders in many, but not all, people. However, they also have side effects which may be considered worse than the original symptoms of the disorder. The fact that chemotherapy is effective in reducing symptoms of mental disorders is regarded as sufficient evidence to support the theory that chemical imbalance is the cause of the problem. Indeed, it is now known that some chemicals can affect the functioning of particular neurotransmitters, producing the symptoms of certain mental disorders. However, some psychologists disagree, believing the chemical imbalance to be the effect, rather than the cause, of mental problems.

Evaluation of the medical model

Many psychologists criticize psychiatry for focusing its attention primarily on symptoms, and for assuming that relieving symptoms with drugs cures the problem. Unfortunately, in many cases when the drug treatment is ceased, the symptoms recur, suggesting that they are not addressing the true cause of the problem.

Another criticism of the medical model is that people become *patients,* handing over responsibility for their 'wellness' to professionals, who may or may not accurately diagnose the problem. Prescribed treatment may not be appropriate and yet there is an expectation that patients will comply with medication, despite the fact that, as the British National Formulary (an index of pharmaceutical drugs and preparations) indicates, most medication carries side effects and often long-term dependency upon the drugs. If you go on to study psychology at A level, you may have the opportunity to explore other biological treatments.

Psychodynamic model

Basic assumptions

The psychodynamic model was developed by Freud and others in the latter part of the nineteenth century through clinical work with mentally disordered patients. Freud believed that problems arose directly from the dynamics of the psyche, rather than through physical malfunction. In his 'Introductory lectures on psychoanalysis' (1915–1918), Freud stated that humans are born with insatiable, demanding instincts – what Freud called the *id* part of our personality. People are then subsequently socialized into the moral standards of their culture and these become a second part of our personality – what Freud called the *superego.* Freud explained that these two parts of our personality are in direct conflict and therefore need to be managed and channelled in a rational way. The well-adjusted person develops a strong *ego* that is able to manage the personality, by allowing both the id and the superego expression at appropriate times. If the ego is weakened, then the personality may be dominated by either the id or the superego, whichever is the stronger. If id impulses emerge unchecked, then they are expressed in destructiveness and immorality, which may result in conduct disorders in childhood and psychopathic behaviour in adulthood. A powerful superego rigidly restricts the id to such an extent that the person will be deprived of even socially acceptable pleasures. Freud maintained that this would create neurosis, which could be expressed in the symptoms of anxiety disorders, such as phobias and obsessions. Psychological disturbance, therefore, results from the inability of the ego to manage conflict within the psyche. Freud postulated the concept of the *unconscious* and maintained that internal psychodynamics and conflicts occur at an unconscious level, so that at a conscious level, we are unaware of their influence.

Childhood trauma

Although psychical conflict can occur at any time in our life, it is most marked in early childhood because the ego is not developed fully enough to mediate between the id and the superego. Nor is it developed fully enough to deal with external events such as maternal absences, parental shortcomings and competition with siblings. Events in childhood of a traumatic or confusing nature are pushed into the unconscious – a process which Freud called *repression* – because they are too painful for the ego to bear, or because the child hasn't developed sufficient knowledge of the world to make sense of the event (A. Freud 1936). Distressing feelings around traumatic events do not disappear, however, simply because they are repressed. They find expression in dreams and irrational behaviour and may eventually erupt and express themselves in psychological and psychosomatic problems.

Defence mechanisms

The role of the ego is important in balancing the id and superego, both of which are very powerful. In order to do this, the ego employs 'defence mechanisms' (see Table 4.1). *Defence mechanisms* distort or deny reality and are essential ways of protecting the ego from distress and allowing the person to cope with life. They have a powerful, yet unconscious, influence upon our behaviour, and everyone uses them. Freud said that they are perfectly natural and normal and offer a way of satisfying the demands of the id without upsetting the superego. Whilst useful for protecting the ego, however, they do not offer a long-term solution, and if defence mechanisms are adopted too frequently, or get out of proportion, they themselves can create psychological problems.

According to Freud, the behaviour of all people is to some extent 'abnormal', in that none of us is free from the dynamic conflicts relating to our unconscious drives, nor from the influence of repressed memories. Therefore it is perfectly 'normal' to experience anxiety. Abnormality is therefore both inevitable and beyond our conscious control. Try Activity 3 now.

Evaluation of the psychodynamic model

Unfortunately, the psychodynamic model has proved to be difficult to subject to scientific, empirical analysis, which has led some theorists to claim that the theory is lacking in *validity*. However, Kline (1988) claims that a theory is not invalidated because it cannot be tested scientifically; it merely means that no one has yet found

---

Activity 3: Using defence mechanisms

Discuss in pairs:

◆ Can you identify occasions when you might have used defence mechanisms?
◆ Can you identify occasions when others have used defence mechanisms with you?

Try to provide additional examples of each defence mechanism.

---

a way to do it. Many of the observations made by psychodynamic theorists, such as those concerning the use of defence mechanisms, appear to be borne out in everyday life. Although early traumatic experiences may not necessarily emerge in adulthood as psychological problems, research indicates that many people with psychological problems do recollect experiences of emotional trauma in childhood.

The psychodynamic model holds that abnormal behaviour results from unconscious psychic conflict related to innate, biological drives. The model also holds that early relationships with parents are important to psychological development. For these reasons, it has been claimed the theory is *deterministic,* i.e. that individuals appear to have very little conscious involvement in their own personality development. The implicit assumption, therefore, is that people are not to blame for their *own* abnormal behaviour, but may be partially responsible for the development of abnormal behaviour in their offspring. This may prove to be a heavy burden for parents who feel they have 'done their best' and, according to the model, may also be grappling with their own inner emotional conflicts.

Implications for treatment

Freud was instrumental in changing ways of thinking about the mentally ill, by pointing out that physical symptoms could have psychological causes. He developed a method of treatment for psychological distress, known as 'psychoanalysis', which is often called the 'talking cure'. From this, many other psychodynamic therapies have evolved. These therapies seek to uncover unconscious psychodynamic processes in order to facilitate insight into the conflicts and anxieties that are the underlying causes of abnormal behaviour. The belief is that if someone can better understand what happened in the past and what is going on at an unconscious level within their psyche, then they can better deal, at a conscious level, with situations that are happening in their life now. Within

Table 4.1	Defence mechanisms
Repression	Preventing unacceptable desires, motivations or emotions from becoming conscious. Repression does not mean that you consciously cover up guilty secrets; it means that you make them unconscious so that you are not even aware of them. The repressed drives do not disappear; they remain in the unconscious where they influence behaviour in ways that we are unaware of, and may cause emotional difficulties.
	Example: A person who is normally placid acts in a violent way towards someone else and subsequently has no recollection of this.
Projection	When people's own unacceptable faults or wishes are attributed to someone else. In the extreme, this defence mechanism can become paranoia.
	Example: Accusing someone else of being angry, or secretive, or thoughtless, when it is you yourself who feels angry, is being secretive, or being thoughtless.
Rationalization (intellectualizing)	This is when rational reasons, or excuses, are found to justify actions that have unconscious motives.
	Example: A parent who beats their child may rationalize their actions by saying it is for the child's own good.
Denial	People sometimes refuse to believe events or to admit they are experiencing certain emotions that provoke anxiety.
	Examples: A person may refuse to believe that their partner has died and continue to talk to them, set a place at the dinner table, etc. An alcoholic may deny that they are dependent on alcohol.
Regression	Sometimes people respond to anxiety by behaving in childish ways, such as adults who resort to stamping or kicking, which, as children, may have been successful for them. People may also regress to an earlier type of behaviour when they suffer a traumatic experience.
	Example: A 9-year-old child whose parents are getting divorced may revert to thumb-sucking or bed-wetting.
Displacement	Diverting emotions on to someone else because the emotions cannot be expressed to the person concerned, or alternatively because accepting faults in ourselves will cause anxiety. In each case the emotion is displaced on to someone else.
	Examples: A child who feels angry towards their parents may resort to bullying a younger or weaker child at school. A student who fails an exam may blame the teacher.
Sublimation	Diverting emotions onto something else (rather than someone else). It is the socially acceptable form of displacement and a defence mechanism that is encouraged in our society.
	Examples: Playing a vigorous sport, or punching a cushion (rather than kicking the cat).
Reaction formation	Where the conscious mind adopts the opposite of what is in the unconscious mind. This can lead to adopting certain outward behaviours in order to conceal unacceptable (although unconscious) desires and urges.
	Example: A person with a strict moral upbringing reacts against unconscious sexual desires by becoming actively involved in an antipornography campaign.

psychodynamic theory, the unconscious is thought to be revealed in dreams; therefore, one of the techniques of psychoanalysis is the analysis of dreams. If you go on to study psychology at A level you may have the opportunity to explore psychodynamic therapies in more detail.

Behavioural model

Basic assumptions

This model focuses on the 'behaviour' of an individual in order to explain psychological problems. Advocates of the behavioural model would not use the term 'mental disorder' or 'mental illness', since they have no interest in mental structures, only in overt behaviour. Accordingly, they argue, abnormal behaviour is not genetically inherited, nor a physical illness, nor the consequence of psychodynamic conflicts. For the behaviourist, abnormal behaviour is quite simply learnt in the same way as most other behaviour, largely through the ways that people have been conditioned to respond in certain situations. The behavioural model provides explanations for the emergence of specific, maladaptive, or dysfunctional behaviours such as phobias, anxiety, depression and eating disorders, through the processes of *classical conditioning*, *operant conditioning*, and *social learning*.

Classical conditioning

Pavlov (1927, 1941), in his theory of *classical conditioning*, explained how behaviour is learned through what he called 'stimulus-response' associations. An event in the environment (stimulus) results in a physiological reaction (response) in the individual. The event and the reaction are then forged into an association. Phobias (pathological fears of objects or situations) are thought to develop in this way. For example, a person may climb to the top of a high building and, when looking down (environmental stimulus), experience nausea and dizziness (physiological response). This association may then develop into a fear of heights so strong that it becomes a phobia and the person will then be so afraid of heights that they will avoid all situations that involve heights.

In classical conditioning, it is not the object, or the situation, which is the cause of the fear but the conditioned response to the object or situation. For example, it is the response of feeling sick and dizzy when looking down from a high building that causes the fear of heights, not the height itself. What is important is that the person must have first experienced a fearful reaction to the situation or event which is so extreme that they will avoid at all costs putting themselves in that, or any other similar situation, in the future. This may be fine if the person can avoid being in high places, but dysfunctional if the person works in a tall office block for example, or has a job which involves airline travel. In such cases, the person would either have to seek alternative employment or seek help from a therapist to overcome their phobia. In a classic study, Watson and Raynor (1920) conditioned a young boy to fear white rats in order to illustrate how phobias are the consequence of learned behaviour (see *In Focus*).

Activity 4: Counterconditioning

Can you think of a way in which Little Albert could have been counterconditioned? The clue lies in the way in which he was originally conditioned.

Operant conditioning

In his theory of *operant conditioning*, Skinner (1974) explained how our behaviour is influenced by the consequences of our own actions. We learn the likely consequences of our own actions at a very early age, through whether they are rewarded or punished by those who are caring for us. Conduct disorders and antisocial personality disorders have been explained in operant conditioning terms. If childhood aggression is rewarded, then that behaviour is likely to be repeated

---

in focus

'Little Albert' study by Watson and Raynor (1920)

Watson and Raynor (1920) attempted to show how a phobia could be conditioned. With his parents' consent, they conducted an experiment on an 11-month-old child – known as Little Albert. Albert was first introduced to a tame white rat and showed no fear. During the experiment, each time Albert reached out to touch the rat the experimenters made a loud noise by striking two metal bars together. The noise startled Albert and soon he became afraid to touch the white rat. In this classic study, Watson and Raynor showed that an association had been formed between touching the white rat and fear of the noise. This conditioned fear then became generalized to other stimuli that resembled the white rat, such as other fluffy animals and objects such as cotton wool. Unfortunately, Little Albert's parents became concerned and withdrew him from the experiment before the experimenters had the opportunity to try and countercondition him. This raises ethical issues around the use of humans in such experiments.

and reinforced again and again. However, behaviours that may appear maladaptive to others may be functional or adaptive for the individual. For example, anxiety or depression might procure a reward (what is called a 'secondary gain') in the form of attention and concern from others.

Social learning

If a child grows up in a violent environment, then, as explained by *Social Learning Theory* (Bandura 1973), the child learns antisocial behaviour by observing and copying violent behaviour in others. A study by Mineka *et al.* (1984) with monkeys showed how a phobia could be developed through observation alone. They first of all observed that monkeys raised by parents with a fear of snakes did not automatically acquire this fear themselves and concluded that it was not genetically inherited. Those monkeys who observed their parents showing fearful reactions to real and toy snakes did, however, acquire an intense and persistent fear themselves.

Individual and cultural issues

The behavioural model emphasizes individual differences in that we are all subject to our own unique learning experiences. This in turn means that the gap between 'normal' and 'abnormal' is reduced. According to Skinner (1953), cross-cultural studies reveal that what is regarded as abnormal in one culture may be regarded as normal in another. For example, hallucinations are viewed as a symptom of psychosis in the Western world, whereas in some African tribes these are regarded as 'visions'.

Evaluation of the behavioural model

The behavioural model provides explanations for psychological problems that overcome the ethical considerations of labelling someone as 'ill' or 'abnormal'. Instead, the model advocates a consideration of whether behaviour is 'adaptive' or 'maladaptive'. This model also allows individual and cultural differences to be taken into account. Providing the behaviour is presenting no problems to the individual, or to other people, then there is no reason to regard the behaviour as a mental disorder. It is the behavioural model that gave rise to the definition of abnormality previously outlined as 'a failure to function adequately'. However, whilst this philosophy is embodied in the theoretical model, it is not always adhered to in practice. Behavioural methods of reshaping behaviour have been forced on people who are not in a position to give informed consent, for instance, because they are institutionalized, often under sectioning laws, where their individual rights have been withdrawn.

Implications for treatment

If maladaptive or dysfunctional behaviours have been learned, then they can equally be changed through the same methods of classical and operant conditioning. New and more 'healthy' associations can be made, such as replacing a 'fear' response with one of feeling more relaxed in previously fearful situations. In addition, maladaptive antisocial behaviour can be reshaped through a system of rewards and punishments, known as *behaviour modification*. Behavioural therapy, therefore, takes a practical, problem-solving approach. The role of the therapist is to identify maladaptive learning and then to educate the person into more adaptive learning strategies.

Advocates of the psychodynamic model claim that the behavioural model focuses only on symptoms and ignores the causes of abnormal behaviour. They claim that symptoms are merely the tip of the iceberg – the outward expression of deeper underlying emotional problems. Whenever symptoms are treated without any attempt to ascertain the deeper underlying problems, then the problem will only manifest itself in another way, through different symptoms. This is known as 'symptom substitution'. Behaviourists counter this criticism by claiming that they need not look beyond the symptoms because the symptoms *are* the disorder. Thus, there is nothing to be gained by searching for internal causes, either psychological or physical. If you go on to study psychology at A level you may have the opportunity to explore behavioural treatments in more detail.

Cognitive model

Basic assumptions

The cognitive approach to understanding abnormality was founded by Albert Ellis (1962) and Aaron Beck (1963), who thought that the weakness of the behavioural model was that it did not take mental structures into account. The rationale behind the cognitive model is that the *thinking* (cognition) processes that occur between a stimulus and a response are responsible for the *feeling* component of the response. The cognitive model holds that emotional problems can be attributed directly to distortions in our cognitions or thinking processes. These take the form of negative thoughts, irrational beliefs and illogical errors, such as polarized (black and white) thinking and overgeneralization. These maladaptive thoughts, it is claimed, usually take place automatically and without full awareness. Ellis (1962) maintained that everyone's thoughts are rational at times and irrational at other times. Psychological problems occur only if people engage in faulty thinking to the extent that it becomes maladaptive for themselves and others around them (see Fig. 4.2).

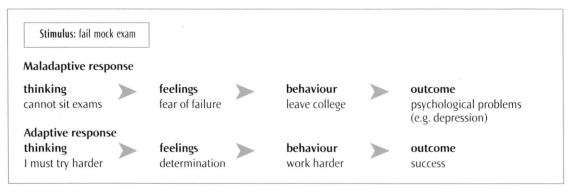

Figure 4.2 Rationale behind cognitive theory

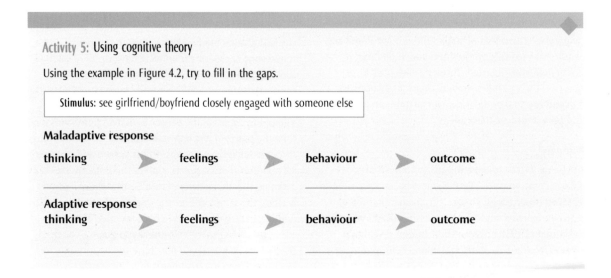

Activity 5: Using cognitive theory

Using the example in Figure 4.2, try to fill in the gaps.

Rational-Emotive Behaviour Therapy

Ellis developed Rational-Emotive Therapy (RET), which he renamed Rational-Emotive Behaviour Therapy (REBT) based on his theoretical model of how psychological problems emerge. He claimed that thinking and emotion are interrelated in a circular cause and effect relationship, in that thinking affects emotion and emotion affects thinking (Ellis 1958). This occurs because *emotion* is largely *evaluative thinking* based on illogical deductions. In turn, negative thinking arouses negative emotions, such as anger, guilt and anxiety.

According to Ellis, when we think rationally, we behave rationally, and as a consequence, we are happy, competent and effective. When we think irrationally, however, the result can be psychological disturbance, because people become habituated to their disturbed thoughts.

Ellis observed that irrational thinking is often revealed in the language that people use, in particular the use of words such as *'should', 'ought'* and *'must'*: for example, 'I *ought* to be good for my parents', 'David *should* be nice to me', 'I *must* do well in my A levels'.

He also claimed that people tend to exaggerate or *'catastrophize'* events: for example, 'I *must* be an *awful* person because Mary ignored me when I spoke to her this morning'. Ellis said that all of these statements are based on irrational beliefs or faulty logic, and yet the things we tell ourselves *become* our thoughts and feelings because we tend to ignore rational alternatives. Such alternatives might be that Mary was engrossed in thought, or feeling ill, or that she may be a moody type of person, or even that she doesn't like you, but that still doesn't make you an *awful* person, because there are other people who do like you.

Evaluation of the cognitive model

Research has shown that many people suffering from mental disorders do exhibit thought patterns associated with maladaptive functioning. For example, Gustafson (1992) found that maladaptive thinking processes were displayed in many people with psychological disorders such as anxiety, depression and sexual disorders. However, Beck (1991) has pointed out that, although cognitive processes are involved in many psychological disorders, they may well be a consequence rather than a cause of their problems. Thus, a criticism of the model is that it does not attempt to examine the origins of irrational thinking, nor does the treatment address these origins.

The cognitive model has also been criticized because it suggests that everyone should be self-sufficient. Indeed, Ellis himself had little sympathy with those suffering from depression, regarding it as an 'indulgence' of self-defeating thoughts (1962). A belief in self-sufficiency tends to devalue social support systems. It lays the blame for psychological problems firmly within the individual, rather than with the social environment. Consequently, attention may be drawn away from the need to improve social conditions that have a significant effect on quality of life. The cognitive model also ignores the possibility that some so-called irrational thoughts might actually be true and therefore rational.

Implications for treatment

Cognitive therapy takes a practical, problem-solving approach, by scientifically challenging and changing faulty cognitions. Therapists teach people to recognize their maladaptive thinking patterns, and how to counter these by replacing them with more adaptive ones. Therapists and clients work together to set new goals for the clients in order that more realistic and rational beliefs are incorporated into their ways of thinking. Ellis (1980) claimed that his Rational-Emotive Behaviour Therapy helps people to 'cure' themselves in an *elegant* way because they become less disturbed and less anxious and they maintain this over a long period, or even permanently. The ultimate aim is that REBT should be incorporated into a person's way of life, in order to overcome procrastination and eradicate self-defeating thoughts. The cognitive approach offers a 'model for living' which promotes psychological wellbeing and avoids the stigma of 'mental illness'.

Cognitive therapies are becoming more and more popular and diverse in their applications. For example, they are increasingly being applied in stress management, as well as with marital and family problems and in educational settings. Cognitive therapies are also being applied to eating disorders, which will be considered later on in this chapter.

If you go on to study psychology at A level, you may have the opportunity to explore other cognitive therapies.

Humanistic model

Basic assumptions

The humanistic model is based on the work of Carl Rogers (1951) and of Abraham Maslow (1968). The model proposes that people are able to make choices in life freely and that in the main those choices are channelled towards fulfilment and happiness and a healthy sense of *self-worth*.

Development of self-worth

Rogers maintained that the development of self-worth begins in infancy. Humans have a basic need to feel nurtured and valued by significant people in their lives, such as parents. This nurturing comes in the form of love, praise and acceptance – what Rogers called positive regard. Rogers claims that if this is given freely, without conditions (*unconditional positive regard*), then people will develop a healthy sense of self-worth, recognizing their abilities and their difficulties. However, when there are conditions placed upon positive regard, such as 'We will love you only if you are a good girl', then those people learn that they cannot be accepted and loved unless they fulfil standards set by others. As the child grows up, conditions for acceptance become self-imposed and are often too rigid and impossible to meet. Children who receive only negative regard, such as criticism and blame, develop low self-esteem. Such people are usually quick to recognize faults in themselves and to take blame readily upon themselves, but they are very reluctant to accept their good qualities and to praise themselves. Rogers maintains that, in order to avoid this, parents should criticize the behaviour not the child, e.g. 'That was a naughty thing to do' rather than 'You are a bad boy.'

A sense of wellbeing

Humans establish a healthy sense of *wellbeing* by maintaining reasonable consistency between ideal-self and actual behaviour – what Rogers called *congruence*. However, the person's self-imposed *conditions of worth*, developed in childhood, may create a discrepancy between these. In striving for self-fulfilment, people often set themselves goals, or ideal standards, that are difficult or even impossible to meet, and thus set themselves up for failure. Rogers called this *incongruence*; the greater the gap between ideal-self and actual-self, the greater the incongruence. He maintained that this could generate feelings of low self-worth, which in turn can affect psychological wellbeing and can even lead to maladjustment.

Humanistic model and 'abnormality'

Strictly speaking, humanistic theory does not offer a 'model of abnormality' because it is diametrically opposed to any form of classification. Humanistic psychologists believe that it is fruitless to differentiate between 'normal' or 'abnormal', because people are unique individuals with their own idiosyncratic modes of behaviour. Therefore, everyone's experience of problems is individual and it is this unique experience that is important and not the labels attached to it.

Evaluation of the humanistic model

The humanistic model offers an optimistic view by focusing on mental health and wellbeing, rather than illness, and on personal growth, rather than mental disorder, although some would argue that this is overly optimistic. It has been regarded as the most ethical of all the models because of its particular emphasis on the *person* rather than on the *label*. This avoids any of the problems associated with labelling, such as stigma and misdiagnosis. However, the model places much of the responsibility on significant others in the child's life, yet it is very difficult for parents to provide consistent unconditional positive regard and always to limit their criticizing to behaviour, rather than the person.

Implications for treatment

Humanistic therapy, often called 'person-centred therapy', concentrates on the *person* rather than the *problem*, and in particular on levels of incongruence (i.e. distorted self-perceptions and low self-worth). The therapist should provide 'unconditional positive regard', which entails being accepting and non-judgemental, which will give the person permission to talk through their problems openly. Given the human tendency towards growth and self-fulfilment, the aim of therapy is to facilitate the human capacity for self-cure.

The belief in personal responsibility, however, carries an implicit assumption that people *ought* to be able to help themselves (self-cure), which may not always be the case, especially for someone with a severe psychological problem. The emphasis on personal freedom and the reluctance to diagnose, if adhered to too rigidly, may mean that some disorders requiring medical assistance go untreated.

Summary: Models of abnormality

Each of the models (medical, psychodynamic, behavioural, cognitive and humanistic) explains the origins of abnormality in different ways. However, these models are not necessarily mutually exclusive, since each is effectively examining a different aspect of the individual.

The medical model focuses on the physical dimension, whilst the psychodynamic model emphasizes the psychological dimension. The behavioural model observes that learned behaviour can be maladaptive, while the cognitive model claims that thoughts can be irrational and therefore also maladaptive.

The humanistic model focuses on the person's ability to fulfil their potential and, like the psychodynamic model, claims that early environmental experience is important to later development.

CRITICAL ISSUE: Eating disorders

Two subtypes of eating disorder – *anorexia nervosa* and *bulimia nervosa* – will be described in this section. A number of explanations for the cause of eating disorders will then be considered. Each explanation has its origins in one of the models of abnormality already outlined in this chapter. Biological and psychological models all offer different explanations and each will be considered in the light of research. There is no one model that is firmly accepted as the definitive explanation for eating disorders.

in focus

Case study of anorexia nervosa

Jenny was in her first year at university but abandoned the course and returned home having been diagnosed with anorexia nervosa. This was not the first diagnosis. As a child she was chubby and remembers several hurtful remarks from teachers. Jenny is the middle child of three siblings and recalls a sense of always being left out as a child and of not getting her needs met, especially by her mother. She also recalls that she was sent to ballet lessons, piano lessons and singing lessons, and although she enjoyed these, there was always an expectation that she would do better than she felt able to do.

Although Jenny is currently back to a normal weight, she is totally preoccupied with food. For several years, her dreams have been symbolic of her disorder, for example drowning in a pool of spaghetti. She also makes a ritual of the way that she eats food, daydreams about food and is constantly reading recipes for meals. She feels that she desperately needs to understand her psychological condition.

Anorexia nervosa

The term *anorexia nervosa* means literally a nervous loss of appetite. However, *loss of appetite* does not mean that the person is never hungry. Indeed, people with anorexia usually have normal appetites and may often be very hungry, but will nevertheless behave as if they have lost their appetite. The main characteristic of anorexia is a refusal to maintain a minimum average expected body weight. Even though the person is underweight, there is an intense fear of gaining weight or becoming fat. Food intake is restricted to around 600 to 800 calories or less per day, with an avoidance of any food regarded as fattening. Food is often cut up into small pieces and eaten in a ritualistic way. There is usually a preoccupation with food, such as constantly reading cookery books and working in environments involved with food. There is also a disturbance in the way anorexic people perceive their body weight and shape; they tend to believe themselves to be overweight or deny that they are seriously underweight.

Ninety per cent of cases of anorexia occur in females, usually between the ages of 13 and 18. Anorexia rarely begins before puberty and in its diagnosis it is expected that, in females, there would have been an absence of at least three consecutive menstrual cycles. The American Psychiatric Association (1994) states that anorexia occurs in 0.5 to 1.0 per cent of females in late adolescence and early adulthood. In the UK, surveys indicate around 1 per cent prevalence among schoolgirls and female university students (Gelder *et al.* 1998). Although still low by comparison, cases of eating disorders in males are becoming more frequent. Currently in the UK, figures are between 5 and 10

per cent of those diagnosed with anorexia nervosa (Gelder *et al.* 1998).

The course and outcome of anorexia are variable:

◆ Around 20 per cent of anorexics have one single episode with full recovery.

◆ Around 60 per cent follow an episodic pattern of weight gain and relapse over a number of years.

◆ The remaining 20 per cent continue to be severely affected and, in many cases, hospitalization is required to restore weight, as well as fluid and electrolyte balance.

Studies (e.g. Lambe *et al.* 1997) with weight-recovered anorexics have found significantly reduced grey matter, which affects cognitive functioning, and that this brain damage is irreversible. For some people with anorexia, it is a chronic unremitting course until death. The mortality rate of those admitted to hospital is over 10 per cent, with deaths occurring from starvation, suicide or electrolyte imbalance.

Bulimia nervosa

Bulimia nervosa is characterized by episodes of secret binge eating, followed by inappropriate behaviours designed to compensate for weight gain, such as self-induced vomiting, misuse of laxatives, diuretics, enemas, medications, excessive exercise or fasting. With bulimia, unlike anorexia, the person is usually within the normal weight range but, like anorexia, this is accompanied by a disturbance in self-perception of body weight, size, or shape. There is an irresistible urge to overeat, usually precipitated by stress and accompanied by a loss of control. A release of tension occurs immediately after huge amounts of food have been eaten. However, this is accompanied by feelings of guilt and disgust, followed by an extreme need to control body weight, and the person then engages in purging. Thus there is both a loss of control and a need to control. (See *In Focus*, 'Princess Diana's confession of bulimia'.)

Ninety per cent of cases are female, with bulimia being very uncommon in men. This condition is more common in a slightly older age group than anorexia. Bulimia nervosa is diagnosed in around 1 to 2 per cent of women aged between 16 and 40 (Gelder *et al.* 1998). Between 1 and 3 per cent of women diagnosed are in their twenties and thirties. Bulimia frequently follows on from months or years of anorexia. Whilst people with bulimia nervosa are not likely to die from starvation, their continual purging has long-term effects on their physical health. See Table 4.2 for the consequences of anorexia and bulimia.

The effects of anorexia

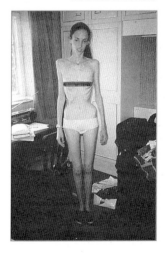

Table 4.2	Consequences of anorexia and bulimia

Anorexia and bulimia are very serious, life-threatening disorders. Not only is there a high mortality rate through starvation or suicide, there are other long-term consequences, some of which may lead to death. The consequences of starvation, vomiting and the use of laxatives are listed below:

Starvation	*Vomiting*	*Laxatives*
Amenorrhoea (absence of menstruation)	Stomach acid dissolves the enamel on teeth	Persistent stomach-pain
Brittle bones which break easily	Puffy face (due to swollen salivary glands)	Swollen fingers
Muscles become weak		Damage to bowel muscles which may lead to long-term constipation
Difficulty in concentrating and thinking straight	Irregular heartbeats	
Broken sleep	Muscle weakness	
Constipation	Kidney damage	
Depression	Epileptic fits	
Loss of interest in sex		

Source: free publication by the Royal College of Psychiatrists on anorexia and bulimia

Explanations of eating disorders

Biological explanations

Biological explanations for eating disorders fall into two categories:

◆ genetic inheritance

◆ biochemical dysfunction of neurotransmitters in the brain.

A biochemical dysfunction or imbalance, may have been genetically inherited or may be due to other causes.

Genetic explanation for eating disorders

As yet, genetic science has not been able to identify genes for specific behaviours, such as those associated with eating disorders. Research is based, therefore, on examining whether a particular disorder runs in families. The American Psychiatric Association (1994) reports that, from diagnostic statistics, there is an increased risk of eating disorders among first-degree biological relatives (parents, children and siblings) of those diagnosed, with a number of studies showing a

much higher prevalence rate than in the general population. However, since relatives usually share the same environment, this does not necessarily support a genetic cause, as the behaviour may have been learned from other family members.

Twin studies provide more reliable evidence. The nature of this research is to compare monozygotic (MZ) twins with dizygotic (DZ) twins. MZ twins have identical genes, whereas DZ twins need be no more alike genetically than any other siblings. Therefore, environmental factors could be largely eliminated if a significantly higher concordance rate were found among MZ twins compared with DZ twins. (Concordance means that both twins have the same disorder.) Twin research into anorexia nervosa by Holland *et al.* (1984) found a 55 per cent concordance rate for MZ twins, compared with only a 7 per cent concordance rate in DZ twins. Kendler *et al.* (1991) found a similar result for bulimia nervosa, among 2,163 female twins, with a 23 per cent concordance rate in MZ twins compared with 8.7 per cent in DZ twins.

There is clearly a significantly higher concordance in MZ twins compared with DZ twins in these studies,

<table>
<tr><td>in focus</td><td>

Princess Diana's confession of bulimia

In a television interview on the BBC programme *Panorama* in 1995, the late Princess Diana confessed that she had suffered from bulimia for many years, although she had managed to hide it because bulimia does not involve weight loss. The Princess said that she and other sufferers inflict it upon themselves because their self-esteem is at such a low ebb and they have no sense of value or worth. The Princess explained that bulimia is a 'cry for help, although it is often giving the wrong signals'.

</td></tr>
</table>

but, even with the Holland study reporting 55 per cent concordance, this still leaves 45 per cent of the MZ twins in their study who were discordant (that is, one twin had the disorder, but the other twin did not). Hsu (1990) has suggested, on the other hand, that the genetic element may relate to personality traits such as emotional instability, which make the person more susceptible to stressful life events. These could manifest in an eating disorder or, alternatively, in some other mental disorder. In many cases of anorexia and bulimia, there is a family history of mood or personality disorders. Other studies have not supported a genetic base. For example, Wade *et al.* (1998) studied both genetic and environmental risk factors in 325 female twins. They found a significant environmental influence in shaping women's attitudes towards weight, shape, eating and food, but little evidence of a genetic component.

Biochemical explanations for eating disorders

One view of the medical profession is that eating disorders may be associated with a biochemical imbalance. Research in the biological field has focused on the region of the brain known as the *hypothalamus*. Animals have been found to stop eating – and even to starve themselves to death – when the hypothalamus is damaged. According to Keesey and Corbett (1983) the *lateral hypothalamus* (LH) and the *ventromedial hypothalamus* (VMH) work alongside each other to provide a 'weight thermostat'. When activated, the LH produces hunger and the VMH depresses hunger. If weight falls below the set point on the 'thermostat', the LH is activated; if weight rises above the set point, the VMH is activated. Once either the LH or the VMH is activated, the hypothalamus will send messages to areas of the brain responsible for thinking and behaviours that will satisfy whichever is activated (LH or VMH). A malfunction in this part of the hypothalamus offers a possible explanation for eating disorders, although there is as yet no conclusive evidence.

Amenorrhoea (loss of menstrual cycle) can occur *before* weight loss, which suggests a primary disorder of low endocrine levels, again associated with a hypothalamus dysfunction. Also, the endocrine levels of anorexics of around 19 years of age are similar to those of a healthy 9-year-old. However, post-mortems have not revealed damage to the hypothalamus, and eating disorders do not appear to be accounted for by any known physical disease.

More recent research has focused on certain hormonal chemicals, including norepinephrine, dopamine and, most especially, low levels of serotonin, which has been found to be associated with binge eating. Walsh *et al.* (1997) have found that the most effective drug treatment for bulimia is serotonin-active antidepressant medication which decreases binge eating. In the light of such findings, Jimerson *et al.* (1997) conducted clinical tests comparing serotonin function in patients with bulimia and in healthy controls. They did find considerable differences and concluded that impaired serotonergic responsiveness may contribute to the onset, persistence or recurrence of abnormal eating patterns in people with bulimia nervosa. The problem with biochemical research is that it is difficult to differentiate between the cause and the effect, since the behavioural symptoms of anorexia and bulimia have a direct, and significant, adverse effect on the person's physiology, which, in turn, may affect their biochemistry. In simple terms, starvation may eventually cause an imbalance in biochemical functioning.

Psychological models

Behavioural explanations

Advertising in teenage magazines and on television promotes the message that 'slim is beautiful'; it is not surprising, therefore, that so many people turn to diets with such frequency. This has led to the layperson's view of anorexia as 'slimming that got out of hand'.

Classical conditioning incorporates the layperson's view, suggesting that slimming becomes a 'habit', just like any other habit, through stimulus-response mechanisms. The person first goes on a diet and after a while receives admiration from others, either for their endeavour or their new, slimmer appearance. They learn, in other words, to associate being slim with feeling good about themselves. *Operant conditioning* comes into play as admiration from others further reinforces the dieting behaviour. Refusing to eat may also provide an additional reward in the form of attention gained from parents, and starving oneself can even be rewarding as an effective way of punishing parents.

Cross-cultural studies appear to support the behavioural explanation. It has been noted that anorexia and bulimia are more prevalent in industrialized societies, mainly Europe, USA, Canada, Australia, Japan, New Zealand and South Africa. In these societies, there is an abundance of food and yet, at the same time, being attractive is associated with being slim. The American Psychiatric Association (1994) states that immigrants from cultures where these disorders are rare have been found to develop anorexia just as frequently as those born in industrialized societies, once these ideals of attractiveness are assimilated. A study by Nasser (1986) compared 50 Egyptian women in London universities with 60 Egyptian women in Cairo universities. Twelve per cent of those in London developed an eating disorder. None of those in Cairo did so. However, another study by Mumford *et al.* (1991) of Asian schoolgirls living in Bradford, found that concerns about weight and body shape were more associated with their Asian culture than their Western experience.

There are still very few studies conducted in non-industrialized countries, so it is quite difficult to provide adequate comparisons. The idea that pressures to be slim in Western cultures play a part in eating disorders is supported in studies conducted on groups of people for whom slimness is essential, such as gymnasts and ballet dancers. For example, Garner *et al.* (1987) found that in a group of 11- to 14-year-old ballet students, 25 per cent developed anorexia over the two-year period of their study. Other studies, such as that by Pike and Rodin (1991) have identified family pressures on daughters to be thin, particularly from mothers who are perfectionist, overly concerned with external appearance and who continually diet themselves.

Cognitive explanation

Given that people with anorexia and bulimia often have a *distorted body image*, it is not surprising that the cognitive model offers a possibly valid explanation for eating disorders. The main tenet of this view is an irrational belief system whereby the person firmly believes they cannot be valued unless they have an ideal physical appearance. To be a glamorous actor, this belief system may have some validity, but for most people a preoccupation with physical appearance to the exclusion of other personal characteristics may be misguided. Nevertheless, films, television and popular magazines continue to exacerbate such faulty beliefs. People with eating disorders often have a distorted body image and perceive themselves to be unattractive (owing to their being fat). It is ironic, therefore, that those with the most severe anorexia nervosa are the most likely to be perceived as unattractive by other people because of their excessive thinness.

However, most people who diet because of social pressure don't become anorexic, which is why distorted perceptions may offer a valid explanation. Bemis-Vitousek and Orimoto (1993) found a consistent pattern of distorted thinking among people with anorexia. They noted their cognitive convictions, which were consistent with the cognitive model of abnormality. For example, 'I must lose more weight since I am not yet thin'. They also found irrational attitudes about control, for example, 'I must continue to lose weight so I can continue to be in control of my body', yet at the same time, they were clearly not in control because they were losing weight to a dangerous degree. Fairburn *et al.* (1999) conducted an interview study comparing 169 people with eating disorders, 102 people with other psychiatric disorders and 204 healthy controls. They identified 'perfectionism' and 'negative self-evaluation' as high-risk factors for both anorexia and bulimia. A study conducted by Lovell *et al.* (1997) found that cognitive bias, in relation to shape, food and adolescent issues, was still present in women who had recovered from an eating disorder at least two years previously. What is not clear in the cognitive model, however, is where irrational beliefs come from in the first place. Perhaps the behavioural model and the humanistic model offer the most plausible explanations for their emergence and perpetuation.

Psychodynamic explanations

Freud maintained that eating is a substitute for sexual expression and therefore, in *psychoanalytic* terms, anorexia could be viewed as the person's way of *repressing sexual impulses*. Hilde Bruch (1979) has been particularly influential in applying psychodynamic theory to anorexia. She suggested that anorexia is associated with psychosexual immaturity in a number of ways. One suggestion is that women have fantasies of oral impregnation and confuse fatness with pregnancy. They then unconsciously believe that eating will lead to pregnancy and therefore starve themselves. Another suggestion is that eating becomes equated with taking on an adult sexual role and that those women who cannot face this, starve themselves in order either to remain children or to regress to childhood. Bruch (1981) suggested that there is a mutual reward to be gained by both mothers and daughters. The mother may become over-anxious about her daughter and therefore curtail her independence and thus retain her 'child'. For the daughter, her behaviour has secured a way of continuing to be dependent upon her mother.

Eating disorders have been strongly related to early traumatic experiences, and psychotherapy studies indicate that a large proportion of patients report early experience of *sexual abuse*. A study conducted in an eating disorder clinic by McLelland *et al.* (1991) reported that 30 per cent of clients had a history of childhood sexual abuse. The suggestion is that such experiences are repressed into the unconscious and express themselves in adolescence and adulthood through the symptoms of anorexia or bulimia. Sexual abuse in childhood can lead to a rejection by victims of their own bodies; in adolescence this rejection can turn to disgust and an unconscious desire to destroy their bodies. It is, however, difficult to obtain evidence to support or refute these ideas. Added to this, not all people who have experienced childhood sexual abuse develop an eating disorder and not all people with eating disorders report having been sexually abused as children.

An interesting suggestion is that early traumatic experiences are repressed and then become expressed in later life in ways associated with *gender socialization*. Females are taught to be subservient and self-critical and, as such, early trauma is turned inwards upon the self, in the form of self-harm. Males on the other hand, are taught to be dominant and outwardly expressive. Thus their early trauma is more likely to be directed outward in hostility towards others. This could explain why eating disorders are predominantly a female disorder and why most violent crimes are perpetrated by males. A study of anorexia and bulimia in males was conducted by Carlat *et al.* (1997) on 135 patients in Boston, USA from 1980 to 1994. They observed that 42 per cent of the bulimia group were either homosexual or bisexual, and 58 per cent of the anorexia group were identified as asexual. They concluded that sexual orientation was a major factor in male eating disorders.

Humanistic explanations

In humanistic terms, eating disorders relate to family relationships, and in particular to the adolescent's struggle to gain a sense of *individual identity*. In some family relationships, the parents exert such a strong level of control that children grow up without a sense of their own identity and, consequently, with a low self-esteem. In adolescence, this control is maintained through roles within the family, such as the mother cooking the meals and the daughter dutifully eating them. This may form the arena in which the daughter struggles for her identity by refusing to eat.

Anorexia is much more prevalent in middle-class families, particularly among those whose parents have a professional background. It is also more prevalent in those who go on to higher education. Consequently, it is suggested that family pressure to 'succeed' may be too great for some young people and may lead to psychological problems, such as depression and anorexia.

The study by Fairburn *et al.* (1999), previously mentioned under the cognitive explanation, also supports the humanistic explanation. They found that *negative self-evaluation* was identified as a high-risk factor for bulimia nervosa, along with parents who had high expectations for their daughters and yet had low contact with them. A study by Joiner *et al.* (1997) also supports the humanistic, along with the psychodynamic, view. They conducted a 10-year study from 1982 to 1992 on 459 females diagnosed with bulimia, aged 18 to 22 years at the beginning of the study. What they found to be the most significant factors sustaining the disorder over the 10-year span were a drive for thinness, maturity fears, perfectionism and interpersonal distrust.

Family Systems Theory implicates family factors in a quite different way. Minuchin *et al.* (1978) suggest that the development of anorexia serves the function of preventing dissension within the family. For example, it may be the adolescent's way of preventing a marriage break-up by diverting attention onto themselves. In so doing, the hope is that joint concern for the child will bring the parents back together. A study by Hill and Franklin (1998) found little evidence of mothers influencing their daughters regarding issues of weight and attractiveness. However, they did find that there were perceived problems in family functioning.

The ways in which families may be involved in eating disorders have been explained in psychodynamic, humanistic and family systems terms. Family relationships are thought to be a central feature in eating disorders, so much so that family therapy (based largely on family systems theory) is currently the most significant form of intervention for eating disorders.

Summary: Eating disorders

Eating disorders are very serious mental disorders because of their enormous danger to physical health. There are serious and irreversible physical consequences resulting from starvation and the continued use of laxatives, diuretics, etc. There is a risk of becoming infertile and also a high risk of death from either suicide or the effects of starvation.

There is little evidence to suggest that eating disorders are caused by any known disease. There is some evidence for a genetic link, although it is difficult to isolate this from environmental influences. Biochemical imbalances are just as likely to be the effect as the cause, of eating disorders.

The behavioural model has traditionally been the most predominant explanation because it appears to make common sense. This view incorporates social and cultural ideals of 'slim is beautiful' and suggests that eating disorders result from slimming habits, conditioned via the media. The cognitive model extends the behavioural view to incorporate faulty, irrational thinking and perceptions regarding body weight and shape. Currently, however, the bulk of the evidence trying to explain eating disorders comes from psychodynamic and humanistic theories, identifying links with early sexual abuse, socialization of gender and family relationships.

Chapter summary

◆ There are various ways in which **abnormality** can be defined, including **statistical infrequency**, **deviation from social norms** and the concept of **'ideal mental health'**. These offer a useful general guide for distinguishing forms of functioning which might be regarded as pathological. However, **their use is limited** because there are no universal definitions of 'normality' and 'abnormality'. Such concepts are **culturally relative**.

◆ A **'failure to function adequately'** offers the most practical working definition. This view is that people should be offered suitable treatment if their daily functioning is seriously affected, but left alone if they are functioning adequately, even if their behaviour may appear strange to others.

◆ **Biological (medical)** and **psychological** (**psychodynamic, behavioural, cognitive** and **humanistic**) **models of abnormality** are based on very different assumptions about the nature of human functioning and the origins and **causes of abnormality**.

◆ Each model offers quite different **implications for treatment** (or **therapeutic strategies**), based upon their relative orientations. Since each model is addressing a different aspect of functioning, it is possible that they all have a valid place in explaining abnormality of psychological functioning.

◆ **Eating disorders**, such as **anorexia nervosa** and **bulimia nervosa**, have very serious consequences for physical health and as such it is important to understand the causes of these disorders.

◆ Research into **biological explanations** has found no links with disease, and biochemical dysfunction is more likely to be a consequence of the disorder, rather than the cause. Genetic links are considered weak and difficult to prove, because members of a family tend to share the same environment.

◆ Amongst **psychological explanations**, **behavioural** and **cognitive models** provide a theoretical framework which elaborates upon the layperson's view of 'slimming that got out of hand', although this may be too simplistic.

◆ **Psychodynamic** and **humanistic models** are currently offering the most plausible explanations, examining relationships within the family.

Exam summary

The AQA examination will test your understanding of the following areas:

◆ definitions of abnormality – statistical infrequency (pp. 81–3), deviation from social norms (pp. 83–5), failure to function adequately (pp. 87–90) and deviation from ideal mental health (pp. 85–7)

◆ limitations of definitions of psychological abnormality including cultural relativism (pp. 81–90)

◆ assumptions of biological models of the causes of abnormality (pp. 90–1), including implications for treatment (p. 91)

◆ assumptions of psychological models of the causes of abnormality – psychodynamic (pp. 91–3), behavioural (pp. 94–5), cognitive (pp. 95–7), including implications for treatment (pp. 91–7)

◆ clinical characteristics of anorexia nervosa (p. 99) and bulimia nervosa (pp. 99–100)

◆ biological explanations and research studies of anorexia nervosa and bulimia nervosa (pp. 100–1)

◆ psychological explanations and research studies of anorexia nervosa and bulimia nervosa (pp. 101–3).

Example question

The question below is typical of one drawn from the material above, and should take you 30 minutes to answer:

(a) Outline the 'statistical infrequency' and 'deviation from social norms' definitions of abnormality.
(3 + 3 marks)

(b) Describe the assumptions of one psychological model of the causes of abnormality and its implications for treatment. *(6 + 6 marks)*

(c) 'Clinical assessment must also take a person's cultural background into account.'

To what extent have definitions of abnormality been limited by problems of cultural diversity?
(12 marks)

Suggested answer structure

(a) Dividing up the 30 minutes available for this part of the question should tell you that you have just 6 minutes to answer it. Further dividing this part tells you that you have 3 minutes to outline the 'statistical infrequency' definition and 3 minutes to outline the 'deviation from social norms' definition. This is not as overpowering as it might appear to be, although finding that you are not very good at précis in the middle of an examination just may be! The 'statistical infrequency' definition is described on pp. 81–3, and the 'deviation from social norms' definition on pp. 83–5, although you are just required to pick out the main points of these definitions here. Try to be precise and selective rather than packing your answer with interesting illustrations or unnecessary (in this part of the question) evaluation.

(b) Using the same technique of dividing up your time as you used in part (a), you can work out that this part gives you 12 minutes of the overall 30 minutes allowed for the whole question. That is 6 minutes to describe the main assumptions of your chosen psychological model, and 6 minutes to consider its implications for treatment. Again, you should be careful about what you include, as all material must earn its inclusion rather than simply making up the word length. A good exercise is to take a psychological model (e.g. the behavioural model on pp. 94–5) and practise describing its main assumptions in about 100 to 120 words (the 'Basic assumptions' section for this model on p. 94

is exactly 125 words long). If you had chosen the behavioural model, its implications for treatment can be found on p. 95. Notice that the instruction to write about the 'implications' for treatment is not an open invitation to describe a range of behavioural therapies, but merely to suggest how, if the model was correct, problem behaviour might be treated.

(c) This part of the question constitutes the AO2 component of the question (see Chapter 8). It is a fairly open invitation to consider some of the different ways in which definitions of abnormality are limited in their validity by issues of cultural diversity. This may involve considering differences between cultures – for example, the observation that mental disorders may appear to be statistically infrequent in a particular culture merely because people are more reluctant to seek professional help in that culture (p. 82). Alternatively, you might consider some of the other forms of cultural diversity included in this chapter, such as gender, historical and social class issues (pp. 82–90). It is important that you engage with this material, and constantly consider whether such issues do actually limit the validity of definitions of psychological abnormality.

Further resources

Comer, R.J. (1997) *Abnormal Psychology*, New York: Freeman.

This comprehensive text has chapters which include definitions of abnormality, models of abnormality and specific mental disorders, including eating disorders. This text will also be useful for the Individual Differences sections in A2 A-level psychology.

Tyrer, P. and Steinberg, D. (1993) *Models for Mental Disorder*, Chichester: John Wiley.

This text provides easy-to-read explanations of each model along with their practical implications. The text is sprinkled with amusing illustrations.

Lemma-Wright, A. (1994) *Starving to Live*, London: Central Book Publishing (Gateways to Counselling Series).

Although written for counsellors, this text provides a sensitive overview of anorexia, covering research, theory and practice.

Rack, P. (1982, reprinted 1993) *Race, Culture and Mental Disorder*, London: Routledge.

Fernando, S. (1991) *Mental Health, Race and Culture*, London: Mind Publications/Macmillan.

Worell, J. and Remer, P. (1992) *Feminist Perspectives in Therapy*, Chichester: John Wiley.

The last three texts are suitable for those who wish to extend their studies on cultural and gender issues in relation to mental health in considerable depth beyond the requirements of the AS syllabus.

Website

www.eating-disorders.org.uk/index.htm

*The website of the **National Centre for Eating Disorders:** Here you can find information on anorexia, bulimia, obesity, the psychology of dieting, and body image.*

Chapter 5

Social influence

Claire Meldrum

Preview

In this chapter we shall be looking at:

◆ explanations and research relating to conformity and minority influence

◆ explanations and research relating to obedience to authority and how people resist pressures to obey

◆ ethical issues in social influence research.

Introduction

Social influence can be defined as the process by which an individual's attitudes, beliefs or behaviours are modified by the presence or actions of others (Saks and Krupat 1988). Some forms of social influence, such as when a teacher insists that you hand in work on time, are obvious (though not always successful). Other types of social influence are more subtle, sometimes unintended and, on occasions, even unnoticed by those who are influenced.

In this chapter we shall look at several types of social influence by examining the research studies carried out to investigate them. Specifically, we shall consider the topic of conformity – or how majority social pressure may influence individuals. More recently psychologists have become increasingly interested in how minority positions become influential and we shall examine some of the findings from research in this area.

Next, we shall explore the research studies of obedience, one of the most challenging and controversial topics in social psychology. Not only are the results of such studies unsettling, but the methods used by those who have researched this area (e.g. Stanley Milgram) have come in for much criticism. Consequently, we shall look at some of the ethical issues that have arisen in psychological investigations and particularly those that are evident in social influence research.

Conformity and minority influence

Conformity

Conformity is defined by David Myers (1999) as 'a change in behaviour or belief as a result of real or imagined group pressure'. Zimbardo *et al.* (1995) define it as a 'tendency for people to adopt the behaviour, attitudes and values of other members of a reference group'. You may find it easier to identify with Myers' definition because it focuses upon the kind of experience most of us have had at one time or another: the feeling that others are putting pressure on us to change our minds or behaviour. However, the Zimbardo definition proposes that we tend to go along with those people with whom we compare ourselves when we are evaluating our status (i.e. our reference groups). If you accept that the process of conformity can occur without your being aware of it, then you may prefer the wording of the Zimbardo definition.

Although most people think of themselves as autonomous individuals, they nevertheless tend to go along with (conform to) the social norms (rules and expectations) that their groups and societies have evolved. The social norms that indicate how we ought to behave may be explicit (e.g. a 'No Smoking' sign in a restaurant), or they may be implicit (e.g. the unspoken but well understood norm in the UK of not standing too close to strangers).

Activity 1: Conformity

Think back to an occasion when you have conformed to the views or behaviours of others.

◆ What was it about the situation that caused you to conform?

◆ Were you aware at the time that you were under pressure to conform?

Why do people conform?

Dual process dependency model

According to this influential model (Deutsch and Gerard 1955), there are two powerful psychological needs that lead people to conform to social norms:

◆ the desire to be liked which underlies *normative social influence* – we conform because we think that others will approve and accept us

◆ the desire to be right which forms the basis for *informational social influence* – we look to others whom we believe to be correct, to give us information about how to behave, particularly in novel or ambiguous situations.

The dual process dependency model as an explanation for social influence is sometimes criticized for implying that the two processes are separate and independent. Instead, Insko *et al.* (1983) claim that they often complement each other, both forms of influence working together to affect levels of conformity.

Referent informational influence

Another challenge to the dual process dependency model relates to the claim that it underestimates the psychological importance that people attach to being part of a group. According to Turner (1991) this sense of 'belonging' to a group makes us conform to its social norms. In other words, we identify with a group, define ourselves as having *category membership* and adopt the values of that group. Moving from school to university, defining oneself as a student, observing how other students conduct themselves and behaving in similar ways is an example of this process and is called *self-stereotyping*. It is caused by a process called *referential informational influence*. Turner proposed three stages involved in this process:

◆ Individuals acknowledge their membership of the group.

◆ They then learn the group's norms.

◆ They behave according to these norms.

Therefore, referent social influence sets the conditions for normative and informational influence to be most effective. Newcomb investigated the importance of reference groups as sources of social influence in an interesting longitudinal study carried out many years ago (see *In Focus* opposite and then do Activity 2).

Types of conformity

As long ago as 1958, Kelman identified three types of conformity (that is, three responses to social influence):

Activity 2: Influence today

Do you think that universities and colleges have as much influence on their students today as Bennington college had on its student when Newcomb carried out his research? If not, why not?

◆ *Compliance* – publicly conforming to the behaviour or views of others but privately maintaining one's own views. Compliance may result from normative social influence.

◆ *Identification* – adopting the views or behaviour of a group both publicly and privately because one values membership of that group. However, the new attitudes and behaviours are dependent on the presence of the group and are often temporary, i.e. are no longer maintained on leaving the group.

◆ *Internalization* – a conversion, or true change of private views to match those of the group. Internalization may be the result of informational social influence. What distinguishes this type of conformity from identification is that the new attitudes and behaviours have become part of one's value system and are not dependent on the presence of the group.

There are occasions when people appear not to conform. There are at least two ways of explaining their behaviour:

◆ The person might be displaying true *independence*, that is, being unresponsive to the norms of the group. An example of this type of behaviour might be the case of a student who ignores the dress norms of her fellow students and who dresses only to please herself. Note that sometimes this student might dress like her friends if their dress sense happened to coincide with hers. She is not reacting against their code; she is just unaffected by it.

◆ *Anticonformity*, on the other hand, occurs when someone consistently opposes the norms of the group. Anticonforming behaviour is not uncommon, such as deliberately choosing to dress or wear one's hair in a way that is different from others. It may seem paradoxical, but anticonformity is, in fact, a type of conformity as it is determined by the norms of the group; if the group favours long hair, anticonformists will wear theirs cut short; if the group decides that short hair is cool, anticonformists will wear theirs long.

Membership and reference groups in a women's college (adapted from Brown 1985)

Bennington is an expensive college in America. It was a college for women only in the 1930s when Newcomb began a study to see if new students, coming from wealthy, conservative backgrounds, would change their social and political views after spending four years at Bennington where staff and most senior students held liberal (radical) views. Not surprisingly, the views of these new students, at the start of their courses, tended to be conservative. However, while at the college they were exposed to discussion of a wide range of social problems. The teaching staff believed that all students should be aware of the social problems of their contemporary world.

As a consequence of their four years at college, most of the girls showed a marked shift in their attitudes, from relatively conservative to relatively liberal views. This is not very surprising. The college was close-knit and quite small (250 students), and the academic staff were actively liberal in their views. However, since not all students became more liberal, the effect cannot be explained simply in terms of their physical presence in the group. In other words, just because Bennington College was a girl's membership group does not explain her shift in attitude. The crucial variable seems to be whether or not the student adopted the college as a positive reference group for her own political attitudes. A membership group consists of people who are members by virtue of their presence in it. A reference group, on the other hand, is a group with whom we identify. We use it to evaluate our opinions and actions. Interviews revealed that some girls felt hostile towards the college (took it as a kind of *negative reference group*) and maintained home and family as their positive reference group. Their original views on entering college were unaffected by their four years at Bennington.

The vast majority of the women, however, did alter their political views, and Newcomb (1952) concluded that attitudes change as a function of how an individual relates to the total membership group and to one or more reference groups. The probability of change also depends on the strength of the initial attitude and the discrepancy between that and the attitudes of the people in one's new membership group. It is possible that personality differences may also play a part in the extent to which people yield to perceived group expectations.

Twenty-five years later, Newcomb *et al.* (1967) carried out a follow-up study. He found that very few of the women he contacted had reverted to the conservative attitudes they held before attending Bennington College. Both the women and their husbands tended to have more liberal views than a comparable sample of American women of the same socio-economic level. A much later survey, indeed, showed that in the 1984 presidential election, 73 per cent of Bennington College graduates preferred the Democratic candidate, Walter Mondale, to the Republican candidate, Ronald Reagan. This compares with only 26 per cent of American women of the same age and educational level who voted for Mondale. The persistence of these liberal attitudes many years after the students left college can be accounted for in a number of different ways:

◆ The values adopted while at college were internalized (see Kelman's three types of conformity).

◆ The college remained a positive reference group in their lives.

◆ Their later liberal associations, such as their friends and husbands who were chosen in the first place because they shared the liberal attitudes of the women, caused the persistence of their liberal views.

Today, we might also use some aspects of Turner's concept of referent informational influence to explain why most of the women remained influenced by Bennington's liberal attitudes. They categorized themselves as 'Bennington women'; they embraced the norms of the college; when these norms became salient (important and relevant) at election times, they behaved in a normative way and voted Democrat.

Comedian Eddie Izzard – displaying anticonformity or independence?

Activity 3: Types of conformity

Revisit the occasion you thought of for Activity 1. Using Kelman's three types of conformity, decide which type best applies in your case: compliance, identification or internalization.

Research into conformity

The Sherif study

Sherif (1935) investigated the emergence of group norms using the autokinetic effect. This is an optical illusion experienced when a person is placed in a totally dark room in which a stationary point of light appears to move because the person's perceptual system has no frame of reference for it. Sherif asked individual participants to judge how far the light appeared to move on a number of trials. Each individual's estimates were relatively stable but between participants there was considerable variation. When the same participants then worked in groups of three people, announcing their estimates aloud, their judgements converged until a group norm emerged. When Sherif altered his procedure so that participants made their first judgements in the group situation, he found that group norms emerged even more quickly than in the previous procedure. The study showed that when faced with an ambiguous situation, the participants looked to others in the group for guidance, that is, they experienced informational influence. Furthermore, this occurred even though they were asked to give their *own* estimates and despite the fact that, at the end of the study, they stated that they had not seen themselves as members of a group.

Strictly speaking, Sherif was studying the process of norm formation in new groups, not the process of conformity. Nevertheless, his results suggest that people will adjust their judgements to bring them into line with those of other people even when they do not perceive themselves and the others as constituting a group.

The Asch studies

Asch (1956) argued that the convergence of judgements found in the Sherif study was attributable to the ambiguity of the situation. What would happen, Asch wondered, if participants were exposed to normative social influence in a situation where there could be no doubt about the correct answer to a question? In Asch's original study he showed a pair of cards to people seated around a table. On one card was a 'test' line and on the other, three lines of differing lengths. The participants' task was to say aloud which of the three lines (1, 2 or 3) matched exactly with the test line (see Fig. 5.1). The correct judgements were always obvious. Fifty male college students were studied in the first round of experiments.

Apart from one naive participant, all other members of the group were confederates (accomplices) of the experimenter. Asch used groups of seven to nine confederates. He instructed them to give the same wrong answer unanimously on 12 of the 18 trials. All participants sat at a table with the naive participant answering last but one (see Fig. 5.2). How many participants would conform to the group, deny the evidence of their own eyes and give the wrong answer when it was their turn?

Main results of Asch studies

◆ On 32 per cent of the critical trials (those when the confederates had given the wrong answers), naive participants conformed to the unanimous view of the majority. This might not strike you as a particularly high figure, but remember that the correct answer was always obvious.

Figure 5.1 A sample of the stimulus material used in Asch's experiments on conformity

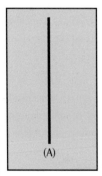
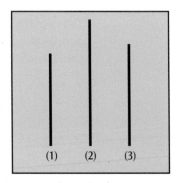

Standard line   Comparison lines

Figure 5.2
The set-up in Asch's studies, in which a minority of one (answering last but one) faces pressure to conform to an otherwise unanimous majority

◆ 74 per cent of naive participants conformed at least once.

◆ 13 out of 50 participants never conformed. Some of these 'independent' participants were confident in their judgements. More often, however, they experienced tension and doubt but managed to resist the pressure being exerted by the unanimous majority.

◆ During post-experimental interviews with his participants, Asch found that conformity occurred at three levels:

– A few conforming participants experienced *distortion of perception* and were unaware that their estimates had been distorted by the majority. These participants claimed that they had actually perceived the line identified by the majority as the correct answer.

– Most conforming participants experienced a *distortion of judgement*: they thought that their perception must be inaccurate and for that reason they yielded to the majority view.

– Some conforming participants did not undergo a distortion of perception or think that their judgement must be wrong. Rather, they yielded to the majority (*distortion of action*) because they could not bear to be in a minority of one and risk being ridiculed or excluded by the group.

Asch sums up these findings from the debriefing interviews thus: 'Independence and yielding [conformity] are not psychologically homogeneous ... [they] can be the result of different psychological conditions' (Asch 1952, p. 179). In other words, people may go along with the views of others for different reasons. Similarly, there may also be different reasons why people resist pressures to go along with the majority (see section on 'Resisting pressures to conform' on p. 115).

In addition to his interest in individual differences between participants, Asch was also interested in how variations to situational factors might affect levels of conformity.

Effects of varying Asch's procedures

◆ *A non-unanimous majority* – Asch found that levels of conformity dropped dramatically when just one other participant dissented from the majority and supported the naive participant. A number of studies investigating the effects of dissenters have shown that a dissenter only had to give a different answer from the majority, even a different wrong answer, for conformity levels to be reduced. Morris and Miller (1975) found that when the dissenter's judgement was heard near the beginning of the procedure, there were lower levels of conformity than when it was given nearer the end. A unanimous majority of three was more effective in producing conformity than a majority of eight with one dissenter.

◆ *The size of the majority* – When the majority consisted of only two people, conformity responses in naive participants dropped to 12.8 per cent of their total judgements. Optimum conformity effects (32 per cent of responses) were found with a majority of three. Increasing the size of the majority beyond three did not increase the levels of conformity found. Baron and Byrne (1997) suggest that people may suspect collusion if the majority rises beyond three or four. When only one confederate was used, no conformity effects were elicited.

◆ *Losing or gaining a partner* – The effect of losing a partner was tested by having the naive participant start with a 'partner' who responded correctly to begin with but who 'deserted' to the majority in the middle of the procedure. This resulted in conformity levels of 28.5 per cent on critical judgements. When a participant who had started the procedure as a minority of one received a 'partner' part way through, this reduced conformity responses to 8.7 per cent.

◆ *The nature of the task* – As Asch reduced the clarity of the task or increased its difficulty, the levels of conformity increased (see also Crutchfield's results in the next section).

◆ *Mode of response* – When Asch asked his participants to write their answers rather than call them out loud, conformity levels dropped sharply. This illustrates the difference between *public compliance* (overtly adhering to social norms) and *private acceptance* (actually thinking as others do).

Studies of conformity after Asch

One of the strengths of Asch's work is the amount of subsequent research it generated. Some subsequent researchers have been interested in whether reliable individual differences could be identified between those who conformed and those who did not. Others have replicated Asch's procedures to check the reliability of the so-called 'Asch effect' in different countries and at different historical periods. Some psychologists have questioned the validity of Asch's procedure. We shall look at each of these in turn.

Individual differences

Are certain types of people more likely to conform than others? Crutchfield (1955) tried to answer this question in a series of studies that he conducted. He also thought that the face-to-face arrangement of participants in the Asch procedure might be responsible for the levels of conformity found. Therefore, he arranged his participants in booths out of sight of each other, but all able to see the stimulus cards. This enabled him to collect data in a more economical fashion by running several naive participants at the same time. Participants sat individually in booths with a row of switches and lights

Figure 5.3 Crutchfield's conformity-testing procedure: people sit in adjacent booths and answer questions shown on the wall in front of them after apparently being told of other people's responses

in front of them. They had to press the switch that corresponded to their judgement when their turn came to answer. They were told that the lights on the display panel showed the responses of the other participants. In fact, the experimenter controlled these lights and each participant saw an identical display. Despite the absence of an actual face-to-face group, Crutchfield found 30 per cent conformity levels when using Asch's line comparison tasks. When the task was made more difficult, conformity increased. In addition to using more difficult perceptual tasks (see Fig. 5.3), this was demonstrated also using attitude items. For example, when college students were asked to express private agreement with the statement, 'Free speech being a privilege rather than a right, it is proper for a society to suspend free speech whenever it feels itself threatened', only 19 per cent expressed agreement. However, when confronted with a unanimous majority, 58 per cent expressed agreement.

Crutchfield was also interested in individual differences and how these might affect conformity. Some of his participants (over 600 in total) were drawn from business and military men on a three-day assessment course, where they had been tested for a number of qualities including intelligence, leadership ability and ego strength. The participants who scored highly on these characteristics displayed lower levels of conformity during Crutchfield's study. It may, therefore, appear that there is a conforming type of personality. However, there has been a lack of evidence subsequently to support Crutchfield's findings.

Historical and cultural context

Some observers have suggested that Asch's findings tell us more about the historical and cultural climate of the United States in 1951 than they do about fundamental psychological tendencies; some more recent studies of conformity have failed to confirm Asch's findings. For example, Larsen (1974) found significantly lower rates of conformity among American students than Asch had two decades earlier. Perrin and Spencer (1981) who replicated Asch's procedure, using British students, found only one conforming response in 396 trials. They proposed that this dramatic reversal of Asch's findings could be explained in terms of the cultural changes that had occurred in the interim. In the 1950s the USA was very conservative, involved in an anticommunist witchhunt against anyone who was thought to hold left-wing views (this became known as McCarthyism, named after the senator who spearheaded the witchhunt) and its educational institutions were more

Which is bigger?

hierarchical than they are today. By the time of the Larsen study in 1974, the USA had undergone considerable social change, including a period of student militancy.

Another factor that might have influenced the Perrin and Spencer results is the type of students used. They were British and drawn from engineering, chemistry and mathematics courses and it is possible that the knowledge and skills acquired in their courses had equipped them to resist conformity pressures during a task of this sort. Another study by Perrin and Spencer (1981) using youths on probation as participants and using probation officers as the confederates demonstrated levels of conformity similar to those found by Asch in 1952. The researchers concluded that where the perceived costs for people of not yielding were high, conformity effects would still be demonstrated.

Perrin and Spencer speculated that either historical or cultural differences might have accounted for the differences in their results compared with those found by Asch. To investigate this, Nicholson *et al.* (1985) collected data from students in the United States and in Great Britain, using the Asch paradigm (procedure). No significant differences were found between the US and British students, suggesting similarity in British and US student cultures. When the British and US data were combined and compared with Asch's data, the 1985 students were found to be significantly less conformist than their 1952 counterparts. Nevertheless, conformity remained observable in both British and US students. Nicholson and colleagues proposed, therefore, that there remained a minority of students in both countries who were willing to conform, though the proportion was less than in 1952. They can only speculate as to why their results were so discrepant with those of Perrin and Spencer. They suggested that the experience of the Falklands War (when Britain went to war with Argentina, in 1982, over the occupancy of the Falkland

Islands), which took place between the collection of Perrin and Spencer's data and the collection of their own data, might have contributed to group cohesiveness and, in turn, to a higher degree of conformity.

Further to this debate, Smith and Bond (1998) have reviewed 31 studies of conformity conducted in different cultures using Asch's paradigm. They concluded that people in collectivistic cultures (e.g. Africa and Asia) show a higher level of conformity compared with those who live in individualistic cultures such as Britain and the United States. (See Table 5.1 for differences between collectivistic and individualistic societies.) Hedy Brown (1996) sums this area up well when she says:

> 'The fact that experimental social psychologists may not provide us with universal truths ... does not make their work unimportant or uninteresting. They help us understand our own times and our own place in it ... When we are trying to understand psychological processes we may still arrive at valid and possibly long-lasting insights, even though the extent to which such processes operate may vary from one historical period or one society to another and indeed from one individual to another.'
> (Brown 1996, p. 20)

Validity of the Asch paradigm

Asch's experimental situation is sometimes criticized for being unlike real life (lacking ecological validity). Why choose a task where the correct answer was so obvious? Well, he did not want a situation where participants might genuinely have doubts about the correct response. In his later studies, he actually showed that conformity levels were higher when the answers were less obvious.

Several studies examining conformity in more real-life situations have demonstrated how others may be a

---

Table 5.1 Features of collectivistic and individualistic cultures

Collectivistic cultures	Individualistic cultures
◆ Emphasis on loyalty to the group; in turn, the group looks after wellbeing of the individual	◆ Emphasis on promoting self-interest of oneself and one's immediate family
◆ Emotional dependence on groups and organizations	◆ Stress on rights, not duties, of individual
◆ Less personal privacy	◆ Privacy
◆ Group decisions preferred to individual decisions	◆ Individual initiative
◆ Personal identity = one's place in the group	◆ Personal identity = the characteristics of the individual
◆ Concern about needs and interests of others	◆ Less concern about needs and interests of others

Source: adapted from Baron and Byrne (1997)

source of influence, especially when people were uncertain how to act. For example, Furman and Duke (1988) asked students to listen to two versions of each of 10 orchestral excerpts. The students were either majoring in music on their degree programme or were majoring in another subject. Each student, on their own, selected a preferred version for each of the ten pairs. They were then individually tested in the presence of three confederates who unanimously stated a verbal preference from each pair of excerpts. Music majors were not influenced to change their already stated preferences. However, the publicly stated preferences of non-music majors were significantly affected by the preferences of the confederates. When a group of students, acting as controls (a comparison group), wrote their responses instead of stating them aloud after hearing confederates' preferences, no conformity effects were found. You might consider to what extent those around you influence your tastes in music and fashion.

Zimbardo's prison simulation study (1973)

Philip Zimbardo and colleagues conducted one of the best-known and most controversial studies of conformity. He used a simulated prison set-up to see to what extent normal, well-balanced people would conform to new social roles when they took part in a role-playing exercise. Simulations attempt to imitate some aspect of a real-world situation. Participants are asked to act (role-play) as though the simulation was real. Psychologists use simulations in order to study behaviours to which they would not normally have access. (See *In Focus* for an outline of the procedures used in Zimbardo's study.)

How can we account for the guards' overzealous behaviour and the capitulation of the prisoners to the regime imposed by the guards? According to Zimbardo, these results demonstrate how easily people can come to behave in uncharacteristic ways when placed in new situations and given new roles. The adoption of new role-related behaviours might have been facilitated by the stereotypic expectations that the participants brought with them of how guards and prisoners should behave. Another possible explanation is that the volunteers might have tried to be 'good subjects' and behaved in the ways they thought the researcher wanted.

Many criticisms have been levelled against this study, including the following made by Savin (1973):

◆ Participants did not give fully informed consent; they did not know, for example, they would be arrested at home, although they did sign an agreement drawn up by Stanford University to act as volunteers.

◆ Participants were humiliated and dehumanized by the initiation procedure when they arrived at the 'prison'.

◆ The ends do not justify the means and this study became 'too real' for those participating; it should not have been carried out.

Zimbardo responded to these criticisms as follows:

◆ After the simulation had been ended, Zimbardo and his colleagues held several sessions with the participants to help them deal with their emotional reactions to the experience.

◆ During the year after the study ended, contact was maintained with all the student participants involved to prevent any negative effects persisting.

◆ The reality of this study and its findings made people uneasy because they preferred not to consider that they might have behaved in the same way!

Ethical issues in Zimbardo's prison study are discussed further on p. 129.

---

in focus

Conforming to social roles

To investigate how readily people would adopt a new role and exercise the power that went with it, Zimbardo *et al.* (1973) recruited 25 male volunteers to participate in a two-week study of prison life. Volunteers, who would be paid $15 a day during the study, were clinically examined, judged to be both physically and mentally healthy, and allocated randomly to the roles of prisoners or guards. Local police were recruited to help and nine 'prisoners' were arrested at their homes, without any warning, taken blindfolded to the 'prison' (basement of Stanford University, California), stripped, sprayed with disinfectant and given prison smocks to wear and their numbers to memorize. From then on they were referred to by number only, their toilet visits were supervised, they were assigned work shifts and they were lined up three times a day for a count. There were three 'guards' who wore khaki shirts and trousers, dark glasses and carried long wooden batons. The guards, who were permitted to devise most of the rules (though no physical aggression was allowed) conformed to their perceived roles with such zeal that the study had to be discontinued after six days. Some prisoners exhibited passive behaviour, depression, crying and anxiety.

Resisting pressures to conform

Pressures to conform, however, are not irresistible. Asch's experiments demonstrated quite the opposite. Most of his participants held out against the social influence exerted by the majority; 13 out of 50 *never* conformed. It is unfortunate that the conformity demonstrated in his experiments has become known as the 'Asch effect'. This implies that most people will tend to give in to majority pressure, a misrepresentation of Asch's findings. As Harris (1985) has pointed out, 'there is little evidence in these studies of any general tendency among Asch's subjects to conform to the majority ... this appears to be true of only a minority of his subjects' (p. 229). Remember:

◆ On the critical trials there were around twice as many correct responses as wrong ones.

◆ More than half of the errors were made by a minority of the participants.

◆ Around 26 per cent of participants remained independent on all critical trials compared with fewer than 5 per cent of participants who conformed on all trials.

Of course, as Asch has made clear, this does not mean that the participants were unaffected by the experimental situation. We can see from Asch's post-experimental interviews that even participants who remained independent were deeply disturbed by the situation they had faced.

Why doesn't everyone conform?

People resist pressures to conform to majority views for a number of different reasons and they use different techniques or strategies to help them maintain their independence. Asch, for example, distinguished three main categories of independent behaviour:

◆ Independence based on participants' *confidence* that their perceptions were correct. This probably contributed in part to the results found by Perrin and Spencer (see p. 113) when they used mathematics, engineering and science students as participants.

◆ Independence accompanied by *withdrawal.* These participants reported the need to act as individuals no matter what the others did. They tried to isolate themselves from the others by avoiding eye contact.

◆ Independence accompanied by *tension* and *doubt.* These participants felt they had to deal with the requirements of the task no matter what discomfort they were experiencing.

Therefore, we see that the reasons for not yielding to conformity pressure are no more homogeneous than those for conforming behaviour. Asch's findings still beg the question: 'Do some people possess certain characteristics that enable them to resist group pressure?' There is very limited evidence concerning such individual factors. Crutchfield's early results concerning differences in intelligence, for example, have not received support. Two reasons for individuals resisting majority pressure, however, have been proposed more recently.

Individuation

The desire for *individuation* is the wish to be distinguished in some way from others. Maslach *et al.* (1987) claim that, while we want to be like others generally, we still wish to be individuals in certain respects. Therefore, we will sometimes risk the disapproval of the group in order to proclaim our unique individuality. The power of social influence may be tempered by our need to maintain our personal identity.

Control

You may have noticed that some people seem to have a greater need for personal control than others do. One common difference often observed concerns people's willingness to ask for advice (e.g. when they cannot find a street or a shop that they want). Some will readily ask for help while others will struggle on rather than lessen their sense of control by seeking aid from another person. Burger (1992) has demonstrated that people who score highly in desire for personal control are more likely to resist conformity pressures than those who have a lower need to feel in control. One way in which this has been investigated is by looking at how people react to unasked-for help when working in pairs on a set of puzzles (Daubman 1993). The reactions of two groups were examined: those who had a high score when tested on a *Desirability of Control Scale* and those who had a low score. All participants were given the same feedback: that they had achieved an average performance and that their partner had done better. Some participants were then given hints on how to do better. As predicted, those who scored low on the Desirability of Control Scale tended to welcome these hints. On the other hand, those with a high score felt worse after help was offered, over half of them expressing irritation at this unwelcome incursion into their personal control. These results support Burger's contention that other people's offers of advice or attempts at influence are seen as threats to the personal freedom of people who have a high need for personal control.

Asch is sometimes criticized for implying that conforming behaviour is intrinsically 'bad' and that resisting (not yielding) to majority influence is somehow always good. Clearly, there are dangers involved if people are too conformist. Nevertheless, without widespread conformity, society could not function effectively. Conformity to prosocial norms, such as helping others in distress, is obviously highly desirable.

Minority social influence

Activity 4: Minority social influence and you

Before reading the section 'Minority social influence', try making a list of minorities that have been influential in your lifetime, e.g. gay-rights or environmental groups. What was it about their behaviour, point of view or timing that made them influential? Now read this section in the textbook and compare your ideas with those discussed here.

The research of Asch (1952) was concerned with the influence of majorities. There are, however, many instances where small minorities – or even lone dissenters – have influenced majority opinion. These people may be dismissed initially by the majority as eccentrics or extremists. However, under certain circumstances, these small groups or individuals can eventually become very influential. The term *snowball effect* (Van Avermaet 1996) is used to describe a typical occurrence in minority influence. Once a few members of the majority start to move towards the minority position, then the influence of the minority begins to gather momentum as more people gradually pay attention to the potential correctness of the minority view. As Wood *et al.* (1994) state, 'majorities are not only sources of influence, but they are also influence targets; deviant minorities are not simply targets refusing to conform but also sources actively challenging the validity of the majority position' (p. 323). One explanation for the slowness of minority influence is given on p. 118 (see *In Focus*, 'The dissociation model of minority influence').

Experiments on minority influence

Moscovici *et al.* (1969) asked six participants to estimate the colour of 36 slides. All the slides were blue but adding filters varied their brightness. Each participant had good eyesight. Two of the six participants were accomplices of the experimenter. They constituted the minority whose influence would be assessed in two conditions. In the *consistent condition*, the two confederates called the slides green on all trials. Results showed that naive participants (128 in total) called the slides green (i.e. they yielded to the consistent minority) in 8.42 per cent of the trials and 32 per cent of all naive participants reported a green slide at least once. In the *inconsistent condition*, the confederates called the slides green 24 times and blue 12 times. In this condition, naive participants (44 in total) yielded on only 1.25 per cent of the trials (Moscovici and colleagues do not give the number of

participants in this condition who yielded at least once). Clearly, consistency on the part of the minority is important. Although the levels of yielding found in the consistent condition are nothing like as high as those found by Asch in his studies of majority influence, they do indicate that minorities can exert some degree of influence, even when yielding is measured publicly and immediately after the influence attempts. Furthermore, minorities may be even more influential with the passage of time provided they adopt the appropriate style of behaviour.

Behavioural styles

Following his investigations, Moscovici (1985) identified the behavioural styles which minorities must possess if they are to exert social influence on majorities:

◆ They must be consistent in their opposition to the majority. Consistency, according to Moscovici, comprises 'resolution, certainty, clarity of definition, and coherence'.

◆ They must not appear dogmatic by rigidly reiterating the same arguments. They need to demonstrate a degree of flexibility.

Others psychologists (e.g. Hogg and Vaughan 1995) have also claimed that minorities are more likely to be influential if they:

◆ appear to be acting from principle (not out of self-interest)

◆ have had to make sacrifices in order to maintain their position

◆ are similar to the majority in terms of class, age and gender

◆ are propounding views that are consistent with current social trends (e.g. as our society becomes more concerned with environmental issues, so the views of certain minority groups, once derided, attract a wider audience and become more persuasive).

Why do people yield to minority influence?

Consistency

Consistency is generally recognized as the single most important factor for a minority to be influential. There are two types of consistency:

◆ *intra-individual* – where a person maintains a consistent position over time

◆ *inter-individual* – where there is agreement among members of the minority group.

Although most research confirms Moscovici's claim for the importance of consistency, there have been certain qualifications. If a consistent message also appeared dogmatic (i.e. arrogantly inflexible), it did not have the same impact as a consistent but flexible message (Mugny and Papastamou 1980). It is necessary, therefore, for a minority to be consistent but to avoid appearing rigid if it is to be influential or else the majority may write it off as too extreme or fanatical.

Finding an explanation for the crucial role of consistency is more problematic than finding evidence of its importance. Nemeth (1986) has suggested that a minority that consistently disagrees with the majority changes what the majority *pays attention to* and may encourage more creative thinking. Nemeth has proposed that this may partly explain why juries required to reach unanimous decisions concerning a defendant's guilt or innocence may consider cases more carefully than those required only to reach a majority verdict. If any disagreement exists among jurors required to reach a unanimous decision, then a consistently held minority position will encourage the other jurors to examine their own views in order to be able to explain why they hold them. Furthermore, the views of the minority will have to be attended to by the majority if counterarguments are to convince the minority that it is wrong. This process of

attending to the minority view may result in a closer examination of the details of a case. In 1994, Clark carried out an unusual experiment to see what aspects of minority influence had the greatest effects on an individual's views (see *In Focus*). He concluded that it was a combination of convincing arguments and a shift by other majority members that resulted in the minority exerting the greatest influence.

Dual process theory

According to Moscovici (1980) majorities and minorities achieve influence through different processes. Majority influence, he claims, involves public compliance where the person is more concerned with how they appear in front of others than with the issue itself. By contrast, minority influence evokes a process aimed at trying to understand why the minority holds its viewpoint. By focusing on the issue, the majority comes to examine the arguments proposed by the minority. In turn, this may start the process of *conversion* whereby, at least in private, attitudes genuinely begin to shift, resulting in influence that, albeit delayed, is more lasting than majority influence. Moscovici has proposed that minorities produce a greater amount of *cognitive activity* than do majorities. However, Wood *et al.* (1994), in their extensive review of minority influence research, found

---

in focus

Clark's (1994) research on *Twelve Angry Men*

In the famous film, *Twelve Angry Men*, Henry Fonda played a member of a jury in a murder trial where a young man was accused of stabbing his father to death. The prosecution presented three major pieces of evidence against him; two of these were supposed eyewitnesses and the third was the shopkeeper who claimed to have sold the defendant the 'unique' knife used to kill his father. Despite the pressure exerted on him by all the other jurors, Fonda's character alone held to the belief that the man was innocent. Gradually, by sticking to his guns, refusing to be browbeaten and consistently and reasonably presenting his arguments, he compelled his fellow jurors to re-examine carefully all the evidence proffered by the prosecution. Neither of the eyewitnesses was in fact reliable and the knife used in the murder could be easily bought in several stores. Fonda demonstrated this by purchasing one himself. Eventually he succeeded in persuading the other jurors to change their minds and the innocent young man was found not guilty. Clark (1994), in a study of how minority influence works in jury settings, had student jurors read a summary based on the case presented in the film. The students, who were unfamiliar with the film, had to decide whether or not the accused was guilty.

◆ Some of the students received no information about Fonda's arguments but knew he was unconvinced about the man's guilt.

◆ Some did not receive information about the other jury members changing their opinions but they knew of Fonda's arguments.

The results showed that both types of information affected the students' verdicts. Although at first convinced of the man's guilt, they were more inclined to reconsider when they read that one juror (Fonda) was unconvinced. Once they read his arguments, they were even more inclined to change their initial views. Likewise, students were also more apt to change their own opinion when they learned that other jurors had changed their minds also.

little difference between majority and minority sources of influence in the amount of cognitive activity elicited. Another challenge to the conversion (or dual process) theory comes from those who claim that *self-categorization* plays an important role in the process of social influence.

Self-categorization theory

According to this theory, we are most likely to be influenced by those who are perceived to be like us (called an *in-group*). David and Turner (1996) have reported a number of studies that have supported this contention. In one experiment, participants (186 in total) were categorized as either proconservation or anticonservation on the basis of their answers to a questionnaire. They then read a message about logging in the rainforests that challenged their views. Half the participants thought the message came from an in-group with which they could identify. The other half thought the message came from an *out-group* (people holding opposing views to them). Half the participants were led to believe that the message they read represented the views of 85 per cent of either prologgers or proconservationists (majority message), while the other half believed that only 8 per cent of prologgers or proconservationists agreed with the message (minority message). The participants' attitudes to logging were re-measured immediately after they had read the messages and again three weeks later. Results showed that:

◆ Majority and minority messages from in-groups were influential in changing the attitudes of the participants.

◆ Messages from out-groups, however, did not lead to conversion, but rather pushed participants into more extreme in-group positions. For example, those who were anticonservation and read a message purportedly from an antilogging, proconservation

group were not influenced to change their views, even if the views in the message were described as those of 85 per cent of proconservationists.

◆ In-group majority messages had the most immediate impact on participants' views, as shown in the measures taken immediately after participants had read the messages.

◆ In-group minority messages had the most delayed impact on participants' views, as shown in measures taken three weeks later.

These results challenge Moscovici's belief that 'deviant' minorities (or out-groups) help liberate and propel majorities into more innovative ways of thinking. David and Turner suggest that participants may be less willing to listen to out-group views (be they minority or majority views), if they deal with issues that are important to them. The logging issue was very important to David and Turner's participants who were Australian students some of whose families depended upon logging for their livelihood.

Theory of social impact

Another explanation for the limited effect of minority social influence has been proposed by *social impact theory* (Latane 1981). This states that social influence effects depend upon the number of people exerting influence, their status and their immediacy (both in space and time). This model predicts a decrease in minority influence in both private and public as the number of the majority increases. Findings of Clark and Maass (1990) suggest that a ratio of 2:4 between minority and majority (such as that used by Moscovici) is the optimal ratio for minority influence to occur. When the size of the majority was increased, the influence effects of the minority diminished. However, it is difficult to apply this theory to observations of minority influence in real life, where virtually whole populations may

---

◆ **in focus**

The dissociation model of minority influence

Mugny and Perez (1991) and Perez *et al.* (1995) propose that minority groups influence majority group members through a process called *social cryptoamnesia*, meaning that minority ideas are assimilated into the majority viewpoint without acknowledgement or memory of their source. In other words, the content and the source become dissociated. The model presupposes that minority ideas are so strongly associated with their source that to adopt the message is to assume a negative identity in allowing oneself to be influenced by a non-normative source. If, on the other hand, the ideas can be dissociated from their source, the majority can resist overt identification with an out-group while still drawing inspiration from their ideas. This may account for why the conversion effect (outlined by Moscovici) generated by minority groups is often delayed. The process of assimilating ideas is slow because initially they have been resisted vigorously, purely because of their source. Over time, the ideas become detached from their source and begin to reappear in the individual's mind as their own.

Source: adapted from Millward (1998)

eventually be persuaded to adopt what were once minority views, e.g. attitudes to slavery, universal suffrage and animal welfare.

The dissociation model

The *In Focus* gives an account of this more recent explanation of minority influence. The model does not lend itself to experimental testing, but it does provide an appealing explanation as to how *zeitgeists* (dominant ideas or trends within a culture) can be launched by minority groups despite the strong resistance they encounter from majority positions.

To conclude, investigations into minority influence continue to flourish. Most research uses laboratory experiments that may lack ecological validity, given the slowly evolving, long-term effects of the minority-influence process. Despite these shortcomings and the different explanations proposed for observed effects, minorities *can* exercise influence over majorities. The majorities in the world may exercise most social power, but minorities can and do bring about social change and innovation.

Section summary

Because we look to other people for guidance and approval, we are likely to conform to their attitudes and behaviours in many situations. Conformity may occur at one of three levels: compliance, identification or internalization.

Sherif has demonstrated how norms may emerge in small groups, while Asch has shown how a unanimous majority of three can produce optimum conformity effects. Using a longitudinal field study, Newcomb noted the important role of reference groups.

More recent research into conformity has underlined the importance of historical and cultural factors. The influence on behaviour of social roles has been demonstrated in the prison simulation study of Philip Zimbardo.

However, not only majorities are influential; Moscovici and others have shown how even small minorities who act consistently may exert social influence.

Obedience

Obedience is a type of social influence where somebody acts in response to a direct order from another person (Cardwell 1996). Obedience may sometimes be destructive, as when people comply with the orders of a malevolent authority.

> 'It has been reliably established that from 1939 to 1945, millions of innocent persons were slaughtered on command; gas chambers were built, death camps were guarded, daily quotas of corpses were produced with the same efficiency as the manufacture of appliances. These inhumane policies may have originated in the mind of a single person, but they could only have been carried out

on a massive scale if a very large number of persons obeyed orders.' (Milgram 1963, p. 371)

Similarly appalling events have occurred since then (e.g. the My Lai massacre during the Vietnam war, the slaughter of Kurds in Iraq, ethnic cleansing in Kosovo and slaughter in East Timor). The list seems endless. What induces people to obey their leaders' orders to torture and kill innocent human beings? Milgram was one of the first psychologists who tried to answer this question. He placed the issue of obedience in a social-psychological context, proposing that it is a *normative process*, a basic feature of human interaction:

> 'Obedience is as basic an element in the structure of social life as one can point to. Some system of authority is a requirement of all communal living and it is only the man dwelling in isolation who is not forced to respond ... to the commands of others ... It must not be thought all obedience entails acts of aggression ... [It] may refer to acts of charity and kindness as well as to destruction.' (p. 371)

Some of the 53,000 participants at a Nazi rally, Nuremberg 1937

Milgram's studies of obedience

Stanley Milgram carried out a series of studies between 1960 and 1963 to try to shed some light on this aspect of human behaviour. In all, he studied over 1,000 participants who were representative of the general population. He discovered that, under certain situational influences, most of us would obey orders that went against our conscience.

Milgram's original procedure

In his original experiment in 1960, 40 male participants were recruited by means of newspaper advertisements. Each was paid $4.50 for volunteering. Participants believed that they were taking part in a study on the role of punishment in learning and memory. The study took place in a laboratory at Yale University in the USA. The experimenter (who wore a grey lab coat to reinforce his status and authority) introduced two participants to each other and they each drew lots to determine who would be the 'teacher' and who would be the 'learner'. In fact, the draw was fixed so that the real participant was always the teacher and the other person, an accomplice of the researcher, was always the learner. The teacher's role was to administer a shock each time the learner made a mistake on a simple learning task. The learner was strapped into an 'electric chair' in a room next door to where the teacher sat. The teacher was told that the shocks were painful but not dangerous, and he was given a sample shock of 75 volts to feel the amount of pain it caused. The learner-accomplice was a mild-mannered 47-year-old man who mentioned that he had had a heart complaint in the past but that he was willing to participate in the study none the less. His task was to memorize pairs of words. When tested, the 'learner' would indicate his choice using a light system. The teacher sat in front of the shock generator which had 30 levers, each of which indicated the level of shock to be given. The first shock was 15 volts. Each subsequent shock was increased by another 15 volts. Shocks ranged from 15 volts to 450 volts (labelled 'Danger: Severe Shock XXX').

To begin with, the accomplice answered correctly, but then began to make mistakes. As the level of shock administered increased, the accomplice was heard to protest until, at 180 volts he shouted that he could bear the pain no longer. At 300 volts he screamed and complained that his heart was troubling him. At 315 volts he refused to continue and from then on he made no responses to the teacher's requests that he answer. In reality, of course, the accomplice never received any shocks. His responses and pleadings were prerecorded.

You will not be surprised to learn that this procedure was very stressful for the 'teacher' participants. Most protested and wanted to stop. Many showed signs of extreme anxiety, biting their lips and trembling.

However, whenever the teacher hesitated, the experimenter gave standardized prods to encourage him to continue:

◆ Prod 1: 'Please continue' or 'Please go on'

◆ Prod 2: 'The experiment requires that you continue'

◆ Prod 3: 'It is absolutely essential that you continue'

◆ Prod 4: 'You have no other choice, you must go on'.

The experiment continued either until the teacher refused to continue or until 450 volts were reached and given four times. All participants were then debriefed and taken to meet the learner.

Activity 5: Obedience

List the particular features of Milgram's procedure that you think most contributed to the high levels of obedience he found. What variations to this procedure do you think would (a) reduce, and (b) increase obedience?

Look at Table 5.2 to compare your ideas with what Milgram found.

Milgram's main results

◆ Most participants dissented verbally but obeyed behaviourally.

◆ All participants went to at least 300 volts.

◆ When the learner was in the next room to the 'teacher' and answering via the light system, 65 per cent of the participants went to the end of the shock generator, i.e. they believed that they had administered the full 450 volts!

Milgram was as surprised by these results as anyone. Prior to conducting his study, he had asked a number of people, including psychiatrists, how far they thought the participants would go in a study of this sort. They predicted that only a tiny handful would proceed to 450 volts. They were wrong. What was it about the situation that caused the participants to obey?

In order to answer this question, Milgram systematically varied a number of the features of his procedure. These variations and their consequences for the participants' behaviour are listed in Table 5.2. It is clear from the results given in Table 5.2 that obedience levels can be manipulated by controlling situational variables. Where participants were unsure how to disobey or what the consequences of disobedience might be, they tended to obey. When others modelled disobedience for them, they were quick to follow suit. When participants

Table 5.2 Variations on Milgram's basic procedure

Variation	Obedience rate (those going to 450 volts)
Original experiment	65%
Venue moved to seedy offices in nearby town	47.5%
Teacher and learner in same room	40%
Teacher had to force learner's hand on to plate to receive shock	30%
Teacher given support from two other 'teachers' (confederates) who refuse to continue	10%
Teacher paired with an assistant (confederate) who threw the switches	92.5%
Experimenter instructs and prods teacher by telephone from another room	20.5%

were forced to see as well as hear the consequences of their actions (i.e. the learner's distress), they were less likely to obey the experimenter. When they were less closely supervised by the experimenter, obedience levels declined. When someone else 'did the dirty work' of throwing the switches, obedience levels soared. A study by Rosenhan (1969), using school children as participants, showed that when the relative status of the experimenter to the participant is increased, obedience levels rose (to 80 per cent in this case).

Psychological processes in obedience

Why do people obey? A number of explanations have been offered that look at the psychological processes involved in obedience.

Legitimate authority

One suggestion is that we feel obligated to those in power because we respect their credentials and assume they know what they are doing. Legitimate social power is held by authority figures whose role is defined by society, which usually gives the person the right to exert control over the behaviour of others, and others usually accept it (see the study by Hofling *et al.* described on p. 123). Although respect for authority permits orderly social interaction, there is the danger that it may be so deeply ingrained in us that we obey, even when we believe we are being asked to do something that is unethical or immoral. Clearly, the authority conveyed by a legitimate researcher at a prestigious university impressed the participants in Milgram's original experiment. When the location of the study was moved downtown to a run-down office building, the level of

obedience dropped (see Table 5.2). Respect for authority varies from country to country. For example, in an Australian study, (Kilham and Mann 1974), where there is a greater tradition of questioning authority than was the case in early 1960s United States, only 40 per cent of participants went to 450 volts on the shock generator. On the other hand, a German study (Mantell 1971) found 85 per cent obedience levels.

Gradual commitment

An important feature of Milgram's procedure was the gradual way in which participants became sucked into giving greater and greater levels of shock. They found it difficult to decide when to disengage from the procedure because each voltage increment was fairly small. Psychologists call this gradual commitment the *foot-in-the-door effect*. Once people comply with a trivial, seemingly harmless, request they find it more difficult to refuse to carry out more serious, escalating requests. This is explained by the desire to appear consistent. Milgram also pointed out that participants felt that they had 'contracted' to help with the study. By coming along to the laboratory, they saw themselves as helpful people, willing to aid scientific research. If they then were to refuse to continue, they might have to re-evaluate this flattering self-perception.

Agency theory

Milgram's agency theory states that people operate on two levels:

- as *autonomous* individuals, behaving voluntarily and aware of the consequences of their actions
- on the *agentic level*, seeing themselves as the agents of others and not responsible for their actions.

The consequence of moving from the autonomous to the agentic level (known as the *agentic shift*) is that individuals attribute responsibility for their actions to the person in authority. At this agentic level, Milgram argued, people mindlessly accept the orders of the person seen as responsible in the situation. In effect, their responsibility is to the person in charge and not to the target of their actions. Milgram believed that this explained the behaviour of the participants in his study; they denied personal responsibility, merely 'doing what they were told'. You probably know that when those responsible for atrocities during the Second World War were asked why they did what they did, their answer was simply: 'I was only obeying orders' (Arendt 1963). Similar defences have been offered more recently by ex-torturers at the South African Truth and Reconciliation Commission.

What causes people to undergo the agentic shift? Milgram suggested that it is part of the socialization process: we train children from a very early age to be obedient to authority at home, in school and in society. Many rules and regulations exist to reinforce obedience, so that eventually we tend to accept unquestioningly what we are told to do because most requests are perceived to be both reasonable and appropriate. Additionally, there are factors that operate to keep one in the agentic state. These are known as *binding factors.* They include:

◆ fear of appearing rude or arrogant by disrupting a well-defined social situation such as a laboratory experiment. This would involve a breach of etiquette and require courage.

◆ fear of increasing one's anxiety levels (likely to be high already among Milgram's participants) by challenging the authority figure.

Passivity

Moriarty (1975) has suggested that the desire many people have to avoid confrontation may result in *passivity.* Laboratory and field studies have confirmed that people will, for example, tolerate loud and intrusive music rather than confront the offender. It is little wonder then that people tend passively to obey those they perceive as being in authority.

Buffers

The term *buffer* is used here to describe any aspect of a situation that protects people from having to confront the consequences of their actions. Remember that the participants in Milgram's studies did not enjoy what they were doing. Why then did they continue? Milgram suggested that, in addition to the factors already described, buffers acted as a mechanism to help people reduce the strain of obeying an immoral or unethical command. In turn, these buffers served to facilitate obedience. In the original Milgram study, the 'teacher' and 'learner' were in different rooms; the teacher was buffered (protected) from having to see his victim. In some real-life situations where obedience is required, the person merely has to press a button – the resulting destruction may not even be observed. In other cases, those carrying out orders are not told full details of their mission. This was the case with the aircrew who dropped the atomic bomb on Hiroshima.

Normality versus psychopathology thesis

The explanations described so far support Milgram's contention that, given the right (or wrong) circumstances, anyone is capable of obedience to a malevolent authority. This is called the *normality thesis* (Miller 1986). Others, who propose the *psychopathology thesis,* have suggested that there are individual differences between those who commit atrocities and the rest of us. Miale and Selzer (1975), for example, claimed that results from Rorschach tests (a psychodynamic personality test) showed that many Nazi war criminals were characterized by depression, violence, concern for status, a rejection of responsibility and an absence of guilt or concern for others. In other words, they were psychopaths.

Miale and Selzer interpreted the obedience of Milgram's participants as a socially acceptable expression of their violent impulses. Milgram refuted this account completely. He reminded us that when participants were able to select their own voltage levels they gave lower levels of shock. Another supporter of the normality thesis was Hannah Arendt who covered the trial of Nazi war criminal Adolf Eichmann for crimes against humanity. She wrote:

'It would have been comforting indeed to believe that Eichmann was a monster ... The trouble with Eichmann was precisely that so many were like him and the many were neither perverted nor sadistic ... [but] terrifyingly normal.' (1963, p. 276)

The normality thesis focuses on situational factors that produce obedience but it also recognizes that people play a part in producing situations. 'It simply denies that doers of evil are necessarily different from the rest of us in terms of basic psychological functioning.' (Miller 1986, p. 185)

Evaluating Milgram's work

Orne and Holland (1968) have criticized Milgram's studies on two counts:

◆ lacking *experimental (internal) validity,* that is the extent to which the situation forced participants to take the study seriously

◆ lacking *ecological validity,* that is the extent to which the results could be generalized to other situations, e.g. to real life.

Experimental (internal) validity

Orne and Holland claimed that the participants in Milgram's studies were 'going along with the act' when they 'shocked' the learner. They argued that participants did not believe they were really giving electric shocks and that they were not really distressed, just pretending in order to please the experimenter and to continue to play their role in the study. Milgram has disputed both these claims. He cited evidence from films made of some of his investigations that clearly showed participants undergoing extreme stress. He also referred to evidence from postexperimental interviews and questionnaires to support his belief that the majority of participants believed they were administering real shocks. Furthermore, Orne and Holland do not explain why some participants refused to continue giving shocks if they were merely role-playing in the first place or why altering the location of the study (to downtown Bridgeport) reduced the levels of obedience.

Ecological validity (mundane realism)

As we have already seen, Milgram's procedures have been replicated in other countries with higher levels of obedience found in Germany and lower levels found in Australia. In a Jordanian study, children aged between 6 and 16 exhibited high levels of obedience with 73 per cent believing that they were administering the full 450 volts (Shanab and Yahya 1977). Therefore, there is plenty of evidence to support Milgram's contention that high levels of obedience can be readily obtained in laboratories other than his own.

However, Orne and Holland have challenged the generalizability of Milgram's findings, claiming that the situation within Milgram's laboratory bore little resemblance to real-life situations where obedience is required. Given this criticism, it is interesting to look at the results of a study by Hofling *et al.* (1966) which showed that blind obedience to an authority figure could occur just as readily in real life. The situation used was a hospital. They arranged for a nurse (the participant) to receive a phone call from an unknown doctor who asked her to administer 20 milligrams of a drug called Astroten to a patient so that it would have taken effect before he arrived. If the nurse obeyed, she would be breaking several hospital rules:

◆ giving twice the maximum dose allowable for this drug

◆ administering a drug not on the ward stock list for that day

◆ taking a telephone instruction from an unfamiliar person

◆ acting without a signed order from a doctor.

Despite all this, 95 per cent of the nurse participants started to give the medication (a harmless placebo, in fact) until another nurse, who had been stationed nearby but out of sight, stopped them. When interviewed afterwards, all the nurses said that they had been asked to do this type of thing before and that doctors became annoyed if they refused. This study provided evidence for the ecological validity of Milgram's findings. However, not all studies conducted in real-life settings do so.

Rank and Jacobson (1977) were uneasy about two aspects concerning the ecological validity of the Hofling study – that the nurses had no knowledge of the drug involved and that they had no opportunity to seek advice from anyone of equal or higher status. Therefore, Rank and Jacobson replicated the procedure but this time the doctor required the nurse to use the common drug Valium at three times the recommended level. The doctor who telephoned gave the name of a real doctor on the staff and nurses were able to speak to other nurses before they proceeded. Results showed that only two out of 18 nurses proceeded to prepare the medication as requested. Rank and Jacobson concluded that 'nurses aware of the toxic effects of a drug and allowed to interact naturally ... will not administer a medication overdose merely because a physician orders it' (p. 191).

On the other hand, the study by Dutch researchers Meeus and Raaijmakers (1986) strengthens the claim for the ecological validity of Milgram's experiments. They modelled their procedure on that used by Milgram, but placed it in a real-life setting. In their investigation, a participant acted the role of an interviewer. The experimenter told them that they wanted to see how job applicants handled stress. The participants were required to make 15 'stress remarks' during the job interview on an escalating scale from mild to utterly humiliating. An example of a stress remark was 'This job is too difficult for you'. The job applicants were actually confederates of the experimenter although the participants believed them to be genuine applicants. At the time, unemployment was very high in Holland and participants knew that anyone doing badly at an interview was unlikely to find a job. Therefore, if the participant disrupted the interviewee's performance, the consequences would be serious. At the start of the interview the applicants seemed confident, but as the interview proceeded and the stress remarks became more demeaning, the interviewees' performance deteriorated and they looked distressed. They pleaded that the interviewer should stop interrupting and eventually refused to answer any more questions. Nevertheless, 22 out of the 24 participants delivered all 15 'stress remarks'. In this realistic business setting, participants appeared willing to impose psychological torture on their victims merely at the request of an experimenter, despite believing that the stakes were high for the job seekers.

More recently, in a role-playing study, Brief *et al.* (1995) found US business studies students willing to discriminate against African-American job applicants if they were told that the 'company president' wanted the job to go to a White American.

The research studies discussed so far looked at how people respond when they are required to obey. The other side of the obedience coin concerns how people behave when placed in the position of being able to make others obey them. The Zimbardo prison simulation study (discussed earlier) investigated both these issues. Zimbardo's study, while primarily concerned with conformity to social roles, also sheds light on what people will do when they are given the power to make others obey and how those who are ordered to obey will react. The answers were clear cut and dramatic. Those who were given power abused it, and those who were powerless became helpless and apathetic. Not only should we ask ourselves how we might have behaved as participants in Milgram's experiment, but also how we might have behaved if we had been a guard or prisoner in Zimbardo's study. Ethical issues in Zimbardo's study are discussed on p. 129.

Resisting pressures to obey

In this section we have been focusing on the power of social influence in making people obey, but it is important to remember that some participants did actually disobey the instructions given them. What factors help one resist pressures to obey?

Feeling responsible

In Milgram's study, some participants disobeyed the experimenter and refused to continue giving shocks when they thought the learner was in distress. One such participant, when asked why, said that she had experienced too much pain in her own life, having grown up in Nazi Germany, and did not wish to inflict pain on someone else. According to Milgram, the triggering of painful memories had 'awakened' her from her agentic state. She felt responsible for any harm produced. The arrangement whereby the learner was in a separate room was an insufficient buffer for this particular participant who could imagine all too clearly the pain he must be suffering.

Moral reasoning

In these investigations, no differences between men and women or between social groups have been found in obedience levels. However, Kohlberg (1969), a colleague of Milgram's, found that those who used more advanced stages of moral reasoning were more able to resist the exhortations of the experimenter and consequently showed higher levels of disobedience. Kohlberg also found that American students in the 1960s who possessed high levels of moral reasoning were more likely to be among those who disobeyed college regulations and conducted sit-ins in protest against government policy in Vietnam.

Disobedient models

Exposing people to the actions of disobedient models, i.e. seeing others refuse to obey instructions from an authority figure, encourages disobedience. For example, when confederate teachers refused to continue giving

shocks, only 10 per cent of participants continued (see Table 5.2).

Questioning motives

Questioning the motives, legitimacy and expertise of authority figures has been proposed as a way to prevent automatic obedience. Remember that when Milgram's study was transferred to a run-down office block, the levels of obedience dropped (see Table 5.2). The lack of prestigious surroundings made it easier for participants to question the legitimacy of the experimenter. See also Gamson et al.'s study next.

Education

A study conducted by Gamson et al. (1982) provided one particularly nice example of the effectiveness of education. It involved people making a video and signing statements that could be used in court proceedings. As the study progressed, participants became more suspicious about the real purpose of the experimenters. Participants, who worked in groups, refused to obey the requests of the experimenter and one person actually quoted Milgram's findings as a reason for disobedience. He became aware that he was becoming victim of the foot-in-the-door effect (gradual commitment – see p. 121). However, in this study, participants had plenty of time to share information and to discuss their suspicions. They eventually began to question the legitimacy and the motives of the authority figures. One explanation given for their disobedience was the psychological process called *reactance*.

Reactance

The process of reactance may occur when we want to protect our sense of freedom. Blatant attempts to restrict people's freedom can sometimes produce a *boomerang effect,* causing people to do the opposite of what is being asked (Nail and Van Leeuwen 1993). It has been suggested that reactance might contribute to underage drinking and the increase in cigarette-smoking among young people, although peer pressure and conformity effects probably play a part as well. This type of reactance to social pressure is not necessarily the same as truly independent behaviour and may often be an example of anticonformity.

Section summary

Milgram has shown that levels of obedience can be influenced by a number of factors, including the presence of a legitimate authority, gradual commitment, agentic state, passivity and buffering. In his original study, Milgram showed that 65 per cent of participants were willing to give electric shocks up to 450 volts as punishment to a 'learner' who made an error on a memory test.

The experimental and ecological validity of Milgram's investigations has been hotly disputed and experiments in more real-life settings have added fuel to this debate.

Factors that make it more likely that people will resist pressures to obey include: feelings of responsibility; higher moral reasoning; disobedient models; questioning motives of those giving orders; knowledge of and a reaction against blatant attempts at coercion.

CRITICAL ISSUE: Ethical issues in psychological research

Ethics can be defined as a consideration of what is acceptable or right behaviour in the pursuit of a particular personal or scientific goal (Cardwell 1996). Because human participants are used in much psychological research, ethical issues are a major concern within psychology. Although originally a matter of individual morality and attention (it was expected that psychologists would consider ethical concerns alongside more purely methodological concerns), the need for a clear and unambiguous set of guidelines for research psychologists led to the development of the ethical principles that underlie all psychological research today. To describe something as 'unethical', therefore, not only describes a practice that is morally wrong, but also one that is professionally unacceptable in terms of these guiding principles. The guidelines drawn up by the British Psychological Society (BPS) (1993) stress that psychologists must carry out their work in a way that respects the rights and dignity of all research participants. The work of Milgram and Zimbardo, in particular, has raised many ethical issues that include concerns about:

◆ the use of deception

◆ the inability of participants to give fully informed consent

◆ the adequacy of the debriefing process

◆ the possible harm that might be done to participants.

Dealing with ethical issues

One way in which psychologists have attempted to deal with these ethical concerns has been to devise a set of ethical guidelines. Nowadays, psychology departments in universities, colleges and hospitals have ethical committees that approve or reject proposed research. The decisions of these committees are strongly influenced by the criteria laid down in the ethical guidelines published by bodies such as the British Psychological Society. A summary of the BPS guidelines is shown in Table 5.3. This provides an outline of the guiding principles or 'rules' by which research psychologists operate. Among the important issues that lie behind these principles are those of consent, deception, debriefing and protection of participants.

Consent

If someone volunteers for an experiment, we might believe that they are doing so because they know exactly what is going to happen to them. In other words, they are able to give their *informed consent* to take part in the study. Unfortunately, this is not always the case. Epstein and Lasagna (1969) discovered that only one third of participants volunteering for an experiment really understood what was involved. Gaining a participant's informed consent is a very important aspect of any research investigation. Without full disclosure prior to obtaining their consent, it becomes impossible for participants to make any informed decision about their willingness to take part. Of course, we might argue that full disclosure (of procedures to be used, reasons for the research, and so on) is not a feasible requirement in a piece of psychological research. Put it another way, however, would you accept a job when you did not fully know what you were required to do? Some participants may initially give their consent to take part in a study, but if they later realize that they would like to withdraw that consent (for whatever reason), they are free to do so, even if they have previously accepted payment for their participation. An 'I pay you – you do as you are told' relationship between investigator and participant can never be justified.

There are alternatives to informed consent that may be used when to reveal the purpose of the investigation to participants would invalidate the study. One solution is to gain *presumptive consent*. For example, we may take a large random sample from the population to be studied and introduce them to the research design, including the use of deception. If they agree that they would still have given voluntary informed consent, had they known the true aims of the investigation, then we may assume that they represent the views of that population group. Another sample from that population would then be selected for use in the study without being told its true purpose. A second solution involves the use of *prior general consent*. In this case, people who might be used as participants in a study are told that sometimes participants are misinformed about the true purpose of a study. Only those who agree that such a

1 Introduction

Participants in psychological research should have confidence in the investigators. Good psychological research is possible only if there is mutual respect and confidence between investigators and participants. Although investigators are potentially interested in all aspects of human behaviour, for ethical reasons some areas of human experience and behaviour may be beyond the reach of psychological investigation. Ethical guidelines are necessary to clarify the conditions under which psychological research is acceptable.

2 General

In all circumstances investigators must consider the ethical implications and psychological consequences for the participants in their research. The essential principle is that the investigation should be considered from the standpoint of all participants; foreseeable threats to their psychological wellbeing, health, values or dignity should be eliminated. Where investigations involve individuals of different ages, gender and social background, the investigators may not have sufficient knowledge of the implications of any investigation for the participants. The best judges of whether an investigation will cause offence may be members of the population from which the participants in the research are to be drawn.

3 Consent

Whenever possible, investigators should inform all participants of the objectives of the investigation. The investigators should inform the participants of all aspects of the research or intervention that might reasonably be expected to influence their willingness to participate. Research with children or with other vulnerable participants requires special safe-guarding procedures. Investigators are often in a position of authority or influence over participants who may be their students, employees or clients. This relationship must not be allowed to pressurize the participants to take part in, or remain in, an investigation. The payment of participants must not be used to induce them to risk harm beyond that which they risk without payment in their normal lifestyle.

4 Deception

Withholding information or misleading participants is unacceptable if the participants are typically likely to show unease once debriefed. Where this is in any doubt, appropriate consultation must precede the investigation. Intentional deception of the participants over the purpose and general nature of the investigation should be avoided whenever possible, although it may be impossible to study some psychological processes without withholding information about the true object of the study or without deliberately misleading participants.

5 Debriefing

In studies where the participants are aware that they have taken part in an investigation, when the data have been collected, the investigator should provide the participants with any necessary information to complete their understanding of the nature of the research. The investigator should discuss with the participants their experience of the research in order to monitor any unforeseen negative effects or misconceptions.

6 Withdrawal from the investigation

At the outset, investigators should make plain to participants their right to withdraw from the research at any time, irrespective of whether or not payment or other inducement has been offered. In the light of experience of the investigation or as a result of debriefing, the participant has the right to withdraw retrospectively any consent given, and to require that their own data, including recordings, be destroyed.

7 Confidentiality

Except in circumstances specified by the law, information obtained about a participant during an investigation is confidential unless otherwise agreed in advance. Participants in psychological research have a right to expect that information they provide will be treated confidentially and, if published, will not be identifiable as theirs.

8 Protection of participants

Investigators have a primary responsibility to protect participants from physical and mental harm during the investigation. Normally the risk of harm must be no greater than in ordinary life. Where research may involve behaviour or experiences that participants may regard as personal and private, the participants must be protected from stress by all appropriate measures, including the assurance that answers to personal questions need not be given.

9 Observational research

Studies based upon observation must respect the privacy and psychological wellbeing of the individuals studied. Unless those being observed give their consent to being observed, observational research is only acceptable in situations where those observed would expect to be observed by strangers. Additionally, particular account should be taken of local cultural values and of the possibility of intruding upon the privacy of individuals who, even while in a normally public space, may believe they are unobserved.

10 Giving advice

During research, an investigator may obtain evidence of psychological or physical problems of which a participant is apparently unaware. In such a case the investigator has a responsibility to inform the participant if the investigator believes that by not doing so the participant's future wellbeing may be endangered. If the issue is serious and the investigator is not qualified to offer assistance, the appropriate source of professional advice should be recommended.

11 Colleagues

Investigators share responsibility for the ethical treatment of research participants with their collaborators, assistants, students and employees. A psychologist who believes that another psychologist or investigator may be conducting research that is not in accordance with the principles above should encourage that investigator to re-evaluate the research.

practice is acceptable would be selected as participants for this type of study. Therefore, they have given general informed consent but they do not know whether or not the actual study they participate in uses misinformation.

Deception

To those within the psychological profession, and to many outside it, the idea of deceiving research participants would be unacceptable. Quite apart from the immorality (or even illegality) of deception by a professional psychologist, the experience of deception can make research participants cynical about the activities and attitudes of psychologists. By deceiving research participants, we may also remove their ability to give fully informed consent to take part in the investigation we have in mind. This is not an open and shut case, however, as total honesty throughout an investigation may lead participants to modify their behaviour in some way because of the knowledge they have about the real aims of the investigation. You may like to consider the implications of complete research honesty in the investigation carried out by Stanley Milgram on obedience to authority. There are clearly some situations where deception is inappropriate and some where it may be acceptable. There is a difference, for example, between withholding some of the research details and deliberately misleading the participants into believing the purpose of the research is more innocent than it actually is. There are a number of issues here:

◆ The consequences of some deceptions are more damaging than others. The amount of discomfort or anger expressed by participants when deception is revealed is normally a good guide to this.

◆ Deception in investigations of a trivial nature is less acceptable than in investigations that make significant contributions to psychological knowledge. Although this may seem a case of the ends justifying the means, it should be clear that the importance of some research means that the ethical concerns spread far beyond the immediate context of the investigation. You might like to consider how Milgram might have justified deceiving his participants.

◆ There are alternatives to deception. Deception should only be used if such alternatives are considered inappropriate. We may, for example, provide participants with complete information about the purpose of the investigation. In a study by Gallo et al. (1973), participants were told that the study concerned to what extent people were conformers. The results for these informed participants were no different from those for deceived participants who thought they were involved in an investigation of depth perception.

However, a second study by the same researchers produced opposite findings. Another alternative to deception is to tell participants about the general nature of the study (though not the detailed hypothesis being tested) and ask them to role-play the experimental procedure as though they were naive participants. Mixon (1972) used this method in a set-up similar to that used in Milgram's obedience studies. He found that provided the role-playing participants were led to believe that the experimenter carried the responsibility for any distress caused to the 'learner', they behaved much as Milgram's participants did. However, if the role-players were led to assume responsibility, their levels of obedience were significantly lower than those found by Milgram. More often than not, studies using role-play procedures result in different findings from those where investigators have concealed their true purpose from participants.

Debriefing

An important aspect of any research design, especially when deception has taken place, is the process of debriefing. Sometimes it is seen as sufficient merely to inform participants of the true nature of the investigation, but at other times such perfunctory debriefing would be inadequate. Consider again Stanley Milgram's research into obedience. His research participants either obeyed and gave the maximum electric shock, or disobeyed and declined to give further shocks. Either way, the participants had done something they may have perceived as being wrong. (See p. 129 for an account of the debriefing measures used by Milgram.) As a general rule, debriefing aims to restore participants to the same state as when they entered the investigation. It also offers the researcher the opportunity to provide additional information about the research so that the whole thing becomes an educational experience for the participant. Debriefing does not, of course, provide a justification for any unethical aspects of the investigation. A good researcher regards participants as colleagues, not as objects to be used solely for the ends of the experimenter.

Protection of participants

Another general concern of the BPS is the protection of participants from undue risk during psychological research. The definition of undue risk is based on the risks that individuals might be expected to encounter in their normal lifestyle. Thus, the risks that an individual may be exposed to during a psychological investigation should not be greater than the risks they might already be expected to face in their everyday life. The concept of risk includes risk to self-respect or risk of mental harm. You might like to consider whether the risks to self-respect encountered by Asch's, Milgram's or Zimbardo's participants were greater than those you would expect them to meet in their normal life.

Ethical issues in social influence research

The question is often asked whether the scientific knowledge gained or the moral lessons learned by social influence research have outweighed the costs and potential harm done to participants. The studies carried out by Milgram and Zimbardo have received most attention.

Milgram's obedience studies

Milgram's procedures have attracted much criticism. His work, however, has also received considerable support and has been stoutly defended by Milgram himself.

Activity 6: Evaluating Milgram's research

After you have read the sections in the chapter on obedience and the two quotations below, consider what it is about Milgram's research that made Bettelheim describe it as 'vile' whilst, at the same time, others describe it as a study of great moral significance.

'These experiments are so vile, the intention with which they were engaged in so vile, that nothing these experiments show has any value.' (Bruno Bettelheim, quoted in Miller 1986)

'Milgram, in exploring the external conditions that produce such destructive obedience, the psychological processes that lead to such attempted abdications of responsibility, and the means by which defiance of illegitimate authority can be promoted, seems to me to have done some of the most morally significant research in modern psychology.' (Alan Elms, quoted in Miller 1986)

The case for the prosecution

Baumrind (1964) believed that Milgram showed insufficient respect for his participants, that there were inadequate steps taken to protect them and that his procedures had the potential for causing long-term harm. The studies, it has been claimed, involved lack of informed consent, deception and possible psychological harm to his participants.

◆ Voluntary *informed consent* and *lack of deception* are important principles to be adhered to if psychological research is to be ethical. Without doubt, Milgram's participants did not know the true purpose of his experiment and therefore they could not give informed consent. For the experiment to work, deception was essential. The point at issue, however, is whether or not the deception can be justified in this case. Some researchers (e.g. Mixon 1979) have advocated the use of role-playing to avoid the need for deception.

◆ The criticism most often levelled against Milgram's experiments concerns the *psychological damage* that might have been done to participants. This harm, it is claimed, could result from several aspects of the procedure, including the stress of carrying out the instructor's orders to continue giving the shocks to the learner. For example, Milgram (1963) recorded that his participants often trembled, stuttered and sweated. Furthermore, there were the possible long-term psychological effects of learning that they had been willing to give potentially lethal shocks to fellow human beings, and feeling stupid and 'used' when they learned the true nature of the experiment and how they had been *deceived*. Allied to this is the likelihood that they would not trust psychologists or people in authority in the future.

◆ John Darley (1992), in his thought-provoking paper, 'Social organization for the production of evil', argues that the possibility of being evil is latent in all of us and it can be made active by a conversion process. He invites us to consider the possibility that Milgram may have begun the process of converting innocent participants into evil people. To support this theory, he draws our attention to the reports of Lifton's (1986) interviews with physicians who participated in the Nazi death camps. He reported that the Nazi doctors were initially banal, ordinary individuals. What they did, however, was not ordinary, and in performing their evil acts, they changed. Their encounter with a 'demonic killing machine' began a process that morally altered them. Could the same be true of those people who gave 450-volt shocks to the learners in Milgram's experiments?

Case for the defence

Milgram has responded to his critics. The major plank of his defence is that participants themselves do not agree with the criticisms.

◆ Milgram responded to Baumrind's accusation that he had not respected his participants sufficiently, by drawing attention to the questionnaire distributed to participants. Eighty-four per cent replied that they were glad they had been involved and claimed it had been an enriching and instructive experience. Seventy-four per cent said they had learned something of personal importance. Only 1.3 per cent reported negative feelings. Furthermore, one year after the study, a university psychiatrist interviewed 40 participants and reported no evidence of emotional harm that could be attributed to participation in the study.

◆ After each experimental session, a careful debriefing session was held when the reasons for the *deception* were explained and the true purpose of the study was revealed. Milgram claimed that the debriefing process was instrumental in helping to reassure and *protect the participants*. Obedient participants were reassured that their behaviour was the norm in that investigation (i.e. there was not anything wrong with them). Disobedient participants were reassured that their behaviour was actually socially desirable, because they had stood up against a malevolent authority figure trying to coerce them into doing something they felt was wrong.

◆ As regards the criticism that people might be distrustful of psychologists or others in authority in the future, Milgram (1964) replied that he thought it would be 'of the highest value if participation in the experiment could inculcate a scepticism of *this* [inhumane] kind of authority' (p. 852).

◆ Supporters of Milgram (e.g. Zimbardo 1974) have rallied to his defence, agreeing with him that had the results of his studies been different, with participants declining to continue at the first sign of learner discomfort, no one would have protested. But, of course, we cannot be sure what the results of research will be. Milgram had not intended to cause discomfort to his participants. Indeed, the survey carried out beforehand predicted that few people would give shocks after the learner began to protest. Therefore, few participants should have experienced any discomfort. Even when participants did show distress, however, Milgram did not believe it sufficient to justify stopping the experiment. After Milgram's research was published, the American Psychological Association investigated it and found it ethically acceptable. He was, in fact, awarded a prize for his outstanding contribution to social psychological research.

◆ Elliot Aronson (1999) has suggested that psychologists face a particularly difficult dilemma when their wider responsibility to society conflicts with their more specific responsibilities to each individual research participant. This conflict is greatest when the issues under investigation are issues of social importance.

◆ Darley's proposition that those who took part in Milgram's experiments may have entered on the slippery slope towards evil was made after Milgram's death (1984) and so Milgram did not have an opportunity to respond. He did, however, as already mentioned, arrange for a psychiatrist to interview a sample of his participants to see if any psychological damage could be detected. None was reported.

◆ A very positive outcome of Milgram's experiments has been the increased awareness among psychologists since then concerning how they should treat their participants. This, in turn, has led psychologists to draft guidelines to be used for research. Remember that the ethical guidelines used by research psychologists today were not formulated when Milgram carried out his research.

Zimbardo's prison simulation study

On p. 114 we listed the ethical charges made against Zimbardo's procedure and his initial responses to these criticisms. You must decide for yourself whether or not Zimbardo's rebuttals are adequate. Less than 36 hours after the arrests, one of the 'prisoners' began to cry uncontrollably and became depressed. In the days that followed, four other prisoners developed stress-related symptoms. After six days the simulation, originally planned to last two weeks, was ended because of the unexpectedly extreme emotional and behavioural effects. You might consider whether it should have ended sooner. Did the knowledge gained justify the means by which it was acquired? Zimbardo thinks it did. He reports that follow-ups over many years revealed no lasting negative effects; that student participants were healthy and able to bounce back from their 'prison' experience; that they had learned the important lesson that even the most intelligent and well-intentioned among us can be overwhelmed by social influences.

In recent years, Zimbardo has acknowledged that he should not have acted as 'prison superintendent' as well as principal researcher, because he became trapped by the day-to-day business of his superintendent role, rather as the 'guards' and 'prisoners' became trapped in their roles. However, he argues that instead of banning research of this type, what is needed is better research – that is, where experiments are ethically sensitive, there should be an *independent monitor* and *more vigilant surveillance* by the institution concerned. In this way, he claims, participants could be protected while valuable information was acquired.

After the surprising results of the prison simulation study, Zimbardo proposed another study be undertaken to investigate ways in which prison guards might be trained to be less dehumanizing towards their

<table>
<tr><td>in
focus</td><td>**Zimbardo: Ethics and research in social psychology**</td></tr>
</table>

In an interview with Mark McDermott (1993), Zimbardo said:

'One of the subtle dangers arising out of the increase in concern for the ethics of experiments, is it gives social psychologists an easy out. To do behavioural experiments is very difficult. Its time consuming, it's labour intensive and you can replace it with an "as if" paper-and-pencil, 30-minute self-report. The question arises, "is that the same thing?" If, in fact, you could discover the same things about human nature from asking people to imagine how they would behave in a situation instead of observing how they do, it clearly doesn't make sense to do the behavioural simulation. I think what you get from the Milgram study and my Prison study is very different from self-report based ones. Indeed, Milgram asked 40 psychiatrists how people would behave in his conformity experiment. To a person they all got it wrong: they predicted that fewer than one per cent of the subjects would go all the way in shocking the innocent victim, when in actuality two-thirds blindly obeyed the unjust authority figure. There are situations you cannot imagine what it would be like until you are in them. So, if we are going to have a psychology of "as if", of "imagine this were the situation and how would you predict you would behave?", I think you are missing out on some of the powerful yet subtle dynamics of situational control ...

'The contribution social psychologists make is [in] understanding what people will or won't do in certain situations. Typically, even if you describe the situation, people will underestimate its power. There is no way until you are in it, that you begin to feel and become entrapped in the power of the situation.'

prisoners. His proposal was turned down, he claims, because he could not guarantee that the training would be successful. Zimbardo points out, of course, that in research the outcome is never certain – that is why research is done!

Some critics of both Milgram and Zimbardo have suggested that deceiving participants is really not necessary in research and is particularly unethical when it might leave them feeling foolish or humiliated. They have proposed that other more ethically

acceptable methods could be used, e.g. asking people to imagine how they or others would behave in certain situations. You may recall that Milgram did this by asking people how many participants they thought would go to 450 volts on his shock generator. Their predictions grossly underestimated the levels of obedience found by Milgram in his actual experiments. Zimbardo is scathing about the use of 'as if' procedures to replace simulations or experiments (see *In Focus*).

Activity 7: Applying ethical guidelines

Ethical guidelines, such as those published by the British Psychological Society did not exist when the early studies on conformity (e.g. Asch, Zimbardo), minority influence (e.g. Moscovici) and obedience (e.g. Milgram) were carried out.

Try to list the arguments for and against such studies being permitted today. Is it possible to gain informed consent, avoid deception and protect the wellbeing of participants in these studies? If yes, how can this be done? If not, should such research be carried out?

Section summary

Psychologists must attend to the ethical issues that arise from their research. One way this has been done is by developing ethical guidelines. Among the issues that the guidelines address are: deception, informed consent, debriefing and protection of participants.

Critics of Milgram have accused him of deception and subjecting the participants in his obedience studies to psychological harm. Others have defended his actions by referring to the importance of his findings and to the extensive debriefing and follow-up procedures he employed. Similar accusations have been lodged also against Zimbardo for his prison simulation study. Zimbardo responds by advocating that such research should be done but done better, e.g. by using surveillance procedures.

Chapter summary

- In the chapter we have looked at some of the different ways social psychologists have studied **social influence**. These include studies of norm development (Sherif); majority influence/conformity effects (e.g. Asch; Perrin and Spencer); effects of social roles (Zimbardo); minority influence (e.g. Moscovici, Clark); and obedience (e.g. Milgram; Hofling; Meeus and Raaijmakers).

- Many studies have demonstrated the effects of **majority influence**, but some more recent research has failed to find **conformity effects**. **Situational factors** that influenced levels of conformity included: losing/gaining a partner; nature of the task; mode of response; context of study. People with a strong desire for control may be better able to resist conformity pressures.

- **Newcomb** has demonstrated how **social norms** may influence our attitudes and **Zimbardo's prison simulation study** vividly showed the power of social roles.

- **Minority pressure** can also exert social influence and the work of **Moscovici** showed how important it is for minorities to behave consistently, if they want to influence majority members. Other possible **factors in minority influence** are: the type of cognitive activity generated; the size of the majority;

whether the minority view is perceived to come from an in-group; the role of cryptoamnesia.

- **Milgram's** original study demonstrated **obedience** caused by the role of the authority figure, the gradual commitment of and agentic shift in the participant, a tendency to passivity and the buffering effects of not having to see the distress of the 'learner'. Milgram's work has been criticised for **lacking experimental and ecological validity**, but some later investigations have produced comparable results.

- People with **higher levels of moral reasoning** have been found more able to resist pressures to obey, as have those who felt responsible for their actions or who observed disobedient models. Similarly, the chance to question the motives of an authority figure and learning about obedience-effects can lead to a reaction against pressure to obey.

- In order to deal with **ethical issues** that arise in research, psychologists have devised **ethical guidelines** to help them look after the welfare of their participants. The criteria contained in these guidelines are sometimes used to criticize the research methods of social psychologists. However, such guidelines did not exist when the famous studies of Milgram and Zimbardo were carried out.

Exam summary

The AQA examination will test your understanding of the following areas:

- research studies of conformity (pp. 110–15)
- research studies of minority influence (pp. 116–17)
- explanations of why people yield to majority influence (i.e. why they *conform*) (pp. 108–10)
- explanations of why people yield to minority influence (pp. 116–19)
- research studies of obedience (pp. 119–21, 123–4)
- experimental and ecological validity in obedience research (pp. 122–4)
- explanations of the psychological processes involved in obedience (i.e. why people obey) (pp. 121–2)
- resisting obedience (p. 124)
- ethical issues in psychology (pp. 125–30).

Example question

The question below is typical of one drawn from the material above, and should take you 30 minutes to answer:

(a) Explain what is meant by the terms 'conformity' and 'obedience'. *(3 + 3 marks)*

(b) Describe one study of obedience. *(6 marks)*

(c) Describe two psychological processes that might be involved in obedience. *(3 + 3 marks)*

(d) 'Not only does research into the psychology of obedience have little application to the horrors seen in wartime, but the abuse of human participants in such research must also be ethically unjustifiable.'

To what extent might we justify obedience research such as that carried out by Milgram and others? *(12 marks)*

Suggested answer structure

(a) This question uses the injunction *explain*, and therefore requires an accurate and detailed response to guarantee maximum marks. *Conformity* is defined on p. 107, and a suitable elaboration of this definition might be to include Kelman's three types of conformity (p. 108). *Obedience* is defined on p. 119, and you may like to elaborate this definition by adding the essence of Milgram's own views of obedience as a 'normative process' (p. 119).

(b) Although this appears to be a dream question, it is easy to get bogged down doing nothing other than describing the procedural details of (for example) Milgram's obedience research (pp. 119–21). When describing research, it is best to cover the aims (what was Milgram trying to find out?), methods (what did he do?), results (what did he find?) and conclusions (what did this tell him?).

(c) This is an attempt to see if you can explain *why* people obey. There are a number of psychological processes that have been proposed for obedience. These include the *gradual commitment* imposed by the experiment (p. 121), *agentic shift* (pp. 121–122) and the use of *buffers* (p. 122).

(d) Obedience research, particularly that carried out by Milgram, has been criticized for lacking *validity* and for being *unethical*. The quotation alludes to both these criticisms. Remembering that this is the AO2 requirement of this question (see Chapter 8), you might elaborate either or both of these criticisms. Orne and Holland's criticisms regarding the validity of Milgram's work can be found on pp. 122–3, and a discussion of the ethical issues in Milgram's work can be found on pp. 128–9. It is a good idea to include some of the points raised in defence of Milgram's research (pp. 128–9).

Further resources

Baron, R.A. and Byrne, D. (1997) *Social Psychology: Understanding Human Interaction* (7th edn), Boston: Allyn and Bacon.

> *An excellent, well-established text that provides many applied examples of social psychology research.*

Myers, D.G. (1999) *Social Psychology* (6th edn), Boston: McGraw-Hill College.

> *This provides clear, concise accounts of the classic studies in social influence. It lacks the depth and range of Baron and Byrne's text, but you may find it easier to digest.*

Pennington, D.C., Gillen, K. and Hill, P. (1999) *Social Psychology*, London: Arnold.

> *This is a very accessible text that is suitable for an A-level audience. Chapter 8 will reinforce and extend many of the issues in this chapter.*

Websites

www.bps.org.uk/charter/codofcon.htm

> *This provides the up-to-date code of conduct for chartered psychologists, and supplements the Ethical Guidelines published by the BPS.*

www.sonoma.edu/people/g/goodman/zimbardo.htm

> *Contains the text of the lecture that Zimbardo gave to the Holocaust Studies Centre in March 1999.*

www.stanford.edu/dept/news/relaged/970108prisonexp.html

> *Includes an interesting account by Christina Maslach of some of the ethical issues arising in Zimbardo's prison simulation study.*

Chapter 6

Quantitative and qualitative research methods

Graham Davies

Preview

In this chapter we shall be looking at some of the research methods used by psychologists, and in particular at the nature and use of:

◆ experimental investigations, including:
  – laboratory experiments
  – field experiments
  – natural experiments

◆ non-experimental investigations, including:
  – investigations employing correlational analysis
  – naturalistic observational studies
  – questionnaire surveys
  – interviews.

Introduction

The function of the wide range of research methods used in psychological investigations is to provide techniques which can help psychologists to gather and make sense of their data. The data produced can be either quantitative or qualitative. *Quantitative* data have a numerical basis (e.g. time in seconds, stress ratings), whereas *qualitative* data are non-numerical (e.g. verbal reports of how research participants feel about something).

For many years the experiment, and in particular the laboratory experiment, has been a leading method used in psychology. However, dissatisfaction concerning the realism and applicability of the results achieved from experimental research has stimulated a search for alternative methods and has led to a recent increase in the use of non-experimental methods producing qualitative data. Nevertheless, although the latter have increased in importance, it is true to say that the experiment still remains a vital research tool for psychologists. Both experimental and non-experimental approaches to investigation have their place and can be considered complementary to each other, since different types of research situations require different methods of investigation. The different viewpoints of those advocating the use of experimental or non-experimental methods also reflect fundamental differences in perception about what psychologists should be doing and how they should go about it.

This chapter discusses only a selection of methods that you are likely to meet as an AS-level student and makes no attempt to cover the complete range of methods used by psychologists. You should bear in mind that, although research methods can be divided into specific categories, these methods often merge into each other. For example, the boundary between experimental and non-experimental research is far from clear cut. What really matters, however, is that the appropriate method is used for a given research situation, rather than the descriptive label placed on that method.

Experimental investigations in psychology

The *experiment* is regarded by many as the preferred method of scientific enquiry, because by using it, a researcher can intervene directly in the situation which is being investigated. It is the most powerful of the research methods at the disposal of psychologists, as its potential to seek and find the causes of events is greater than that of other methods. The true experiment has three key features:

◆ An *independent variable* is manipulated by the researcher in an attempt to produce a change in a *dependent variable.*

◆ All *other variables,* which might influence the results, are *held constant* or *eliminated.*

◆ Participants are *allocated* to the experimental conditions *randomly.*

A *variable* is, quite simply, anything which can change. In the simplest form of an experiment, one crucial variable, called the *independent variable*, is deliberately manipulated by the researcher in an attempt to change the performance of participants on another variable, referred to as the *dependent variable*. For example, consider an experiment set up to investigate which of two methods is more successful at teaching children to read. In this case, the independent variable would be the teaching method that the participants (in this case the children who took part in the study) were exposed to. The dependent variable would be some measure of their reading ability (such as scores derived from a standard test of reading ability).

However, if the experimenter is to be sure that it is the independent variable that has produced a change in the dependent variable, it is necessary also to ensure that all other variables, which might provide alternative explanations for the results, are either held constant or, if they cannot be held constant, eliminated. These unwanted variables are known as *confounding variables*, and might include the following:

◆ differences in the instructions given by an experimenter or in the stimulus materials being used (which can be overcome by standardizing the instructions and materials for all those taking part in the experiment)

◆ differences between participants, e.g. in their age (which can be eliminated as a variable by using a single age group, or alternatively it can be made constant by ensuring that the age structure of each of the groups taking part in the experiment is very similar).

A particularly important variable is the nature of the participants themselves. This is dealt with in the next chapter in the section on experimental design. The logic of the experiment is that if all variables other than the independent variable have been successfully controlled or eliminated, then any change that is produced in the dependent variable must be the result of manipulating the independent variable.

As a principle of good design, it is necessary either to allocate participants randomly to conditions (i.e. give all those taking part an equal chance of being selected for each), or permit all participants to experience each condition.

Sometimes, however, it is not possible to meet all three of the requirements for a true experiment. The term *quasi-experiment* (the prefix 'quasi' means 'resembling but not really the same as') is sometimes used for research which is broadly similar in approach to experimental research but in which the investigator lacks complete control over the independent variable and / or allocation of participants to groups. For

example, a quasi-experiment might be set up to investigate the application of an antitruancy strategy in schools. This might be studied by comparing the truancy levels in schools where the strategy has been applied, to the truancy levels in similar schools where it has not. This is a quasi-experiment as there is no control over the allocation of participants to the two conditions.

The laboratory experiment

The laboratory experiment gives the researcher 'complete control over the experiment: the who, what, when, where and how' (McBurney 1983). It can be used to test theories, determine the conditions under which certain events occur, or extend current research by proposing new research problems.

Laboratory experiments provide the psychologist with the highest possible level of control over variables. However, it must be remembered that not all experiments are carried out in laboratories and that not all investigations carried out in laboratories are experiments. For example, field experiments (see later in this chapter) are carried out in natural settings, and non-experimental techniques such as naturalistic observation may be carried out in a laboratory setting (e.g. an observational study of the strategies used by people to deal with boredom might be carried out in a laboratory).

Uses of the laboratory experiment

The laboratory experiment is used very widely as a research tool in psychology. Examples are some of the experiments by Loftus (1975, 1978 *et al.*) on eye witness testimony and by Baddeley *et al.* (1975) on memory span for short or long words (see Chapter 1). See *In Focus*, 'The Stroop Effect', for a detailed example of a laboratory experiment.

Activity 1: Variables in laboratory experiments

Identify the independent and dependent variables in the above two studies. What variables did the researchers need to control in each case?

Advantages of the laboratory experiment

◆ *Replicability of procedures* – A major advantage of the properly carried out and reported laboratory experiment is that its procedures can be repeated (replicated) by other researchers to see if they obtain similar results. Without this ability to replicate procedures, research might wait

<table>
<tr><td>in focus</td><td></td></tr>
</table>

The 'Stroop Effect' (Stroop 1935)

The 'Stroop Effect' is a term that has come into common usage in psychology since the findings from a series of experiments by J. Ridley Stroop were published in the 1930s. The term refers to how colour name words have an interfering effect on the time taken to name the ink colours of non-matching colours. For example, naming the ink colour of the word 'blue' written in green ink takes longer than it does for the same word written in blue ink. Two of Stroop's experiments are described below.

In one of these experiments, the colour names red, blue, green, brown and purple were selected. For the experimental condition, each word was printed in a grid such that each word occurred twice in each column and twice in each row. No word appeared in the colour that it named, but an equal number of times in each of the other four colours. No word or colour immediately succeeded itself in any column or row. A second sheet of words was produced using the same words in reverse order.

The control condition used the same arrangement of ink colours, but this time each ink colour was represented by a coloured block. The independent variable was therefore whether the stimulus sheets consisted of words in ink colours which conflicted with the colour names or were in the form of colour blocks.

The times taken to name the ink colours for each condition (the dependent variable) were compared. On average, it took participants 47 seconds longer to name the ink colours of a stimulus sheet from the experimental condition, than from the control condition.

In another of the experiments, the same words and format were used for the experimental condition as in Experiment 1. The control condition used the same word arrangements as the experimental condition but printed in black type. This time the participants were asked to read the sheets of words in each condition. In this experiment it took participants an average of 2.3 seconds longer to read a sheet of words from the experimental condition.

indefinitely for the precise set of circumstances which are obtained in the experiment to be repeated by chance.

◆ *Forcing the pace of research* – Experimentation allows the pace of research to be forced, making it unnecessary to wait for natural events to reproduce the appropriate scenario. As a result, it is possible to study behaviour which is uncommon, rarely observed by psychologists or which cannot be studied easily in another way, for example, bystander attitudes to an emergency. Also, it permits the researcher to select when, and possibly where, to undertake an experiment.

◆ *Control over variables* – The control of variables is less difficult in the laboratory than in other settings or with other research methods, so high levels of precision can be achieved. If all variables other than the independent variable are controlled successfully, then cause and effect can be established.

◆ *Generalizing results* – It is possible to generalize experimental results to the rest of the population from which the participants have been drawn, if a representative sample of participants has been selected to take part.

◆ *Quantitative data* – An experiment yields quantitative data (numerical amounts of something) which can be analysed using inferential statistical tests. These tests permit statements to be made about how likely the results are to have occurred through chance.

◆ *Use of technical equipment* – The laboratory may be the only place where sophisticated technical equipment can be used and accurate measurements made. For some research at least, the fact that the laboratory situation may be artificial does not really matter – examples here include research on newborn children, or on auditory perception.

Limitations of the laboratory experiment

◆ *Drawbacks of experimental designs* – These include the potential for order effects resulting from the order of presentation of the experimental conditions or, alternatively, the effects of individual differences between participants. These drawbacks are discussed further in Chapter 7.

◆ *Loss of validity* – A serious problem with experiments is that by establishing high levels of control, and narrowly defining independent and dependent variables, an experimental situation may become artificial and recognizably different from real-life situations. *Ecological validity* is concerned with the extent to which results may be generalized to settings other than the one in which the research took place, such as those outside the laboratory. For example, memory experiments have often been conducted using word lists, which are rarely learned in everyday life. A fuller discussion of ecological validity can be found in Chapter 7.

♦ *Demand characteristics* – These occur when participants try to make sense of the situation they find themselves in and act accordingly (Orne 1962). These may seriously threaten the validity of an experiment. The demands placed on participants in a laboratory situation are not helped by the experimenter sticking rigidly to a standardized procedure and acting in an unemotional way (necessary if confounding variables are to be avoided). Participants may respond to specific cues made by an investigator, such as differences in the tone of voice used, and this may present a problem. Another possible demand characteristic is that participants may try to behave in some way that they perceive as being helpful to the researcher (alternatively, if feeling awkward, they may set out deliberately to confound the results). With most participants, however, this is probably relatively unimportant. Other potential problems with those taking part may result from evaluation apprehension, where participants demonstrate concern over what an experimenter might find out about them, or social desirability effects, where participants change their everyday behaviour so that they may be perceived more favourably by others. A further possible problem concerns the level of public knowledge (or the lack of it) about psychology – how psychology is perceived by an individual may affect their responses in the research setting.

♦ *Sampling bias* – The participants in many experimental investigations reflect an overrepresentation of males and of specific cultures, and have often been volunteers drawn from university campuses. This raises the question of the extent to which it is reasonable to generalize the results of such experimental studies to other groups of people.

♦ *Ethical issues* – Finally, ethical issues may present problems: for example, concern may arise over the issues of informed consent and deception of participants. However, it may be impossible to carry out an experiment without the researcher using some degree of deception or failing to provide full information on the procedures involved. These issues are discussed more fully in Chapter 5, *Social influence*.

Good research design can help overcome many of the potential problems associated with laboratory experiments. We will return to this issue in Chapter 7.

The field experiment

Field experiments are experimental investigations in which there is an attempt to improve realism by carrying them out in the natural environment of those being studied, e.g. in homes or schools, or on the street. As with the laboratory experiment, an independent variable is still deliberately manipulated by the researcher. Therefore, much of what has been written in the previous section about the laboratory experiment also applies to the field experiment, so this part of the chapter focuses on a discussion of the key differences.

Uses of the field experiment

The field experiment is used in situations where it is considered particularly important for research to take account of the natural environment. For example, the method is used widely when studying non-human animals (one example is the field experiment by Andersson (1982) on the behaviour of the long-tailed widow bird). A further example from the study of human behaviour comes from the study by Klaus and Kennell (1976) (see *In Focus*, 'Two examples of field experiments').

Activity 2: Looking at field experiments

Read the accounts of the field experiments undertaken by Andersson (1982) and Klaus and Kennell (1976) (see *In Focus*). Suggest reasons why you think a field experiment was used in preference to a laboratory experiment in each case.

Advantages of the field experiment

♦ *Improved ecological validity* – By avoiding the artificiality of the laboratory environment, the field experiment helps to eliminate the common criticism made of the laboratory experiment that it is difficult to generalize the findings to real-life situations. Therefore, validity is better.

♦ *Reduction of demand characteristics* – Participants may be unaware of taking part, and if this is the case, demand characteristics may be minimized.

Two examples of field experiments

Mating success of the long-tailed widow bird (Andersson 1982)

In this field experiment, Andersson demonstrated the importance of tail length to the mating success of the long-tailed widow bird, a species in which the males have very long tails. The independent variable was tail length – some individuals had their tails lengthened, others had them shortened and some had normal length tails as controls. Mating success was measured by the mean number of nests per male (the dependent variable). Those with the longest tails were the most successful; those with the shortest had the least success.

Infant-mother bonding (Klaus and Kennell 1976)

In this field experiment, the independent variable was the random allocation of mothers to one of two groups following the birth of their infants. In one group, mothers were given extra contact with their infants; in the second group, infants were separated from their mothers until their first feed (the normal hospital procedure). The dependent variable was how the mothers reacted towards their babies. Amongst the findings from the research were that mothers in the first group reacted more positively to their infants in a number of ways, such as holding their babies closer and establishing eye contact more often.

Limitations of the field experiment

◆ *Establishing controls* – It is more difficult to establish high levels of control in a field experiment than it is in a laboratory setting. This applies to the precise control over the independent variable, measuring the dependent variable and controlling any potentially confounding variables (for example, conversation from any non-participants or even their mere presence).

◆ *Generalization to other situations* – Although realism is higher in a field experiment, results cannot be generalized to other real-life situations different from the one in which the field experiment took place.

◆ *Ethical issues* – A particular ethical issue arises if participants are unaware of taking part in a psychological investigation (see Chapter 5 for more discussion of ethical issues).

◆ *Time and cost* – Field experiments may cost more than those undertaken in laboratory settings and may take longer to complete.

Activity 3: Ethical issues in field experiments

How would you feel if you had participated in a field experiment without having given your consent to take part? In what circumstances (if any) could a researcher be justified in withholding information about the purpose of a field experiment from participants? Would there be any circumstances in which deception of the participants could be justified?

◆ *Use of technical equipment* – It may be more difficult to use sophisticated equipment than it is with experiments undertaken in a laboratory setting.

◆ *Replicability* – Due to the increased difficulty of establishing control, it may be harder to replicate a field experiment than a laboratory experiment.

The natural experiment

In a natural experiment, the researcher exploits naturally occurring differences in the independent variable – therefore it is not directly controlled by the researcher. The approach can therefore best be described as *quasi-experimental* – indeed some purists might regard the method as non-experimental. For example, within a hospital setting one ward might be managed according to one management style, with a second ward adopting a different style. A natural experiment might then be carried out which compares the two styles of management. This approach would not be a true experiment as the participants would not be allocated randomly to the two conditions.

Uses of the natural experiment

The natural experiment is a method used in situations in which the psychologist can exploit a naturally occurring event. Examples can be found in the adoption studies discussed in Chapter 2, *Attachments*. An example based on witnessing violent crime is included in Fig. 6.1. Occasionally, an unforeseen event in the environment permits a natural experiment to be undertaken. Berkowitz (1970) hypothesized that

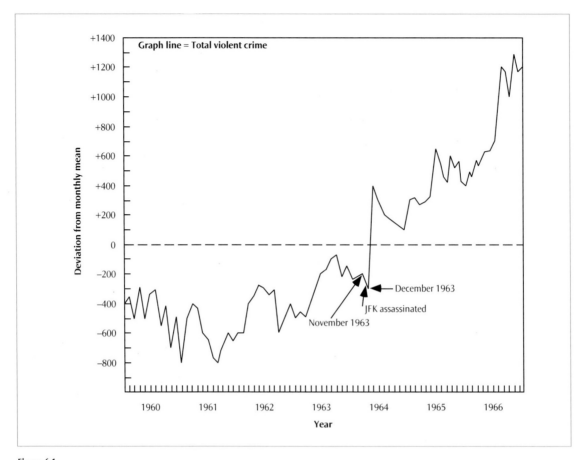

Figure 6.1
The assassination of President Kennedy and recorded levels of violence in the USA
Source: Berkowitz 1970

witnessing violence makes people more violent. He recorded and examined data on violent crime before and after the assassination in 1963 of President Kennedy in the USA, which appeared on TV in America and throughout the world. Berkowitz was able to demonstrate a sudden rise in violent crime after the assassination, thereby supporting his hypothesis. Note that the researcher here was not in full control over the independent variable.

Advantages of the natural experiment

◆ *Reduction of demand characteristics* – This approach has the advantage that participants may be unaware that they are taking part in an experiment, so demand characteristics may be avoided.

◆ *Lack of direct intervention* – The experimenter does not intervene directly in the research situation (although it is possible that the researcher's mere presence may still produce an effect).

Limitations of the natural experiment

◆ *Loss of control* – As the independent variable is not controlled by the investigator, the degree of control

exercised by the researcher is less than in both the laboratory experiment and the field experiment.

◆ *Likelihood of the desired behaviour being displayed* – The naturally occurring situation that the researcher wishes to study may occur only rarely.

◆ *Ethical issues* – If the participants are unaware of taking part, there is an issue relating to informed consent.

Summary: Experimental investigations

The experimental method is an important and powerful research tool available to the psychologist. A true experiment involves the deliberate manipulation of an independent variable by a researcher to produce a change in a dependent variable, complete control over potentially confounding variables and the random allocation of participants to conditions.

The greatest levels of control are possible in laboratory settings, but experimental research may take place outside laboratories as field experiments, or may investigate the effect of a naturally occurring event in a natural experiment. In cases such as these, the experimenter's control over events is reduced.

Non-experimental investigations in psychology

This section examines research in which an independent variable is not deliberately manipulated by a researcher. The selection of research methods outlined here allows psychologists to study behaviour in more natural settings. This potential benefit, nevertheless, has its costs: as a result of reduced levels of control, it is much harder for the researcher to reach any conclusions concerning cause and effect. The non-experimental methods discussed here are investigations employing correlational analysis, naturalistic observations, questionnaire surveys and interviews.

Investigations employing correlational analysis

The term *correlation* refers to descriptive statistical techniques which measure the relationships between variables. Literally, these techniques measure 'co-relationships' between variables – i.e. the extent to which high values on one variable are associated with high values on another (known as a *positive correlation*) or the extent to which high values on one variable are associated with low values on another (a *negative correlation*). Many correlational techniques calculate a *correlation coefficient*, a statistic which has a value on a scale between +1 (which is known as a *perfect positive correlation*) and –1 (which is known as a *perfect negative correlation*). The strength of the correlation (i.e. the degree of the relationship) increases as the calculated correlation coefficient becomes closer to +1 or –1.

The concepts associated with correlation coefficients are discussed more fully in Chapter 7.

As it is correctly a statistical technique, correlation is not strictly a research method in the truest sense of the word. Indeed, correlational techniques may be – and often are – used within experimental investigations. However, the term is also used to refer to the overall design of a non-experimental investigation which specifically attempts to identify relationships.

Uses of investigations employing correlational analysis

Correlational analysis is often used to measure the extent of relationship between variables that are thought likely to co-vary. For example, research by Bryant and Bradley (1985) established a correlation between nursery school children's rhyming abilities and their later reading skills. A further example is the research by Murstein on attractiveness (see *In Focus*).

in focus   Physical attractiveness and marital choice (Murstein 1972)

Murstein's stimulus-value-role hypothesis of marital choice proposed that individuals tend to select marital partners of comparable physical attractiveness to themselves. In two studies published in 1972, he set out to demonstrate that partners forming premarital couples show greater similarity with regard to physical attractiveness than one would expect by chance.

In the second of these studies, 98 couples described as 'engaged' or 'going steady' participated as paid volunteers. All participants were asked to rate the physical attractiveness of their partner and to estimate their own physical attractiveness, using a five-point scale. Photographs of each partner were also taken using a Polaroid camera.

The following correlation coefficients were obtained:

Relationship between:	Correlation coefficient achieved:
Male participants' perception of their own and their partners' attractiveness	+0.50
Female participants' perception of their own and their partners' attractiveness	+0.45
Independent judges' ratings of the physical attractiveness of partners	+0.38

All correlations obtained were highly significant ($p < 0.01$, meaning the likelihood of the results being due to chance was less than 1 in 100), indicating support for Murstein's hypothesis.

Another major use of correlation is in the early stages of research into a particular area, especially where it is desirable to isolate relationships from a web of complex variables. An example involves the use of the Social Readjustment Rating Scale, a technique developed by Holmes and Rahe (1967) to measure the impact of life events. Studies using this measuring instrument have found a correlation between life change units (scores derived from using the Social Readjustment Rating Scale) and, for example, the incidences of sickness or depression (see Chapter 3, *Stress*).

The correlational technique plays a major role in establishing the reliability and validity of psychological measuring instruments. For example, these techniques have played an important part in establishing the reliability and validity of psychometric tests of intelligence and personality (the concepts of reliability and validity are discussed in Chapter 7).

Advantages of investigations using correlational analysis

◆ *Measuring the strength of relationships* – Correlational techniques provide valuable information on the strength of the relationship between specific variables.

◆ *Value to exploratory research* – Correlational techniques allow for the measurement of many variables and their relationships at the same time. They are useful, therefore, when trying to unravel complex relationships and are a powerful tool for exploratory research. Conducting tests of correlation in such circumstances may suggest appropriate directions for future research.

Limitations of investigations using correlational analysis

◆ *The issue of causality* – It is impossible to establish cause and effect through research investigations using correlational analysis, which can only measure the degree of interrelationship between different variables. The presence of correlations which it would be very hard to explain causally shows that the technique only measures relationships. For example, Snedecor (1956) reported a correlation of −0.98 between production of pig iron in the USA and the birth rate in Britain for the years 1875 to 1920! This ability to detect spurious

relationships is a real drawback of the technique, so it is important that there is some link to underlying theory when a researcher decides to analyse the correlation between specific variables.

As an illustration of problems with the issue of causality, let us look briefly at the correlation which exists between the presence of symptoms of schizophrenia and the high availability of the neurotransmitter dopamine. This is a well-established correlation, but there is at the present time insufficient evidence to state that excess dopamine *causes* schizophrenia. It remains possible that it is schizophrenia which causes the increase in available dopamine, or indeed that there are other links in the causal chain which have yet to be discovered. Nevertheless, the existence of this correlation has provided an avenue for further research.

◆ *Measurement of non-linear relationships* – Non-linear relationships cannot be measured by commonly used techniques such as Spearman's Rank Order Correlation Coefficient. For example, Fig. 6.2 shows the relationship between time of day and attention level in a group of students. Initially, there is a positive correlation between the two variables, but as lunchtime approaches this changes into a negative relationship. The result is that when such data are analysed, the positive and negative relationships tend to cancel each other out, with the result that no meaningful relationship is indicated by the calculated correlation coefficient.

Figure 6.2
Relationship between time of day and attention level in students

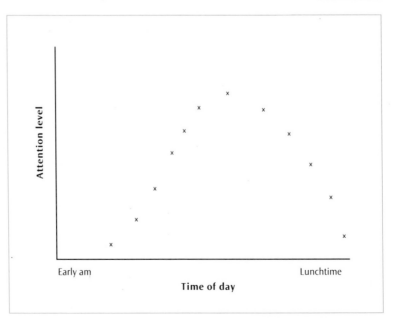

Naturalistic observation

Observation is a relatively loose term in itself, implying the scrutiny of ongoing behaviour. In this sense, it would be true to say that all psychological research involves observation. This section, however, will look at research where the deliberate manipulation of variables does not take place, and the research involves recording behaviour in its natural setting. You will remember from the discussion of experimental research earlier in this chapter that rigidly controlled research methods can be criticized on the grounds of their artificiality. Research methods such as *naturalistic observation* provide a counter to this by placing the emphasis on how people or non-human animals behave in natural situations, with no attempt being made to influence the behaviour that is being investigated. Nevertheless, this does not imply that naturalistic observation cannot be laboratory based. For example, some species adapt well to laboratory conditions, and the behaviour displayed in laboratory settings may be considered to be natural. Also, although naturalistic observation is a relatively simple concept, it must be remembered that this kind of research presents its own particular difficulties.

A distinction is usually made between *participant observation*, in which the observer actually joins the group of people being studied and *non-participant observation* in which the observer remains external to those being observed. Observers may remain *undisclosed* (where those observed remain unaware of the research being undertaken) or may be *disclosed* to those taking part (where participants are aware of the research taking place).

Uses of naturalistic observation

The very wide range of uses of naturalistic observation includes topics such as driver behaviour, the behaviour of children in nursery settings, and studies of the workplace. It is also useful where behaviour might be difficult to recreate in a laboratory setting or as a preliminary to laboratory investigation. Examples of naturalistic observational research include that by Rosenhan (1973) (see *In Focus*). Also, naturalistic observation has always been popular in ethological research with non-human animals. Examples of these include the classic research by Lorenz on imprinting (see Chapter 2, *Attachments*), and the example contained in the *In Focus* on the acquisition of new behaviours in Japanese macaques by Kawamura (1963).

Advantages of naturalistic observation

◆ *Value as a preliminary research tool* – Careful observation can lead to the suggestion of appropriate hypotheses for further investigation or, on the other hand, may help to prevent time being wasted in carrying out unrealistic experiments.

---

in focus

Two examples of naturalistic observational research

On being sane in insane places (Rosenhan 1973)

Eight individuals, all free of any psychiatric symptoms, presented themselves at different psychiatric hospitals in the USA. All reported the same symptom – they said they heard a voice say 'dull', 'empty' and 'thud'. Apart from this single symptom they were instructed to behave normally, and give honest answers to any other questions asked. All were believed to be genuine patients and were admitted to the psychiatric hospitals concerned, seven with a diagnosis of schizophrenia. On admission, they immediately ceased reporting that they had been hearing voices. They were subsequently discharged 7 to 52 days later with diagnoses of 'schizophrenia in remission'. Rosenhan attributed these diagnoses to the context in which their behaviour was observed. None actually displayed symptoms of schizophrenia, but the context in which the symptoms were reported led to an expectation that these 'pseudopatients' were indeed mentally ill.

Study of Japanese macaques (Kawamura 1963)

This study recorded the spread of new behaviours through a population of Japanese macaques on Koshima Island. Researchers observing this group of monkeys spread sweet potatoes on a beach in an attempt to lure monkeys into a situation in which their behaviour could be observed more easily. One female macaque called Imo began to use a stream to wash sand from these sweet potatoes before eating them. This habit was imitated by other members of the group, and within ten years the behaviour had been acquired by the majority of the population. Subsequently, Imo started another procedure for washing food – cleaning handfuls of grain mixed with sand in the sea. This procedure was also learned by other members of the group in a similar way.

It is a useful technique for studying unknown or little-known behaviour. For example, Clutton-Brock and his research associates have provided much of our knowledge about the behaviour of red deer through their pioneering studies carried out on the island of Rum in the Hebrides (e.g. Clutton-Brock and Albon 1979).

◆ *Validity* – Naturalistic observation can provide a useful check on whether experimental findings apply outside the laboratory. Realism and ecological validity can be good, provided that the observer remains undetected. If this is so, then it is assumed that it is natural behaviour which is being displayed. The overall quality of the research may be improved through increased familiarity with the research setting, i.e. the researcher can become a 'predictable and familiar part of the environment' with both human and non-human participants (Coolican 1999), resulting, it is hoped, in natural behaviours being observed.

◆ *Avoidance of demand characteristics* – Behaviour is affected neither by anxiety nor by inhibition which results from being in a laboratory situation. Also, with undisclosed naturalistic observation, there will be no feeling of a need to impress the researcher (providing, of course, the observer remains undetected).

◆ *Use where experimentation is inappropriate* – The method can be used where experimental intervention is inappropriate (e.g. when studying weddings or funerals) or unethical (e.g. intervention with children). Also, it may be used where it is desirable to acknowledge the wider social context of observed behaviour.

◆ *Study of species which do not adapt to laboratory conditions* – With non-human animals, naturalistic observation is also of value when studying species which fail to thrive in laboratory conditions (e.g. red deer or marine mammals).

Limitations of naturalistic observation

◆ *Control* – Controls over potentially confounding variables are poor (although some degree of control is often possible), and cause and effect cannot be established with any certainty.

◆ *Observer effects* – It is possible that the presence of an observer may change behaviour, especially when it is a small group that is being studied. This can also be an issue when observing non-human animals. For example, breeding patterns may be disturbed by the mere presence of an observer (e.g. when recording the breeding patterns of seabirds on uninhabited islands).

◆ *Ethical issues* – Ethical issues such as deception and the invasion of privacy can be a problem, especially if the observation remains undisclosed to those taking part. The need to respect private behaviour in public places presents particular difficulties. As a general rule, an observer should not carry out research if it is considered that participants would refuse to take part if they were given the opportunity to do so (see Chapter 5 for a discussion of the ethical principles governing such research).

◆ *Observer bias* – The potential exists for bias on the part of observers, deriving from their expectations or interpretations of events.

Activity 4: **Observing people**
Imagine you observe someone screaming in the street. Write down the different ways in which you might interpret this behaviour.

◆ *Costs* – There may be problems with costs: for example, the costs of travel or of transporting recording equipment.

◆ *Difficulty of replication* – Replication may be difficult due to the problems which arise in controlling variables, such as differences in naturalistic settings.

◆ *Structuring of data* – There may be limitations concerning how any data gathered are structured. This then places restrictions on the interpretations of behaviour which can be made (i.e. behaviour which doesn't fit into the categories which have been used).

◆ *Missing behaviour* – While the researcher is recording behaviour, there is a potential problem that further behaviour may be missed. This problem may be minimized with the use of sound or video recordings.

◆ *Generalizability of the findings* – It may be difficult or impossible to generalize results to other occasions or other settings.

◆ *Studying unusual phenomena* – This may prove to be difficult: for example, the responses of individuals to events such as natural disasters. Indeed, even relatively common behaviours might not be produced within the timespan of an observational study.

◆ *Reliability* – Low inter-observer reliability may be a problem, even after observer training has taken place, since we all see the world from our own unique viewpoint. For example, identical behaviour in children might be classified as 'aggressive' by one researcher or as 'rough and tumble play' by another.

◆ *Study of non-human animals* – Certain practical difficulties exist when studying non-human animals: for example, when individual members of a species appear very similar to each other (e.g. small brown birds) or when species live up trees, underground, under water, fly, move quickly or are nocturnal.

We will return to some of the ways in which some of these difficulties may be overcome in Chapter 7.

Questionnaire surveys

A questionnaire survey involves asking participants questions about, for example, their attitudes, behaviours or intentions. The use of a questionnaire allows the researcher to gain information from large numbers of participants relatively quickly and efficiently. The aim is to obtain information from a specified population of interest to the researcher, usually by administering a questionnaire to a sample of this population. The method can be used to gain information where a pen-and-paper method is appropriate. The researcher does not need to be present when the questionnaire is administered (although the researcher's presence may be helpful to answer any queries). Questionnaire surveys can be conducted by post, telephone, via the Internet or left for participants to collect from some central point.

Questions can be of two broad types:

◆ *Closed questions* are those where the researcher determines the range of possible answers (respondents often reply by ticking boxes or circling appropriate answers). These questions are best used when factual information is required. They produce information which is easy to analyse but which may lack realism due to the forced choices of answers available to the respondents. Examples of different forms of closed questions are shown in Fig. 6.3.

◆ *Open-ended* questions are those in which the researcher does not restrict the range of available answers (e.g. 'What are your views on the use of corporal punishment by parents?'). This produces a greater depth of qualitative information, but at a cost – answers are often harder to analyse as the range of possible answers is so wide.

Good practice when carrying out questionnaire surveys is to keep the number of questions to a minimum, use short questions and phrase these questions clearly in

Figure 6.3 Some forms of closed questions

◆ *Checklists* – where respondents tick any items that apply.

For example: 'Please tick the subjects in the following list which you studied at GCSE level.'

☐ Art   ☐ English   ☐ History
☐ Geography   ☐ Mathematics   ☐ Psychology
☐ Science   ☐ Sociology

◆ *Placing items in rank order*

For example: 'Place a number against each of your GCSE subjects, placing them in rank order from most liked (given the number 1) to least liked.'

◆ *Attitude scales*

For example: Underline the response that best reflects your attitude to the statement: 'A University education is essential if you are to succeed in the employment market.'

Do you: Strongly disagree
Disagree
Neither disagree or agree
Agree
Strongly agree.

◆ *Likert scales* – based on a numerical rating.

For example: 'How important are the following factors to the relationship between you and your partner? (Please circle the appropriate number.)'

	Very Important	Neither important nor unimportant		Very unimportant
Sense of humour	1	2	3	4	5
Common interests	1	2	3	4	5
Mutual respect	1	2	3	4	5

◆ *Semantic differential scales* – where respondents are asked to rate items on scales based on a series of pairs of opposite adjectives.

For example: 'How would you rate your feelings about your A-level Psychology course? (Place a tick at the appropriate point on each scale)'

Warm | | | | | | | | *Cold*
Satisfied | | | | | | | | *Dissatisfied*

order to avoid any misunderstandings. Emotionally charged questions should be avoided.

Ideally, any questionnaire should be properly piloted before it is administered. (Pilot studies are discussed in Chapter 7.)

Uses of questionnaire surveys

Questionnaire surveys are very widely used by psychological researchers. They produce descriptive and/or explanatory information that can be tailored to fit a very wide range of research situations. They can be carried out as a 'one-off', or more powerfully, they can be conducted both before and after some event in order to examine the impact of that event. Their flexibility is also demonstrated by the fact that they are valuable both as a preliminary research tool and as a source of in-depth information on some topic of interest. Examples of well-known questionnaires include the Social Readjustment Rating Scale (Holmes and Rahe 1967), described in Chapter 3, *Stress*, and the Hassles and Uplifts Scale (Kanner *et al.* 1981) (see *In Focus*).

The advantages of questionnaire surveys

◆ *Versatility* – Questionnaires can be used in a very wide range of research situations.

◆ *Simplicity* – Once they have been constructed, questionnaires involve a well-understood technology and can be carried out with a minimum of training.

◆ *Speed* – A large amount of information can be gathered from a large number of respondents in a short time.

◆ *Ease of analysis* – Data from closed questions are often easy to analyse. It is often easy to compare answers from different individuals or groups of respondents.

◆ *Range of data* – Both qualitative and quantitative data may be produced.

◆ *Cost* – Large amounts of data can be gathered relatively cheaply.

Limitations of questionnaire surveys

◆ *Untruthful answers* – There is no guarantee that respondents answer questions truthfully (see also 'Social desirability bias' below).

◆ *Researcher effects* – If a researcher administers the questionnaire personally, then respondents may be influenced by such factors as the researcher's ethnic origin, age, appearance or gender. Even unintentional nods, smiles or frowns may have an effect.

◆ *Difficulty with controls* – It is hard to ensure that survey data are collected under controlled conditions and that other uncontrolled variables do not influence responses.

◆ *Imprecise wording of questions* – Different respondents may answer in different ways if questions are at all ambiguous.

◆ *Leading questions* – These may influence responses. For example, it is quite clear what answer is being encouraged by the question: 'Don't you think that spending money on education is good?'

◆ *Different interpretations of language* – For example, there may be different interpretations of the term 'rarely' with regard to a question on days off work due to illness. To one person, 'rarely' may mean once or twice a month, to another, once or twice a year.

◆ *Social desirability bias* – Respondents may not provide truthful answers, especially to personal or potentially embarrassing questions. They may wish their answers to be seen in the best possible light.

◆ *Researcher bias* – This may be a problem when data are interpreted. Imagine a situation where a

---

Hassles and Uplifts (Kanner *et al.* 1981)

This scale was developed as an alternative to the Social Readjustment Rating Scale for predicting the onset of psychological symptoms. *Hassles* are the irritations and frustrations of everyday life, whereas *uplifts* are positive experiences. The particular version developed by the researchers for this study consisted of 117 hassles and 135 uplifts that might occur regarding health, work, the family, friends or through chance. Participants were asked to rate how often each hassle or uplift had occurred in the last month on a 3-point scale.

Examples of hassles included misplacing or losing things, filling out forms, being exploited and traffic. Uplifts included being lucky, friendly neighbours, eating out and buying clothes. The researchers concluded that this scale may be better at predicting the onset of psychological symptoms than the Social Readjustment Rating Scale.

researcher provides one possible answer on a questionnaire that is perceived as being more socially desirable than other possible answers. Responses in this category might be wrongly interpreted as providing genuine support for the researcher's particular (biased) viewpoint. (See Chapter 7 for more about wording questionnaires.)

Interviews

The interview is a common way of carrying out research; it may form the basis of a case study or may be used as one of the ways of conducting a survey. Most research establishes some kind of distance between the researcher and the researched, but this kind of approach is challenged by the face-to-face nature of the interview, which is both personal and public in its nature. An important tool for the research psychologist, the interview needs an explicit purpose and aims to encourage the flow of information from the interviewee to the interviewer. In some instances, the focus of an interview may be negotiated between interviewer and interviewee – notice the key difference here from the experimental approach, in which the research focus is always predetermined by the researcher. Consequently, interviews are both diverse in their nature and specific to a particular research situation. Their diversity also means that interviewing is a skill that requires careful development.

Interviews need careful planning and piloting (see Chapter 7), and vary in the extent to which they are structured or unstructured. At one end of this continuum, *structured interviews* usually aim to produce quantitative data and include questions which are decided in advance with the aim of structuring the interviewee's responses. The structured interview has several *advantages*. The interviewer and interviewee are less likely to deviate from the topic that is the subject of the interview. Also, data analysis may be simpler, results are easier to generalize, less training is needed for interviewers and there is less risk of the results being affected by interviewer bias, since the interviewer is more likely to be objective. However, there are *costs* as well as benefits. The researcher cannot follow up any new lines of enquiry which become apparent during the interview, and validity may be threatened by participants reacting to the formality of the research situation.

At the other end of the continuum are *unstructured interviews*. These are far less rigid and very little, if anything, concerning their nature will be decided in advance. These can be more difficult to analyse, but have greater validity as interviewees will be more likely to report whatever they wish to say and the interviewers can be flexible in their approach.

Activity 5: Conducting interviews
Try conducting two interviews on a topic of your choice. Obtain two volunteers; use a structured interview technique with the first and an unstructured interview technique with the other person. What differences do you note in your findings?

The *semi-structured interview* is often the most successful approach, with the use of some prepared questions by the interviewer, supplemented by opportunities for the interviewee to expand the answers that have been given.

Uses of the interview

An interview may provide information additional to that obtained from other research methods. For example, Milgram (1963) enriched his work on obedience by interviewing his participants after they had completed the experimental procedure. Two areas where the approach has been of particular value are social psychology (see, for example, the use of interviews in the research on conformity by Asch, discussed in Chapter 5) and psychopathology (for example, in exploring the family histories of sufferers from anxiety disorders). See *In Focus*, 'Cognitive maps', for a further example showing the use of interviews.

The advantages of the interview

Two of the major reasons for using interviews have been outlined by Banister *et al.* (1994):

◆ Interviews enable the researcher to *gain subjective meanings* (those that participants attribute to the topic of the interview) rather than obtaining responses within a standard format.

◆ The interview can *permit complex issues to be explored*. These are difficult to investigate through quantitative techniques, which may lead to an oversimplification of the issues in hand (i.e. making the participants' real views hard to represent). Interviewing, however, may explore precisely those areas where other research methods present difficulties. The interviewer can also tailor questions to the responses of the interviewee so that issues can be explored which the researchers had not envisaged initially. In other words, interviews allow *flexibility* in questioning and the possibility of uncovering perspectives unobtainable by other research methods.

In addition, interviews may permit researchers to *identify personal aspects of behaviour*. If carried out

in focus

Cognitive maps (Lynch 1960)

Lynch (1960) was interested in environmental perception and, in particular, in the cognitive maps people have of their home areas. He interviewed residents in three American cities (Boston, Jersey City and Los Angeles) about their feelings for local landmarks, and also about major routes and the areas that they passed through when driving around. From his interviews, he was able to produce a general image of each city that identified the basic units of the urban landscape. Often, participants were able to point out distinctive features of the urban landscape, which were not always the tallest or skyline features but rather things on a more human scale, such as a well-known building or open space. However, interviewees also tended to have been to areas of the cities which they were unable to describe. Information gained in this way of the knowledge that people have about their own cities has been used to practical effect in urban planning. For example, the work of Goodey (1971) on residents' cognitive maps of Birmingham was used to help planners develop their future vision of the city.

sensitively, the interview will permit knowledge to be gained about aspects of behaviour which are private or personal to the individuals concerned.

Limitations of the interview

'Conducting interviews is a complex, labour intensive and uncertain business, fraught with tricky issues that social scientific researchers, and particularly psychologists, are often ill-equipped to address' (Banister *et al.* 1994).

◆ *Interpreting data* – Misinterpretation or partial interpretation of data may take place. The interviewer needs to be detached from the interviewee, which can be difficult to achieve in face-to-face situations with their potential for bias.

◆ *Limitations in interviewees' responses* – A particular problem with interviews is that interviewees may be unable to put their thoughts precisely into words.

◆ *Ethical issues* – Ethical issues arise, e.g. participants may be deceived if the true purpose of the interview is disguised. There is a need to understand the position of power that the interviewer is in and to show respect for participants' views. This is particularly important in relation to potentially sensitive topics, such as asking parents about how they brought up their children, including the use of discipline within the home.

◆ *Interviewer effects* – The appearance of the interviewer may produce effects (e.g. as a result of their ethnic group, age, gender, physical attractiveness or mode of dress).

◆ *Demand characteristics* – There may also be effects on the interviewees such as social desirability bias,

where a participant gives answers which are considered to be 'socially acceptable' and which may not actually represent their personal views on the topic under investigation.

◆ *Difficulties of analysing data* – Qualitative data obtained from unstructured interviews may not be easy to analyse.

Summary: Non-experimental investigations

Psychologists use a wide range of non-experimental methods and techniques to study behaviour. These include correlational studies, naturalistic observations, questionnaire surveys and interviews.

The aim of investigations using correlational analysis is to establish relationships between variables. It is not possible to establish cause-and-effect links in research using correlational analysis.

Naturalistic observation has been widely used in studies of animal behaviour. When used to study human behaviour, naturalistic observation raises ethical issues concerned with privacy and consent.

Questionnaire surveys enable psychologists to collect large amounts of data quickly. Possible limitations of questionnaire surveys include researcher bias, difficulties of wording questions precisely and respondents wishing to present themselves in a favourable light.

Interviews can be structured, semi-structured or unstructured. Interviews can be used to explore issues which other techniques cannot investigate.

Both naturalistic observation and interview techniques have the advantage of increased ecological validity when compared with experimental methods.

Chapter summary

◆ Psychologists have adopted a range of research methods when investigating their subject matter. No single method is appropriate or successful in all circumstances and in all contexts.

◆ **Experimental methods** rely on the manipulation and control of independent, dependent and confounding variables, and the random allocation of participants, to produce quantifiable results and establish cause-and-effect relationships.

◆ **Experimental methods** provide the highest levels of control, but at the cost of a reduction in ecological validity.

◆ The experimenter usually has greatest control in **laboratory** settings. **Field experiments** can give greater validity, but usually at the cost of some control and possibly replicability. **Natural**

experiments are sometimes regarded as quasi-experimental, using naturally occurring events over which the researcher does not have full control.

◆ Investigations using **correlational analysis** allow researchers to obtain measures of the relationship between variables, but do not allow the research to establish cause-and-effect relationships.

◆ **Naturalistic observational** studies provide the researcher with an ecologically valid technique. However, establishing controls may be difficult, making it difficult to generalize the results.

◆ **Questionnaire surveys** allow the gathering of a large amount of information quickly and efficiently.

◆ **Interviews** allow the flexible exploration of detailed issues, some of which may not have been envisaged at the outset by interviewer or interviewee.

Exam summary

The AQA examination will test your knowledge of the following (in conjunction with the topics covered in Chapter 7):

◆ the experimental method, its advantages and disadvantages – laboratory (pp. 134–6), field (pp. 136–7) and natural experiments (pp. 137–8).

◆ investigations using correlational analysis, their advantages and disadvantages (pp. 139–40)

◆ naturalistic observations, their advantages and disadvantages (pp. 141–3)

◆ questionnaire surveys, their advantages and disadvantages (pp. 143–5)

◆ interviews, their advantages and disadvantages (pp. 145–6)

◆ the use of ethical guidelines (pp. 125–30).

You will find two example Research Methods questions at the end of Chapter 7 (see pp. 176–8).

Further resources

Banister, P., Burman, E., Parker, I., Taylor, M. and Tindall, C. (1994) *Qualitative Methods in Psychology: A Research Guide*, Buckingham: Open University Press.

An advanced text which covers observations and interviews.

Foster, J.J. and Parker, I. (1995) *Carrying out Investigations in Psychology: Methods and Statistics*, Leicester: BPS Books.

A detailed and advanced text which is useful for reference purposes.

Coolican, H. (1995) *Introduction to Research Methods and Statistics in Psychology*, London: Hodder & Stoughton.

A condensed version of the Coolican (1999) text.

Coolican, H. (1999) *Research Methods and Statistics in Psychology*, London: Hodder & Stoughton.

A clearly written text which covers the research methods included in the AEB syllabus.

continued on p. 148

Dyer, C. (1995) *Beginning Research in Psychology: A Practical Guide to Research Methods and Statistics,* Oxford: Blackwell.

> *A detailed text with useful sections on non-experimental methods.*

Searle, A. (1999) *Introducing Research and Data in Psychology,* London: Routledge.

> *An easily accessible text that provides a basic introduction to research methods.*

Websites

See the suggestions given at the end of Chapter 7 (p. 179)

Research design and implementation, and data analysis

Graham Davies

Preview

In this chapter we shall be looking at the following aspects of psychological investigations:

◆ generating aims and formulating hypotheses

◆ research designs: experimental (independent groups, repeated measures and matched participants) and non-experimental (naturalistic observational studies, questionnaire surveys and interviews)

◆ factors associated with research design: the control of variables, operationalization of independent and dependent variables, conducting pilot studies, techniques for assessing and improving reliability and validity, ethics

◆ methods of selecting participants

◆ the relationship between researchers and participants

◆ the analysis of qualitative data derived from naturalistic observational studies, questionnaire surveys and interviews

◆ descriptive statistical techniques, including measures of central tendency and measures of dispersion

◆ the use and interpretation of graphs and charts

◆ the nature of positive and negative correlations, and the interpretation of correlation coefficients.

Introduction

Chapter 6 discussed some of the research methods most widely used by psychologists. This chapter covers a wide range of issues associated with the design and implementation of these research methods and examines some of the ways that the results of investigations can be analysed.

We begin by considering the generation of appropriate aims and the formulation of appropriate hypotheses. We then move on to examine different experimental designs as well as the designs of non-experimental investigations. A range of factors associated with research designs are discussed, including the operationalization and control of variables, the nature of pilot studies and how two extremely important factors in research – reliability and validity – can be assessed and improved. The major sampling methods that psychologists use to obtain their participants are discussed. The chapter continues by examining the relationship between researchers and participants in psychological research.

The last part of this chapter looks at some of the ways in which psychologists analyse their data, and some of the issues which arise from this analysis. You may recall from Chapter 6 that the data derived from psychological investigations can be of different types. *Quantitative data* are measured on a numerical basis – for example, something is categorized, placed in rank order or measured in units of measurement. On the other hand, *qualitative data* do not have numbers attached to them, but consist of descriptions of what took place, e.g. transcripts of conversations. It is possible that such data may subsequently be quantified, although it is their very qualitative nature that may help to provide insights that would not be apparent with a quantitative approach. To a certain extent, whether quantitative or qualitative data are obtained depends on the standpoint of the person conducting the research – an issue which has already been discussed in Chapter 6. It also depends on the aims of the research and the topic under investigation.

In considering the different ways in which psychologists analyse their data, this chapter explores some of the opportunities available. It examines the qualitative methods of analysis used in association with naturalistic observational studies, questionnaire surveys and interviews. It also looks at the interpretation of quantitative data using descriptive statistical techniques. Analysis using inferential statistical techniques is also widely employed in psychology but this is beyond the scope of the AS specification. However, those of you continuing to study psychology at A level will become familiar with one or more of these inferential tests when you analyse the data from your coursework.

Aims and hypotheses

Generating appropriate aims

The starting point for any piece of psychological research is generating appropriate *aims* for the idea that you wish to investigate. In order to generate these aims successfully, you need to know the intended purpose of the investigation, i.e. what the research investigation in question is actually trying to discover. In some non-experimental studies, the aims may be fairly wide, particularly in investigations in which qualitative data are being analysed. In experimental investigations (and indeed in others where quantitative data are produced), the aim may be to test one or more hypotheses.

Formulating hypotheses

A *hypothesis* can be defined simply as a testable statement. The *research hypothesis* is a general prediction made at the beginning of an investigation about what the researcher expects to happen. However, in order to assist the analysis of data obtained from any research investigation, it is essential to phrase the hypothesis carefully, so that it is clear and testable. This is the process of *hypothesis formulation*, i.e. stating it in precise terms. For example, consider the research hypothesis that 'leading questions affect eyewitness testimony'. In the form presented here, this begs too many questions to be tested precisely. For instance, what kind of leading question are we talking about, or in what ways is the testimony of witnesses affected? If this statement is to be converted into a format useful for the analysis of results data, then its wording must be completely free from ambiguity. Try Activity 1 before reading any further.

Activity 1: Phrasing hypotheses

Try to rephrase the above hypothesis about eyewitness testimony in a precisely testable form.

You probably came up with a more specific statement – something along the lines of 'More witnesses report seeing a knife in a given scene when a leading question suggests the existence of a knife as a murder weapon'. This formulation process serves to highlight a fundamental issue concerning experimental research. On the one hand, the original statement is so general in its nature that it is difficult to test. On the other hand, the version based on operationalized variables, despite having the important advantages of being more clearly defined and testable, may lack more general

application (see p. 158 for a discussion of the operationalization of variables).

Null and alternative hypotheses

Researchers refer to two different hypotheses when analysing their data: the null hypothesis and the alternative hypothesis. The *null hypothesis* predicts that the results obtained from an investigation are due to chance alone. For example, in an experiment investigating the effect of an mnemonic on memory recall, the null hypothesis would predict that any differences in observed outcome are due to chance, rather than to the effect of the *independent variable* (the mnemonic). The task of the researcher is to decide whether the null hypothesis should be retained or rejected. If the likelihood of the results occurring by chance is remote, then the null hypothesis can be rejected and we may prefer to accept the *alternative hypothesis* (in an experiment this may be termed the *experimental hypothesis*). This predicts that something other than chance alone has played a part in producing the results obtained. Only if the design of the investigation is completely watertight will we be left with just one explanation for the results (i.e. that the independent variable is responsible for the outcome). In practice, reaching such a definite conclusion can be difficult.

Alternative hypotheses can be described as being directional or non-directional:

◆ A *directional hypothesis* predicts the direction in which results are expected to occur: for example, 'rehearsal using a mnemonic technique improves the recall of words'.

◆ A *non-directional hypothesis*, however, does not predict the expected direction of outcome. For example, 'there is a difference in the number of words recalled from word lists presented with or without background music'.

Directional and non-directional hypotheses are referred to in many texts as *one-tailed* and *two-tailed* hypotheses respectively. However, the terms directional and non-directional hypothesis are preferred.

The null hypothesis can thus be regarded as the hypothesis which states that the alternative hypothesis is untrue. It is the most important of the hypotheses, as it is the null hypothesis which is actually tested when inferential statistical tests are applied to data. Knowledge of this is beyond the scope of the AS Psychology specification, but those of you continuing to A level will need to apply one or more of these tests in your coursework.

Activity 2: Devising hypotheses

Select four areas of psychological research which you have studied.

1 Devise research hypotheses for each, together with null and alternative hypotheses which might be appropriate in these areas.

2 Provide an example of a directional and a non-directional alternative hypothesis in each case.

Summary: Aims and hypothesis

The aims of a piece of psychological research reflect the purpose of the investigation; they can be fairly wide, or more specific, to test one or more hypotheses.

A hypothesis can be defined as a testable statement. A null hypothesis predicts that the results obtained from an investigation are due to chance alone. An alternative hypothesis, which can be directional or non-directional, attributes the results to a factor other than chance, such as to the effects of the independent variable.

Research designs

This section begins with a review of some of the key decisions that the psychological researcher must take. After looking at some of the most common experimental designs, we shall then discuss design issues associated with naturalistic observations, questionnaire surveys and interviews.

Key decisions

When undertaking research, a number of key decisions need to be taken. These may include the following.

Deciding on an appropriate research method

The researcher must decide which research method(s) to use and when it is appropriate to use them.

Deciding how many participants to use

The researcher conducting an experiment or questionnaire survey will usually decide how many participants to use. However, the non-experimental researcher will sometimes have no control over this and will need to use whoever is available. In some examples of qualitative research (e.g. research based on interviews), there will be only a single participant. However, there will be occasions when the researcher does have a choice. As a general rule, the larger the sample, the less biased it is likely to be; 25 or 30 is often regarded as a reasonable number in a small-scale study when quantitative data are to be collected and analysed.

Using an appropriate sampling method

Where a sample of participants is selected to represent some larger population, the researcher will need to decide on a sampling method that is appropriate for the task in hand. Also, the researcher will need to decide how representative the participants are of a particular target population.

(Sampling methods are discussed later in this chapter.)

Deciding how to brief participants

An important question is whether participants should be aware or unaware of taking part in research, or of the specific nature of the investigation. This raises the ethical issue of informed consent (see Chapter 5). Sometimes researchers disclose their intent to participants (this is usual in the case of questionnaire surveys, interviews and many experiments) and may even spend a period of time getting to know them before the research is carried out. It is hoped that this will encourage more natural behaviour. With naturalistic observation, the researcher may choose whether or not to let participants know that an investigation is being carried out on them.

Deciding the medium for recording data

The researcher will need to have a clearly defined medium for recording data. A written record may be made (often by the participant in the case of questionnaire surveys or many experiments), or behaviour may be recorded, e.g. on video or audio tape, for subsequent analysis. A combination of these methods is commonly used. The researcher will need to decide which behaviour to record and which to ignore. If a written record is made, the researcher may need to devise an appropriate coding system for recording behaviour (an example is provided later in the chapter (see Fig. 7.3).

Deciding the techniques for recording behaviour

The method used may be highly structured, as in many experiments, questionnaire surveys and some naturalistic observational studies; or may be unstructured, as in some interviews. The aim is to obtain data which are sufficiently explicit to enable appropriate analysis of the results.

Designing experiments

Selecting an appropriate experimental design is a crucial decision which is essential for the success or otherwise of an experimental investigation. The selection process involves balancing the advantages and disadvantages of the different designs which are available to the psychologist. When planning an experiment, it should be borne in mind that the aims of a successful design are to:

◆ provide an overall plan for the experiment

◆ try and ensure precision of measurement

◆ enable experimental results to be analysed to their full potential

◆ avoid potential sources of ambiguity or confusion

◆ ensure high levels of control over the different variables.

When deciding on an appropriate design to use, the researcher must consider carefully the precise nature of the experimental task to be undertaken, how to control relevant variables and the availability of participants. This section considers the three experimental designs that AS level students are likely to come into contact with:

◆ the independent groups design

◆ the repeated measures design

◆ the matched participants design.

These are only three of the many designs available to the experimenter. You can find out further information by looking at specialist texts such as those by Coolican (1995, 1999) or Dyer (1995).

Independent groups design

An *independent groups design* involves using different participants in each of the conditions of the experiment. (You may see this referred to as an independent measures/participants/subjects/samples design, or as a between groups/participants/subjects/samples design.) Experiments with this design may consist of:

◆ a control condition and one or more experimental conditions, or

◆ two (or more) experimental conditions.

See Fig. 7.1 for an example of how this design might appear in practice.

In the former case, the group of participants that is given the experimental treatment is referred to as the *experimental condition*, and the group that exists for comparison and which receives no treatment is the *control condition*.

In true experiments, participants are allocated *randomly* to each of the conditions (i.e. allocated to the conditions in such a way that each participant stands an equal chance of being selected for each condition). The random allocation of participants aims to ensure that participant variables do not differ systematically between each condition. Otherwise, individual differences relevant to the experiment concerned might lead to results being *confounded*. (A discussion of confounding can be found on p. 158.)

For example, if an experiment was carried out on learning ability, it would be undesirable to have all the fastest learners allocated to the same condition. However, you should not interpret this as suggesting that random allocation will produce groups of participants which have identical characteristics. You may still, through chance, fail to eliminate differences as a factor and allocate all the fastest learners to one group. However, the chance of this happening is minimal. For example, imagine the likelihood of the numbers one to six inclusive coming up in that order on the National Lottery, or the probability of dealing out all four suits of a pack of cards in both suit and number order. The chances of these happening are extremely remote – but of course any single combination, such as those just described, is as likely to

Figure 7.1 Allocation of participants in three different experimental designs

1   The independent groups design:

Participants (Ps) may be allocated to the conditions randomly. For example:

Condition A	Condition B
P1	P3
P2	P5
P4	P6 ..... *and so on.*

2   Repeated measures design:

Each participant undertakes all conditions of the experiment. For example:

Condition A	Condition B
P1	P1
P2	P2
P3	P3 ..... *and so on.*

3   Matched participants design:

Pairs of participants are matched on appropriate variables relevant to the experiment; the members of each pair are then allocated to each condition (sometimes randomly). For example:

Condition A	Condition B
P1a	P1b
P2a	P2b
P3b	P3a ..... *and so on.*

happen as any other single combination. However, by randomly allocating participants, the researcher avoids any conscious or subconscious bias in participant allocation. Provided that the independent groups design is suitable for the proposed experiment, the probability is high that individual differences will not be significant as a confounding factor.

The random allocation of participants to conditions can be achieved in several ways. The simplest method is to draw names from a hat. A more sophisticated way is to employ a random number table. (The Appendix on p. 180 contains a random number table together with an explanation of how to use it.)

In *natural experiments* (see Chapter 6), the allocation of participants to conditions is decided by the naturally occurring event, which is treated as the independent variable. For example, if the independent variable is the management style of two different hospital wards, then the experimenter will not have complete control over the allocation of participants to conditions. This kind of technique is properly regarded as *quasi-experimental.*

An independent groups design has a great *advantage* resulting from the different participants used in each condition – there is no problem with *order effects*. These occur when participants' performance is positively affected by their taking part in two or more experimental conditions. For example, their performance in a second or subsequent condition may be helped through the practice of a task which they undertook in a previous condition. Alternatively, order effects may have a negative effect occurring through fatigue or boredom. This freedom from order effects means that the independent groups design has a wide range of potential uses and can be used freely where problems with order effects would make a repeated measures design impractical.

However, the design also has *disadvantages.* The most serious is the potential for error resulting from individual differences between the groups of participants taking part in the different conditions. Also, if participants are in short supply, then an independent groups design may represent an uneconomic use of those available to participate, since twice as many participants are needed to obtain the same amount of data as would be required in a two-condition, repeated measures design.

Repeated measures design

A *repeated measures design* involves exposing every participant to each of the experimental conditions, so, in effect, participants are used as their own controls. (You may also see this referred to as related measures/samples, or within participants/subjects design). Figure 7.1 provides an example of how participants might be

arranged in an experiment using this design. One of the conditions in experiments using this design may be a control condition, which serves the same purpose as the control condition in an independent groups design, i.e. to provide a baseline against which responses from any experimental condition can be compared.

Activity 3: Assessing the repeated measures design

Look back at the advantages and disadvantages of an independent groups design. Bearing in mind these strengths and weaknesses, what do you think are the advantages and disadvantages of the repeated measures design?

The key *advantage* of a repeated measures design is that individual differences between participants are removed as a potential confounding variable (you may recall that this was a major drawback of the independent groups design). Also, the repeated measures design requires fewer participants, since data for all conditions derive from the same group of participants.

This design also has its *disadvantages.* The range of potential uses is smaller than for the independent groups design. For example, it simply is not possible to use two different reading schemes to teach young children to read within the same group of children. Only an independent groups design could be employed. Also, there is a potential disadvantage resulting from order effects which may result when participants take part in more than one experimental condition. (You may remember that order effects can confound experimental results in two ways: either negatively through the effects of fatigue or boredom, or positively through the effects of learning or practice.)

There are, however, ways in which the potential risks of order effects on results in a repeated measures design can be minimized. These are known as counterbalancing and randomization. The *counterbalancing* concept is simple, and involves equal numbers of participants undertaking the tasks required of them in different orders. Figure 7.2 shows two examples of how this might take place, with participants performing the conditions alternately until all participants have been tested.

Notice from Fig. 7.2 that there needs to be an even number of participants if counterbalancing is to be implemented fully. In the first example, a multiple of two participants would be required and in the second a multiple of six, reflecting in each case the number of possible task orders.

Counterbalancing in a two-condition experiment:

Participant number	First condition undertaken	Second condition undertaken	
1	A	B	
2	B	A	
3	A	B	
4	B	A	... and so on

Counterbalancing in a three-condition experiment:

Participant number	First condition undertaken	Second condition undertaken	Third condition undertaken
1	A	B	C
2	B	C	A
3	C	A	B
4	A	C	B
5	B	A	C
6	C	B	A
			... and so on

Figure 7.2
Examples of how counterbalancing might take place in two- and three-condition experiments

Occasionally, however, it is not possible to apply counterbalancing as a strategy for minimizing order effects. Problems can occur when order effects influence one condition more than another. This can take place, for example, when performing one condition helps the performance of another more than the other way round.

Consider the following memory experiment:

◆ Condition A: Learning a set of words presented randomly.

◆ Condition B: Learning a matched set of words using a mnemonic technique to assist memory.

There may be no problem when participants undertake condition A first, followed by condition B. However, when condition A is presented after condition B, it is likely that participants still have the mnemonic technique fresh in their minds. As a result, condition B might help performance on condition A more than A helps B, which is likely to lead to confounding of the results. In such circumstances, counterbalancing would be inappropriate and a researcher would be advised to use an independent groups design.

Randomization is an alternative technique to counterbalancing for dealing with the potential problems resulting from order effects. It involves adopting a random strategy for deciding the order of presentation of experimental conditions by, for example, drawing lots or tossing a coin. This procedure,

however, fails to provide a guarantee that presentation order of conditions will not influence results, because it is still possible, through chance, that differences will remain in the numbers of participants experiencing the conditions in particular orders.

Randomization can also be used as a technique for deciding the order of presentation of, for example, individual stimuli within experimental conditions. It works best when there is a large number of items within each condition. For example, suppose an investigation involves each participant rating 20 photographs for their attractiveness. If the same presentation order is followed by all participants, then some biases in rating may occur (for example, the picture presented first is likely to be given an average rating by many participants, simply because they are rating this picture conservatively as they feel they may wish to use more extreme ratings for subsequent pictures).

Finally, before leaving the repeated measures design, it is worth pointing out that it is possible to combine an independent groups and a repeated measures design. Such mixed designs are in frequent usage. For example, children from two different age groups might be given two different cognitive tasks. The independent element of the design would involve a comparison of the two age groups, and the repeated measures element would be a comparison of performance on the two cognitive tasks.

Matched participants design

A *matched participants design* (or matched subjects/ pairs design) aims to gain the key advantages of both an independent groups design (no problems with order effects as different people are used in each condition), and a repeated measures design (a greatly reduced risk of problems resulting from individual differences as participants are matched). It involves matching each participant in one of the experimental conditions as closely as possible with another participant in the second condition on variables which are considered to be relevant to the experiment in question. For example, pairs of participants might be matched for age, gender and their scores from intelligence or personality tests. Once pairs of participants have been identified, members of each pair can be randomly allocated to the conditions (see Fig. 7.1). The assumption made is that members of each pairing are so similar on the relevant variables that they can, for research purposes at least, be treated as if they are the same person. At the same time, however, participants perform in one condition of the experiment only.

Although this design combines the key *advantages* of both an independent groups and a repeated measures design, there is a *disadvantage*. Achieving matched pairs of participants is a difficult and time-consuming task which may be too costly to undertake. Successful use of a matched participants design is heavily dependent on the use of reliable and valid procedures for pre-testing participants to obtain the matched pairs. Complete matching of participants on all variables which might affect experimental performance can rarely be achieved. As a result of this difficulty, a matched participants design is relatively uncommon, with its use being restricted to specific situations where a matching process is highly desirable in order that experimental success can be achieved.

Non-experimental design issues

These non-experimental methods – naturalistic observations, questionnaire surveys and interviews – were introduced in Chapter 6. Some of the design issues associated with these methods were also dealt with at the start of this section (see 'Key decisions' on p. 151).

Naturalistic observational studies

A key design issue with *naturalistic observational studies* concerns deciding how to sample the behaviour to be studied. The possibilities include:

- ◆ *time interval sampling* (observing and recording what happens in a series of fixed time intervals)
- ◆ *time point sampling* (observing and recording the behaviour which occurs at a series of given points in time)
- ◆ *event sampling* (observing and recording a complete event each time it occurs).

A further issue is how data are to be recorded. Likely methods are written notes, the production of a checklist or tally chart, or using a rating scale. Figure 7.3 is a simplified example of the tally chart devised by Bales (1970) as part of his technique of Interaction Process Analysis (IPA) and is used for plotting changes in the interactions within small groups. Figure 7.4 shows a simpler tally chart, developed for an observational study on the state of a baby.

Questionnaire surveys and interviews

Questionnaire surveys and *interviews* are widely used by research psychologists. They can produce qualitative and/or quantitative data, and the range of design

Figure 7.3 A simplified version of a tally sheet used by Bales (1970) to record social interaction among problem-solving discussion groups.

Each observer records the interactions of one participant for the period of the discussion, which lasts for 10 minutes. This 10-minute period can be divided into two 5-minute halves to allow comparison between behaviours over time. From this sheet, the total number, type and direction of a participant's interactions can be calculated and compared with those of other participants.

Name of observed person _____

Categories	Person being addressed											
	Person A		Person B		Person C		Person D		Person E		The group	
	1st half	2nd half	1st half	2nd half	1st half	2nd half	1st half	2nd half	1st half	2nd half	1st half	2nd half
Seems friendly												
Jokes												
Agrees												
Gives suggestion												
Gives opinion												
Gives guidance												
Asks for guidance												
Asks for opinion												
Asks for suggestion												
Disagrees												
Shows tension												
Seems unfriendly												

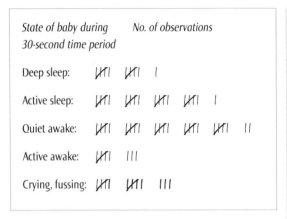

State of baby during 30-second time period	No. of observations
Deep sleep:	ЖI ЖI I
Active sleep:	ЖI ЖI ЖI ЖI I
Quiet awake:	ЖI ЖI ЖI ЖI ЖI II
Active awake:	ЖI III
Crying, fussing:	ЖI ЖI III

Figure 7.4
Specimen checklist of behaviours and tally chart
(behaviour categories taken from Bee 1999, p. 90)

options available to the researcher is wide. The *In Focus* on p. 156 introduces some design decisions that need to be taken into account when designing questionnaires.

A checklist for interview planning, and an example of an interview schedule prepared for a study of gender identity which would produce qualitative data, are shown in Figs 7.5 and 7.6 respectively.

Activity 4: Asking suitable questions

◆ What are the advantages and disadvantages of asking open or closed questions?

◆ Work through any questions given in the *In Focus*. Can you suggest a more suitable question in each case?

◆ Write a brief questionnaire that is designed to investigate respondents' health over the last six months. Check the design issues raised in the *In Focus* and review your questions. Have you asked the questions in the best possible way?

Summary: Research designs

The experimental designs available to the researcher include independent groups, repeated measures and matched participants designs.

Key design issues with non-experimental research include deciding how behaviour is sampled, the method(s) used for recording data and the phrasing and organization of questions.

---

in focus

Design issues in questionnaire surveys

◆ *Open questions or closed questions?*

See Chapter 6, p. 143, if you need to remind yourself of this issue or the different types of closed question available.

◆ *Question order*

It is conventional to ask questions on demographic data (e.g. age, gender) at the end of a questionnaire. Questions asking about highly sensitive issues are rarely placed right at the start.

◆ *Avoiding unnecessary jargon*

For example: 'Do you favour affirmative action in employment practices?' It is important that your respondents are familiar with the language that has been used for phrasing the questions. Plain English should be used wherever possible, or an explanation of terms given before the question is asked.

◆ *Avoiding leading questions or value judgements*

For example: 'Was the suspect's shirt blue or green?' A question should not lead the respondent towards a particular response.

◆ *Avoiding double-barrelled questions*

For example: 'Do you think that life is generally more stressful than it was 30 years ago, or do people find that modern technology reduces the stresses of life?' More than one item should not be included within the same question as participants may wish to give different answers to each part.

◆ *Avoiding emotive questions*

For example: 'Do you think that the killing of defenceless animals in laboratories should stop?' If emotive language is included, it may serve to bias the response made.

◆ *Avoiding vagueness or ambiguity*

For example: 'Do you take time off work? (please tick one)'

Never ☐   Rarely ☐   Sometimes ☐   Often ☐

These categories may mean different things to different people. It is important that all participants need to treat any particular question in the same way.

◆ *Avoiding unwarranted assumptions*

For example: 'What is your occupation?' may cause embarrassment if people are unemployed.

1 The preliminaries to the interview:

Have you:

- clearly described the research problem?
- stated the aim of the interview?
- linked the problem to an appropriate theory?
- identified the general categories of data which you will need to collect?

2 The questions:

Have you:

- generated an appropriate set of questions?
- planned the order in which the questions will be presented?
- planned the interview to obtain the required balance between structured and unstructured interviewing?

3 The interview procedure:

Have you:

- considered the issues of self-presentation?
- identified and approached potential respondents?
- planned the pre-interview meeting?
- planned the post-interview debriefing?
- decided how the information is to be recorded in the interview?
- considered the ethical issues raised by the proposed research and sought advice if necessary?

Figure 7.5
A checklist for planning interviews
Source: Dyer (1995, p. 65)

Figure 7.6
An example of an interview schedule
Source: Dyer (1995, p. 72)

The following is an example of a schedule of questions on the subject of the contribution of early school experience to the development of gender identity. The extreme right-hand column is used to place a tick against each question as it is asked, to prevent the embarrassing possibility of asking the same question twice. Note the heading to the schedule which ensures that you have a record of the basic details of the research stored with the questions, and the range of question types covered.

Title of project: A study of the development of gender identity

Topic: Contribution of early school experiences

Date of interview:

1 Can you begin by giving me a general description of the school you attended at the age of five, so I can begin to understand what kind of a place it was?

2 Looking back, how did your school deal with the issue of gender in general? For example, were boys and girls treated in very different ways? Could you give me some examples of that?

3 How did this compare with what you experienced at home?

4 How was children's behaviour dealt with? For example, was a clear distinction made between what was considered appropriate behaviour for boys compared to girls?

5 Did the school generally reinforce or challenge stereotyped gender definitions? Examples?

6 How do you now think this affected you during your early school life? Can you give some examples?

7 Can you give me some examples of the kind of thing that would have happened if a boy behaved in a way the teachers thought was more appropriate to a girl?

8 Can you give me any examples of the ways in which the rules about appropriate behaviour were enforced? How do you feel about them now?

9 What would have happened if you had been found breaking a rule like that?

Factors associated with research design

This section will examine some of the key factors that are associated with research design. It looks at:

◆ how variables in research can be defined, controlled and operationalized

◆ how pilot studies help to improve research quality

◆ techniques for assessing and improving reliability and validity

◆ ethical issues associated with research.

Defining, operationalizing and controlling variables

A *variable* is, quite simply, anything that may change or alter in any way. You may recall from Chapter 6 that the control, manipulation and observation of variables are central to psychological research. Psychologists need to be able to define variables successfully if their research is to be treated as scientifically worth while. This is not as easy as it may sound.

Activity 5: Defining variables

Try writing down a definition for the term 'aggressive behaviour'.

When you wrote your definition, you probably included different forms of violent behaviour – but did you include things such as spitting, swearing, glaring or invading personal space? Even a smile can sometimes have aggressive intent! It is even more difficult to define variables when they are less tangible, for example, 'stress' or 'concentration levels'. We may be able to measure the visible signs of their effect on a person, and we may endeavour to measure their effects on an aspect of behaviour, but can we be confident that we are actually measuring the variable?

Operational definitions

Operational definitions of variables or factors being investigated are precise descriptions of what researchers understand by particular terms.

In experimental research, the key variables are the *independent variable* and the *dependent variable* (see Chapter 6). Operationalizing these variables usually results in a narrowing-down of the research focus. For example, the general statement that 'mnemonics improve memory' might be refined into an independent variable that specifies the presence or

Activity 6: Operationalizing variables

Imagine that you are about to undertake an observational study of aggressive behaviour in young children. Refine the definition of aggressive behaviour that you generated for Activity 5 into a fully operationalized definition that could be used in a research situation.

absence of imagery, and a dependent variable that specifies the number of words correctly recalled. This process has wide implications for the extent to which research findings can be generalized, as it follows that the narrower the research focus, the narrower the area to which results can be generalized.

The control of variables

Unwanted variables (i.e. those which cause the potential confounding of results) are also known as *extraneous variables*. They may obscure the effect of an independent variable on a dependent variable, or provide a false impression that an independent variable has produced changes when in fact it has not. Unwanted variables can result from either *random error* or *constant error*, and need to be eliminated or controlled as far as possible. If a variable other than the independent variable produces a change in a dependent variable, then results are said to be *confounded*.

The effects of random errors cannot be predicted. Possible sources of random errors might include:

◆ a participant's state of mind

◆ a participant's level of motivation

◆ incidental noise

◆ room temperature

◆ previous experiences on the day of the experiment.

It is hoped that errors which might result from variables such as these will not systematically affect one condition of an experiment more than another. By allocating participants randomly to experimental conditions, psychologists will assume that such errors balance out across the experimental conditions. Such errors might, however, result in some loss of sensitivity.

Constant errors affect the dependent variable in a consistent way and are, therefore, a much more serious problem for the researcher than random errors, since they may not affect all conditions of an experiment equally.

Such errors might include:

◆ a failure to counterbalance or randomize the presentation order of experimental conditions

◆ participant differences

◆ errors of measurement which affect one condition more than another.

Wherever possible, such sources of error are eliminated by good experimental design.

Conducting pilot studies

A *pilot study* is a small-scale prototype of a particular piece of research. It is carried out on a small number of participants in order to find out whether there are any problems with the design, the instructions for participants or the measuring instruments used. Also, a pilot study may provide information on how long the study takes to complete and enable the researcher to become practised at carrying out the research task. The researcher can inform participants that it is a pilot study and may ask them to draw attention to any problematic areas or ambiguities that they come across. In the light of experience gained with the pilot study, the researcher can make revisions before the final research is carried out.

A questionnaire survey or interview-based investigation will need to be piloted on people from the appropriate target population.

Activity 7: A pilot study

Pilot the brief questionnaire that you devised for Activity 4 on a small number of friends. In the light of this experience, how would you change the questions?

Assessing and improving reliability

The term *reliability* means dependability or consistency, which are vital attributes if the psychologist is to obtain meaningful data. The term can be applied in a general way to the findings from psychological research. If the findings are replicated consistently, then the outcome can be said to be reliable. The term is used also in specific contexts. Assessing reliability often involves using correlational analysis (discussed in Chapter 6) in an attempt to assess the consistency of observer ratings or psychological measuring instruments such as psychometric tests. There are several ways in which reliability can be assessed and improved, and we will now move on to consider some of these.

Assessing and improving observer reliability

Observer reliability is assessed by measuring the extent to which researchers, scoring the same participants, achieve consistency of measurement between each other. Scorers record their own data individually and then the sets of data obtained from each scorer are correlated. Observer reliability is achieved if highly significant positive correlations are obtained between the scorers.

Inter-rater reliability is a form of observer reliability. Ideally, in observational studies, more than one observer should be used. This procedure allows a researcher to measure the extent to which observers agree on the behaviours they have observed. Independent checks for reliability can often be made easier by the use of audiotaping or videotaping. Correlational analysis is often used to establish inter-rater reliability.

Observer reliability may be improved by, for example, the thorough pretraining of observers in the techniques being used and by ensuring that operational definitions of the key terms involved in the research are both clear and understood fully. Consider, for example, an observational study of aggressive behaviour in children's playgrounds. If more than one observer is being used, it is important that they all understand exactly which behaviours can be categorized as examples of 'aggressive behaviour'. In other words, they need to operationalize the term 'aggressive behaviour', as you were asked to do in Activity 6.

Assessing and improving test reliability

Another important aspect of reliability concerns the reliability of tests employed by psychologists (such as those which attempt to measure intelligence or personality). The *split half* method can be used as a way of assessing the extent to which individual items in a particular test or questionnaire are consistent with other items in the same test. The method involves splitting the test concerned into two parts after data have been obtained from the participants. This splitting might be done by, for example:

◆ comparing the results obtained from odd- and even-numbered questions

◆ comparing the results from the first half of the test with those from the second half

◆ splitting the test into two at random.

The two sets of responses (however they are obtained) are then correlated, and a highly significant positive correlation would indicate reliability. An insufficiently high correlation would result in carefully checking the procedure used for constructing the test and very possibly by revising the test items. This should then produce an improvement in reliability.

The *test–retest* method is used to assess another important aspect of consistency: the stability of a test or questionnaire over time. This method involves presenting the same participants with the same test or questionnaire on different occasions, with no feedback given after the first presentation. The time interval between presentations needs to be selected carefully. If it is too short, participants may remember their previous answers, but, on the other hand, if it is too long, then it is possible that the participants may have changed in some way relevant to the test or questionnaire over the intervening time period. Again, correlational techniques will indicate test stability if there is a highly significant positive correlation between the scores obtained from the test and retest phases. Test items and/or testing procedures can be revised (e.g. by rephrasing instructions) if a sufficiently high correlation is not obtained.

Assessing and improving validity

Validity is concerned with the extent to which something measures what it sets out to measure. This is not as simple as it first appears. For example, there is considerable debate over issues such as whether personality tests are valid measures of personality, or whether diagnostic classification schemes used in the mental-health field really are valid. A distinction may be drawn between internal validity, external validity and test validity.

Internal and external validity

Internal validity is concerned with the extent to which we can be sure that research findings are due to the mechanisms suggested. For example, in an experiment the key issue might be whether we can be certain that differences in the results obtained are due to manipulation of the independent variable and not to the action of some other unwanted variable, such as participant variables or the effects of practice. Internal validity is also compromised if no effect is found within research when in fact an effect actually exists.

External validity is concerned with the extent to which results can be generalized to other settings beyond that of the study concerned. A distinction can be drawn here between *population validity* (the extent to which results from research can be generalized to other groups of people) and *ecological validity* (the extent to which research findings can be generalized to situations outside the setting in which the research was conducted). There are sometimes misconceptions with ecological validity. Laboratory experiments do not lack ecological validity by the mere fact that they are carried out in laboratories. They *sometimes* do, but many laboratory studies are ecologically valid and have results that can be generalized beyond the lab.

Similarly, the fact that research is carried out in a natural setting does not guarantee ecological validity. This may or may not be achieved – it all depends on whether results can be generalized or not.

Test validity

There are several different techniques which are available to help the psychologist assess *test validity*:

◆ *Face validity* is the simplest technique, and is concerned with assessing whether a measuring instrument looks correct in the eyes of independent experts – who may suggest improvements to the researcher. Because of its subjectivity, assessment of face validity usually only takes place in the earliest phases of constructing a measuring instrument, e.g. when a draft examination paper is submitted for approval.

◆ *Content validity* is, superficially, similar to face validity. Again, independent experts are asked to assess the validity of the measuring instrument concerned. This time, however, the procedures are more rigorous, and there is a detailed and systematic examination of all the component parts of the measuring instrument concerned.

◆ *Concurrent validity* involves obtaining two sets of scores at the same time, one from the new procedure with unknown validity, and the other from an alternative procedure or test for which validity has already been established. The scores obtained from both of these measures will then be correlated with each other to assess the validity of the new procedure. If a highly significant positive correlation is obtained, this would suggest that the procedure of interest is valid. For example, a new diagnostic procedure for the diagnosis of a psychopathological condition might be compared with an existing method of diagnosis for which the success rate is already known. Further refinement of the criteria in order to improve concurrent validity might be necessary if the correlation obtained is not high enough.

◆ *Predictive validity* involves a similar strategy to that used to establish concurrent validity. However, this time, the two sets of scores are obtained at different points in time. An example of this method in practice comes from abnormal psychology, where initial diagnoses may be correlated with information gained in the light of experience with the patients concerned over a period of time. In other words, a diagnostic procedure or test with high predictive validity would allow fairly accurate forecasts to be made about future behaviour. If the test indicates that certain behaviours should occur and they do not occur, then the test has low predictive validity.

◆ *Construct validity* involves a more complex procedure concerned with the validation of hypothetical constructs which cannot be directly observed, for example, extroversion. It is important that this validation occurs, because if this does not take place, the construct concerned will remain purely hypothetical. When establishing construct validity, it is assumed that the constructs concerned are derived from a sound theoretical base, but this can be difficult to establish. One method which researchers have used to help them establish construct validity is *factor analysis*. This is the name given to a series of statistical procedures which are used to determine the smallest number of factors (dimensions) that can explain any correlations between participants and responses obtained on a large number of different tests. Readers wishing to know more about construct validity are referred to the discussion in Coolican (1999).

Ethics

The ethical issues associated with research are dealt with in other chapters: specifically, Chapter 5, which contains a section on ethical guidelines, and Chapter 6, where particular issues are raised in association with the different research methods.

Activity 8: **Appropriate ethical issues**

Describe one ethical issue which is important with each of the following research methods: laboratory experiment, naturalistic observation, questionnaire survey and interview. Select a different issue for each.

Summary: Factors affecting research design

The control of variables is fundamental to scientific research in psychology. Psychologists need to define precisely all the variables that they are investigating, to ensure that they are properly operationalized. Small-scale pilot studies can be carried out before research takes place in order to identify any potential problems.

Reliability refers to the consistency of a test or procedure. Key aspects of it are observer reliability and test reliability.

The validity of measuring instruments can be established by the extent to which they measure what they set out to measure. Key aspects are internal validity, external validity and test validity. It is essential that all psychological research is carried out ethically, i.e. it respects the rights and feelings of those taking part.

Selecting participants

When selecting participants to take part in research investigations, two key concepts are the *population* and the *sample*. A *target population* is a group of people that share a given set of characteristics, about which a researcher wishes to draw conclusions (e.g. all students registered for A-level psychology examinations in a given year). However, a target population is usually too large for each individual to be investigated, so a subset of the population – a sample – is investigated instead. A *representative sample* forms part of a target population, sharing the characteristics of the population despite its smaller size. Only if a sample is truly representative can it be used by psychologists as a basis for generalizing their conclusions to the remainder of the target population. If a sample is not truly representative, then time and effort may have been wasted.

As a general principle, the larger the sample, the more likely it is to give an accurate estimate about the nature of the population from which it has been drawn. Deciding on the size of a sample, therefore, reflects a delicate balancing act between the need for accurate representation of the target population on the one hand, and practical considerations such as time and money on the other. In practice, if a sample is used instead of an entire population, some degree of

sampling error is likely to result. The researcher's task is to minimize the sampling error. Generally, the larger the sample the better; the smaller the sample, the greater the potential bias. It is possible to determine sample size precisely – statistical tables exist which advise on the sample size needed to achieve acceptable levels of sampling error in target populations of different sizes.

There are several different ways in which samples can be taken. We shall discuss some of them below.

Random samples

In a *random sample*, every person or item in a given target population stands an equal chance of being selected for inclusion. This means that it is necessary to have a list of every person or item in the target population in order to generate a random sample. Selection must take place in a completely unbiased way. However, it is important to recognize that selecting a random sample neither guarantees the researcher a sample which is totally representative of the population concerned, nor that any two random samples which are drawn from the same target population will share identical characteristics. By its very nature, a random sample can only come with a guarantee that it has been selected in an unbiased manner (a random sample can be selected from a target population using one of the techniques described for randomly allocating participants to conditions earlier in this chapter). However, as long as the target population and sample size have been chosen carefully, the laws of probability predict that the chance of selecting a biased sample through random-sampling techniques is minimal.

Other sampling methods

Stratified samples

A *stratified sample* is more complex than a random sample and its selection is undertaken through a multistage process. The term 'stratified' means 'arranged in layers'. First, factors (the 'strata') which are considered important to the research are identified by the investigator. Then the precise proportions of these factors in the total population are ascertained. A sample size is decided on and subsets of the sample are preselected which represent the distribution of these factors in the target population. For example, if social class was considered to be an important factor in a particular investigation, then the subsets selected for study would contain the exact proportions of people within each social class in the total target population. Within each of these subsets of the target population, the actual sample taken would then be selected on a random basis. The extra effort involved in taking this kind of sample will cost the researcher time and money, but the outcome is likely to be improved accuracy and more representative results.

Quota samples

A *quota sample* is similar to a stratified sample but a preset number of individuals (the quota) is drawn from each stratum. Random sampling is not involved and the sampling method can be used when a complete list of individuals in the target population is unavailable. For example, a quota sample could be selected representing A-level and GCSE students. The sample would be proportional in size to the total number of students in each of these two groups. The quotas would then be selected opportunistically, with each quota proportional in size to the number of students who actually study each subject. The researcher, however, would have no way of knowing how representative the selected students were of their particular subject groups.

Systematic samples

A common way of selecting a *systematic sample* is to select as participants those present at fixed intervals, for example, every twentieth person from a list which represents the target population, such as a class register, or every tenth person alighting from a train. Strictly, this kind of sample should not be regarded as a random sample as each person does not stand an equal chance of selection. However, selection is substantially unbiased and the term *quasi-random* is sometimes applied to this kind of sample.

Self-selected samples

A *self-selected sample* (or volunteer sample) involves participants selecting themselves, often through replying to an advertisement. Much university research uses this kind of sample. A well-known example of this technique was Milgram's selection of participants for his research on obedience in the 1960s (see Chapter 5). The potential disadvantages of using a self-selected sample are:

◆ selectivity of response (the majority of a given target population are unlikely to respond)

◆ biased response (those who do respond may be atypical of the target population in some way).

Opportunity samples

An *opportunity sample* (or opportunist sample) involves the researcher selecting anyone who is available to take part from any given population (such as available staff or students within a college). This type of sample is very widely used, despite the fact that such samples are very easily biased. However, the risk of bias is often acceptable; for example, in research on the capacity of short-term memory, it might reasonably be concluded that an opportunity sample of the general public would produce results that did not differ in important ways from those obtained from any other kind of sample.

Activity 9: Sampling methods

Consider the population in your local town centre on a weekday at 08.45, 11.00, 16.00 and 23.00. How might the population differ at these differing times of the day?

What sampling method would you use if you were carrying out an investigation embracing all of these times?

Summary: Selecting participants

Different sampling techniques can be used to select participants for research investigations. In a random sample, every person in the target population stands an equal chance of being selected.

Other sampling techniques include stratified, quota, systematic, self-selected and opportunity samples.

The relationship between researchers and participants

The research situation is not a bland one and it is to be expected that a relationship will develop between researchers and participants. A research investigation is a social situation and as such is liable to be influenced by those taking part in it. Research participants may be affected by demand characteristics resulting from the situation that they find themselves in. It is also possible for investigators to have unintended effects on the outcome of research.

Demand characteristics

Demand characteristics have already been described in the section on laboratory experiments (Chapter 6). In that chapter it was pointed out that they occur when participants try to make sense of the research situation that they find themselves in and act accordingly. Demand characteristics are not confined to experiments and may occur in any research scenario in which the participants are aware of taking part. They are a problem as soon as participants act differently from the way that they would outside the research situation. Well-designed research will aim to minimize their effects as much as possible. Demand characteristics might include:

◆ trying to guess the purpose of the research and acting in a way that participants feel is helpful to the researcher

◆ trying to guess the purpose of the research and acting in a way that participants feel is *unhelpful* to the researcher!

◆ acting nervously and out of character because they are in a research situation – for example, participants may feel that they are being evaluated in some way (e.g. that their personality is being assessed) and feel worried about this

◆ displaying a social desirability bias (i.e. wishing themselves to be seen in the most favourable light possible).

Investigator effects

Investigator effects result from the effects of a researcher's behaviour and characteristics on an investigation. There is a wide range of possibilities here. Expectation effects can occur where a researcher is deeply committed to achieving a particular outcome. This may be a particular problem when observing events that can be interpreted in more than one way (an example might be the difficulty in distinguishing between children fighting or indulging in rough and tumble play). Alternatively, even overt fraud ('massaging the data') is a possibility, however remote.

In naturalistic observational studies, the presence of the observer can cause participants to behave in ways different from those that would normally be displayed. For example, behaviour may be more restrained than usual. When research is carried out using questionnaire surveys or interviews, then many different aspects of the investigator may have an influence. These include the investigator's age, gender, ethnic group, appearance, expression and communication style.

Activity 10: Reducing investigator effects

If you were to carry out a questionnaire survey, how might you attempt to reduce the impact of investigator effects?

Summary: Relationship between researchers and participants

Demand characteristics occur when research participants attempt to make sense of the research situation that they find themselves in. Investigator effects result from the effects of a researcher's behaviour and characteristics on an investigation.

Data analysis: Analysing qualitative data

This section looks at ways of analysing and interpreting the qualitative data that could be derived from naturalistic observational studies, questionnaire surveys and interviews. It is important to remember that these research methods often also produce quantitative data, and indeed with questionnaire surveys, quantitative data is very often the only kind of data produced.

Analysis of quantitative data using descriptive statistical techniques is dealt with in the next section of this chapter, but further analysis of quantitative data using inferential statistical tests is outside the scope of the AS-level Psychology specification. If you continue your study of psychology to A level, you will be using inferential statistical tests to help you analyse your coursework data. If you wish to find out more about such tests now, you can refer to the specialist texts listed at the end of this chapter, in the 'Further resources' section.

Interpreting qualitative data from naturalistic observational studies

The use of naturalistic observational techniques is discussed in Chapter 6. These techniques differ widely both in terms of the approaches used and the ways in which behaviour is recorded and classified, so it is unsurprising that they also differ widely in terms of how behaviour is analysed and presented. Interpretation may also aim to produce ideas for hypotheses which can be tested using other research methods.

When qualitative data are obtained, these may be presented in different ways, including diary descriptions and specimen descriptions of behaviour. See *In Focus* for an example of a diary description from an observational study; this illustrates the social rituals through which a child's ability to name can arise.

Although ecological validity may be a strength of observational studies, the categorization of behaviours that takes place in them (and indeed in interview-based research, discussed later) may challenge their validity. Are the operational definitions used the best ways of defining behaviours? For instance, are the definitions comprehensive enough or too comprehensive? It is important, therefore, that the structure of a study is fully justifiable in terms of its theoretical basis, and also sufficiently complete (i.e. it should include all the behaviours of interest).

Other potential threats to validity are inadequate sampling (e.g. too few samples, or sampling undertaken at inappropriate times), mishandling or inadequate handling of the system used (e.g. through a pressure or lack of familiarity in a research situation). These challenges to validity highlight the need for careful analysis and presentation of observational data if the potential benefits from the richness of the data gathered are not to be compromised.

---

in focus

Diary description

Mary, aged 11 months: Mother takes Mary out of her high-chair and puts her on the potty. Her toys are all in a box on the table in front of her chair.

Mother (spontaneously): 'Do you want Teddy?'

Mary: 'aah'

Mother: 'Where is he?'

Mary looks around and makes to get off her potty and go to the table, but Mother restrains her. Mary looks at the table and points.

Mother (going to table opposite and bringing down the box of toys): 'That's right, he's there, isn't he? Here he is. What does he say? What does Teddy say?'

Mary: 'aah'

Mother: 'Yes, he does, doesn't he?'

Mary: 'aah'

Mother pats Teddy.

Mary: 'aah'

Mary's attention moves to the box containing her other toys, which Mother has placed on the floor near her.

Mother: 'Oh, what can you see in there? Doggie? (takes doggie out) Let's see who else is in here. Who's that? Is it duckie? and what does the duck say?'

Mother squeaks the duck.

Mary: 'aah'

Mother: 'He doesn't! What does the duck say? What does he say?'

Mary: 'argh' *(reaching towards it)*

Mother: 'Yes, I know you want it. What does he say?'

Mary: 'woraghagh'

Mother: 'He doesn't, he says *(she squeaks it concurrently)* "quack, quack, quack", doesn't he? "quack, quack, quack".'

Mary: 'gh, gh'

Mother: 'Yes, he does.'

Mary (looking at Teddy): 'aah'

Mother: 'And that's aah is it, that's aah Teddy?'

Mary: 'aah'

Mother: 'And who's this, what does he say? What does duck say? What does duck say?'

No response from Mary. Mother squeaks duck.

Mary: 'gah'

Mother: 'Quack!'

Mary: 'gah'

Mother: 'Ooh, aren't you clever.'

Source: Lock (1980, p. 110)

Interpreting qualitative data from questionnaire surveys

Much of the information that is gained from conducting research using questionnaire surveys is analysed using quantitative methods. However, data from appropriate open questions that invite participants to give different responses may be analysed qualitatively. In contrast to closed questions, such open questions may serve to reduce researcher bias and the impact of the researcher's own views on the design of the survey. The result is a means of analysis that is both flexible and interpretative.

A further possibility for the analysis of data derived from questionnaire surveys is that qualitative data are converted to quantitative by, for example, counting the number of times that a particular item is mentioned. This is a common way of analysing data and shows the extent to which qualitative and quantitative data may be interdependent.

As interviews are often used as a tool for gathering information for a questionnaire survey, further information on qualitative analysis that is applicable to questionnaire surveys is included in the following section.

Interpreting qualitative data from interviews

The use of interviews as a research method has already been discussed in Chapter 6. Interviews are often just one of the techniques used by the researcher in association with other methods in a particular piece of research. As such, they may help to provide a validity check on the results obtained. Interpreting the information gained from interviews is a complex procedure.

Qualitative data might include many elements which need to be taken into account when interpretation takes place. These include description of features of interest, such as:

◆ the actual behaviour observed by the interviewer

◆ the context(s) in which the behaviour occurs

◆ self-reports of behaviour by the participant(s)

◆ self-reports of cognitions which cannot be observed directly: for example, the feelings, thoughts and attitudes of the participants in the study

◆ interpretations made by the researchers

◆ implications of the study for any theory.

From this list it can be seen that distinctions need to be made between the aspects of a report that:

◆ describe what actually happened

◆ are based on the interpretations and inferences made by the researcher

◆ are based on the interpretations and inferences of the participant(s).

If reporting is to be objective, the distinctions between these need to be made clear to the reader when a report of an investigation is published. Inevitably, the potential for bias in reporting is considerable. For example, researchers might report only those aspects of behaviour which support their own theoretical standpoint, or are particularly relevant to their research. Also, decisions about what information to include and what to leave out may be subjective and highly dependent on who makes the decision. Carefully reported investigations will always make clear to the reader the criteria used to select participants and how decisions were made about what information to present.

The close, and often prolonged, relationship between the researcher and the participant(s) in interview-based research may heighten the importance of interpersonal interaction. This interaction may be very productive or it may reduce objectivity.

Whilst the qualitative data generated by interview-based research may add to our existing understanding, they can also produce evidence that challenges theory or our existing understanding, thereby stimulating further research and, perhaps, a new theoretical perspective.

The nature of the data obtained often reflects the extent to which the interview was structured or unstructured (see Chapter 6). Where data are qualitative, the researcher is able to present results more flexibly, but the problem exists of how to organize and present a mass of descriptive data in a meaningful way. Some of the issues the researcher might consider are listed below.

◆ Examine carefully the background theory for a study involving interviews before the research is undertaken, and then decide how the data can be categorized appropriately.

◆ Solicit opinions from the interviewees on how they would wish the material to be presented. Has material been presented in the spirit in which it has been told?

◆ Decide how any selection or paraphrasing of material is going to be undertaken. Particular care needs to be taken with this if bias in reporting is to be avoided.

◆ Decide whether quotations will be used to enrich the presentation of data. If so, how will they be selected?

Categorization of qualitative data is an important task for the person reporting an interview. It involves the grouping of like items together, e.g. statements by the interviewee concerning particular subjects. A good computer database can be an advantage here.

Activity 11: Categorizing interview data

Consider a series of interviews carried out to investigate patients' experiences in hospital. What categories might be used to group data when presenting results?

The interpretation of interview data is, perhaps inevitably because of their nature, partial or incomplete. Something may be lost in terms of reliability and something gained through the sensitivity

and depth of the approach. They may have the important benefit of providing a new basis for interpretation. See *In Focus* for an example which provides interesting insights on the Bristol riots of the early 1980s derived from interviews.

Summary: Analysing qualitative data

The data derived from naturalistic observational studies, questionnaire surveys and interviews can be analysed in a variety of ways, both qualitative and quantitative, reflecting the variety of possible individual research strategies. The qualitative data from naturalistic observational techniques, questionnaire surveys and interviews provides a richness of detail that may be absent when other research strategies are used.

Riots and representations: the Bristol riots of the 1980s (from Foster and Parker 1995)

Qualitative interviewing approaches can add a great deal to our understanding of social processes, and can illuminate events that appear, at first sight, to be incomprehensible. A series of street disturbances in Britain in the early 1980s, for example, raised the spectre of 'mob rule', and the idea that people who get together in crowds are overtaken by a 'group mind'. There is a close similarity here between the ways in which the popular tabloid press portrayed the disturbances and theories of the crowd in social psychology going back to the end of the last century. In both cases the perspective adopted is that of an 'outsider' who focuses attention on the crowd as a kind of mass irrational force. This is also an example, then, of how bad psychology can chime in with mistaken 'common sense'.

Journalists tend to see people in crowds, particularly when they attack the police, as if they were animals who have been stripped of the veneer of civilization that usually holds them in check. Social psychologists who have been influenced by the theories of the French writer Gustave LeBon have been just as negative. LeBon (1947, but first published in 1895) argued that the behaviour of people in crowds fell several rungs down the evolutionary ladder, to the level of 'beings belonging to inferior forms of evolution, women, savages, and children, for instance' (LeBon, 1947, p. 36). These ideas take on a quite nasty political flavour when they are used to describe 'riots' by black people in inner-city areas, and the task of the psychologist should be to look at how popular images work, and how people in the crowd understand their actions. Qualitative interviewing can move to an 'insider' perspective on these events, and so assist in this task.

One of the first 'riots' in the 1980s, in the St Paul's area of Bristol, was studied by Reicher (1984), a social psychologist whose training had been in the experimental tradition. Reicher was carrying out research on social identity at Bristol University when the April 1980 'riot' broke out, and he was able to interview participants. Their accounts did not correspond with either standard social psychological or journalistic images of people who had lost their minds, and the 'inside' story was of a community trying to defend itself against the police. One of the striking aspects of the insider accounts was that both black and white people who were in the crowd refused to accept the outsider claims that this was a racial disturbance. Private homes and shops within the community were left untouched, whereas the banks and the unemployment office were seen as legitimate targets. The stories collected in these qualitative interviews also corresponded with the descriptions of the damage given by the authorities. An examination of the accounts of outsiders and insiders by Reicher and Potter (1985) illustrated the ways in which traditional 'scientific' explanations of crowd behaviour fail to account for the insider perspective which, in the case of St Paul's, stressed the meaningfulness of crowd action, and the feelings of solidarity and emotional warmth that came with defence of the community.

Data analysis: Descriptive statistical techniques

Descriptive statistical techniques provide ways in which the researcher can obtain a summary description of sets of quantitative data. Two types of descriptive statistical techniques are *measures of central tendency*, which give average values, and *measures of dispersion*, which look at the variability of scores. Each of these techniques provides a single value which can help us to summarize a set of data which might otherwise be difficult to interpret. This potential benefit, however, is not without its cost. When any single value is obtained, the process of summation inevitably produces a loss of individual information. Measures of central tendency (see below) and measures of dispersion (see pp. 169–70) are also valuable to the psychologist in that they form the basis for analyses using inferential statistics.

This section also looks at some of the graphs and charts which can be used by psychologists to summarize and clarify their data. The next section (p. 173) looks at scattergraphs, a graphical technique used to illustrate correlational relationships.

Measures of central tendency

You are probably already familiar with measures of central tendency and refer to them as *averages*. A *measure of central tendency* provides a single value which is representative of a set of numbers by indicating the most typical value. Three measures of central tendency are discussed here:

◆ the *mode*, which is the most frequently occurring value
◆ the *median*, which is the middle value of scores arranged in ascending or descending order
◆ the *mean*, which is the arithmetic average.

Each of these has its own particular uses, and therefore advantages and disadvantages, for particular sets of data.

The mode

The *mode* is the value in any set of scores which occurs most frequently. For example, with the following series of numbers:

> 2   4   6   7   7   7   10   12,

the most frequently occurring number is 7, and so the mode = 7.

Although the mode provides information on the most frequently occurring value, it has its limitations and is not widely used in psychological research. One reason for this is that when there are only a few scores representing each value, then even very small changes in the data can radically alter the mode. For example:

| 3 | 6 | 8 | 9 | 10 | 10 | Mode = 10 |
| 3 | 3 | 6 | 8 | 9 | 10 | Mode = 3 |

A further possible problem is that there may not be a single modal value. For example, take the series of numbers:

> 3   5   8   8   8   10   12   16   16   16   20

In this situation, there are two modal values (8 and 16), known as the *bimodal values*. With cases such as this, the bimodal values may still provide a useful summary statistic. It is, of course, possible to have several modal values, in which case the distribution is referred to as *multimodal* and the value of the statistic becomes even more limited. For example:

> 2   2   4   7   7   8   8   10   11   11   13   13

Here, each of five values occurs twice.

The mode has an *advantage* in that it is a figure which actually does occur in a given sequence, which may not be true of other measures of central tendency. However, its *disadvantage* is that it tells us nothing about the other values in the distribution concerned.

The median

The *median* is the middle value of a set of numbers that has been placed in numerical order (i.e. in order from lowest to highest score, or highest to lowest). Therefore, half of the scores in a given set of data will lie above the median, and half below it. When there is an even number of scores, however, there will be two middle values. In these circumstances, the median is calculated by adding the two central values together and dividing by two. Figure 7.7 provides an example of both situations.

Figure 7.7 Calculating the median

> *To calculate the median when there is an odd number of scores:*
>
> Scores placed in numerical order:
>
> $$2\ 4\ 5\ 6\ 8\ 10\ 11$$
>
> Median = 6
>
> *To calculate the median when there is an even number of scores:*
>
> Scores placed in numerical order:
>
> $$2\ 4\ 5\ 6\ 8\ 10\ 11\ 13$$
>
> $$\text{Median} = \frac{6+8}{2}$$
>
> Median = 7

When calculating the median, you may find it helpful to cross out the lowest and highest values alternately until you are left with the middle value(s).

The main *advantage* of the median is that it remains relatively unaffected by any outlying values. It is therefore a safe measure of central tendency to use when we are unsure about the reliability of extreme values. Also, it can be used with data from skewed distributions (i.e. where there is a cluster of values at one end of the range, see *In Focus*). Unlike the mean, it can be used when data are on an ordinal level of measurement, where we cannot be sure that our data are measured in fixed units with an equal distance between each point on the scale concerned.

A *disadvantage* of the median, however, is that it does not work well with small data sets and is affected by any alteration of the central values in a set of values. For example: if we have two sets of data:

10 12 13 14 18 19 22 22   and
10 12 13 14 15 19 22 22,

the median would be 16 in the first case and 14.5 in the second, despite only one value being different in the two sets of data.

in focus

Normal and skewed distributions

A normal distribution curve is a bell-shaped curve which is symmetrical about its mean, median and mode (see diagram below). It is called 'normal' because it describes the theoretical distribution of a great many naturally occurring variables. Various characteristics of individuals are considered to be normally distributed (e.g. height and body weight) and sometimes a particular measure is deliberately constructed in a way that a normal distribution of scores results (e.g. some intelligence tests). In theory, a normal distribution curve should result when a large random sample of measurements is taken from an appropriate population. In practice, however, it would be very rare for a distribution to fit a normal distribution curve precisely – there are always likely to be at least some minor irregularities.

Normal distribution

Mean
Median
Mode

x-axis

Notice the key features of this curve:

◆ The curve is symmetrical about its mean value which occurs at the central point of the distribution. (This value is also the median and mode.)

◆ The curve has a characteristic bell shape, curving downwards close to the mean and outwards further away.

◆ The outer extremities of the distribution (known as the tails) will never touch the *x*-axis.

◆ The properties of this distribution mean that certain statements about probability can be made – a very important feature when a researcher wishes to express clearly the relationship between sample data and data from the population which the sample represents.

However, all variables are not normally distributed – for example, some distributions can be best described as skewed (see below).

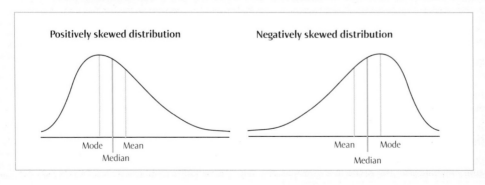

Positively skewed distribution

Mode   Mean
Median

Negatively skewed distribution

Mean   Mode
Median

The mean

The *mean* is the arithmetic average of a set of data, and is probably the average with which you are most familiar. It is calculated by adding all the values together and dividing the total by the number of scores. An example is shown in Fig. 7.8.

To find the mean of:

$$2 \ 4 \ 5 \ 5 \ 6 \ 6 \ 6 \ 7 \ 8 \ 10$$

Add all the values together:

$$2 + 4 + 5 + 5 + 6 + 6 + 6 + 7 + 8 + 10 = 59$$

Divide this sum by the number of scores (there are 10 scores):

$$\text{Mean} = \frac{59}{10}$$

$$\text{Mean} = 5.9$$

Figure 7.8 Calculating the mean

The main *advantage* of the mean is that it makes use of all the data that are available. As such, it is the most powerful of the measures of central tendency available. However, it needs to be used with a certain amount of caution. One *disadvantage* or limitation of the mean is that when it has been calculated, decimal points may be less meaningful if all the data consist of whole numbers (as in the example in Fig. 7.8).

Also, the *distribution of values* needs to be taken into account. The mean can be used appropriately as the measure of central tendency with sets of data (such as normally distributed data – see *In Focus*, 'Normal and skewed distributions') which do not have extreme outlying values. When such extreme values are present, the median should be used instead. For example, calculate the mean of 8, 10, 10, 12, 60. What does the mean tell us about any of these scores?

In this example, the mean is 20, which tells us very little about the four low scores and the single high score. In circumstances where such *outliers* occur, it would be more appropriate to use the median (10), which at least would summarize the first four values reasonably successfully (coincidentally, 10 is also the mode in this example).

The mean can be used most successfully with data on interval or ratio levels of measurement (i.e. data measured in fixed units, where each point on the scale of measurement concerned is an equal distance apart). Caution needs to be used if the mean is used with data on ordinal levels of measurement where data are capable of being placed in rank order but no assumptions can be made about points on the scale concerned being an equal distance apart.

For example, consider the situation where a teacher rates pupils on a seven-point scale which measures how hard they have worked on their psychology coursework. Students are rated from 1 (very hard-working) to 7 (no effort). Given the arbitrary nature of the scale, we have no way of knowing for certain whether all those rated at 4 on this scale (average level of work) actually put in precisely the same amount of work, or whether all the points on the scale are at an equal distance apart. Therefore calculating the mean would be inappropriate. In a similar way, it would be wholly inappropriate to work out a mean GCSE grade – these grades are measured on an ordinal level of measurement, as some mark bands cover a wider range of marks than others.

Activity 12: Calculating measures of central tendency

Examine sets of data in this textbook or from other sources and calculate their mode, median and mean. Try to work out which of these measures of central tendency would be most useful in each case.

Using a measure of central tendency is insufficient on its own to describe a set of data. Take, for example, the following scenario:

Data set A	Data set B
100	100
101	40
99	120
102	60
98	180
100	100

The mean for each set of data is 100, yet the distribution of scores is very different in each case. In data set A, the scores are all very close to 100, while in data set B, they are dispersed much more widely. This is where measures of dispersion come in.

Measures of dispersion

Measures of dispersion enable us to examine the variability within our data sets, and help us to understand whether scores in a given set of data are similar to, or very different from, each other.

The range

The *range* is easy to calculate, being simply the difference between the highest and lowest scores in a given set of data, with one added if the scores are all whole numbers. A sample calculation is shown in Fig. 7.9. Similarly, if values are recorded to one decimal place, then the range is the difference between the lowest and highest values with 0.1 added (to two decimal places, it is the difference plus 0.01, and so on). If values are recorded to the nearest half unit, then the range has 0.5 added to the difference between the lowest and highest value.

To calculate the range of:

3 7 8 10 11 16 18 21 22 26

Find the difference between the highest score (26) and the lowest (3), and add one.

Range = 26 – 3 + 1 = 24

Figure 7.9 Calculating the range

The range has the *advantage* of being quick to calculate, but has some important *limitations*. It does not provide any idea of the distribution of values around the centre, nor does it take individual values into account (it is important to remember that the only values that are used when the range is calculated are the two most extreme values). Following on from this point, the range is seriously affected by any outlying values in a given set of data.

In an attempt to overcome the potential effect of outlying values, calculating the *interquartile range* is often preferred. The interquartile range measures the spread of the middle 50 per cent of values when they are placed in numerical order. The top 25 per cent and the bottom 25 per cent of values are ignored, which has the effect of removing the influence of outlying values, and providing an indication of grouping around the central value. Figure 7.10 explains how this is achieved.

The standard deviation

The *standard deviation* is a measure of the variability (i.e. of the typical deviation) of a given sample of scores from its mean. Calculation, as with the mean, involves using all the scores in a given set of data; this makes the standard deviation the most powerful of the measures of dispersion available to the researcher. Calculation is beyond the scope of the AS-level Psychology specification, although if you continue to A level, you may need to calculate it for data sets in your coursework.

The standard deviation allows us to make statements of probability about how likely (or how unlikely) a given value is to occur. This ability to make inferences is based on the relationship between standard deviation and a *normal distribution curve* (refer back to the *In Focus* on p. 168). The meaningful use of the statistic not only requires data which are approximately normally distributed, but also data measured on interval or ratio levels of measurement (i.e. data measured in fixed units, where each point on the scale of measurement concerned is an equal distance apart). Standard deviation becomes a less effective measure when there are any outlying scores which skew the data distribution.

The percentages of values which lie between the mean and a given number of standard deviations above and below the mean are fixed properties. These fixed properties are:

◆ 68.26 per cent of all values lie within one standard deviation either side of the mean.

◆ 95.44 per cent of all values lie within two standard deviations either side of the mean.

◆ 99.74 per cent of all values lie within three standard deviations either side of the mean.

Figure 7.11 illustrates how this works with some data where the calculated standard deviation is 10. As the mean value is 100, this means that 68.26 per cent of the psychology test scores in the population can be inferred as lying between 90 (minus one standard deviation) and 110 (plus one standard deviation).

Figure 7.10 Calculating the interquartile range

Calculate the interquartile range for the following data:

2 3 7 8 10 11 16 18 21 22 26 26

We first need to calculate the median:

$$\text{The median} = \frac{11 + 16}{2}$$

Median = 13.5

There are six scores above the median, and six below it. The interquartile range will therefore include the six scores which lie closest to the median, and exclude the remaining six. So, for the scores lying above the median, this means that 16, 18 and 21 will be included within the interquartile range, and 22, 26 and 26 excluded. The upper boundary of the interquartile range will therefore be the mean of the values immediately below it (21) and immediately above it (22), i.e. 21.5. Similarly, the lower boundary will be the mean of 7 and 8 (i.e. 7.5). The interquartile range is, therefore, the difference between 21.5 and 7.5 (i.e. 14).

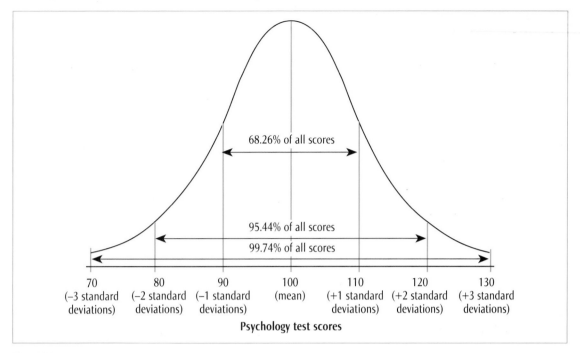

Figure 7.11
The percentage of scores which lie between a given number of standard deviations either side of the mean

Using and interpreting graphs and charts

Graphs and charts act as visual aids which help us to make sense of the data obtained from psychological investigations. They aim to provide an overall picture which helps to summarize the results – when well constructed, they can show us at a glance any patterns which occur in the data.

Be warned, though, that the careful manipulation of the way that the axes in graphs or charts are drawn can easily bias the interpretation. Before reading on, try the exercise in Activity 13 which illustrates the kind of visual deception that can occur.

The graphs will produce very different impressions, even though they are based on identical data – see Figs 7.12 and 7.13, which show the graphs at half actual size. Shortening or extending the axes, or manipulating their labelling, can convey a desired impression and may be highly misleading to the observer. The moral of this exercise is that there is no single correct way to select the scales that are used on the axes of graphs. However, there are certain conventions that serve both to assist the drawer to present their information in an unbiased way, and to reduce the risk of misunderstandings.

◆ *Plot frequency of scores on the y-axis* (as in the examples that you have just drawn). This is the conventional mode of presentation but is not a hard and fast rule – sometimes horizontal bars can provide a pleasing alternative.

A psychology software publisher asks one of its sales representatives to present her sales figures for the last three years to the company's management. Her sales are:

1997	1,000 items,
1998	1,001 items and
1999	1,002 items (evidently a sales boom!).

The company is dissatisfied with the sales performance – but the sales person is desperate to keep her job. Both parties decide to present the sales figures by means of a line graph, with the years 1997 to 1999 on the x-axis (horizontal) and number of items sold on the y-axis (vertical). The sales person draws a graph with 3 cm representing one year, the management opt for 4 cm = one year. The y-axis of the sales person's graph is 16 cm long and extends from 1,000 items sold to 1,002. However, the management draw their y-axis 10 cm long, and label it from 0 items sold to 10,000. Draw or sketch the two graphs and see the bias created.

◆ *Adopt the three-quarter high rule.* This states that when frequencies are plotted, the length of the y-axis should be determined in the following way. It should be organized so that the distance of the highest point on the graph (i.e. the point which represents the score with the highest frequency) from the x-axis is approximately equal to three-quarters of the total length of the x-axis.

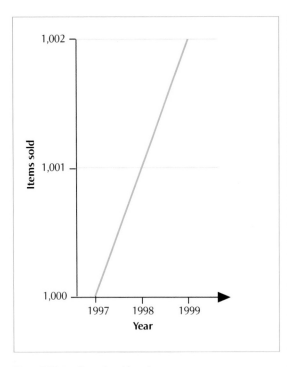

Figure 7.12 Graph produced by salesperson

◆ It is possible to *break the x- or y-axis* of a graph if labelling of the axis from zero would give a poor visual impression due to the large amount of empty space that would result.

◆ Remember that all graphs and charts need to have *each axis clearly labelled* and have an *informative title.*

The ideal situation to aim for is that someone looking at a graph or chart should be able to understand what it is about without any additional explanation.

Histograms

Histograms and bar charts (which we will now look at) are two of the most widely used graphical techniques. Simple forms of these are discussed here, but it is worth remembering that alternative forms exist, such as compound ones which show data from more than one condition simultaneously.

Histograms are a useful form of graphical representation which can be used when presenting data measured on interval or ratio levels.

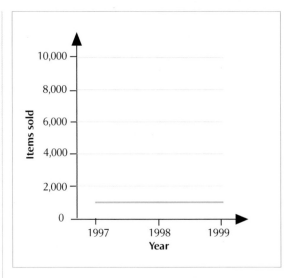

Figure 7.13 Graph produced by management

A histogram consists of a series of vertical bars of equal width, which represent frequencies of the variable placed on the *x*-axis. The height of each bar represents the frequency of occurrence for each point on the scale or each category. A histogram is drawn with the bars representing the frequencies actually touching each other. An ideal number of bars to use is between six and eight. Sometimes, single values can be used for each bar, but if the scale used on the *x*-axis has a large number of points, then the data can be placed into class intervals. (This has been done in the example of a histogram shown in Fig. 7.14.)

Figure 7.14
Histogram showing the number of words recalled in a memory experiment

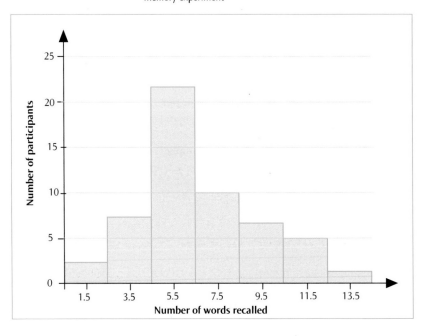

Bar charts

A *bar chart* is superficially similar to a histogram, and consists of a series of vertical bars of equal width which can be used to illustrate the frequencies of a non-continuous variable on the *x*-axis. They are often used to depict data measured on nominal (placed in categories) or ordinal levels of measurement or, for example, to illustrate the means from different samples. Unlike the histogram, it is usual to draw each bar separated from each of the others so that a continuous variable is not implied on the *x*-axis (as in Fig. 7.15). When data are at a nominal level, bias should be avoided in the order in which the bars are presented, as these can logically be presented in any order. They are often presented in alphabetical order to avoid such bias. However, when data are treated at an ordinal level, the *x*-axis can be drawn using the order of the points on the scale concerned.

Frequency polygons

The *frequency polygon* is a particularly useful technique when it is desirable to compare two or more frequency distributions. It is used as an alternative to the histogram. Indeed a frequency polygon can be drawn by linking the midpoints from the top of each bar contained in a histogram, as in the example in Fig. 7.16.

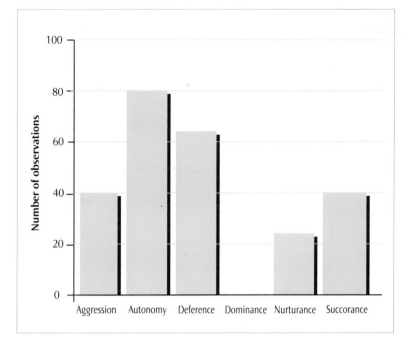

Figure 7.15
Bar chart showing the number of observations of different behaviours in a group of children

It may be the preferred technique when it is necessary to depict results from two or more conditions of an investigation at the same time, because two or more lines can be drawn on the same graph to show direct comparison of results.

Scattergraphs and the interpretation of correlation coefficients

The term *correlation* was introduced in Chapter 6 where the concepts of correlation coefficients, and positive and negative correlations were introduced. Reread that section now to refresh your knowledge of these terms. As far as interpreting correlation coefficients is concerned, the strength of a correlation increases as the obtained coefficient becomes closer to +1 or –1. An important way of depicting correlational relationships is the *scattergraph* (or scattergram), a graphical technique used to illustrate sets of data that are being correlated with each other.

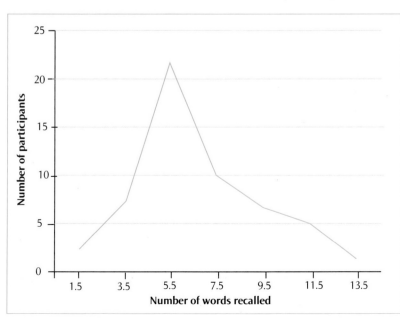

Figure 7.16 Frequency polygon showing the number of words recalled in a memory experiment

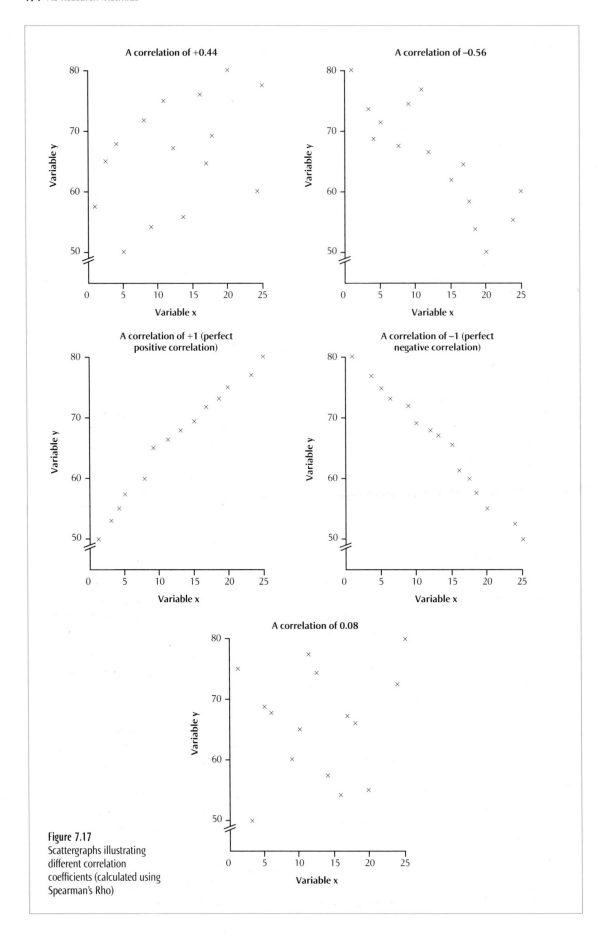

Figure 7.17
Scattergraphs illustrating different correlation coefficients (calculated using Spearman's Rho)

Data from one of the variables being correlated are presented on the *x*-axis and data from the second variable on the *y*-axis (see Fig. 7.17).

In order to interpret a correlation coefficient fully, it is necessary to test the correlation coefficient obtained for statistical significance. If you go on to study psychology at A level, you may have the opportunity to carry out a correlational study and to analyse the results.

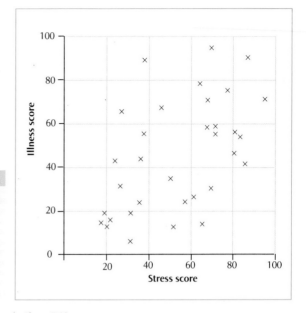

Activity 14: Interpreting scattergraphs

Figure 7.18 is a scattergraph showing the relationship between scores derived from questionnaires measuring ill health and stress levels. How would you interpret this correlation? (See end of chapter for answer.)

Summary: Data analysis

The use of descriptive statistical techniques helps psychologists to summarize quantitative data clearly. There are three principal measures of central tendency: the mean, the median and the mode, each of which provides an average figure to help summarize data and each has its own particular advantages and limitations.

Measures of dispersion permit the psychologist to describe the spread of a set of data by providing a

Figure 7.18
Scattergraph showing the relationship between scores derived from questionnaires measuring ill health and stress levels

single summary statistic. The most important of these measures are the range and, more particularly, the standard deviation. The calculation of the latter enables inferences to be made about probability.

Graphical techniques such as histograms, bar charts, frequency polygons and scattergraphs help the researcher to present sets of data clearly.

Chapter summary

◆ At the start of a psychological investigation, **appropriate aims** and **hypotheses** of the study should be **generated** and clearly stated. Hypotheses are testable statements. **A null hypothesis** predicts that the results obtained from an investigation are due to chance alone. An **alternative hypothesis** attributes results to some factor other than chance, such as the independent variable. Alternative hypotheses may be **directional** or **non-directional**.

◆ The **experimental** designs available to the researcher include **independent groups, repeated measures and matched participants** designs. Key design issues with non-experimental research (e.g. **naturalistic observations, questionnaire surveys and interviews**) include deciding how behaviour is sampled, the method(s) used for recording data and the phrasing and organization of questions.

◆ The **control of variables** is fundamental to scientific research in psychology. Psychologists need

to define precisely all the variables which they are investigating to ensure that they are properly **operationalized**, including both **independent** and **dependent variables**.

◆ Small-scale **pilot studies** can be carried out before research takes place in order to identify any potential problems.

◆ Researchers need to **assess** and, where necessary, **improve** the **reliability** and **validity** of the research measures and techniques. Reliability refers to the consistency of a test or procedure. Key aspects of it are observer reliability and test reliability. The validity of measuring instruments can be established by the extent to which they measure what they set out to measure. Key aspects are **internal validity, external (ecological) validity** and test validity.

◆ It is essential that all psychological research is carried out **ethically**, i.e. it respects the rights and feelings of those taking part.

◆ Different sampling techniques can be used to **select participants** for research investigations. In a **random sample**, every person in the target population stands an equal chance of being selected. Other sampling techniques include stratified, quota, systematic, self-selected and opportunity samples.

◆ **Demand characteristics** occur when research participants attempt to make sense of the research situation that they find themselves in. **Investigator effects** result from the effects of a researcher's behaviour and characteristics on an investigation.

◆ **Naturalistic observational studies, questionnaire surveys** and **interviews** may produce **qualitative** or quantitative data.

Qualitative data can provide a richness of detail which may not be achievable with other methods.

◆ Descriptive statistical techniques for use with quantitative data include **measures of central tendency (mode, median** and **mean)** and **measures of dispersion (range,** interquartile range and **standard deviation).**

◆ **Graphs and charts** available to the researcher include **histograms, bar charts** and **frequency polygons.**

◆ The strength of a **positive** or **negative correlation** increases as the obtained **coefficient** becomes closer to +1 or −1 respectively. The nature of the relationship (correlation) can be shown graphically on a **scattergraph.**

Exam summary

The AQA examination will test your knowledge of the following (in conjunction with the topics covered in Chapter 6):

◆ aims (p. 150) and hypotheses in investigations – directional/non-directional and null hypotheses (pp. 150–1)

◆ experimental designs – independent groups (pp. 152–3), repeated measures (153–4) and matched participants (pp. 154–5)

◆ the design of naturalistic observations, questionnaire surveys and interviews (pp. 155–7)

◆ independent and dependent variables (see p. 134)

◆ pilot studies (p. 159)

◆ reliability (pp. 159–60) and validity – internal and external validity (pp. 160–1)

◆ ethical issues in investigations (see Chapters 5 and 6)

◆ sampling procedures (pp. 161–2)

◆ demand characteristics and investigator effects (p. 163)

◆ analysis of qualitative data (pp. 163–6)

◆ measures of central tendency – medians, means and modes (pp. 167–9)

◆ measures of dispersion – range and standard deviations (pp. 169–70)

◆ positive and negative correlations and the interpretation of correlation coefficients (pp. 173–5)

◆ graphs and charts – histograms (p. 172), bar charts (p. 173), frequency polygons (p. 173), scattergraphs (pp. 173–4).

Example question 1

The question below should take you 15 to 20 minutes to answer (extra time is given for reading Research Methods questions in an exam).

In an attempt to increase the number of books brought back on time to a university library, the psychology department were asked to design a study that would test the effectiveness of smiling when the books were issued on the rate of return within the loan period.

On the first day of the study, half the issuing staff were asked to smile when handing over the books, whereas the other half were asked not to smile.

On the second day of the study, the conditions were reversed (i.e. the non-smiling group now offered a smile when issuing books and the former smiling group did not). Attempts were made to keep all other interactions as normal as possible, so as to minimize the possibility of demand characteristics in the participants taking part in the study.

Two weeks later, when the loan period for these books was up, staff counted up the number of books that had been returned (discounting any that had been renewed). The results are shown in Table 1 opposite.

| Table 1 | Rate of library book return | | | | | |

Condition						
Smiling			**Not smiling**			
Books borrowed	Books returned	% return rate	Books borrowed	Books returned	% return rate	
412	366	88.8	402	317	78.9	

(a) Name the method used in this study.   *(1 mark)*

(b) Give one advantage and one disadvantage of this type of study.   *(2 + 2 marks)*

(c) What was the aim of this study?   *(1 mark)*

(d) Suggest an appropriate directional hypothesis for this study.   *(2 marks)*

(e) Identify the independent variable used in this study.   *(1 mark)*

(f) Why was it important that the conditions were reversed on the second day?   *(2 marks)*

(g) What is meant by 'demand characteristics' and how might they have affected the results of this study?   *(2 marks)*

(h) From the information given in Table 1, what conclusions would you draw about the results of this study?   *(2 marks)*

Suggested answer structure

(a) This is a field experiment because researchers are manipulating an independent variable in a natural setting. In your answer you are simply required to identify the method used, not explain or justify your answer.

(b) The advantages and disadvantages of field experiments are discussed in Chapter 6, pp. 136–7. These include improved ecological validity and reduction of demand characteristics (advantages), and problems of establishing controls and generalization to other situations (disadvantages).

(c) Sometimes the most obvious questions catch students unawares. Do you understand what these researchers were trying to do? The aim of this study is given implicitly in the stimulus material at the beginning of the question. The researchers were trying to find out if smiling at people when they took out library books made it more likely that they would bring them back on time – obvious really, but it still needs thinking about carefully.

(d) Details of how to write effective hypotheses are given on p. 150, so you need to follow this advice carefully. Remember that hypotheses should be precise predictive statements and should use

operationalized variables. This question asks you to suggest a 'directional' hypothesis (see p. 150 for details of what this means when writing your answer to this question).

(e) As with the first part of this question, a simple statement will suffice. Remember the definition of an independent variable (IV) offered on p. 134. The IV being used in this study is, of course, the use of a smile when books were issued. Half of the interactions received the IV and half did not.

(f) Cast your mind back to your own interactions with library staff. Are some of the staff you have come across naturally grumpy? And do others have such a sweet and appealing disposition that you find yourself constantly making excuses to take out books and return them? Given the individual differences of the library staff (for example, students may avoid some staff and actively seek out others), or even the different ways that males and females interact, researchers would need to ensure that the results were actually the result of 'smiling' and not some other factor. That is why conditions were reversed on the second day.

(g) Demand characteristics are discussed on p. 163. Remember that in a question of this type, you have approximately 15 minutes to answer all parts. That is approximately 1 minute per mark. You should bear that in mind when answering this part of the question. You will be given extra time over and above this to read the questions and think about your answers, so this time is simply for writing. Demand characteristics might have been evident in this study if students using the library had guessed (perhaps through the artificial behaviour of some staff) that they were taking part in a psychological investigation. They may then have adjusted their behaviour to in some way match their interpretation of what the study was trying to achieve.

(h) The information in Table 1 tells us that students did indeed bring more books back when they had been smiled at (88.8%) than when they had not (78.9%). This leads us to the conclusion that smiling has increased the rate of return of library books taken out from the university library.

Example question 2

The question below should take you 15 to 20 minutes to answer (extra time is given for reading research methods questions in an exam).

> Insights from evolutionary psychology have suggested that men and women may seek partners for quite different reasons that are important for that sex. Men are thought to seek out partners that are young and attractive (demonstrating good health and good child-rearing capacity) while women are thought to seek mates who are industrious and ambitious (indicating their ability to provide resources later on). Imagine that you have been asked to carry out a questionnaire survey of young married couples to see if there is any support for this proposition.

(a) How would you go about selecting respondents to take part in his study?　　　　　*(2 marks)*

(b) Identify two design issues that would help ensure that questions were appropriate for this study.　　　　　*(2 marks)*

(c) Identify two ethical issues that might arise in this study.　　　　　*(2 marks)*

(d) Explain how you would deal with these ethical issues.　　　　　*(2 + 2 marks)*

(e) How might you test the reliability of your questionnaire?　　　　　*(2 marks)*

(f) How might you move beyond this simple questionnaire approach to a more 'valid' investigation of the sex differences in partner choice outlined above?　　　　　*(3 marks)*

Suggested answer structure

(a) The different methods for the selection of participants are detailed on pp. 161–2. Be careful not to use terms like 'random sampling' if your sampling technique could not reasonably match the definition of this term. You are also asked to explain exactly how you would go about using your preferred sampling method. For example, who would the population be, and how would you choose your sample from that population?

(b) There are a number of ways that you can ensure this. Some of these are described on p. 156. For example, you might avoid leading questions (e.g. 'Most women pick men who have good prospects – is that important to you?') or vague questions (e.g. 'Do you like ambitious men?').

(c) Ethical issues are covered in Chapters 5 and 6. Some of the issues discussed there are more likely to be an issue in questionnaires than others. For example, it would be unacceptable to deceive respondents into thinking they were filling in a questionnaire about something quite unrelated, and it would be equally unacceptable if confidentiality were breached in some way. You should think carefully about matching the ethical issues you have read about to the specific research methodology being used. Remember to look ahead as well, as the next question will ask you how you would deal with these issues.

(d) This question is, of course, linked to the previous question, hence the advice in the previous point. The most likely response is to demonstrate your knowledge of the BPS ethical guidelines for the issues in question (these are covered in Chapter 5). Remember to deal with these guidelines in context rather than merely repeating verbatim the appropriate BPS guideline. Thus, if the BPS guideline for confidentiality offers clear guidance as to what is appropriate practice, what would you do in this context in response to this guidance?

(e) There are different methods for testing reliability in a questionnaire (pp. 159–60). The most likely way in this study is by presenting the same participants with the same 'test' on different occasions (or some variation of this procedure) in order to establish the 'test–retest' reliability of the questionnaire.

(f) This is a slightly more searching question, so you need to ask yourself what other technique you would use, and why this might give a more valid measure of the characteristics under investigation. This may involve a naturalistic observation of people's behaviour at parties and other social gatherings where people 'pair up', an examination of dating agencies, or perhaps looking at the lonely hearts column of a local newspaper. You should then be able to justify why each of these (whichever one you choose) is more valid than the method used in this study. Perhaps they are freer from demand characteristics, or maybe people are simply not very truthful when answering questionnaires (which in this study, may be read not only by the researchers, but also their partners).

Further resources

Banister, P., Burman, E., Parker, I., Taylor, M. and Tindall, C. (1994) *Qualitative Methods in Psychology: A Research Guide*, Buckingham: Open University Press.

> *An advanced text which covers observations and interviews.*

Banyard, P. and Grayson, A. (1996) *Introducing Psychological Research*, Basingstoke: Macmillan.

> *A text which contains shortened versions of key research studies.*

Coolican, H. (1999) *Research Methods and Statistics in Psychology* (3rd edn), London: Hodder & Stoughton.

> *A clearly written text which covers the research methods included in the AQA specification. Chapter 21 provides a very good account of how to analyse qualitative data, including the process of content analysis.*

Coolican, H. (1995) *Introduction to Research Methods and Statistics in Psychology*, London: Hodder & Stoughton.

> *A condensed version of the Coolican (1999) text.*

Dyer, C. (1995) *Beginning Research in Psychology: A Practical Guide to Research Methods and Statistics:* Oxford, Blackwell.

> *A detailed text with useful sections on non-experimental methods.*

Foster, J.J. and Parker, I. (1995) *Carrying out Investigations in Psychology: Methods and Statistics,* Leicester: BPS Books.

> *A detailed and advanced text which is of use for reference purposes.*

Gross, R.D. (1994) *Key Studies in Psychology* (2nd edn), London: Hodder & Stoughton.

> *A further text which provides detailed examples from different methodologies.*

Searle, A. (1999) *Introducing Research and Data in Psychology*, London, Routledge.

> *An easily accessible text aimed at the student new to research methods.*

Websites

www.nov.edu/ssss/QR/AR1-4/wark.html

> *This site provides a list of journals which publish qualitative research.*

www.nov.edu/ssss/QR/text.html

> *This site provides the text of research papers, posters and abstracts using qualitative methods.*

These sites may be a useful starting point if you want to find out more about the areas researched using these methods.

Answers to activities

Activity 14

The scattergraph illustrates that stress and illness scores tend to be positively correlated. In other words, when stress scores increase, then so, generally speaking, do illness scores. The correlation coefficient is in fact around +0.6.

Appendix

Instructions for using a random number table to allocate participants to experimental conditions:

Allocate numbers, with the same number of digits, to all potential participants. For example, you might allocate participants with the numbers 01 to 50. Start at any point in the table below and move in any direction. As you reach numbers between 01 and 50 allocate

them in turn to each condition. For example, if undertaking a two-condition experiment and starting at the top right-hand corner of the random number table and moving down, the first number reached is 17, so participant 17 would be allocated to condition A. Next would come participant 46, who would be allocated to condition B, and so on, until all participants have been allocated.

36	45	88	31	28	73	59	43	46	32	00	32	67	15	32	49	54	55	75	17
90	51	40	66	18	46	95	54	65	89	16	80	95	33	15	88	18	60	56	46
98	41	90	22	48	37	80	31	91	39	33	80	40	82	38	26	20	39	71	82
55	25	71	27	14	68	64	04	99	24	82	30	73	43	92	68	18	99	47	54
02	99	10	75	77	21	88	55	79	97	70	32	59	87	75	35	18	34	62	53
79	85	55	66	63	84	08	63	04	00	18	34	53	94	58	01	55	05′	90	99
33	53	95	28	06	81	34	95	13	93	37	16	95	06	15	91	89	99	37	16
74	75	13	13	22	16	37	76	15	57	42	38	96	23	90	24	58	26	71	46
06	66	30	43	00	66	32	60	36	60	46	05	17	31	66	80	91	01	62	35
92	83	31	60	87	30	76	83	17	85	31	48	13	23	17	32	68	14	84	96
61	21	31	49	98	29	77	70	72	11	35	23	69	47	14	27	14	74	52	35
27	82	01	01	74	41	38	77	53	68	53	26	55	16	35	66	31	87	82	09
61	05	50	10	94	85	86	32	10	72	95	67	88	21	72	09	48	73	03	97
11	57	85	67	94	91	49	48	35	49	39	41	80	17	54	45	23	66	82	60
15	16	08	90	92	86	13	32	26	01	20	02	72	45	94	74	97	19	99	46
22	09	29	66	15	44	76	74	94	92	48	13	75	85	81	28	95	41	36	30
69	13	53	55	35	87	43	23	83	32	79	40	92	20	83	76	82	61	24	20
08	29	79	37	00	33	35	34	86	55	10	91	18	86	43	50	67	79	33	58
37	29	99	85	55	63	32	66	71	98	85	20	31	93	63	91	77	21	99	62
65	11	14	04	88	86	28	92	04	03	42	99	87	08	20	55	30	53	82	24
66	22	81	58	30	80	21	10	15	53	26	90	33	77	51	19	17	49	27	14
37	21	77	13	69	31	20	22	67	13	46	29	75	32	69	79	37	23	32	43
51	43	09	72	68	38	05	77	14	62	89	07	37	89	25	30	92	09	06	92
31	59	37	83	92	55	15	31	21	24	03	93	55	97	84	61	96	85	45	51
79	05	43	69	52	93	00	77	44	82	91	65	11	71	25	37	89	13	63	87

Chapter 8

Preparing for the AS examination

Paul Humphreys

In this chapter we shall be looking at

◆ the nature of the AS course and examination

◆ how to prepare for the examination

◆ how to perform to your full potential in the examination

◆ how your examination work will be marked.

Introduction

The Advanced Subsidiary (AS) examination began life in the mid-1990s as part of the plans for changes in the educational system for 16- to 19-year-olds. The AS is set at a level midway between GCSE and GCE Advanced Level, and the skills that you will need to demonstrate will be different from those at these other levels. It is our aim here to give you the fullest possible understanding of how the examination 'works' – for example, by looking at how questions are set and marked so that you can prepare for the exam with these factors in mind. If you use this chapter in conjunction with the other chapters which contain the psychological knowledge, topic by topic, you should be ideally prepared to achieve your best possible grade. Do remember, though, that we can only provide you with guidance and advice; only *you* can put it into practice and make it work.

Doing well in psychology: 15 exam success tips

Senior examiners are, contrary to a good deal of popular belief, human beings too, and when they put down their marking pens and talk with each other they often exchange examining tales of the good, the bad and the – well – absolutely dreadful! As we go through what you need to know about the AS exam, we will look at some of the tales of *success* and will consider our 'Top 15' exam success tips.

An Olympic sprinter does not win a gold medal by just turning up on the day. He or she will have trained hard for months – probably years – in the build-up to the big day. The same is true for you. But it is not just a matter of hard slog; there are efficient and inefficient ways of preparing and 'getting into shape', just as there are for athletes. Success does not always follow determination and energy. So, our focus throughout this chapter is on efficient preparation and performance, not tears and toil.

Exam tip 1: You

I used an analogy with athletes and sports men and women above. The former World Champion sprinter Linford Christie was not only a formidable athlete but also an extraordinarily highly motivated man. He overcame early mediocrity in his career to dominate the 100 metres across the globe for several years, and become an icon and role model for hundreds of others. In an end-of-century ballot, he was voted British Athlete of the twentieth century. The essential point is that Christie *made* himself great.

There may be a few individuals who are so intelligent and naturally talented that they can just cruise to a grade A without breaking sweat; the majority of us, however, are mere mortals and have to work hard for what we achieve. As Jane Fonda famously said, 'No pain, no gain'. You need to *want* to do well.

Organising and planning

Remember what was just said about efficient versus inefficient preparation. One of the best examples concerns organization and planning. Good students break their work up into manageable chunks and set themselves goals to achieve. These goals may correspond to what your tutor will know as *learning outcomes*. Examples would be:

◆ 'By the end of my revision today/tonight, I will be able to write a detailed essay plan answering an exam question on memory.'

◆ 'By the end of my revision today/tonight I will be able to write accurate and detailed descriptions of two studies of conformity.'

◆ 'By the end of my revision today/tonight I will be able show how stress management has been shown to work.'

Goals will motivate you and will help you keep a check on how you are progressing; what you have achieved and what still remains for you to do. Two final points:

◆ Don't set yourself huge, impossible goals, e.g. 'Tonight I will learn everything about abnormality'! You will miss them by a mile and will become depressed and demotivated.

◆ Remember to revisit what you have already learned. If skills and knowledge are not regularly re-addressed and reviewed, they can decay. This review often only takes a matter of a few minutes. Do this regularly for maximum impact. Remember the old adage: use it or lose it!

Exam tip 2: Gain access to materials

The AQA examining board (at Stag Hill House, Guildford, Surrey GU2 5XJ) makes available a wide range of support material for the AS examination: specimen examination papers, marking schemes, suggestions for reading, and much, much more. Most of this is written for tutors but if you believe (as I think you should) that you should make sure that as much of your future is in your own hands as possible, then reading these will put *you* in the driving seat. Just ask your tutor if you can have a look at what they have and photocopy what you can for yourself. Don't forget to return everything you borrow!

Exam tip 3: Use a wide variety of sources

Of course the writers of this book want to include everything possible that you will need in order to do well, but it is always good practice to cast your net wide. There are a number of magazines and periodicals written for psychologists and psychology students, and you should aim to make good, intelligent use of the World Wide Web. Unfortunately, there is a lot of unmitigated junk on the Web, but this should not blind us to the fact that the Web also contains a wealth of superb and bang-up-to-date material which cannot fail to impress your examiner. (Another useful tip: you can focus your searches, because most British university

sites include 'ac.uk' in their URL whereas most USA ones have 'edu' in theirs.)

During the time I have been writing this chapter, an article has been published in a national newspaper publicizing a forthcoming revision Web site (revise.it) run for current GCSE and A-level students by ex-students. Things update on a week-by-week basis here.

It is inappropriate to list a lot of specific sites here as many disappear overnight, but some which you may find particularly worth a visit are listed in 'Further resources' at the end of the chapter.

You may, of course, find some of the material held on these sites to be quite advanced (a good deal will certainly be written for undergraduates and professionals) but there *will* be plenty to interest and help you. You may like to set up 'swap shops' with your fellow students for good Net materials you have found.

There will also be a number of high-quality television programmes on topics which will be relevant to your AS course. The most likely providers will be BBC2 and Channel 4, but make a point of carefully reading through a decent television programmes magazine each week to see if there is anything of interest. You should video copy any relevant programmes if you can, take detailed notes on them (being particularly careful to note just who is saying what) and then add them to your lecture and reading materials.

Exam tip 4: Make sure you know the specification

There is absolutely no mystery to examination papers. Questions are set clearly and explicitly on material in the *specification* (this is the new word for 'syllabus'). For all parts of the AS course, apart from Research Methods (dealt with later, on pp. 191–4), we can identify question types by general categories and particular topics of psychology. The general categories are:

1 *Terminology* (e.g. definitions – for instance, what do psychologists mean by the term 'attachment'?).

2 *Concepts and contributory factors* (e.g. describe two differences between long-term memory and short-term memory; describe two factors which have been shown to lead to forgetting).

3 *Theories* (e.g. outline the major causes of abnormal behaviour according to any two theories/models of abnormality).

4 *Studies* (e.g. describe one research study which has investigated how people might resist obedience).

5 *Criticisms* (e.g. give two criticisms of a research study which has investigated the accuracy of eyewitness testimony).

6 *Methods* (e.g. in writing about two studies of forgetting, for example Freudian repression and the influence of interference on recall in a laboratory test of memory, you might want to show how the studies used quite different methods and what the consequences of this might be). As such, methods can really be a 'subset' of studies and theories, insofar as many theories develop out of studies which, of course, have been carried out using certain methods. Freudian psychology and Piagetian psychology are good examples. Methods are dealt with explicitly in the Research Methods section of the specification.

Table 8.1 lists the particular topics covered in AS psychology.

(* Indicates what is called the 'Critical Issue'. This refers to areas in which the topic under consideration, i.e. memory, attachments, stress, abnormality and social influence, are looked at in a specified 'real-world' context.)

In preparing for the examination, then, you will need to have learned about five topics – memory, attachments, stress, abnormality and social influence – with three 'subsets' for each. Finally, for each of these you will need to be able to:

◆ offer *definitions* (almost always just a single paragraph), key terms and concepts

◆ know about important *contributory factors*

◆ know about a small number of *theories* (with reference to methods, if appropriate)

◆ know about a small number of *studies* (including their methodologies),

... and that is it!

Be thoroughly prepared for this and you will have everything you will need for the AS examination.

So what does this actually mean in practice? Let's illustrate it with reference to one particular chapter of the book. Let's look at the final third of Chapter 2, *Developmental Psychology: Attachments in development*, where the Critical Issue of Day care is covered (pp. 47–52).

◆ *key terms and concepts* – separation, deprivation and privation, childminding, **day care***, working mothers, interaction effects

◆ *contributory factors* – security, individual variability, enrichment programmes, consistency of care, quality of care, teaching day-care providers, effects of separation on parents

◆ *theories* – Bowlby's maternal deprivation (and responses to this), research (theories and studies) into **social and cognitive development***

◆ *major studies* – Dennis (1973), Mayall and Petrie (1983), Bryant *et al.* (1980), Andersson (1992), Harvey (1999), Operation Headstart, Egeland and Hiester (1995), The NICHD study (1997).

* These terms are stated on p. 19 of the AQA specification. Questions on this topic will make use of these terms and you should, therefore, make sure you feel comfortable with them. The other terms, factors, theories and studies given above are suggestions as to how you might respond to such questions.

Activity 1: Analysing topics

Look again at the list of the list of particular topics in Table 8.1 and select one. Now read the relevant chapter and produce a list like the one for day care above, using the same headings of *key terms and concepts, contributory factors, theories* and *studies.*

You might find it helpful to work with your friends doing this so that you can compare lists and discuss them.

Exam tip 5: Get plenty of exam practice

There is no substitute for practising the skills on which you will finally be assessed, in the actual situation in which they will be assessed. Like most students, you may have a deep hatred of mock exams, but nothing else prepares you better for what you are going to have to do on the big day. If you practise answering questions from mock papers under exam conditions – no books, with time limits, answering questions you have not seen before – every week during your revision building up to the exam, the exam will hold no terrors for you. The best way to prepare for a driving test is to get out on the road as much as you can and rehearse the things you will need to do in the test, not sitting at home reading the Highway Code over and over again.

Exam tip 6: Be able to deliver the exam skills

The AS exam requires you to demonstrate knowledge and skills in three distinct ways, called *assessment objectives*. Different questions cover different assessment objectives, as we shall see later.

◆ Assessment Objective 1 (or AO1): Show *knowledge* and *understanding*

◆ Assessment Objective 2 (or AO2): *Analyse and evaluate*

◆ Assessment Objective 3 (or AO3): *Design, conduct and report*.

Assessment Objective 1

Assessment Objective 1 (or AO1) is the demonstration of knowledge and understanding through clear and effective communication.

Let's stay with the example of day care. In order to do well in the AO1 questions (we look at how to recognize these on p. 187), you will need to know and understand the key concepts and terminology (refresh your memory by looking at the list again), and some contributory factors, theories and studies from the lists given. Don't worry about the vagueness of the term 'some' at the moment; we shall explore this in detail later.

Are knowledge and understanding the same thing? No, they are not. I know that in order to make my car go faster, I have to press my foot down on the accelerator pedal, but I must confess I don't understand how this 'works', i.e. what actually happens as a result of my 'putting my foot down'. By same token, I may 'know' what the main features of Bowlby's theory of attachment are (pp. 37–40), but this knowledge may be quite superficial with no real understanding underpinning it. Take the non-understanding student away from their rote-learning list – attachment as an

adaptive process, social releasers, critical periods, the internal working model – and they're lost. Conversely, if you really understand something, you can look at it from any angle – not just a prelearned sequence – and still feel totally at ease with it. Understanding leads to insight: having a real grasp and comprehension of the thing in question.

The best way to develop understanding (which builds on top of knowledge) is always to try to put things in your own words. If you can do this accurately and with ease, then you have almost certainly achieved understanding.

Before we leave exam skill AO1, note that we said knowledge and understanding are insufficient in themselves; you need to be able to *communicate* them clearly and effectively.

Assessment Objective 2

Assessment Objective 2 (AO2) is analysis and evaluation. We are using the term analysis in the same sense as it is used in psychoanalysis. Freud was interested in analysing the psyche, or the mind, using such questions as:

◆ What are the elements which make it up?

◆ How do they work together?

◆ How do they interrelate?

In the same way, we can take any theory apart, examine the individual parts of it, and then put it back together. It is the opposite of what has been called a *holistic approach*, in which we examine something as a whole entity. Think for a moment about how a Shakespeare play, *Romeo and Juliet* for example, could be viewed in both ways. The same is true for psychological concepts, theories and studies. Think of analysis, then, as taking something apart, stripping it down to its basic elements and then carrying out a detailed examination of these.

There is another aspect of 'analysis' which is not immediately apparent from a literal definition of the word. Imagine you go to see your football team play a match. The odds are you will get sucked into the 'theatre' of the match, and watch it with the heart more than the mind. A football writer, on the other hand, will be watching your team and the game *analytically*. There is, then, a component of critical consideration to analysis too.

What about evaluation? By this term we mean making an informed judgement about the value or worth of something. So, I've just watched *Romeo and Juliet*. How good was it? How did I arrive at that judgement? What were my criteria? It is one thing to know the 'factual features' of Bowlby's theory of attachment, quite another to make an informed judgement about its quality or worth.

Activity 2: Making informed judgements

Imagine you are asked the question: what makes good psychology and what makes bad psychology? We can all imagine extreme cases – 'bad psychology' might be some loudmouth at the pub bar talking utter nonsense about all the 'things I know about the differences between men and women'. Other than obvious physical differences, the rest might be complete gibberish.

But why is it gibberish? A scientist might say, for example, because it is either *wrong* (systematic studies have shown the statements to be inaccurate) or *unsubstantiated* (the studies haven't been carried out). It may be unacceptable for many reasons. For example, the argument may be illogical. It is one thing to say that people differ in terms of skin colour (they obviously do), quite another to say that these differences cause differences in intelligence or personality (they certainly do not).

Make a list of all of the criteria you might use in judging whether a psychological theory is a good one or not. Ten possibilities are listed at the end of the chapter.

Two important points need to be made. You may have noticed that the phrase used was *informed* judgement. This means the judgement is not a whim or 'pulled out of thin air', but is based on solid information and can be substantiated. 'Milgram's work was ethically unforgivable' is an evaluation of sorts but has no substance. (See pp. 128–9 for an informed evaluation of the ethical status of Milgram's work.)

The second point is that evaluation should be *two-sided*. Few things in psychology and life are so one-sided that they have nothing which can be said in their favour or nothing which can be said against them (exceptions might include genocide or paedophilia). In most circumstances, there are two sides to a question and both need evaluating. Evaluation does not mean 'sticking the boot in'; it means giving a balanced appraisal. Make sure you always give both the pros and the cons.

Assessment Objective 3

Assessment Objective 3 (AO3) relates only to the Research Methods part of the course and exam, so we shall deal with it later in this chapter (p. 191).

Exam tip 7: Know what will come up in the exam

We have already discussed the skills and content areas you will need to know about. But we can be even more specific. The detail of the specification shows *exactly* what you need to know. In Table 8.2 you will find all the things you must know about for the examination, i.e. those which are named in the specification. Most importantly, these are the things which the examiners can specify in the exam papers. Put simply, if it's not in the specification, it can't be in a question.

Just one small warning: remember that this is the *bare minimum* you need to cover. You should be looking all the time to draw material out of the relevant chapters to supplement it.

Table 8.2	What you must cover for the exam		

Cognitive Psychology: Human memory

Topic	Key terms and concepts	Research (i.e. theories/explanations and studies)	Analysis and evaluation
Long-term and short-term memory (LTM and STM	1 nature and structure of memory 2 encoding, capacity, duration	1 multistore model (Atkinson and Shiffrin) 2 working memory (Baddeley and Hitch) 3 levels of processing (Craik and Lockhart)	
Forgetting	1 STM forgetting: decay and displacement* 2 LTM forgetting: retrieval failure*; interference*	emotional factors in forgetting: flashbulb memories; repression (Freud*)	
Eyewitness testimony	eyewitness testimony	1 reconstructive memory (Bartlett; Loftus) 2 face recognition	

continued

Table 8.2 *continued*

Developmental Psychology: Attachments in development

Topic	Key terms and concepts	Research	Analysis and evaluation
Development and variety of attachments	attachment	1 explanations (learning theory*, Bowlby's theory*) 2 development (Schaffer*) 3 individual differences: secure and insecure attachments (Ainsworth*) 4 cross-cultural variations	
Deprivation and privation	1 deprivation 2 privation	1 short- and long-term effects of deprivation/separation (including Bowlby's maternal deprivation hypothesis) 2 privation (Tizard and Hodges' study of institutionalization*)	
Day care	day care	1 effects on children's cognitive and 2 social development	

Physiological Psychology: Stress

Topic	Key terms and concepts	Research	Analysis and evaluation
Stress as a bodily response	1 stress 2 stressors	1 body's response to stressors, including General Adaptation Syndrome (Selye) 2 relationship between stress and physical illness, including cardio-vascular disorders and immune system)	
Sources of stress	1 sources of stress 2 workplace stressors	1 life changes (Holmes and Rahe*) 2 workplace (overload*, role ambiguity*) 3 individual differences, including personality (Friedman and Rosenman*), culture, and gender	
Stress management	1 stress management 2 control	1 physical methods, including drugs*, biofeedback* 2 psychological approaches (stress-inoculation*, hardiness*) 3 role of control in stress perception	Critical analysis of 1 strengths 2 weaknesses of methods of stress management

Individual Differences: Abnormality

Topic	Key terms and concepts	Research	Analysis and evaluation
Defining psychological abnormality	abnormality definitions: 1 statistical infrequency 2 deviation from social norms 3 failure to function adequately 4 deviation from ideal mental health		Critical analysis of 1 limitations of named definitions 2 limitations to include cultural relativism
1 Biological and 2 psychological models		1 assumptions relating to causes and 2 implications for treatment of 3 biological (medical) and 4 psychological (incl. psychodynamic, behavioural and cognitive) models	
Eating disorders: 1 anorexia nervosa 2 bulimia nervosa	clinical characteristics of 1 anorexia nervosa 2 bulimia nervosa	1 biological and 2 psychological explanatory models and 3 research studies	

continued

Table 8.2 *continued*

Social Psychology: Social influence

Topic	Key terms and concepts	Research	Analysis and evaluation
1 Conformity 2 Minority influence	1 conformity 2 minority influence	explanations of 1 conformity (majority influence 2 minority influence. research into 1 conformity (Sherif*, Asch*, Zimbardo*) 2 minority influence (Moscovici*, Clark*)	
Obedience to authority	1 obedience to authority 2 experimental and ecological validity	explanations of: 1 obedience processes and why people obey 2 resistance to obedience research studies (Milgram*; Hofling*; Meeus and Raaijmakers*)	
Ethical issues in psychological research	ethical issues related to 1 deception 2 informed consent 3 protection of participants from psychological harm	relevance of named ethical issues to social influence research	Critical analysis of ways in which psychologists have dealt with the ethical issues (e.g. through use of ethical guidelines*)

* These are given as *examples* in the specification (as guidance). You cannot be asked questions directly on them. Consider it good practice, though, to know about them.

Note that the *Analysis and evaluation* column is largely blank. This does not mean that you will not need any; rather, that you can choose your own ways to analyse and evaluate the particular topics.
Remember that analysis and evaluation is AO2 and is only assessed in the last part of each AS question.

Performing well in the examination

Unfortunately, there are always some students who have prepared themselves faultlessly for an exam, but just don't do themselves justice on the day. It's probably rather more complicated than this, but in essence this is likely to be the result of two factors:

◆ stress and tension

◆ not really understanding what skills an exam requires.

It is easy to be glib about the first set of factors and trot out some platitude such as 'just relax – there's nothing to worry about – everything will okay'. Sadly, we all know it's not that easy. Relaxation *is* important, however, and it is true that examiners are not in the business of trying to catch you out. They really do want you to do well. Making use of 'mock' exam practice, mentioned earlier, is probably the best way for you to break up your performance anxiety. Practise, practise,

practise – and you will find a lot of your fear and anxiety will disappear.

The other reason for underachievement is not knowing the exam skills. After you have read the next few pages, there will be no excuse for this!

Exam tip 8: The question structure

In all the sections of the exam papers, except Research Methods (see p. 191), questions have a uniform structure.

Each question carries 18 AO1 marks (effective communication of knowledge and understanding) and 12 AO2 marks (analysis and evaluation), giving a total of 30 marks. The last part of each question carries all of the AO2 marks.

◆ The first section of each question will carry 6 marks (AO1 only).

◆ The middle section will carry 12 marks (AO1 only) – sometimes split into two questions of 6 marks each.

◆ The final section will carry 12 marks (AO2 only).

In the first two sections of the questions, the different possibilities are:

◆ Give definitions...   *(3 marks + 3 marks)*
◆ Describe one study...   *(6 marks)*
◆ Outline two studies...   *(3 marks + 3 marks)*
◆ Describe one theory...   *(6 marks)*
◆ Outline two theories...   *(3 marks + 3 marks)*
◆ Describe two factors which explain ...
                                          (3 marks + 3 marks)
◆ Give two criticisms of ...   *(3 marks + 3 marks)*

In the final section, there will be a short quotation/phrase/vignette, and you will then be asked, for example:

◆ To what extent does ...
◆ Consider what psychologists have shown us about ...
◆ Evaluate research into ... .

Every question will sample the whole topic section. So, in memory, for example, all the parts of the question would *not* be set on forgetting (or the other two subsections), but would be a sample from the section as a whole.

This is a lot to take in and understand, so do reread it several times if you need to. Let's make this 'concrete' by looking at some examples of the sorts of questions that could be set.

Cognitive Psychology: Human memory

1 (a) Explain what is meant by short-term memory and long-term memory.   *(3 marks + 3 marks)*

   (b) Describe one study carried out into reconstructive memory.   *(6 marks)*

   (c) Describe one study carried out into face recognition.   *(6 marks)*

   (d) 'Emotional factors play a very significant part in causing us to forget certain things.'

      To what extent has psychology shown this to be true?   *(12 marks)*

2 (a) Outline two factors which explain why forgetting occurs.   *(3 marks + 3 marks)*

   (b) Describe the working memory and the levels of processing models of memory.
                                          (6 marks + 6 marks)

   (c) 'Factors which have been shown to cause forgetting in short-term memory are different from those which have been found to cause forgetting in long-term memory.'

      To what extent has psychological research supported this view?   *(12 marks)*

Developmental Psychology: Attachments

1 (a) Explain what psychologists mean by cognitive development and social development.
                                          (3 marks + 3 marks)

   (b) Describe one explanation which has been given for attachment.   *(6 marks)*

   (c) Describe one study which has explored the long-term effects of deprivation.   *(6 marks)*

   (d) 'The ways in which children around the world are brought up vary enormously. It should, therefore, come as no surprise to us that typical patterns of attachment will also vary considerably between different countries'.

      Consider what psychological research has shown us about cross-cultural variations in attachments.   *(12 marks)*

2 (a) What is meant by deprivation and privation?
                                          (3 marks + 3 marks)

   (b) Describe two explanations which have been given for attachment.   *(6 marks + 6 marks)*

   (c) 'A child should always be brought up by its mother. No matter how loving and sensitive day carers may be, children will always suffer negative effects from being brought up away from mother'.

      Evaluate research which relates to the effects of day care on children's development.   *(12 marks)*

Physiological Psychology: Stress

1 (a) Outline two of the body's responses to stress.
                                          (3 marks + 3 marks)

   (b) Describe research which has demonstrated the influence of personality on stress modification.
                                          (6 marks)

   (c) Describe research which has demonstrated the influence of gender on stress modification.
                                          (6 marks)

   (d) 'A lot of methods have been put forward to help people manage their stress levels. There is consideration variation, however, in their effectiveness – from almost life-saving to the utterly useless'.

      Consider the strengths and weaknesses of different methods of stress management.
                                          (12 marks)

2 (a) Outline two methods which have been used in stress management.   *(3 marks + 3 marks)*

   (b) Describe Selye's General Adaptation Syndrome.
                                          (6 marks)

   (c) Describe the effects which stress has been shown to have on either the immune system or cardiovascular disorders.   *(6 marks)*

(d) 'Our lives are full of stressors, from major events such as life changes, childbirth and changes in employment, to the daily hassles of the workplace. How can psychology possibly shed light on the stress effects of such a diversity of factors?'

Evaluate what psychology has discovered about the sources of stress. *(12 marks)*

Individual Differences: Abnormality

1 (a) Outline one clinical characteristic of anorexia nervosa and one clinical characteristic of bulimia nervosa. *(3 marks + 3 marks)*

(b) Describe the assumptions made by the psychodynamic model concerning the cause of eating disorders and the implications of these for treatment. *(6 marks + 6 marks)*

(c) 'Abnormality is so diverse and complex that it can never be satisfactorily defined. All attempts by psychologists to do so will inevitably fail.'

Consider the extent to which attempts by psychologists to define abnormality have been shown to have limitations. *(12 marks)*

2 (a) Describe two attempts at defining psychological abnormality. *(3 marks + 3 marks)*

(b) Describe the assumptions about the causes of abnormality made by one biological and one psychological model of abnormality. *(6 marks + 6 marks)*

(c) 'The eating disorders of anorexia nervosa and bulimia nervosa severely damage the day-to-day lives of so many people in our world today and yet psychological research has given us little real insight into these disorders.'

Consider what research studies of anorexia nervosa and/or bulimia nervosa have told us about these eating disorders. *(12 marks)*

Social Psychology: Social influence

1 (a) Define the terms conformity and obedience. *(3 marks + 3 marks)*

(b) Describe two studies into obedience to authority. *(6 marks + 6 marks)*

(c) 'Psychologists must always be mindful of the ethical guidelines intended to regulate their work. Unfortunately, many in the past have not been and psychology as a whole discipline has suffered'.

Consider the ways in which psychologists have dealt with ethical issues. *(12 marks)*

2 (a) Describe the ethical issues of deception and informed consent in psychological research. *(3 marks + 3 marks)*

(b) Describe two factors which explain conformity. *(6 marks)*

(c) Describe two factors which explain how individuals resist obedience. *(6 marks)*

(c) 'Psychologists have spent a lot of time looking at why one person conforms in the presence of a group of others, but very little looking at the equally interesting fact that we are often influenced just as much by a small number of people within a group.'

Evaluate psychological research into minority influence. *(12 marks)*

Activity 3: Understanding exam questions

You have now had the chance to read ten specimen questions. The questions on the exam paper will look very similar to these (the actual content will differ somewhat, of course, but the formats will be the same).

Now try your hand at being an examiner. Look back at the information in Table 8.2, 'What you must cover for the exam', and try to set some exam questions yourself. When you have finished doing this check them against the format 'rules' given at the top of Exam tip 8 (p. 187).

Exam tip 9: Answer the question

This may sound obvious – even patronizing – but many candidates simply don't answer the questions set, as any senior examiner will testify. Some candidates seem to think that the actual wording of a question doesn't really matter too much, as long as they write an answer 'in the general area'. Others seem to prepare too rigidly and go into the exam hall simply intent on reproducing 'prewritten' answers. For whatever reasons, the answers do not 'fit' the questions. You must go into the exam hall prepared to be flexible and deal with the specific demands of the paper in front of you.

Let me illustrate this through two analogies. First the *wrong* one: *don't* think of yourself as an actor in a play whose task it is to repeat the lines they have learned, word perfect, time after time. Second, *do* think of yourself as someone like a doctor who has deal with whatever comes their way in a particular surgery session, no matter what their particular interests and specialisms are.

Make sure you read the questions carefully, and don't start writing your answers until you have really thought about what you are being asked to do and planned your responses. Remember, it isn't just what you put into your answers; it's also to do with what you leave out. Almost certainly you will know a lot more psychology than you can write down in the exam. The trick is to make sure that you offer the examiner those parts of your psychological knowledge that are most relevant to the questions in front of you. Don't fall into the trap of writing what *you* want to; write what *the examiner* wants.

Exam tip 10: Exam structure

Unit 1 (the first exam paper) will contain two cognitive psychology questions and two developmental psychology questions. You will need to answer one cognitive and one developmental question. As with the examples on the previous page, there may be areas of overlap between the questions which makes it more important than ever that you choose your questions carefully. The length of the *assessment unit* (exam paper, in old-speak!) is one hour. Make sure you allocate the time equally (30 minutes) to each question.

Unit 2 will contain two physiological questions and two questions on individual differences. You will need to answer one of each. The time allowance is also one hour.

Unit 3 will contain two social psychology questions (answer one) and two Research Methods (you will need to answer both of these). The examining time allowance for Unit 3 is 75 minutes to allow 15 minutes' reading time for the Research Methods questions.

Exam tip 11: Good time-management

As we have just seen, all the AS questions (excluding those on Research Methods) are set to a specific formula, and we have noted that the allocation of marks is always 18 for AO1 and 12 for AO2.

It is critical to your exam success that you divide your answer to map that of the question. For your answers, you will have a little less than a minute per mark (30 marks available per question; 30 minutes allowed – but reading the questions, planning your answers and then checking them through at the end will, of course, use some of that time allowance, so let's say you have 25 minutes *writing* time). Alternatively, think of it another way: the average candidate is probably capable of writing around 500 words in 25 minutes.

What this means is that each 6 marks unit (refer back to the specimen questions if you wish) should be allocated approximately five minutes of writing time and should generate around 100 words.

Let's imagine a candidate, Alex, in the exam hall. Alex decides to answer Social Psychology Q2 (see p. 189). She writes for about 5 minutes on part (a), and on part (b), although her answer is badly skewed here

as she spends about 4 minutes on the first factor explaining conformity and only about 1 minute on the second. The disaster is still to come, though. Sadly, Alex knows almost nothing about minority influence, but reasons that this only one part (of four) of the question and, since the first part of the quotation is to do with conformity in groups then she can probably get away with writing about that. She loves part (c) with a rare passion – it's the Milgram question – yes!! – so she spends about 12 of the remaining 15 minutes on this. Oh dear, a disaster indeed!

Let's list the separate elements of her demise:

1   Part (a): no problem.

2   Part (b): skewed answer. She should have spent equal time on both.

3   Part (c): unforgivably time-indulgent – she spent two-and-a-half times the time allocation on it. Furthermore, she focuses wholly on Milgram in her answer. This would have been fine had the question been 'Describe one study of obedience to authority', but it wasn't.

4   Part (d): time-starved. Furthermore, Alex is wrong in her interpretation: the quotations are used to 'frame' or 'contextualize' the question, but it is the question itself which must be answered. The question is on minority influence, not conformity.

Hannah, sitting next to Alex, makes none of these mistakes and goes on to get an extremely good mark.

Exam tip 12: Make your answers 'psychological'

The exam is in psychology, so, naturally enough, you will be judged on the quality of your psychology! Again, this may seem an obvious point, but senior examiners know from experience that a large number of candidates ignore this point.

Activity 4: Writing styles

Before reading on, turn to any of the other AS chapters in this book and read a couple of paragraphs.

You will have noticed the style that the authors use, and that it is different to the one used in this chapter. I have written this chapter in a fairly 'chatty', one-to-one style, but this would be inappropriate for other chapters which deal with 'real' psychology. You should try to avoid writing your answers in a chatty, anecdotal way, but should write in the third person ('it can be argued' rather than 'I reckon', for example). Try to write in an objective, logical manner and remember that you should always aim to give evidence to support what you are saying. The bloke down the pub may be able say 'girls have eating problems these days because all the magazines are stuffed with photos of stick-like dolly birds,' but you can't. You need to say, 'Psychological research such as that carried out by XXX has shown that ...'

You may find this difficult to begin with, but it is a classic instance where practice can make perfect, as you will discover.

Exam tip 13: Deliver skill AO3

Earlier in this chapter we examined skills AO1 and AO2. Assessment Objective 3 (AO3) is assessed only in Research Methods, which is the final element of the exam (second half of Unit 3), so you need not concern yourself with it when answering any other questions (i.e. your Cognitive, Developmental, Physiological, Individual Differences and Social Psychology answers).

Some elements of AO3 relate only to the A2 examination, where coursework is carried out, so we need not concern ourselves with those here. What is 'left' is the ability to:

◆ design a psychological investigation

◆ report a psychological investigation (not in the A2 sense of submitting a formal report, but in the sense of 'reporting' various features of a self-designed study in the second Research Methods question)

◆ choose from a range of methods

◆ take account of issues relating to reliability, validity and ethics

◆ draw conclusions from data.

These are dealt with in all the detail you will require in Chapters 6 and 7 in this book. What we need to note here is that these are the abilities which you will be assessed on in the exam.

We can be more exact and examine the *context* in which they will be assessed. The information is given separately in the specification but we have saved you the task of putting the two together. Table 8.3 maps the details of the specification onto the AO3 skills.

Table 8.3 Mapping of AO3 skills with AS specification	
AO3 skill requirement	*What you need to know and be able to do*
Design of psychological investigation	Designs: 1 experimental designs (including independent groups; repeated measures and matched participants) 2 naturalistic observations 3 questionnaire surveys 4 interviews. Factors associated with design: 1 operationalization of the IV/DV 2 conducting pilot studies 3 control of variables 4 selection of participants (including random sampling) where appropriate
Report	Aims and hypotheses: experimental/alternative: 1 directional 2 non-directional 3 null hypotheses
Choose from the methods	1–3 experiments, including 1 laboratory, 2 field and 3 natural experiments 4 investigations using correlational analysis 5 naturalistic observations 6 questionnaire surveys 7 interviews
Take account of:	1 reliability 2 validity 3 ethical issues 4 relationship between researchers and participants (including demand characteristics and investigator effects)
Draw conclusions from data	1 analysis of qualitative data derived from observations, surveys and interviews 2 graphs and charts 3 central tendency and dispersion 4 positive and negative correlations and interpretation of coefficients

Exam tip 14: Performing well in Research Methods

This part of the exam is very different to the others. It focuses on how psychological research is carried out and is what we might call problem-driven, i.e. you have to apply your knowledge of the factors listed in the table above in two particular contexts:

◆ *question style 1:* answering questions relating to a fictitious study (see *In Focus* on this page for an example)

◆ *question style 2:* explaining how you would carry out a study to explore a topic given to you in the exam question (see *In Focus* on the following page).

The two exam questions in Research Methods – and remember that, unlike in all of the other sections of the exam, you have to answer *both* questions this time – make different demands on you. We can see this most clearly by looking at the example of each given below (our gratitude goes to AQA for granting us permission to reproduce these).

Research Methods question style 1

Read through the example question (see *In Focus* below). Note that most of the questions carry 2 marks.

1 mark would be awarded when an answer is muddled or brief. 0 marks would be awarded, of course, if an answer is inaccurate. There are two significant differences between how you need to write your Research Methods answers and how you answer other questions.

1 In Research Methods you need not write in complete sentences/paragraphs. For example, in answering (a) you would gain the mark if you wrote 'The method used in this study was an experiment'; you would also get it if you just wrote 'Experiment'. However, do note what we have just said about brief answers (getting 1 instead of 2, when 2 is available), so you should not aim to be too frugal with your words. The key point is that there is no point in merely putting in words for the sake of it.

2 In all other aspects of the exam, examiners use something known as *positive marking*. What this means is that if you make a mistake, the examiner ignores it and doesn't take any marks away. The logic is that in writing something inaccurate candidates penalize themselves because they have wasted precious time when they could have been writing something which would earn credit. 'Knocking marks off' would therefore be a double penalty. However, this logic isn't used here.

Research Methods question style 1

A psychologist decided to study whether accuracy of eyewitness testimony is influenced by the amount of material a person sees. Each participant in the experiment was taken individually into a lecture room where a number of students were seated. They were instructed to look around the room and then after two minutes were led out. The number of students in the room was either 12 (Small Audience group) or 50 (Large Audience group). The participants were allocated randomly to the two conditions. One week later the participants were asked to identify which of the photographs in the set of 25 were of people who had been in the room.

Before beginning her experiment, the psychologist had hypothesized that the Small Audience group would perform better than the other group.

The median for the Small Audience group was 10 correct identifications; for the Large Audience group it was 7.

(a) Name the method used in this study. *(1 mark)*

(b) Give one advantage and one disadvantage of this method. *(2 marks + 2 marks)*

(c) What is a median? *(2 marks)*

(d) Give one advantage of using the median. *(2 marks)*

(e) Why were the participants taken individually to the room rather than all together? *(2 marks)*

(f) Explain why the psychologist ensured that each student sat in the same seat every time they were in the lecture room. *(2 marks)*

(g) Why was it important that all participants were given the same instruction? *(2 marks)*

Let's look again at (a). You could write: 'survey, interview, experiment, correlation, observation' and under the principles of positive marking you would get the mark because, albeit embedded in a list, you have given the right answer. However, the whole list would have taken you only seconds to write. This is a bit of a cheat and so isn't allowed. The examiner is told to mark only the first answer you give in situations like this.

These two principles also apply to the second type of Research Methods question, to which we shall now turn.

Research Methods question style 2

Read through the example question (see *In Focus*). Note that the two Research Methods questions together carry 30 marks, the same as *one* of your answers in all the other sections of the exam. Remember this if you get stuck – the number of marks carried by each of the parts of these questions is small (generally 3 or less), so it's not a disaster if you can't answer one of them. But if the answer doesn't instantly spring to mind, try to work it out. 'Thinking time' is one of the reasons why this unit carries an extra 15 minutes compared to the other two. Go back to the overall 'theme' of the question, and look again at the questions you *have* been able to answer and you may be able to see the connections. If all else fails, have an intelligent guess – you've nothing to lose and it is disheartening to leave lots of gaps.

Finally, in these examples, both questions carry equal marks (15 each), but they do not have to, so – as ever! – go into the exam prepared to be flexible and adaptable. There does, however, have to be one question of each style set; you could not have two style 1s, for instance.

How your work is marked

A key determinant of success is having a sound understanding of what the examiner is looking for – or to put it another way, how they mark your work.

The uninformed student will write *hoping* that this is what the examiner is looking for; the informed student will write *knowing* that it is what the examiner is looking for.

Before they mark any exam papers (or *scripts*, as they are technically known), all examiners attend a full day's standardization meeting in which they work through a considerable number of candidates' answers. They work alongside all the other examiners and are led by the Principal Examiners who set the question papers. Two factors which are very significant to you emerge from this:

◆ This process ensures that all examiners mark to the same standard, so it makes no difference which examiner marks your work. There are no hard or soft markers!

◆ All the examiners mark to the same set of criteria or guidelines. This is the critical factor, because these criteria are made public by the examining board so you can know in advance what the examiners are looking for.

We will look at the marking criteria shortly, but three other important general points need to be made first.

◆ Examiners mark according to a standard which it is reasonable to expect a notional 17-year-old to display working under examination conditions. They appreciate that you will be anxious and tense. They will bear in mind that you have limited time at your disposal, are answering questions that you have only just encountered and are not allowed to consult your books, notes, etc. Clearly, it's a very different exercise to writing an essay for classwork, and you can rest assured that the examiner will always be mindful of this.

◆ In psychology there are rarely single, right answers (other than occasionally for Research Methods

---

<table>
<tr><td>in focus</td><td>

Research Methods question style 2

Imagine that you have been asked to carry out a questionnaire study of how much stress people feel they are under and how they cope with their stress.

(a) How would you carry out a pilot study on your questionnaire? *(3 marks)*

(b) Why is it necessary to carry out such a pilot study? *(2 marks)*

(c) How would you test the reliability of your questionnaire? *(3 marks)*

(d) How would you select respondents to take part in your study? *(2 marks)*

(e) Why would you choose this particular method of selecting respondents? *(2 marks)*

(f) How would you try to ensure that respondents answered the questions truthfully? *(2 marks)*

</td></tr>
</table>

questions). There are, of course, wrong answers (e.g. 'the concept of attachment was invented by Piaget') but that's a different matter. The consequence of this is that you should bear in mind that there is no single answer to learn when preparing for questions and, perhaps most importantly, no single answer which the examiner is looking for.

◆ Examiners do not mark with pass or fail in mind. They do not even mark with grades in mind. Grades are decided by an Awarding committee of examiners and teachers after the marking has been completed. Examiners award marks solely according to the marking criteria which we will now explore.

Exam tip 15: Understand the marking scheme

Two sets of criteria are used by examiners marking AS exam scripts, one for AO1 questions and one for AO2 questions. (We have already pointed out that AO3 is assessed only in the Research Methods part of the exam, generally in units of 2 marks when 2 is given for accurate answers, 1 for answers which are brief or muddled and 0 for answers which are inaccurate.)

As we have seen from the specimen questions, the AO1 questions tend to be in units of either 3 marks or 6 marks. They are marked as shown in Table 8.4.

You can now clearly see that the examiners are looking for just two things: accuracy and detail. Deliver!

AO2 is always assessed in the final part of the questions (once again excluding Research Methods). This is illustrated in the specimen questions (pp. 187–9) if you wish to refresh your memory. 12 marks are at stake and the marking here is shown in Table 8.5.

Activity 5: Marking your own work

Next time you write an AS piece of work, mark it yourself using the criteria given for AO1 and AO2 in Table 8.4. You may find it hard to begin with, but you will be surprised how quickly you will grasp the principles. Who knows, in the not-too-distant future you may even become a psychology examiner yourself – and then it will be you deciding what mark candidates will be given!

| Table 8.4 | Marking scheme for 3-mark and 6-mark questions |

Marks for 3-mark questions	Marks for 6-mark questions	Criteria
3	6–5	Accurate and detailed (well detailed for 6-mark questions).
2	4–3	Generally accurate but less detailed. Limited.
1	2–1	Basic; lacking in detail; muddled; flawed.
0	0	Inaccurate or irrelevant.

So there you have it – now you know everything you need to know. All that is left is for you to put what you have learned in this chapter into practice. *Good luck.*

| Table 8.5 | Marking scheme for 12-mark questions |

Marks	Commentary (e.g. evaluation)	Analysis	Use of material
12–11	Informed	Thorough	Highly effective
10–9	Informed	Reasonably thorough	Effective
8–7	Reasonable	Slightly limited	Effective
6–5	Reasonable	Limited	Reasonably effective
4–3	Superficial	Rudimentary	Minimal interpretation
2–1	Just discernible	Weak and muddled	Mainly irrelevant
0	Wholly irrelevant	Wholly irrelevant	Wholly irrelevant

Chapter summary

This chapter has focused on how you should prepare for the AS exam in psychology and how to achieve your optimal grade. We have approached this by looking at 15 Exam success tips.

◆ Make sure you get hold of all the relevant materials you can. Make intelligent use of different sources of information, e.g. magazines, television/radio programmes and the Internet.

◆ Make sure you know the exact *subject content* (topics and critical issues) of the specification for

AS level – this will be what you can be examined on.

◆ Ensure that you understand the differences between AO1, AO2 and AO3. These are the *skills* you will need to demonstrate in the exam.

◆ Ensure that you understand the formula for AS questions.

◆ Be familiar with the marking criteria which your examiner will use to mark your work, and practise writing answers with these marking grids in mind.

Further resources

http://www.bps.org.uk/

British Psychological Society: the professional body regulating psychological enquiry in the UK.

http://cogprints.soton.ac.uk

Cogprints: Cognitive Sciences e-print Archive: an electronic archive for papers in any area of psychology. It provides free worldwide access to primary research literature.

http://www.york.ac.uk/inst/ctipsych/

CTI Centre for Psychology: a gateway to a wide-ranging collection of academic sites of interest to students and teachers of psychology.

http://www.cyber-psych.com

Cyber-Psych: high-quality psychological information covering many aspects of mental health.

http://psych.hanover.edu/

Hanover College Psychology Department: links to psychology sites, including on-line tutorials.

http://alabanza.com/kabacoff/Inter-Links/

Inter-Links: an Internet navigator, resource locator and tutorial. Includes a psychology resources section.

http://www.psychnet-uk.com/

PsychNet-UK: aims to enable current and up-to-date web sites to be accessed from one single access point

http://www.psywww.com/

Psych Web: large collection of psychology-related information and resources.

http://www.cop.es/database/

PsychoSearch: a search engine devoted to psychology and related fields.

http://stange.simplenet.com/psycsite

PsycSite: a launch pad providing extensive links to internet sites for the science of psychology.

http://www.psychol.ucl.ac.uk/

University of London Department of Psychology: contains a useful selection of links to psychology-related sites.

www.altavista.com

An excellent general site: simply go to the title page 'education' and then click on 'psychology'.

Answers to activities

Activity 2

Possible criteria for judging a psychological theory:

- corroboration (being supported by the findings of studies)
- consistency with other, well-accepted theories
- the extent to which it is based on very few (or no) assumptions which cannot be tested (such as Freud's belief in the unconscious mind)
- clarity (i.e. transparent and exact)
- comprehensiveness (i.e. wide-ranging, covering many aspects of psychological functioning)
- usefulness (for example, does it enhance of our understanding of human life?)
- logic (what we might technically call 'internal consistency')
- the extent to which it stimulates other good-quality research (technically, 'generativity')
- openness to testing (there should always be some 'acid' test which is capable of disproving it)
- parsimony (is it as uncomplicated as it possibly can be? There is a beauty in scientific simplicity).

Adrenocorticotropic hormone (ACTH): released by the anterior pituitary during stressful situations. ACTH, in turn, triggers the release of corticosteroids (another type of hormone). Corticosteroids produce many of the effects of the stress response.

Agency theory: theory developed by Milgram to explain why people obey orders that go against conscience. When people see themselves as mere agents of another person, they will obey that person's orders, feeling themselves free of individual responsibility.

Aims: when used in the context of psychological investigations, this refers to the general investigative purpose of the study.

Analyse/Critically analyse: show understanding by examining the different components of a topic area.

Anorexia nervosa: (literally, a nervous loss of appetite) a disorder characterized by the pursuit of extreme thinness and by an extreme loss of weight.

Anticonformity: refers to behaviour carried out in order to oppose the norms of the group.

AO1 (Assessment Objective 1): the demonstration of knowledge and understanding through clear and effective communication.

AO2 (Assessment Objective 2): analysis and evaluation.

AO3 (Assessment Objective 3): design, conduct and report.

Applications: actual or possible ways of using psychological knowledge in an applied or practical setting.

Assess/Critically assess: a considered appraisal of an area through a review of the strengths and weaknesses of the information presented.

Attachment: this refers to the result of a bonding process between two individuals (usually the mother and her offspring), characterized by mutual involvement and the desire to remain close to each other.

Autokinetic effect: an optical illusion experienced when a person in a totally dark room sees a stationary spot of light appearing to move.

Autonomic nervous system (ANS): part of the nervous system that maintains the normal functioning of the body's inner environment. The ANS has two subdivisions: (a) the *sympathetic division* whose activity mobilizes energy resources and prepares the body for action, and (b) the *parasympathetic division* whose activity tends to conserve the body's energy resources and restore inner calm.

Bar chart: a way of graphically representing scores on a discrete variable such as the number of cats in the UK belonging to different breeds.

Behaviour therapies: therapeutic techniques of changing behaviour that are based on the principles of classical conditioning. The term 'behaviour modification' is more usually used for techniques derived from operant conditioning.

Behavioural model of abnormality: the view that abnormal behaviours are maladaptive learned responses to the environment which can be replaced by more adaptive behaviours.

Behaviourism: one of the major orientations in psychology that concentrates on overt (observable) events rather than covert (unobservable) mental processing. Behaviours are seen as being acquired through the processes of learning.

Biofeedback: a technique that provides physiological feedback to a person about some bodily process (e.g. heart rate, muscle tension) of which the person is usually unaware.

Bonding: the process whereby the young of a species form a bond with their parent(s). In the bonding process, parents also bond with their offspring and thus safeguard them from abuse or abandonment.

Buffers: term used in social influence research to refer to any aspect of a situation that protects people from having to confront the consequences of their actions.

Bulimia nervosa: characterized by secret binge eating followed by vomiting, misuse of laxatives, diuretics, excessive exercise, etc., in order to lose weight.

Cardiovascular system: consists of two parts, the heart and the blood vessels. It is a system for distributing oxygen and nutrients to the organs in the body. Heart rate, blood pressure and local blood volume are three measures of cardiovascular activity commonly used in research by psychophysiologists.

Central tendency: a single value which is representative of a set of numbers by indicating the most typical value. Three measures of central tendency are the *mean, median* and *mode*.

Chunking: combining individual letters or numbers into larger meaningful units .

Classical conditioning: a basic form of learning – the procedure whereby a neutral stimulus is paired with a stimulus that automatically produces a response. Consequently the neutral stimulus comes to elicit the response.

Cognitive development: the growth of cognitive (thinking) abilities. This may be studied by examining changes in the form and structure of children's thinking as they get older, or by looking at individual differences in the power of children's thinking as measured, e.g. by IQ tests.

Cognitive interview: an interview technique designed to be used by police investigators to help elicit accurate information from eyewitnesses.

Cognitive model of abnormality: the view that stresses the role of cognitive problems (such as illogical thought processes) in abnormal functioning.

Cognitive psychology: research field in psychology that focuses on mental processes used to acquire, store, retrieve and use knowledge.

Cognitive–behavioural therapies: techniques that involve helping clients to identify their negative, irrational thoughts and to replace these with more positive, rational ways of thinking.

Collectivistic cultures: cultures that value group loyalty, prefer group to individual decisions and where the needs of the group outweigh the concerns of the individual.

Compare and contrast: consider both the similarities and the differences between two topic areas.

Compliance: the act of publicly conforming but privately maintaining one's own views.

Concept(s): an idea or group of ideas that might be used as the basis for a psychological theory.

Confidentiality: the ethical concern that information gathered during psychological research or therapy should not be divulged to others unless otherwise agreed in advance or unless there is a legal requirement to disclose it.

Conformity: a type of social influence expressed through exposure to the views of a majority and our submission to those views.

Confounding variable: uncontrolled variable that produces an unwanted effect on the dependent variable. It obscures the effect of the independent variable.

Consent: *see* **Informed consent**

Consider/Critically consider: show knowledge and understanding of the topic area, as well as the strengths and limitations of the material presented.

Content analysis: an investigative technique where people are not studied directly but through the artefacts that they produce, e.g. the

analysis of documents, messages and verbal discourse.

Control (psychological): the sense that one can anticipate events that occur in one's environment – a feeling that one can accomplish things and is not at the mercy of forces beyond one's control. Types of control include: informational, decisional, behavioural, cognitive and retrospective.

Control group: in an experimental design, the group used as a baseline against which to compare the performance of the experimental group.

Correlation coefficient: a statistic that expresses the strength of a correlation. The closer the coefficient is to +1 or –1 the stronger the correlation (relationship).

Correlation: the degree of relatedness between two sets of scores. If two sets of scores are correlated, it enables researchers to predict (with varying degrees of certainty) the approximate value of one score if they know the value of the other. A *positive correlation* exists when high values on one variable are associated with high values on another variable. A *negative correlation* exists when high values on one variable are associated with low values on another variable.

Correlational analysis: a type of analysis used to measure the extent of relationship between variables that are thought likely to co-vary.

Cortical activity: neural activity in the cortex of the brain.

Corticosteroids: *see* **ACTH**.

Counterbalancing: an experimental technique where the sequence in which different conditions are presented is varied to overcome any effect caused by the order of presentation.

Critical period: a crucial period in a person's or animal's development when certain experiences must happen for normal development to proceed. Today it is more common to use the term *sensitive period* to describe the optimum period for certain experiences to happen.

Criticize: evaluate a topic area in terms of its strengths and weaknesses.

Cultural bias: a tendency in psychological theory and research to ignore the differences between cultures and impose understanding based on the study of one culture alone.

Cultural identity: the influence of one's culture on the development of identity. Individualist cultures stress the importance of personal achievement and independence, while collectivist cultures stress the importance of collective achievement and dependence.

Culture: the enduring attitudes and behaviours, etc., shared by a large group of people and passed on from one generation to another.

Debriefing: an ethical requirement in studies where participants are aware that they have taken part in an investigation. Debriefing is carried out after the data have been collected and involves providing information to participants and discussing their experience of the research.

Decay theory: refers to memory traces fading away with time until they can no longer be retrieved.

Defence mechanism: according to psychoanalytic theory, an unconscious strategy used to protect the ego from anxiety by falsifying, distorting or denying reality.

Define: explain what is meant by a particular term.

Demand characteristics: the tendency for experimental participants to adjust their behaviour according to their own interpretation of the aims of the experiment.

Dependent variable: in experimental investigations, this refers to the variable that it assumed to be affected by the independent variable – it is the variable measured at the end of the experimental procedure (*see also* **Independent variable**).

Deprivation: the loss of something. The term is most often used in the field of maternal deprivation, where the child is deprived of the love of the primary attachment figure.

Describe: show knowledge of a topic area.

Diagnostic and Statistical Manual (DSM): a classification, definition and description of over 200 mental health disorders which groups disorders in terms of their common features.

Directional (one-tailed) hypothesis: a predictive statement that specifies the direction of the relationship or difference that will be found in a set of results, for example that participants in one condition will perform *better* than those in another, or that a correlation will be *positive* rather than negative.

Discuss: describe and evaluate a topic area.

Displacement: occurs when material in short-term memory is pushed out by new, incoming information before it has been sufficiently processed to pass on to long-term memory.

Dissociation model of minority influence: refers to the claim that minority ideas are assimilated into the majority viewpoint without people remembering where they came from.

Distinguish between: consider the differences between two topic areas.

Dizygotic (fraternal) twins: twins that develop from different zygotes (eggs) and are no more likely to be similar than any pair of siblings.

Dual process theory: Moscovici's theory that explains minority social influence as a different psychological process to that involved in majority social influence. Majority social influence is seen as producing no more than compliance, but minority social influence is seen as causing a process of conversion.

Eating disorders: a serious disruption of healthy eating habits or appetite.

Ecological validity: the degree to which the findings from a study can be generalized beyond the context of the investigation.

Ego: according to psychoanalytic theory, the part of the personality responsible for decision making and dealing with reality.

Empirical study: almost any form of investigation where the aim is to collect some form of data based on observation or experience.

Encoding: changing sensory input into a form or code to be processed by the memory system.

Enrichment: attempts either to accelerate early learning ('hothousing') or to overcome early deprivation through the provision of compensatory education programmes.

Ethical guidelines: prescriptive guidance on the conduct of psychologists in research and practice. These represent the key issues that face psychologists in their work with humans and animals and are regularly updated by the organizations that issue them.

Ethics: a branch of philosophy that is concerned with what is right or acceptable in the pursuit of a given goal.

Evaluate/Critically evaluate: make an informed judgement as to the value of an argument, theory or piece of research.

Evidence: material that might be drawn from theories or investigations and is used to support or contradict an argument or theory.

Evolution: the change over successive generations in the genetic make-up of a particular group or species. The dominant force in this change is natural selection.

Examine: give a detailed descriptive account of a topic area.

Experiment: an investigative technique which involves the manipulation of an independent variable in order to see its effect on a dependent variable.

Experimental design: a procedure used within an experiment to control the influence of participant variables that might otherwise influence the outcome of the experiment.

Experimental group: the group of participants given the treatment whose effect is being investigated. The performance of these participants is compared with the performance of those in the control group.

Experimental validity: a measure of whether the experimental procedures actually worked, i.e. were the conclusions justified?

Experimental/alternative hypothesis: a testable statement made at the start of an investigation which serves as a prediction of events should statistical analysis dismiss the role of chance factors.

Experimenter effects: aspect of the experimenter's behaviour or characteristics that influence participants and cause them to change their behaviour as a result.

Explain: show understanding of a topic through coherent and intelligible explanation.

Eyewitness testimony: the study of the accuracy of memory following an accident or crime, and the types of errors that are commonly made in such situations.

Family systems theory: the view of the family as a set of interacting and inter-dependent parts. In family systems therapy, the therapist will meet all members of a family, point out problem interactions and help the whole family to change.

Field experiment: an experimental manipulation of an independent variable that takes place in a natural setting rather than in the more artificial setting of the laboratory.

Findings: the outcome of a research investigation.

Flashbulb memory: a detailed, vivid, long-lasting memory of a highly significant event.

Forgetting: the loss of the ability to recall or recognize something that has previously been learned.

Frequency polygon: a frequency distribution that shows the peaks of each of the class intervals.

Gender: term sometimes used to refer to the psychological characteristics of being male and female (as opposed to 'sex' which refers to purely biological characteristics). However, many psychologists use the terms interchangeably.

General Adaptation Syndrome (GAS): a model, described by Hans Selye, of how the body reacts during stressful situations. There are three stages: (a) *alarm* stage when an arousal response is activated (body prepared to expend energy, e.g. to fight or flee); (b) *resistance* stage when body is apparently coping with the stressor; (c) *exhaustion* stage if stress continues for too long – may lead to physical symptoms such as stomach ulcers.

Generalizability: the ability of researchers to offer a justifiable extension of their findings beyond the actual sample of participants used to a wider population of people.

Genetics: the part of biological science concerned with the study of heredity and the role of genes throughout one's life.

Hardiness: personality factors (control, commitment and challenge) identified by Kobasa that provide defence against negative effects of stress.

Hassles and Uplifts Scales: scales devised by Lazarus and Kanner to measure the role of minor stressful events and everyday pleasant events on health and illness.

...ram: a type of frequency ...bution chart or diagram where ...inuous data are divided into proportional intervals.

Hormones: chemicals released by the endocrine system into general circulation.

Humanistic model of abnormality: abnormality seen in terms of blocks and frustrations to an individual's self-growth and development.

Humanistic psychology: a view of human beings that sees every person as unique and possessing an innate potential for positive growth.

Humanistic therapy: a treatment where the therapist tries to see the world through the client's eyes and endeavours to encourage the client to exercise free will and decide on their own life course.

Hypothesis: a specific, testable statement that enables a researcher to predict the results of a study.

Id: according to psychoanalytic theory, the part of the personality present at birth, the mental representation of biological drives.

Ideal mental health: the basis for optimal living as described by Jahoda, comprising positive attitudes to self, self-actualization, resistance to stress, autonomy, accurate perceptions and adaptation to the environment.

Identification: (a) in the area of social influence, this refers to the process of adopting the views of a group because one wants to be with or be liked by the group. Such views may not be maintained if the group is no longer present; (b) in Freud's theory of psychosexual development, the process when the child incorporates the qualities and ideas of the parent of the same sex.

Immune system: system that protects the body against infection; a network of cells and chemicals that seek out and destroy invading particles.

Imprinting: a type of early learning where a young animal forms an attachment to another animal that is difficult to change with subsequent experience (filial imprinting) or where they learn the characteristics of their own species (or a foster species) for later courtship and mating (sexual imprinting).

In-group: a group of which one perceives oneself a member (in contrast to the out-group).

Independent behaviour: behaviour where a person resists the social influence imposed by those around them (e.g. by displaying non-conformity, or disobedience to authority).

Independent groups: a type of experimental design where participants are randomly allocated to the different conditions of the experiment.

Independent variable: in experimental investigations, this refers to the variable deliberately manipulated by the researcher in an attempt to change the performance of participants on the dependent variable.

Individualistic cultures: cultures where self-interest and individual rights are promoted, rather than the needs and interests of others.

Individuation: refers to the desire to be distinguished from others.

Information processing approach: a reference to the belief that the processing of sensory information takes place in a series of stages.

Informational social influence: occurs when we look to others for guidance about what to do or believe. Based on a desire to be right, it is the influence that occurs when one accepts information from others as evidence about reality.

Informed consent: an ethical requirement that participants or clients should have sufficient information about an experiment or therapeutic intervention to enable them to make an informed judgement about whether or not to take part.

Informed consent: see Consent.

Insights: perceptions from theories or investigations that enable us to understand or appraise a topic area.

Intelligence test: a type of assessment that purports to measure intelligence.

Intelligence: an underlying ability which enables an individual to adapt to and function effectively within a given environment.

Interference theory: refers to the process that occurs when memory traces are disrupted or obscured by other incoming information.

Internalization: a social influence process that results in a true and enduring change of views.

Interview: any face-to-face situation where one person (the interviewer) asks questions of another (the respondent).

Investigator effects: arise when a researcher's behaviour or characteristics influence the results of an investigation.

Labelling theory: the view that serious mental illness is caused by society's reactions to unusual behaviour, e.g. diagnostic labels may result in self-fulfilling prophecies, so that the labelled person comes to behave in a way that justifies the label.

Laboratory experiment: an investigative technique where the experimental manipulation of the independent variable takes place within such conditions that careful control of extraneous variables is possible.

Learned helplessness: a psychological state produced as a result of being exposed to uncontrollable events. Observed in people who give up trying to cope because previous attempts have been frustrated and led to failure.

Levels of processing: refers to Craik and Lockhart's proposal that the more deeply information is processed, the better it is remembered.

Life changes (and events): see Social Readjustment Rating Scale, Life Experiences Survey and Hassles and Uplifts Scales.

Life Experiences Survey: devised by Sarason et al., and a modified version of the SRRS, this scale provides respondents with a score for the amount of positive and negative life changes they have experienced. A high score for negative life changes is positively correlated with stress-related health problems.

Locus of control: refers to how much someone perceives that they have personal control over their lives. Individuals with an internal locus are more likely than those with an external locus to believe that they are responsible for what happens in their lives.

Long-term memory: part of memory system that holds large amounts of information for long periods of time (see also Short-term memory).

Matched participants (matched pairs): a type of experimental design where pairs of participants are matched on relevant variables and then the members of each pair allocated randomly to conditions.

Mean: the arithmetic average that is calculated by dividing the sum of all scores by the number of items or participants.

Measures of dispersion: a measurement of the spread or variability in a set of scores.

Median: the middle value in a set of scores when they are arranged in rank order.

Medical model of abnormality: a view of abnormality that sees mental disorders as being caused by abnormal physiological processes such as genetic and biochemical factors. Abnormality, according to this model, is seen as an illness or disease.

Membership group: a group of people who are members because of their *presence* in the group.

Memory: the mental processes involved in registering, storing and retrieving information.

Mental disorder: *see* **Psychological disorder**.

Methods: the different ways that research investigations can be carried out.

Minority influence: the effect when a persuasive minority exerts pressure to change the attitudes, beliefs or behaviours of the majority. Minorities are most influential when they appear consistent and principled.

Mode: the most frequently occurring score in a set of data.

Model: a term that is used synonymously with 'theory', although it may refer to something that is less elaborate or complex.

Models of memory: different explanations concerning the nature of memory and the processes involved in remembering and retrieving information.

Monotropy: an infant's tendency, according to Bowlby, to become attached to one individual. This attachment is seen as qualitatively different from subsequent attachments.

Monozygotic (identical) twins: twins that develop from the same zygote (egg) and are therefore genetically identical.

Multistore model of memory: based on the information-processing approach, the model characterizes

memory as a flow of information through a set of stages in a fixed sequence.

Natural experiment: an example of a 'quasi-experiment' where the allocation of participants to the different experimental conditions is outside the control of the investigator, but rather is manipulated fortuitously by some outside agency.

Naturalistic observation: an observational technique where behaviour is observed in its natural context without intrusion by the person doing the observing.

Non-directional (two-tailed) hypothesis: a statement made at the outset of a research study where a relationship or difference is predicted but the direction of the relationship or difference is not.

Normal distribution: a bell-shaped, continuous distribution, symmetrical about its midpoint.

Normality thesis: refers to Milgram's claim that anyone is capable of obedience to a malevolent authority, given certain circumstances.

Normative social influence: occurs when we conform because we wish to be liked by others.

Null hypothesis: a statement that attributes the results obtained within a research investigation to chance or to some other event that is not covered by the research hypothesis under test.

Obedience: a type of social influence where an individual acts according to the orders of some authority figure. It is normally assumed that without such an order the person would not have carried out that behaviour.

Object permanence: the knowledge that things that are out of sight actually still exist.

Observer reliability: a measure of consistency between observers, i.e. how much two or more observers' ratings (or codings) are in agreement.

Operant conditioning: an explanation of learning that sees the consequences of a behaviour as being of vital importance to the future appearance of that behaviour. If a behaviour is followed by a desirable consequence, it becomes more frequent; if it is followed by an undesirable consequence, it becomes less frequent.

Operation Headstart: an enrichment intervention programme set up for

preschool children in the US in the 1960s. It was designed to reverse the effects of social disadvantage.

Operationalization: the process whereby a variable is defined in terms of the steps or behaviours necessary to measure it. For example, using the behaviour 'laughing' as a measure of 'happiness' or the maximum number of digits a person can recall immediately after learning as a measure of short-term memory capacity.

Out-group: a group of which one is not a member (in contrast to the in-group).

Outline/State: offer a summary description of the topic area.

Participant reactivity: the tendency for participants in a research investigation to alter their behaviour because of the presence of the observer.

Participants: those people who are studied and contribute data in a research investigation.

Perception: the process by which we transform sensory information from the environment into the experience of objects, sounds, movement, etc.

Personality: stable psychological characteristics of a person.

Pilot study: a small-scale preliminary investigation carried out before the main study to detect any problems or ambiguities so that adjustments can be made.

Pituitary: a gland in the skull cavity just below the surface of the brain, responsible for releasing a number of hormones into the bloodstream.

Precocial species: animals that can move about, feed and generally look after themselves shortly after birth.

Privation: refers to a situation where, for example, there is a lack (rather than a loss) of an attachment.

Proactive interference: occurs when an old memory trace interferes with learning and retrieval of new information.

Protection of participants: an ethical requirement that researchers have a duty of care towards their participants. Normally, the risk of harm to participants should be no greater than they would expect to meet in ordinary life.

Psychodynamic models of abnormality: models that view

...nal behaviour as being caused ...derlying psychological forces of ...ch the individual is probably ...aware.

Psychodynamic theories: theories that emphasize change and development in the individual and where 'drive' is a central concept in the process of development.

Psychodynamic therapies: treatments that help clients to uncover past traumatic events and the conflicts that have resulted from them. These conflicts can then be resolved so that the client is able to restore an adaptive level of functioning.

Psychological abnormality: behaviour and psychological functioning that is considered different from the 'normal'. Usually called 'mental disorder'.

Psychological disorder: a term used synonymously with 'mental disorder', it refers to a level of functioning that is harmful or distressing to the individual or to those around them. Psychological disorders are usually defined and described according to some current classification system such as DSM IV.

Psychometric testing: the testing of individuals on items that have been shown to measure competence in some area of functioning, e.g. intelligence, personality or special aptitudes.

Psychopathology thesis: in social influence research the suggestion that people who commit atrocities are psychologically impaired and different to most people (in contrast to Milgram's 'normality thesis').

Psychopathology: the study of the origins and course of psychological disorders such as schizophrenia and depression.

Psychosomatic illness: an illness with physical symptoms but thought to be caused by the continual mobilization of the autonomic nervous system (ANS) under stress.

Qualitative data: information in non-numerical form, e.g. speech, written words, pictures.

Quantitative data: information in numerical form, e.g. number of students in a class, average scores on a quiz.

Quasi-experiment: a type of research that is broadly similar in approach to an experiment but in which the investigator does not directly allocate participants to the different research conditions but makes use of divisions that already exist in terms of the conditions of interest.

Questionnaire surveys: a technique, using a structured set of questions, for asking a large sample of people about their views and behaviours, etc. Questionnaire surveys may be conducted in person, by telephone, by post, etc.

Random sampling: a technique for selecting members from a population such that every member of the population has an equal chance of being chosen.

Randomization: a way of overcoming order effects by randomizing the order in which participants tackle the different conditions in an experiment.

Range: a measure of dispersion within a set of scores, this refers to the distance between the lowest and the highest score.

Rational-emotive behaviour therapy: a form of psychotherapy, based on the work of Ellis, where the therapist actively confronts clients about their irrational thinking.

Reactance: a psychological boomerang effect, causing people to do the opposite of what has been asked. Occurs when attempts to restrict freedom are made too blatantly.

Reconstructive memory: refers to Bartlett's view of memory – an imaginative construction influenced by schemas.

Reductionism: the tendency to reduce human behaviour to simpler levels of analysis, such as the effects of genes or environmental reinforcement.

Reference group: refers to a group with whom we *identify*.

Reinforcement: the process by which a response is strengthened. This can be *positive*, when a response produces a pleasant outcome or *negative* when the response leads to the removal of something unpleasant. Each outcome strengthens the response it follows.

Reliability: the degree to which a description or score is consistent over time or across different observers. If the findings of research are consistently replicable then they can be called reliable.

Repeated measures: a type of experimental design where the same participants are used in all conditions of the experiment.

Representative sample: a selected group from a target population that reflects the characteristics of the population, e.g. same proportions of people in different social classes or in different age groups.

Repression: (a) defence mechanism (unconscious process) in which a distressing memory or impulse is excluded from conscious awareness; (b) a theory of forgetting.

Research: the process of gaining knowledge, either by an examination of appropriate theories or through empirical data collection.

Retroactive interference: occurs when new information interferes with the ability to retrieve old information from memory.

Role ambiguity: with reference to the workplace, a lack of clarity about the requirements of one's work role. This sometimes results from having no clear (or contradictory) guidelines or standards of performance – a major factor contributing to work-related stress.

Scattergraph (or scattergram): a graphical representation of the correlation between two sets of measurements.

Schemas: knowledge packages built up through experience of the world. In theories of memory and thinking, the term 'schema' refers to a cognitive structure which can be used to interpret information.

Self-categorization theory: states that people are most likely to be influenced by those perceived to be like themselves (members of their in-groups).

Sensitive period: *see* **Critical period**.

Sensory memory: storage system that holds information in relatively unprocessed form for fractions of a second after the physical stimulus is no longer available.

Separation anxiety: distress shown by infants when separated from their main caregiver.

Short-term memory: system for storing information for short periods of time (*see also* **Long-term memory**).

Sociability: a child's willingness to interact with others and to seek their attention or approval.

Social class: term used to describe the broad variations in economic and social positions within a society.

Social development: refers to the growth of social behaviours, such as the ability to form attachments, develop healthy self-esteem and form appropriate relationships.

Social drift theory (hypothesis): the attempt to explain the relationship between social class and serious mental illness by proposing that those who are seriously mentally ill 'drift' down the socio-economic scale.

Social impact theory: a social influence theory proposing that influence effects depend upon the number of people exerting influence, their status and their immediacy.

Social influence: the process by which a person's attitudes, beliefs or behaviours are modified by the presence or actions of others.

Social learning theory: an explanation of the way in which people learn through observing and imitating the behaviour of others.

Social norms: the rules for behaviour established by a society.

Social Readjustment Rating Scale (SRRS): a rating scale, devised by Holmes and Rahe, that scores major life events and life changes according to their psychological impact, proposing that higher scores on the SRRS increase the chances of stress-related health breakdown.

Social releasers: social behaviours that elicit a caregiving reaction (e.g. smiling) from another person.

Social support: people and/or services one can turn to when in need. May take the form of tangible support (actual goods and services), information (e.g. advice) or emotional support (e.g. reassurance that one is cared for).

Standard deviation: a statistical measure of the variation from the mean in a set of scores.

Statistical significance: a conclusion drawn from the data collected in a research study that the results are unlikely to have been caused by chance, and can therefore be attributed to the particular relationship under study.

Statistically infrequent behaviour: behaviour that occurs rarely.

Stereotypes: a fixed and often simplistic generalization about a group or class of people. Stereotypes are frequently unflattering and may *underlie* prejudice and discrimination.

Strange situation: A laboratory-based structured observation method of assessing how securely or insecurely attached an infant is to its caregiver.

Stress reduction: techniques used by an individual to cope with stress and reduce its adverse effects.

Stress-inoculation training: a cognitive-behavioural strategy used in stress management. It has three phases: *Conceptualization* – client relives stressful event and analyses its features to achieve a more realistic understanding of the demand being made; *Skills training and practice* – to help overcome key elements causing stress; *Real-life application* – put training to test in real-life situations.

Stress: three ways of defining stress: (a) as *a response or reaction* to something in the environment; (b) as a *stimulus or stressor* – a feature of the environment that produces a 'stress' response; (c) as a *lack of fit* between the perceived demands of the environment and the perceived ability to cope with those demands. This *transactional model* of stress is the most popular among psychologists.

Stroop effect: refers to how colour name words have an interfering effect on the time taken to name the ink colours of non-matching colours.

Studies: usually these refer to empirical investigations, although in a general sense they refer to any attempt to study a person or persons (or any other organism) in order to find out something about them.

Superego: according to psycho-analytic theory, the part of the personality that acts as the conscience.

Survey: a method of obtaining information by questioning a large sample of people.

Temperament: refers to a person's typical energy level or characteristic mood. Temperament is usually viewed as a genetic predisposition because of the wide differences seen in new-borns in terms of their reactivity to stimulation and general mood.

Theory: a set of interrelated ideas or principles that can be used to explain observed phenomena.

Type A behaviour: a behaviour pattern characterized by impatience, competitiveness, constant time pressure, etc. Some correlation found between Type A behaviour and coronary heart disease.

Validity: the degree to which a test, measurement or experimental manipulation is doing the job it has been designed to do.

Variable: something that alters or can be changed.

Weapon focus: refers to the finding that eyewitnesses to a crime who see a weapon are distracted by it and less able to identify the perpetrator of the crime later on.

Westermark effect: refers to the finding that children who are reared closely together before the age of six avoid sexual relationships later.

Withdrawal from investigation: an ethical requirement of psychological research that participants have the right to withdraw at any time from the investigation.

Work overload: having too much work to do in the time available.

Working memory: a model of memory formulated by Baddeley and Hitch to replace the concept of short-term memory. It proposes a multicomponent, flexible system concerned with active processing and short-term storage of information.

References

Ainsworth, M.D.S. (1967) *Infancy in Uganda: Childcare and the Growth of Love*, Baltimore: John Hopkins University Press.

Ainsworth, M.D.S. (1972) 'The effects of maternal deprivation: a review of findings and controversy in the context of research strategy', in *Deprivation of Maternal Care: A Reassessment of its Effects*, Geneva: World Health Organisation.

Ainsworth, M.D.S. and Bell, S.M. (1970) 'Attachment, exploration, and separation: illustrated by the behavior of one-year-olds in a Strange Situation', *Child Development*, 41, pp. 49-65.

Ainsworth, M.D.S., Bell, S.M. and Stayton, D.J. (1974) 'Infant/mother attachment and social development as a product of reciprocal responsiveness to signals', in M.P.M. Richards (ed.) *The integration of the child into a social world*, Cambridge: Cambridge University Press.

American Psychiatric Association (1994) *Diagnostic and Statistical Manual of Mental Disorders* (4th edn), Washington, DC: American Psychiatric Association.

Andersson, B.-E. (1992) 'Effects of daycare on cognitive and socio-emotional competence of thirteen-year-old Swedish schoolchildren', *Child Development*, 63, pp. 20-36.

Andersson, M. (1982) 'Female choice for extreme tail length in widow bird', *Nature*, 299, pp. 818–19.

Antoni, M.H. (1987) 'Neuroendocrine influences in psychoimmunology and neoplasia', *Psychology and Health*, 1, pp. 3-24.

Arendt, H. (1963) 'Eichmann in Jerusalem: a report on the banality of evil', New York: Viking Press, cited in A.G. Miller (1986) *The Obedience Experiments*, New York: Praeger Publishers.

Aronson, E. (1999) *The Social Animal* (7th edn), New York: W.H. Freeman.

Asch, S.E. (1952) *Social Psychology*, Englewood Cliffs, NJ: Prentice Hall.

Asch, S.E. (1956) 'Studies of independence and conformity: a minority of one against a unanimous majority', *Psychological Monographs*, 70 (9).

Atkinson, R.C. and Shiffrin, R.M. (1968) 'Human memory: a proposed system and its control processes', in K.W. Spence and J.T. Spence (eds) *The Psychology of Learning and Motivation*, Vol. 2, London: Academic Press.

Attanasio, V., Andrasik, F., Burke, E.J., Blake, D.D., Kabela, E. and McCarran, M.S. (1985) 'Clinical issues in utilising biofeedback with children', *Clinical Biofeedback and Health*, 8, pp. 134-41.

Baddeley, A.D. (1966) 'Short-term memory for word sequences as a function of acoustic, semantic and formal similarity', *Quarterly Journal of Experimental Psychology*, 18, pp. 362-5.

Baddeley, A.D. (1986) *Working Memory*, Oxford: Clarendon Press.

Baddeley, A.D. (1988) 'But what the hell is it for?', in M.M. Gruneberg, P.E. Morris and R.N. Sykes (eds) *Practical Aspects of Memory: Current Research and Issues*, Vol. 1, Chichester: John Wiley & Sons.

Baddeley, A.D. (1990) *Human Memory: Theory and Practice*, Hove: Psychology Press

Baddeley, A.D. (1997) *Human Memory: Theory and Practice* (revised edition), Hove: Psychology Press.

Baddeley, A.D. (1999) *Essentials of Human Memory*, Hove: Psychology Press.

Baddeley, A.D. and Hitch, G.J. (1974) 'Working memory', in G.H. Bower (ed.) *The Psychology of Learning and Motivation*, Vol. 8, London: Academic Press.

Baddeley, A.D. and Hitch, G.J (1977) 'Recency re-examined', in S. Dornic (ed.) *Attention and Performance*, New Jersey: Erlbaum.

Baddeley, A.D., Grant, S., Wight, E. and Thomson, N. (1973) 'Imagery and visual working', in P.M.A. Rabbitt and S. Dornic (eds) *Attention and Performance V*, London: Academic Press.

Baddeley, A.D., Thomson, N. and Buchanan, M. (1975) 'Word length and the structure of short-term memory', *Journal of Verbal Learning and Verbal Behaviour*, 14, pp. 575-89.

Bahrick, H.P. (1984) 'Memory for people', in J.E. Harris and P.E. Morris (eds) *Everyday Memory, Actions and Absentmindedness*, London: Academic Press.

Bahrick, H.P. and Phelps, E. (1987) 'Retention of Spanish vocabulary over eight years', *Journal of Experimental Psychology: Learning, Memory and Cognition*, 13, pp. 344-9.

Bales, R.F. (1970) *Personality and Social Behaviour*, New York: Holt, Rinehart & Winston.

Bandura, A. (1973) *Aggression: A Social Learning Analysis*, London: Prentice Hall.

Banister, P., Burman, E., Parker, I., Taylor M. and Tindall, C. (1994) *Qualitative Methods in Psychology: A Research Guide*, Buckingham: Open University Press.

Baron, R.A. and Byrne, D. (1997) *Social Psychology* (8th edn), Boston: Allyn & Bacon.

Barrett, H. (1997) 'How young children cope with separation: toward a new conceptualization', *British Journal of Medical Psychology*, 70, pp. 339-58.

Bartlett, F.C. (1932) *Remembering*, Cambridge: Cambridge University Press.

Baumrind, D. (1964) 'Some thoughts on ethics of research after reading Milgram's "Behavioural study of obedience"', *American Psychologist*, 19, pp. 421-3.

Beck, A.T. (1963) 'Thinking and depression', *Archives of General Psychiatry*, 9, pp. 324-33.

Beck, A.T. (1991) 'Cognitive therapy: a 30-year retrospective', *American Psychologist* 46, pp. 382-9.

Bee, H. (1995) *The Developing Child* (7th edn), London: HarperCollins.

Bee, H. (1999) *The Developing Child* (9th edn), Boston: Allyn & Bacon.

Bekerian, D.A. and Bowers, J.M. (1983) 'Eye-witness testimony: were we misled?', *Journal of Experimental Psychology: Learning, Memory and Cognition*, 9, pp. 139–45.

Bekerian, D.A. and Dennett, J.L. (1993) 'The cognitive interview: reviving the issues', *Applied Cognitive Psychology*, 7, pp. 275-97.

Belsky, J. and Rovine, M. (1987) 'Temperament and attachment security in the Strange Situation: a rapprochement', *Child Development*, 58, pp. 787-95.

Bemis-Vitousek, K. and Orimoto, L. (1993) 'Cognitive-behavioural models of anorexia nervosa, bulimia nervosa and obesity', in K.S. Dobson and P.C. Kendall (eds) *Psychopathology and Cognition*, San Diego: Academic Press.

Bennett, M. (1995) 'Why don't men come to counselling? Some speculative theories', *Counselling*, 6 (4), pp. 310-13.

Berkowitz, L. (1970) 'The contagion of violence: an S-R meditational analysis of observed aggression' in W.J. Arnold and M.M. Page (eds) *Nebraska Symposium on Motivation* (Vol. 18), Lincoln: University of Nebraska Press.

Blaney, P.H. (1986) 'Affect and memory: a review', *Psychological Bulletin*, 99, pp. 229-46.

Bower, G.H and Winzenz, D. (1969) 'Groups structure, coding and memory for digit series', *Journal of Experimental Psychology*, Monograph 80 (No. 2, Pt 2), pp. 1-17.

Bowlby, J. (1944) 'Forty-four juvenile thieves: their characters and home lives', *International Journal of Psychoanalysis*, 25, pp. 107-27.

Bowlby, J. (1953, 2nd edn 1965) *Child Care and the Growth of Love*, Harmondsworth: Penguin.

Bowlby, J. (1969) *Attachment and Loss*, Vol. 1, *Attachment*, London: Hogarth Press.

Bowlby, J. (1981) 'Psychoanalysis as a natural science', *International Review of Psychoanalysis*, 8 (3), pp. 243-56.

Bowlby, J. (1988) *A Secure Base: Clinical Applications of Attachment Theory*, London: Routledge.

Bowlby, J., Ainsworth, M., Boston, M. and Rosenbluth, D. (1956) 'The effects of mother–child separation: a follow-up study', *British Journal of Medical Psychology*, 29, pp. 211-47.

Bowlby, J., Robertson, J. and Rosenbluth, D. (1952) 'A two-year-old goes to hospital', *The psychoanalytic study of the child*, VII, pp. 82-94.

Bradley, B.P. and Baddeley, A.D. (1990) 'Emotional factors in forgetting', *Psychological Medicine*, 20, pp. 351-5.

Brady, J.V., Porter, R.W., Conrad, D.G. and Mason, J.W. (1958) 'Avoidance behavior and the development of gastroduodenal ulcers', *Journal of the Experimental Analysis of Behavior*, 1, pp. 69-72.

Brandimonte, M.A., Hitch, G.J. and Bishop, D.V.M. (1992) 'Influence of short-term memory codes on visual image processing: evidence from image transformation tasks', *Journal of Experimental Psychology: Learning, Memory and Cognition*, 18, pp. 157-65.

Bransford, J.D. and Johnson, M.K. (1972) 'Contextual prerequisites for understanding; some investigations of comprehension and recall', *Journal of Verbal Learning and Verbal Behaviour*, 11, pp. 717-26.

Bransford, J.D. and Johnson, M.K. (1973) 'Considerations of some problems of comprehension', in W.G. Chase (ed.) *Visual Information Processing*, New York: Academic Press.

Bretherton, I. and Waters, E. (eds) (1985) *Growing Points in Attachment Theory and Research*, Monographs of the Society for Research in Child Development, 50 (1-2), Serial No. 209.

Brewer, W.F. and Treyens, J.C. (1981) 'Role of schemata in memory for places', *Cognitive Psychology*, 13, pp. 207–30.

Brief, A.P., Buttram, R.T., Elliott, J.D., Reizenstein, R.M. and McCline, R.L. (1995) 'Releasing the beast: a study of compliance with orders to use race as a selection criterion', *Journal of Social Issues*, 51, pp. 177-94.

British Psychological Society (1993) *Code of Conduct, Ethical Principles and Guidelines*, Leicester: BPS.

Broverman, I.K., Broverman D.M., Clarkson, F.E., Rosencrantz, P.S. and

Vogel, S.R. (1981) 'Sex role stereotypes and clinical judgements of mental health', in E. Howell and M. Bayes (eds) *Women and Mental Health*, New York: Basic Books.

Brown, A.S. (1991) 'A review of the tip-of-the-tongue experience', *Psychological Bulletin*, 109, pp. 204-33.

Brown, G.W. and Harris, T.O. (1978) *Social Origins of Depression*, London: Tavistock.

Brown, H. (1985) *People, Groups and Society*, Milton Keynes: Open University Press.

Brown, H. (1996) 'Themes in experimental research on groups from the 1930s to the 1990s', in M. Wetherell (ed.) *Identities, Groups and Social Issues*, London: Sage

Brown, J.A. (1958) 'Some tests of the decay theory of immediate memory', *Quarterly Journal of Experimental Psychology*, 10, pp. 12-21.

Brown, R. and Kulik, J. (1977) 'Flashbulb memories', *Cognition*, 5, pp. 73–99.

Bruch, H. (1979) *The Golden Cage*, New York: Vintage Books.

Bryant, B., Harris, M. and Newton, D. (1980) *Children and Minders*, London: Grant McIntyre.

Bryant, P.E. and Bradley, L. (1985) *Children's Reading Problems*, Oxford: Blackwell.

Buckhout, R. (1974) 'Eyewitness testimony', *Scientific American*, 231, (6), pp. 23-31.

Buckhout, R. and Regan, S. (1988) 'Explorations in research on the other-race effect in face recognition', in M.M. Gruneberg, P.E. Morris and R.N. Sykes (eds) *Practical Aspects of Memory*, Chichester: Wiley.

Burchinal, M., Lee, M. and Ramey, C. (1989) 'Type of day-care and preschool intellectual development in disadvantaged children', *Child Development*, 60, pp. 128-37.

Burger, J.M. (1992) *Desire for Control: Personality, Social, and Clinical Perspectives*, New York: Plenum.

Bushnell, I.W.R., Sai, F. and Mullin, J.Y. (1989) 'Neonatal recognition of the mother's face', *British Journal of Developmental Psychology*, 7, pp. 3-15.

Camras, L.A., Malatesta, C. and Izard, C. (1991) 'The development of facial expression in infancy', in R. Feldman and B. Rime (eds) *Fundamentals of Non-verbal Behavior*, Cambridge: Cambridge University Press.

Cannon, W. (1914) 'The interrelations of emotions as suggested by recent physiological researches', *American Journal of Psychology*, 25, pp. 256-63.

Cardwell, M.C. (1996) *The Complete A-Z of Psychology Handbook*, London: Hodder & Stoughton.

Carlat, D.J., Carlos, M.D., Camargo, A. Jr and Herzog, D.B. (1997) 'Eating disorders in males: a report on 135 patients', *American Journal of Psychiatry*, 154, pp. 1127-32.

Christianson, S.A. and Hubinette, B. (1993) 'Hands up! A study of witnesses' emotional reactions and memories associated with bank robberies', *Applied Cognitive Psychology*, 7, pp. 365-79.

Christie, D.F. and Ellis, H.D. (1981) 'Photofit constructions versus verbal descriptions of faces', *Journal of Applied Psychology*, 66, pp. 358-63.

Clark, D.M. and Teasdale, J.D. (1982) 'Diurnal variatons in clinical depression and accessibility of memories of positive and negative experiences', *Journal of Abnormal Psychology*, 91, pp. 87-95.

Clark, R.D. III (1994) 'A few parallels between group polarization and minority influence', in S. Moscovici, A. Mucchi-Faina and A. Maass (eds) *Minority Influence*, Chicago: Nelson Hall.

Clark, R.D. III and Maass, A. (1990) 'The effects of majority size on minority influence', *European Journal of Social Psychology*, 20, pp. 99-117.

Clarke, A.D.B. and Clarke, A.M. (1979) 'Early experience: Its limited effect upon later development', in D. Shaffer and J. Dunn (eds) *The First Year of Life*, Chichester: John Wiley.

Clarke, A.M. and Clarke, A.D.B. (1998) 'Early experience and the life path', *The Psychologist*, 11 (9), pp. 433-6.

Clarke-Stewart, K.A., Gruber, C.P. and Fitzgerald, L.M. (1994) *Children at Home and in Day Care*, Hillsdale, NJ: Erlbaum.

Clutton-Brock, T.H. and Albon, S.D. (1979) 'The roaring of red deer and the evolution of honest advertisement', *Behaviour*, 69, pp. 145–70.

Cochrane, R. (1977) 'Mental illness in immigrants to England and Wales: an analysis of mental hospital admissions, 1971', *Social Psychiatry*, 12, pp. 25-35.

Cochrane, R. (1983) *The Social Creation of Mental Illness*, London: Longman.

Cochrane, R. (1995a) 'Mental illness and the built environment',

Psychology Review, 1 (4), pp. 12-15.

Cochrane, R. (1995b) 'Women and depression', *Psychology Review*, 2 (1), pp. 20-4.

Cochrane, R. and Sashidharan, S.P. (1995) 'Mental health and ethnic minorities: a review of the literature and implications for services', Paper presented to the Birmingham and Northern Birmingham Health Trust.

Cochrane, R. and Stopes-Roe, M. (1980) 'Factors affecting the distribution of psychological symptoms in urban areas of England', *Acta Psychiatrica Scandinavica*, 61, pp. 445-60.

Cockett, M. and Tripp, J. (1994) 'Children living in disordered families', *Social Policy Research Findings*, no. 45, Joseph Rowntree Foundation.

Cohen, D. (1988) *Forgotten Millions: The Treatment of the Mentally Ill – A Global Perspective*, London: Paladin.

Cohen, G. (1993) 'Everyday memory', in G. Cohen, G. Kiss and M. LeVoi, *Memory: Current Issues* (2nd edn) Buckingham: Open University Press.

Cohen, G. (1996) *Memory in the Real World* (2nd edn), Hove: Psychology Press.

Cohen, S., Tyrrell, D.A.J. and Smith, A.P. (1993) 'Negative life events, perceived stress, negative affect, and susceptibility to the common cold', *Journal of Personality and Social Psychology*, 1993, 64, pp. 131-40.

Comer, R.J. (1997) *Abnormal Psychology*, New York: W.H. Freeman.

Connell, C.M. and Gibson, G.D. (1997) 'Racial, ethnic, and cultural differences in dementia caregiving: Review and analysis', *Gerontologist*, 37, pp. 355-64.

Conrad, R. (1964) 'Acoustic confusions in immediate memory', *British Journal of Psychology*, 55, pp. 75-84.

Constable, J.F. and Russell, D.W. (1986) 'The effect of social support and the work environment upon burnout among nurses,' *Journal of Human Stress*, 12, pp. 20-6.

Conway, M.A. (1995) *Flashbulb Memories*, Hove: Erlbaum.

Conway, M.A., Anderson, S.J., Larsen, S.F., Donnelly, C.M., McDaniel, M.A., McClelland, A.G.R. and Rawles, R.E. (1994) 'The formation of flashbulb memories', *Memory and Cognition*, 22, pp. 326–43.

Coolican, H. (1995) *Introduction to Research Methods and Statistics in Psychology*, London: Hodder & Stoughton.

Coolican, H. (1999) *Research Methods and Statistics in Psychology*, London: Hodder & Stoughton.

Cowan, N. (1995) *Attention and Memory: An Integrated Framework*, New York: Oxford University Press.

Craik, F.I.M. and Lockhart, R.S. (1972) 'Levels of processing: a framework for memory research', *Journal of Verbal Learning and Verbal Behaviour*, 11, pp. 671–84.

Craik, F.I.M. and Lockhart, R.S. (1986) 'CHARM is not enough: comments on Eich's model of cued recall', *Psychological Review*, 93, pp. 360-4.

Crutchfield, R.S. (1955) 'Conformity and character', *American Psychologist*, 10, pp. 191-8.

Curtiss, S. (1977) *Genie: A Psycholinguistic Study of a Modern-day 'Wild Child'*, London: Academic Press.

Darley, J.M. (1992) 'Social organization for the production of evil', *Psychological Inquiry*, 3 (2), pp. 199-218.

Darwin, C.J., Turvey, M.T. and Crowder, R.G. (1972) 'An auditory analogue of the Sperling partial report procedure: evidence for brief auditory storage', *Cognitive Psychology*, 3, pp. 255-67.

Daubman, K.A. (1993) 'The self-threat of receiving help: a comparison of the threat-to-self-esteem model and the threat-to-interpersonal-power model', Unpublished manuscript, Gettysburg College, Gettysburg, PA, cited in R.A. Baron and D. Byrne (1997) *Social Psychology*, Boston: Allyn & Bacon

David, B. and Turner, J.C. (1996) 'Studies in self-categorization and minority conversion: is being a member of the out-group an advantage?', *British Journal of Social Psychology*, 35 (1), pp. 179-200.

Davis, G., Ellis, H. and Shepherd J. (1978) 'Face recognition accuracy as a function of mode of representation', *Journal of Applied Psychology*, 63, pp. 180-7.

Davis, K. (1947) 'Final note on a case of extreme isolation', *American Journal of Sociology*, 52, pp. 432-7.

Davison, G.C. and Neale, J.M. (1997) *Abnormal Psychology*, New York: Wiley and Sons.

DeLongis, A., Coyne, J.C., Dakof, G., Folkman, S. and Lazarus, R.S. (1982) 'Relationship of daily hassles, uplifts, and major life events to health status', *Health Psychology*, 1, pp. 119-36.

Dennis, W. (1973) *Children of the Creche*, New York: Appleton-Century-Crofts.

Deutsch, M. and Gerard, H.B. (1955) 'A study of normative and informational influence upon individual judgement', *Journal of Abnormal and Social Psychology*, 51, pp. 629-36.

Dollard, J. and Miller, N.E. (1950) *Personality and Psychotherapy: An Analysis in terms of Learning, Thinking and Culture*, New York: McGraw-Hill.

Dyer, C. (1995) *Beginning Research in Psychology: A Practical Guide to Research Methods and Statistics*, Oxford: Blackwell.

Egeland, B. and Hiester, M. (1995) 'The long-term consequences of infant day-care and mother-infant attachment', *Child Development*, 66, pp. 474-85.

Eich, J.E. (1980) 'The cue-dependent nature of state-dependent retrieval', *Memory and Cognition*, 8, pp. 157-73.

Elicker, J., Englund, M. and Sroufe, L.A. (1992) 'Predicting peer competence and peer relationships in childhood from early parent-child relationships', in R. Parke and G. Ladd (eds) *Family–Peer Relationships: Models of Linkage*, Hillsdale, New Jersey: Erlbaum.

Ellis, A. (1958) *Rational Psychotherapy*, New York: Institute for Rational-Emotive Therapy.

Ellis, A. (1962) *Reason and Emotion in Psychotherapy*, New Jersey: Citadel.

Ellis, A. (1980) 'Discomfort anxiety: a new cognitive-behavioural construct. Part 2', *Rational Living*, 15 (1), pp. 25-30.

Ellis, A. (1993) 'Reflections on Rational-Emotive Therapy', *Journal of Consulting and Clinical Psychology*, 61 (2), pp. 199-201.

Ellis, H.D. and Shepherd, J.W. (1992) 'Face memory – theory and practice', in M.M. Grinegerg and P.E. Morris (eds) *Aspects of Memory, Vol 1: The Practical Aspects* (2nd edn), London: Routledge.

Epstein, L.C. and Lasagna, L. (1969) 'Obtaining informed consent', *Archives of Internal Medicine*, 123, pp. 682-8.

Erikson, E.H. (1963) *Childhood and Society*, New York: Norton.

Evans, P. (1990) 'Type A behaviour and coronary heart disease: when will the jury return?', *British Journal of Psychology*, 81, pp. 147-57.

Evans, P. and Edgerton, N. (1991) 'Life events and mood as predictors of the common cold', *British Journal of Medical Psychology*, 64, pp. 35-44.

Evans, P., Bristow, M., Hucklebridge, F., Clow, A. and Walters, N. (1993) 'The relationship between secretory immunity, mood and life events', *British Journal of Clinical Psychology*, 32, pp. 227-36.

Fairburn, C.G., Cooper, Z., Doll, H.A. and Welch, S.L. (1999) 'Risk factors for anorexia nervosa', *Archives of General Psychiatry*, 56, pp. 468-76.

Fernando, S. (1988) *Race and Culture in Psychiatry*, London: Croom Helm.

Fisher, R.P., Geiselman, R.E. and Amador, M. (1989) 'Field test of the cognitive interview: enhancing the recollection of actual victims and witnesses of crime', *Journal of Applied Psychology*, 74, pp. 722-7.

Flanagan, C. (1996) *Applying Psychology to Early Child Development*, London: Hodder & Stoughton.

Fleischman, E.A. and Parker, J.F. Jr (1962) 'Factors in the retention and relearning of perceptual motor skill', *Journal of Experimental Psychology*, 64, pp. 215-26.

Foster, J.J. and Parker, I. (1995) *Carrying out Investigations in Psychology: Methods and Statistics*, Leicester: BPS Books.

Foster, R.A., Libkuman, T.M., Schooler, J.W. and Loftus, E.F. (1994) 'Consequentiality and eyewitness person identification', *Applied Cognitive Psychology*, 8, pp. 107-21.

Fox, N. (1977) 'Attachment of Kibbutz infants to mother and metapelet', *Child Development*, 48, pp. 1228-39.

Frankenhaeuser, M., Dunne, E. and Lundberg, U. (1976) 'Sex differences in sympathetic-adrenal medullary reactions induced by different stressors,' *Psychopharmacology*, 47, pp. 1-5.

Freud, A. (1936) *The Ego and the Mechanisms of Defence*, London: Chatto & Windus.

Freud, A. and Dann, S. (1951) 'An experiment in group upbringing', *Psychoanalytic Study of the Child*, 6, pp. 127-6.

Freud, S. (1915-18) *Introductory Lectures on Psychoanalysis*, London: Hogarth Press.

Friedman, M. and Rosenman, R.H. (1974) *Type A Behavior and Your Heart*, New York: Knopf.

Friedman, M., Thorensen, C.E., Gill, J.J. and Ulmer, D. (1986) 'Alteration of Type A behavior and its effect on cardiac recurrences in post myocardial infarction patients: summary results of the Recurrent Coronary Prevention Project', *American Heart Journal*, 112, pp. 653-65.

Furman, C.E. and Duke, R.A. (1988) 'Effect of majority consensus on preferences for recorded orchestral and popular music', *Journal of Research in Music Education*, 36 (4), pp. 220-31.

Gallo, P.S., Smith, S. and Mumford, S. (1973) ' Effects of deceiving subjects upon experimental results', *Journal of Social Psychology*, 89, pp. 99-107.

Gamson, W.B., Fireman, B. and Rytina, S. (1982) *Encounters with Unjust Authority*, Homewood, IL: Dorsey Press.

Garner, D.M., Garfinkel, P.E., Rockert, W. and Olmsted, M.P. (1987) 'A prospective study of eating disturbances in the ballet', *Psychotherapy and Psychosomatics*, 48, pp. 170-5.

Gathercole, S.E. (1992) 'The nature and uses of working memory', in P. Morris and M. Gruneberg (eds) *Theoretical Aspects of Memory* (2nd edn), New York: Routledge.

Gathercole, S.E. and Baddeley, A.D. (1993) *Working Memory and Language*, Hove: Erlbaum.

Gauld, A. and Stephenson, G.M. (1967) 'Some experiments relating to Bartlett's theory of remembering', *British Journal of Psychology*, 58, pp. 39-50.

Geiselman, R. (1988) 'Improving eyewitness testimony through mental reinstatement of context', in G.M. Davies and D.M. Thomson (eds) *Memory in Context: Context in Memory*, Chichester: Wiley.

Geiselman, R., Fisher, R., Mackinnon, D. and Holland, H.L. (1985) 'Enhancement of eyewitness testimony with the cognitive interview', *American Journal of Psychology*, 99, pp. 385-401.

Gelder, M., Gath, D., Mayou, R. and Cowen, P. (1998) *Oxford Textbook of Psychiatry* (3rd edn), Oxford: Oxford Medical Publications/ Oxford University Press.

Glass, D. and Singer, J. (1972) *Urban Stress: Experiments on Noise and Social Stressors*, New York: Academic Press.

Godden, D. and Baddeley, A. (1975) 'Context-dependent memory in two natural environments: on land and under water', *British Journal of Psychology*, 66, pp. 325–31.

Goffman E. (1968) *Stigma: Notes on the Management of Spoiled Identity*, Harmondsworth: Penguin.

Goodey, B. (1971) *City Scene: An Exploration into the Image of Central Birmingham as Seen by Area Residents*, Research Memorandum No. 10, Birmingham: Centre for Urban and Regional Studies.

Goodwin, D.W., Powell, B., Bremer, D., Hoine, H. and Stern, J. (1969) 'Alcohol and recall: state dependent effects in man.', *Science*, 163, p. 1358.

Graesser, A.C. and Nakamura, G.V. (1982) 'The impact of a schema on comprehension and memory', in G. Bower (ed.) *The Psychology of Learning and Motivation: Advances in Research and Theory*, 16, New York: Academic Press.

Green, S. (1994) *Psychobiology*, Hove: Erlbaum.

Grossman, K., Grossman, K.E., Spangler, G., Suess, G. and Unzer, L. (1985) 'Maternal sensitivity and newborn's orientation responses', in Bretherton, I. and E. Waters (eds) *Growing Points in Attachment Theory and Research*, Monographs of the Society for Research in Child Development, 50, Serial No. 209, pp. 3-35.

Guarnaccia, P.J., Good, B.J. and Kleinman, A. (1990) 'A critical review of epidemiological studies of Puerto Rican mental health', *American Journal of Psychiatry*, 147, pp. 1449-56

Gustafson, R. (1992) 'The relationship between perceived parents' child-rearing practices, own later rationality, and own later depression', *Journal of Rational-Emotive and Cognitive Behaviour Therapy*, 10 (4), pp. 253-8.

Haaga, D.A. and Davison, G.C. (1993) 'An appraisal of Rational-Emotive Therapy', *Journal of Consulting and Clinical Psychology*, 61 (2), pp. 215-20.

Halpern, D. (1995) *More than Bricks and Mortar? Mental Health and the Planned Environment*, London: Taylor and Francis.

Harlow, H.F. and Harlow, M.K. (1962) 'Social deprivation in monkeys', *Scientific American*, 207 (5), p. 136.

Harlow, H.F. and Zimmerman, R.R. (1959) 'Affectional responses in the infant monkey', *Science*, 130, pp. 421-32.

Harris, P.R. (1985) 'Asch's data and the "Asch effect": A critical note', *British Journal of Social Psychology*, 24, pp. 229-30.

Harvey, E. (1999) 'Short-term and long-term effects of early parental employment on children of the National Longitudinal Survey of Youth', *Developmental Psychology*, 35 (2).

Hazen, N.L. and Durrett, M.E. (1982) 'Relationship of security of attachment to exploration and cognitive mapping abilities in 2-year-olds', *Developmental Psychology*, 18, pp. 751-9.

Hebb, D.O. (1949) *Organisation of Behaviour*, New York: Wiley.

Hill, A.J. and Franklin J.A. (1998) 'Mothers, daughters and dieting: investigating the transmission of weight control', *British Journal of Clinical Psychology*, 37, pp. 3-13.

Hiroto, D.S. and Seligman, M.E.P. (1975) 'Generality of learnt helplessness in man', *Journal of Personality and Social Psychology*, 31, pp. 311-27.

Hodges, J. and Tizard, B. (1989) 'Social and family relationships of ex-institutional adolescents', *Journal of Child Psychology and Psychiatry*, 30 (1), pp. 77-97.

Hofling, C.K., Brotzman, E., Dalrymple, S., Graves, N. and Pierce, C.M. (1966) 'An experimental study in nurse-physician relationships', *Journal of Nervous and Mental Disease*, 143, pp. 171-80.

Hogg, M.A. and Vaughan, G.M. (1995) *Social Psychology: An Introduction*, Hemel Hempstead: Prentice Hall/Harvester Wheatsheaf.

Hogg, M.P., Nadler, R.D., Hoff, K.T. and Maple, T.L. (1994) 'Separation and depression in infant gorillas', *Developmental Psychobiology*, 27 (7), pp. 439-52.

Holland, A.J., Hall, D.J., Murrey, R., Russell, G.F.M. and Crisp, A.H. (1984) 'Anorexia Nervosa: A study of 34 twin pairs and one set of triplets', *British Journal of Psychiatry*, 145, pp. 414-18.

Holmes, D.S. (1990) 'The evidence for repression: an examination of sixty years of research', in J. Singer (ed.) *Repression and Dissociation: Implications for Personality Theory, Psychopathology and Health*, Chicago: University of Chicago Press.

Holmes, D.S. (1993) 'Aerobic fitness and the response to psychological stress' in P. Seraganian (ed.) *Exercise Psychology: The Influence of Physical Exercise on Psychological Processes*, New York: Wiley.

Holmes, J. (1993) *John Bowlby and Attachment Theory*, London: Routledge.

Holmes, T.H. and Rahe, R.H. (1967) 'The social readjustment rating scale', *Journal of Psychosomatic Research*, 11, pp. 213–18.

Howell, E. (1981) 'The influence of gender on diagnosis and psychopathology', in E. Howell and M. Bayes (eds) *Women and Mental Health*, New York: Basic Books.

Howes, C. and Hamilton, C.E. (1992) 'Children's relationships with caregivers: Mothers and child care teachers', *Child Development*, 63 (4), pp. 859-66.

Howes, C., Galinsky, E. and Kontos, S. (1998) 'Caregiver sensitivity and attachment', *Social Development*, 7 (1), pp. 25-36.

Howes, C., Matheson, C.C. and Hamilton, C.E. (1994) 'Maternal, teacher, and child care correlates of children's relationships with peers', *Child Development*, 65 (1), pp. 264-73.

Hsu, I.K.G. (1990) *Eating Disorders*, New York: Guildford Press.

Hunt, R.R. and Elliott, J.M. (1980) 'The role of non-semantic information in memory: orthographic distinctiveness on retention', *Journal of Experimental Psychology: General*, 109, pp. 49-74.

Hunter, M., Philips, C. and Rachman, S. (1979) 'Memory for pain', *Pain*, 6, pp. 35-46.

Hyde, T.S. and Jenkins, J.J. (1973) 'Recall for words as a function of semantic, graphic and syntactic orienting tasks', *Journal of Verbal Learning and Verbal Behaviour*, 12, pp. 471–80.

Immelmann, K. (1972) 'Sexual and other long-term aspects of imprinting in birds and other species', in D.S. Lehrmann, R.A. Hinde and E. Shaw (eds) *Advances in the study of behaviour, Vol. 4*, New York: Academic Press.

Ineichen, B., Harrison, G. and Morgan, H.G. (1984) 'Psychiatric hospital admissions in Bristol: 1. Geographical and ethnic factors', *British Journal of Psychiatry*, 145, pp. 600-4.

Insko, C.A., Drenan, S., Soloman, M.R., Smith, R. and Wade, T.J. (1983) 'Conformity as a function of the consistency of positive self-evaluation and being liked and being right', *Journal of Experimental Social Psychology*, 19, pp. 341-58.

Insko, C.A., Smith, R.H., Alicke, M.D., Wade, J. and Taylor, S. (1985) 'Conformity and group size: the concern with being right and the concern with being liked', *Personality and Social Psychology Bulletin*, 11 (1), pp. 41-50.

Isabella, R.A., Belsky, J. and Von Eye, A. (1989) 'Origins of infant–mother attachment: an examination of interactional synchrony during the infant's first year', *Developmental Psychology*, 25, pp. 12-21.

Jahoda, M. (1958) *Current Concepts of Positive Mental Health*, New York: Basic Books Inc.

Jennings, G., Nelson, L., Nestel, P., Esler, M., Korner, P., Burton, D. and Bazelmans, J. (1986) 'The effects of changes in physical activity on major cardiovascular risk factors, hemodynamics, sympathetic function, and glucose utilization in man: a controlled study of four levels of activity', *Circulation*, 73, pp. 30-40.

Jimerson, D.C., Wolfe, B.E., Metzger, E.D., Finkelstein, D.M., Cooper, T.B. and Levine, J.M. (1997) 'Decreased seratonin function in bulimia nervosa', *Archives of General Psychiatry*, 54. pp. 529-33.

Johansson, G., Aronsson, G. and Linstrom, B.O. (1978) 'Social psychological and neuroendocrine stress reactions in highly mechanised work', *Ergonomics*, 21, pp. 583-99.

Johnstone, L. (1989) *Users and Abusers of Psychiatry: A Critical Look at Traditional Psychiatric Practice*, London: Routledge.

Joiner, T.E. Jr, Heatherton, T.F. and Keel, P.K. (1997) 'Ten-year stability and predictive validity of five bulimia-related indicators', *American Journal of Psychiatry*, 154, pp. 1133-8.

Jones, D.N., Pickett, J., Oates, M.R. and Barbor, P. (1987) *Understanding Child Abuse* (2nd edn), London: Macmillan.

Kagan, J. (1982) *Psychology Research on the Human Infant: An Evaluative Summary*, New York: W.T. Grant Foundation.

Kagan, J., Kearsley, R.B. and Zelazo, P.R. (1980) *Infancy: Its Place in Human Development*, Cambridge, MA: Harvard University Press.

Kamarck, T.W., Peterman, A.H. and Raynor, D.A. (1998) 'The effects of the social environment on stress-related cardiovascular activation: current findings, prospects, and implications', *Annals of Behavioral Medicine*, 20, pp. 247-56.

Kamen, L.P. and Seligman, M.E.P. (1989) 'Explanatory style and health', in M. Johnston and T. Martineau (eds) *Applications in Health Psychology*, New Brunswick: Transaction.

Kanner, A.D., Coyne, J.C., Schaefer, C. and Lazarus, R.S. (1981) 'Comparison of two modes of stress measurement: daily hassles and uplifts versus major life events', *Journal of Behavioural Measurement*, 4, pp. 1-39.

Kawamura, S. (1963) 'The process of sub-culture propagation among Japanese macaques', in C.H. Southwick (ed.) *Primate Social Behaviour*, New York: Van Nostrand, pp. 82-90.

Keesey, R.E. and Corbett, S.W. (1983) 'Metabolic defence of the body weight set-point', in A.J. Stunkard and E. Stellar (eds) *Eating and Its Disorders*, New York: Raven Press.

Kelman, H.C. (1958) 'Compliance, identification and internalisation: three processes of attitude change', *Journal of Conflict Resolution*, 2, pp. 51-60.

Kendler, K.S., McLean, C., Neale, M., Kessler, R., Heath, A. and Eaves, L. (1991) 'The genetic epidemiology of bulimia nervosa', *American Journal of Psychiatry*, 148, pp. 1627-37.

Kessler, R.C., McGonagle, K.A., Zhao, S., Nelson, C.B., Highes, M., Eshleman, S., Wittchen, H.U. and Kendler, K.S. (1994) 'Lifetime and 12-month prevalence of DSM-III-R psychiatric disorders in the United States', *Archives of General Psychiatry*, 51, pp. 8-19.

Kiecolt-Glaser, J.K., Fisher, L.D., Ogrocki, P., Stout, J.C., Speicher, C.E. and Glaser, R. (1987) 'Marital quality, marital disruption, and immune function', *Psychosomatic Medicine*, 49, pp. 13-34.

Kiecolt-Glaser, J.K., Garner, W., Speicher, C., Penn, G.M., Holliday, J. and Glaser, R. (1984) 'Psychosocial modifiers of immunocompetence in medical students', *Psychosomatic Medicine*, 46, pp. 7-14.

Kiecolt-Glaser, J.K., Glaser, R., Cacioppo, J.T. and Malarkey, W.B. (1998) 'Marital stress: immunologic, neuroendocrine, and autonomic correlates', *Annals of the New York Academy of Sciences*, 840, pp. 656-63.

Kilham, W. and Mann, L. (1974) 'Level of destructive obedience as a function of transmitter and executant roles in the Milgram obedience paradigm', *Journal of Personality and Social Psychology*, 29, pp. 696-702.

Kim, H.K. and McKenry, P.C. (1998) 'Social networks and support: A comparison of African Americans, Asian Americans, Caucasians, and Hispanics', *Journal of Comparative Family Studies*, 29, pp. 313-36.

Kintsch, W. and Buschke, H. (1969) 'Homophones and synonyms in short-term memory', *Journal of Experimental Psychology*, 80, pp. 403-7.

Klaus, M.H. and Kennell, J.H. (1976) *Parent–Infant Bonding*, St Louis: Mosby.

Kline, P. (1988) *Psychology Exposed, or, The Emperor's New Clothes*, London: Routledge.

Knight, R. and Knight, M. (1959) *A Modern Introduction to Psychology*, London: University Tutorial Press.

Kobasa, S.C. and Maddi, S.R. (1977) 'Existential personality theory', in R. Corsini (ed.) *Current Personality Theories*, Itasca: Peacock.

Kobasa, S.C., Maddi, S.R., Puccetti, M.C. and Zola, M.A. (1985) 'Effectiveness of hardiness, exercise and social support as resources against illness', *Journal of Psychosomatic Research*, 29, pp. 525-33.

Kohlberg, L. (1969) 'Stage and sequence: the cognitive-developmental approach to socialization', in D.A. Goslin (ed.), *Handbook of Socialization Theory and Research*, Chicago: Rand McNally.

Koluchová, J. (1976) 'A report on the further development of twins after severe and prolonged deprivation', in A.M. Clarke and A.D.B. Clarke (eds) *Early Experience Myth and Evidence*, London: Open Books.

Koriat, A. and Goldsmith, M. (1996) 'Memory metaphors and the real life/laboratory controversy: correspondence versus storehouse conceptions of memory', *Behavioural and Brain Sciences*, 19, pp. 167-228.

Kübler-Ross, E. (1969) *On Death and Dying*, New York: Macmillan.

Kulik, J.A. and Mahler, H.I.M. (1989) 'Social support and recovery from surgery', *Health Psychology*, 8, pp. 221-38.

Lamb, M.E. (1977) 'The development of mother–infant and father–infant attachments in the second year of life', *Developmental Psychology*, 13, pp. 637-48.

Lamb, M.E. (1981) 'The development of father-infant relationships', in M.E. Lamb (ed.) *The Role of the Father in Child Development*, New York: Wiley.

Lambe, E.K., Katzman, D.K., Mikulis, D.J., Kennedy, S.H. and Zipursky, R.B. (1997) 'Cerebral gray matter volume deficits after weight recovery from anorexia nervosa', *Archives of General Psychiatry*, 54, pp. 537-42.

Langner, T.S. and Michael, S.T. (1962) *Life Stresses and Mental Health: The Midtown Study*, Illinois: Free Press.

Larsen, K.S. (1974) 'Conformity in the Asch experiment', *Journal of Social Psychology*, 94, pp. 303-4.

Latane, B. (1981) 'The psychology of social impact', *American Psychologist*, 36, pp. 343-56.

Lazar, I. and Darlington, R. (1982) *Lasting Effects of Early Education: A Report from the Consortium of Longitudinal Studies*, Monographs of the Society for Research in Child Development, 47 (2-3), Serial No. 195.

LeBon, G. (1947, first published 1895) *The Crowd: A Study of the Popular Mind*, London: Ernest Benn.

Levinger, G. and Clark, J. (1961) 'Emotional factors in the forgetting of word associations', *Journal of Abnormal and Social Psychology*, 62, pp. 99-105.

Lichstein, K.L. (1988) *Clinical Relaxation Strategies*, New York: Wiley.

Lifton, R.J. (1986) *The Nazi Doctors: Medical Killing and the Psychology of Genocide*, New York: Basic.

Lindsay, D.S. (1990) Misleading suggestions can impair eyewitnesses' ability to remember event details', *Journal of Experimental Psychology: Learning, Memory and Cognition*, 16, pp. 1077-83.

List, J.A. (1986) 'Age and schematic differences in reliability of eyewitness testimony', *Developmental Psychology*, 22, pp. 50-57.

Lock, A.J. (1980) *The Guided Reinvention Of Language*, London: Academic Press.

Loftus, E.F. (1975) 'Leading questions and the eyewitness report', *Cognitive Psychology*, 7, pp. 560-72.

Loftus, E.F. (1979) 'Reactions to blatantly contradictory information', *Memory and Cognition*, 7, pp. 368–74.

Loftus, E.F. (1997) 'Creating false memories', *Scientific American*, September, pp. 50-5.

Loftus, E.F. and Ketcham, K. (1991) *Witness for the Defence*, New York: St Martin's Press.

Loftus, E.F. and Loftus, G.R. (1980) 'On the permanence of stored information in the human brain', *American Psychologist*, 35, pp. 409-20.

Loftus, E.F. and Palmer, J.C. (1974) 'Reconstruction of automobile destruction: an example of the interaction between language and memory', *Journal of Verbal Learning and Verbal Behaviour*, 13, pp. 585-9.

Loftus, E.F., Miller, D.G. and Burns, H.J. (1978) 'Semantic integration of verbal information into a visual memory', *Journal of Experimental Psychology: Human Learning and Memory*, 4, pp. 19–31.

Lorenz, K. (1937) 'The companion in the bird's world', *Auk*, 54, pp. 245-73.

Lorenz, K. (1952) *King Solomon's Ring: New Light on Animal Ways*, London: Methuen & Co.

Lovell, D.M., Williams, J.M.G. and Hill, A.B. (1997) 'Selective processing of shape-related words in women with eating disorders and those who have recovered', *British Journal of Clinical Psychology*, 36, pp. 421-32.

Lynch, K. (1960) *The Image of the City*, Cambridge, MA: MIT Press.

McBurney, D.H. (1983) *Experimental Psychology*, Belmont, California: Wadsworth.

McCloskey, M., Wible, C.G. and Cohen, N.J. (1988) 'Is there a special flashbulb memory mechanism?', *Journal of Experimental Psychology: General*, 117, pp. 171-81.

Maccoby, E.E. (1980) *Social Development: Psychological Growth and the Parent-child Relationship*, San Diego: Harcourt Brace Jovanovich.

McDermott, M. (1993) 'On cruelty, ethics and experimentation: profile of Philip G. Zimbardo', *The Psychologist*, 6 (10), pp. 456-9.

McGeoch, J.A. and MacDonald, W.T. (1931) 'Meaningful relation and retroactive inhibition', *American Journal of Psychology*, 43, pp. 579-88.

McGovern, D. and Cope, R. (1987) 'The compulsory detention of males of different ethnic groups, with special reference to offender patients', *British Journal of Psychiatry*, 150, pp. 505-12.

McKenna, S.P. and Glendon, A.I. (1985) 'Occupational first aid training: decay in cardiopulmonary resuscitation (CPR) skills', *Journal of Occupational Psychology*, 58, pp. 109-17.

McLelland, L., Mynors-Wallis, L. and Treasure, J. (1991) 'Sexual abuse, disordered personality and eating', *British Journal of Psychiatry*, 158, pp. 63-8.

Main, M. and Cassidy, J. (1988) 'Categories of response to reunion with the parent at age six: predicted from infant attachment classifications and stable over a one-month period', *Developmental Psychology*, 24, pp. 415-26.

Mantell, D.M. (1971) 'The potential for violence in Germany', *Journal of Social Issues*, 27, pp. 101-12.

Maslach, C., Santee, R.T. and Wade, C. (1987) 'Individuation, gender role and dissent: personality mediators of situational forces', *Journal of Personality and Social Psychology*, 53, pp. 1088-94.

Maslow, A.H. (1954) *Motivation and Personality*, New York: Harper & Row.

Maslow, A.H. (1968) *Toward a Psychology of Being*, New York: Van Nostrand-Reinhold.

Mason, M.K. (1942) 'Learning to speak after six and one-half years of silence', *Journal of Speech and Hearing Disorders*, 7, pp. 295-304.

Masters, J.C., Burish, T.G., Hollon, S.D. and Rimm, D.C. (1987) *Behavior Therapy: Techniques and Empirical Findings* (3rd edn), San Diego: Harcourt Brace Jovanovich.

Matas, L., Arend, R.A. and Sroufe, L.A. (1978) 'Continuity of adaptation in the second year: the relationship between quality of attachment and later competence', *Child Development*, 49, pp. 547-56.

Matthews, K. and Haynes, S. (1986) 'Type A behavior pattern and coronary disease risk', *American Journal of Epidemiology*, 123, pp. 923-7.

Maurer, D. and Maurer, C. (1989) *The World of the Newborn*, London: Viking.

Mayall, B. and Petrie, P. (1983) *Childminding and Day Nurseries: What Kind of Care?* London: Heinemann Educational Books.

Meeus, W.H.J. and Raaijmakers, Q.A.W. (1986) 'Administrative obedience: carrying out orders to use psychological-administrative violence', *European Journal of Social Psychology*, 16, pp. 311-24,

Meichenbaum, D.H. and Cameron, R. (1983) 'Stress inoculation training: toward a general paradigm for training coping skills', in D. Meichenbaum and M.E. Jarenko (eds) *Stress Reduction and Prevention*, New York: Plenum.

Meichenbaum, D.H. and Turk, D. (1982) 'Stress, coping, and disease: a cognitive-behavioral perspective', in R.W.J. Neufield (ed.) *Psychological Stress and Psychopathology*, New York: McGraw-Hill.

Melhuish, E.C. (1993) 'Behaviour measures: a measure of love? An overview of the assessment of attachment', *ACPP Review and Newsletter*, 15 (6), pp. 269-75.

Miale, F.R. and Selzer, M. (1975) *The Nuremberg Mind: The Psychology of the Nazi Leaders*, New York: Quadrangle.

Milgram, S. (1963) 'Behavioural study of obedience', *Journal of Abnormal and Social Psychology*, 67, pp. 371-8

Milgram, S. (1964) 'Issues in the study of obedience: a reply to Baumrind', *American Psychologist*, 19, pp. 848-52.

Miller, A.G. (1986) *The Obedience Experiments*, New York: Praeger Publishers.

Miller, G.A. (1956) 'The magical number seven, plus or minus two: some limits on our capacity for processing information', *Psychological Review*, 63, pp. 81-97.

Millward, L. (1998) 'Social Psychology', in M. Eysenck (ed.) *Psychology: An Integrated Approach*, Harlow: Longman.

Milner, B. (1966) 'Amnesia following operation on the temporal lobes', in C.W.M. Whitty and O.L. Zangwill (eds) *Amnesia*, London: Butterworth.

Mineka, S., Davidson, M., Cook, M. and Keir, R. (1984) 'Observational conditioning of snake fear in rhesus monkeys', *Journal of Abnormal Psychology*, 93, pp. 355-72.

Minuchin, S., Rosman, B.L. and Baker, L. (1978) *Psychosomatic Families: Anorexia Nervosa in Context*, Cambridge, MA: Harvard University Press.

Mixon, D. (1972) 'Instead of deception', *Journal of the Theory of Social Behaviour*, 2, pp. 139-77.

Mixon, D. (1979) 'Understanding shocking and puzzling conduct', in G. P. Ginsburg (ed.) *Emerging Strategies in Social Psychological Research*, New York: John Wiley.

Miyake, K., Chen, S.J. and Campos, J.J. (1985) 'Infant temperament, mother's mode of interaction, and attachment in Japan: an interim report', in I. Bretherton and E. Waters (eds) *Growing Points in Attachment Theory and Research*, Monographs of the Society for Research in Child Development, 50 (1-2), Serial No. 209.

Moos, R.H. and Swindle, R.W. Jr. (1990) 'Stressful life circumstances: concepts and measures', *Stress Medicine*, 6, pp. 171-8.

Moriarty, T. (1975) 'A nation of willing victims', *Psychology Today*, April, pp. 43-50.

Morris, W.N. and Miller, R.S. (1975) 'The effects of consensus-breaking and consensus-preempting partners on reduction of conformity', *Journal of Experimental Social Psychology*, 11, pp. 215-223.

Moscovici, S. (1980) 'Towards a theory of conversion behaviour', in L. Berkowitz (ed.) *Advances in Experimental Social Psychology*, London: Academic Press.

Moscovici, S. (1985) 'Social influence and conformity', in G. Lindzey and E. Aronson (eds) *Handbook of Social Psychology* (3rd edn), New York: Random House.

Moscovici, S., Lage, E. and Naffrechoux, M. (1969) 'Influence of a consistent minority on the responses of a majority in a colour perception task', *Sociometry*, 32, pp. 365-80.

Mugny, G. and Papastamou, S. (1980) 'When rigidity does not fail: individualization and psychologization as resistances to the diffusion of minority innovations', *European Journal of Social Psychology*, 10, pp. 43-62.

Mugny, G. and Perez, J. (1991) *The Social Psychology of Minority Influence*, Cambridge: Cambridge University Press.

Mumford, D.B., Whitehouse, A.M. and Plattes, M. (1991) 'Sociocultural correlates of eating disorders among Asian schoolgirls in Bradford', *British Journal of Psychiatry*, 158, pp. 222-8.

Murstein, B.I. (1972) 'Physical attractiveness and marital choice', *Journal of Personality and Social Psychology*, 22, pp. 8-12.

Myers, D.G. (1999) *Social Psychology* (6th edn), Boston: McGraw-Hill College.

Nail, P.R. and Van Leeuwen, M.D. (1993) 'An analysis and restructuring of the diamond model of social response', *Personality and Social Psychology Bulletin*, 19, pp. 106-16.

Nasser, M. (1986) 'Comparative study of the prevalence of abnormal eating attitudes among Arab female students of both London and Cairo universities', *Psychological Medicine*, 16, pp. 621-7.

Naveh-Benjamin, M. and Ayres, T.J. (1986) 'Digit span, reading rate, and linguistic relativity', *Quarterly Journal of Experimental Psychology*, 38, pp. 739-51.

Neisser, U. (1976) *Cognition and Reality*, San Francisco: W.H. Freeman.

Neisser, U. (1978) 'Memory: what are the important questions?', in M.M. Gruneberg, P.E. Morris and R.N. Sykes (eds) *Practical Aspects of Memory*, London: Academic Press.

Neisser, U. (1982) *Memory Observed*, San Francisco: W.H. Freeman.

Nemeth, C. (1986) 'Differential contributions of majority and minority influence', *Psychological Review*, 93, pp. 23-32.

Newcomb, T.M. (1952) 'Attitude development as a function of reference groups: the Bennington study', in G.E. Swanson, *Readings in Social Psychology*, New York: Holt, Rinehart & Winston.

Newcomb, T.M., Koenig, K.E., Flacks, R. and Warwick, D.P. (1967) *Persistence and Change: Bennington College and its Students after 25 Years*, New York: Wiley.

NICHD Early Child Care Research Network (1997) 'The effects of infant child care on infant-mother attachment security: Results of the NICHD study of early child care', *Child Development*, 68 (5), pp. 860-79.

Nicholson, N., Cole, S.G. and Rocklin, T. (1985) 'Conformity in the Asch situation: a comparison between contemporary British and US

university students', *British Journal of Social Psychology*, 24, pp. 59-63.

Orne, M.T. (1962) 'On the social psychology of the psychology experiment with particular reference to demand characteristics and their implications', *American Psychologist*, 16, pp. 776-83.

Orne, M.T. and Holland, C.C. (1968) 'On the ecological validity of laboratory deceptions', *International Journal of Psychiatry*, 6 (4), pp. 282-93.

Palmere, M., Benton, S.L., Glover, J.A. and Ronning, R. (1983) 'Elaboration and recall of main ideas in prose', *Journal of Educational Psychology*, 75, pp. 898-907.

Parke, R.D. (1981) *Fathers*, Cambridge, MA: Harvard University Press.

Parker, K.C. and Forrest, D. (1993) 'Attachment disorder: an emerging concern for school counselors', *Elementary School Guidance and Counseling*, 27 (3), pp. 209-15.

Pavlov, I.P. (1927) *Conditioned Reflexes*, Oxford: Oxford University Press.

Pavlov, I.P. (1941) *Conditioned Reflexes and Psychiatry*, New York: International Publishers.

Perez, J., Papastamou, S. and Mugny, G. (1995) 'Zeitgeist and minority influence – where is the causality? A comment on Clark (1990)', *European Journal of Social Psychology*, 25, pp. 703-10.

Perfect, T.J. and Hanley, J.R. (1992) 'The tip-of-the-tongue phenomenon: do experimenter-presented interlopers have any effect?', *Cognition*, 45, pp. 55-75.

Perrin, S. and Spencer, C. (1981) 'Independence or conformity in the Asch experiment as a reflection of cultural and situational factors', *British Journal of Social Psychology*, 20, pp. 205-9.

Peterson, L.R. and Peterson, M. (1959) 'Short-term retention of individual verbal items', *Journal of Experimental Psychology*, 58, pp. 193-8.

Piaget, J. (1954) *The Construction of Reality in the Child*, New York: Basic Books.

Pike, K.M. and Rodin, J. (1991) 'Mothers, daughters and disordered eating', *Journal of Abnormal Psychology*, 100 (2), pp. 198-204.

Quinton, D., Rutter, M. and Liddle, C. (1985) 'Institutional rearing, parenting difficulties, and marital support', *Annual Progress in Child Psychiatry and Child Development*, pp. 173-206.

Rack, P. (1982) *Race, Culture and Mental Disorder*, London: Routledge.

Rank, S.G. and Jacobson, C.K. (1977) 'Hospital nurses' compliance with medication overdose orders: a failure to replicate', *Journal of Health and Social Behaviour*, 18, pp. 188-93.

Raphael, K.G., Cloitre, M. and Dohrenwend, B.P. (1991) 'Problems of recall and misclassification with checklist methods of measuring stressful life events', *Health Psychology*, 10, pp. 62-74.

Ratcliffe-Crain, J. and Baum, A. (1990) 'Individual differences and health: Gender, coping, and stress', in H.S. Friedman (ed.) *Personality and Disease*, New York: Wiley.

Rattner, A. (1988) 'Convicted but innocent: wrongful conviction and the criminal justice system', *Law and Human Behaviour*, 2, pp. 283-93.

Reicher, S.D. (1984) 'The St Paul's riot: an explanation of the limits of crowd action in terms of a social identity model', *European Journal of Social Psychology*, 14, pp. 1–21.

Reicher, S.D. and Potter, J. (1985) 'Psychological theory as intergroup perspective: a comparative analysis of "scientific" and "lay" accounts of crowd events', *Human Relations*, 38, pp. 167–89.

Reitman, J.S. (1974) 'Without surreptitious rehearsal, information in short-term memory decays', *Journal of Verbal Learning and Verbal Behaviour*, 13, pp. 365–77.

Rhodes, G., Brennan, S.E. and Carey, S. (1987) 'Identification and ratings of caricatures: implications for mental representations of faces', *Cognitive Psychology*, 19, pp. 473-97.

Richardson, J.T.E. (1984) 'Developing the theory of working memory', *Memory and Cognition*, 12, pp. 71–83.

Robertson, J. and Bowlby, J. (1952) 'Responses of young children to separation from their mothers', *Courier Centre International l'Enfance*, 2, pp. 131-42.

Robertson, J. and Robertson, J. (1971) 'Young child in brief separation', *Psychoanalytic Study of the Child*, 26, pp. 264-315.

Robinson, J.O., Rosen, M., Revill, S.L., David, H. and Rus, G.A.D. (1980) 'Self-administered intravenous and intramuscular pethidine', *Anaesthesia*, 35, pp. 763-70.

Rogers, C.R. (1951) *Client-centred Therapy*, Boston: Houghton Mifflin.

Rosenhan, D.L. (1969) 'Some origins of concern for others', in P. Mussen, J. Langer and

M. Covington (eds), *Trends and Issues in Developmental Psychology*, New York: Holt, Rinehart & Winston.

Rosenhan, D.L. (1973) 'On being sane in insane places', *Science*, 179, pp. 250-8.

Rotter, J.B. (1966) 'Generalised expectancies for internal versus external control of reinforcement', *Psychological Monographs*, 80, pp. 1-28.

Rozanski, A., Blumenthal, J.A. and Kaplan, J. (1999) 'Impact of psychological factors on the pathogenesis of cardiovascular disease and implications for therapy', *Circulation*, 99, pp. 2192-2217.

Rutter, M. (1976) 'Parent–child separation: psychological effects on the child', in A.M. Clarke and A.D.B. Clarke (eds) *Early Experience: Myth and Evidence*, London: Open Books.

Rutter, M. (1981) *Maternal Deprivation Re-assessed* (2nd edn), Harmondsworth: Penguin.

Rutter, M., Anderson-Wood, L., Beckett, C., Bredenkamp, D., Castle, J., Dunn, J., Ehrich, K., Groothues, C., Harborne, A., Hay, D., Jewett, J., Keaveney, L., Kreppner, J., Messer, J., O'Connor, T., Quinton, D. and White, A. (1998) 'Developmental catch-up and deficit, following adoption after severe global early privation', *Journal of Child Psychology and Psychiatry*, 39, pp. 465-76.

Rymer, R. (1993) *Genie: Escape from a Silent Childhood*, London: Michael Joseph.

Sagi, A. (1990) 'Attachment theory and research from a cross-cultural perspective', *Human Development*, 33, pp. 10-22.

Saks, M.J. and Krupat, E. (1988) *Social Psychology and its Applications*, New York: Harper & Row.

Sapolsky, R.M. (1994) *Why Zebras Don't Get Ulcers*, New York: Freeman.

Sarason, I.G., Johnson, J.H. and Siegel, J.M. (1978) 'Assessing the impact of life changes: development of the Life Experiences Survey', *Journal of Consulting and Clinical Psychology*, 46, pp. 932-46.

Savin, H.B. (1973) 'Professors and psychological researchers: conflicting values in conflicting roles', *Cognition*, 2 (1), pp. 147-9.

Scarr, S. (1997) 'Why child care has little impact on most children's development', *Current Directions in Psychological Science*, 6 (5), pp. 143-8.

Schaffer, H.R. (1998) *Making Decisions about Children*, Oxford: Blackwell.

Schaffer, H.R. and Emerson, P.E. (1964) *The Development of Social Attachments in Infancy*, Monographs of the Society for Research in Child Development, 29 (3), Serial No. 94.

Schank, R. and Abelson, R. (1977) *Scripts, Plans, Goals and Understanding: An Enquiry into Human Knowledge*, New Jersey: Erlbaum.

Scheff, T.J. (1966) *Being Mentally Ill. A Sociological Theory*, Chicago: Aldine.

Schweickert, R. and Boruff, B. (1986) 'Short-term memory capacity: magic number or magic spell?', *Journal of Experimental Psychology: Learning, Memory and Cognition*, 12, pp. 419-45.

Sebrechts, M.M., Marsh, R.L. and Seamon, J.G. (1989) 'Secondary memory and very rapid forgetting', *Memory and Cognition*, 17, pp. 693-700.

Seligman, M.E.P. (1975) *Helplessness: On Depression, Development and Death*, London: W.H. Freeman.

Selye, H. (1956) *The Stress of Life*, New York: McGraw-Hill.

Shaffer, D.R. (1993) *Developmental Psychology: Childhood and Adolescence* (3rd edn), Pacific Grove, CA: Brooks/Cole.

Shallice, T. (1967) Paper presented at NATO symposium on short-term memory, Cambridge, England.

Shallice, T. and Warrington, E.K. (1970) 'Independent functioning of verbal memory stores: a neuropsychological study', *Quarterly Journal of Experimental Psychology*, 22, pp. 261–73.

Shanab, M.E. and Yahya, K.A. (1977) 'A behavioural study of obedience in children', *Journal of Personality and Social Psychology*, 35, pp. 530-6.

Shedler, J., Mayman, M. and Manis, M. (1993) 'The illusion of mental health', *American Psychologist*, 48, pp. 1117-31.

Shepher, J. (1971) 'Mate selection among second generation Kibbutz adolescents and adults', *Archives of Sexual Behaviour*, 1, pp. 293-307.

Sherif, M. (1935) *The Psychology of Social Norms*, New York: Harper & Row.

Skeels, H. (1966) 'Adult status of children with contrasting early life experiences: a follow-up study', *Monographs of Society for Research of Child Development*, 31 (3), whole issue.

Skinner, B.F. (1953) *Science and Human Behaviour*, New York: Macmillan.

Skinner, B.F. (1974) *About Behaviourism*, New York: Knopf.

Skodak, M. and Skeels, H. (1949) 'A final follow-up study of 100 adopted children', *Journal of Genetic Psychology*, 75, pp. 85-125.

Slamecka, N.J. (1960) 'Retroactive inhibition of connected discourse as a function of practice level', *Journal of Experimental Psychology*, 59, pp. 104-8.

Sluckin, W. (1965) *Imprinting and Early Experiences*, London: Methuen.

Smith, P. and Noble, R. (1987) 'Factors affecting the development of caregiver–infant relationships', in L.W. Tavecchio and M.H. van IJzendoorn (eds) *Attachment in Social Networks*, Amsterdam: North Holland.

Smith, P.B. and Bond, M.H. (1998) *Social Psychology across Cultures: Analysis and Perspectives*, Massachusetts: Allyn and Bacon.

Smith, S.M. (1979) 'Remembering in and out of context', *Journal of Experimental Psychology: Human Learning and Memory*, 5, pp. 460-71.

Snedecor, G.W. (1956) *Statistical Methods*, Iowa State University Press.

Sperling, G. (1960) 'The information available in brief visual presentations', *Psychological Monographs*, 74, pp. 1–29.

Spitz , R.A. (1945) 'Hospitalism: an inquiry into the genesis of psychiatric conditions in early childhood', in A. Freud (ed.), *The Psychoanalytic Study of the Child* (Vol. 1), New York: International Universities Press.

Spitz, R.A. and Wolf, K.M. (1946) 'Anaclitic depression', *Psychoanalytic Study of the Child*, 2, pp. 313-42.

Srole, L., Langner, T.S., Michael, S.T. and Opler, M.K. (1961) *Mental Health in the Metropolis*, New York: McGraw-Hill.

Sroufe, L.A. (1983) 'Individual papers of adaption from infancy to preschool', in M. Perlmutter (ed.) *Minnesota Symposium on Child Psychology*, Hillsdale, New Jersey: Erlbaum.

Stoney, C.M., Mathews, K.A., McDonald, R.H. and Johnson, C.A. (1990) 'Sex differences in acute stress response: lipid, lipoprotein, cardiovascular and neuroendocrine adjustments', *Psychophysiology*, 12, pp. 52-61.

Stroebe, W., Stroebe, M.S. and Abakoumkin, G. (1999) 'Does differential social support cause sex differences in bereavement outcome?', *Journal of Community and Applied Social Psychology*, 1999, 9, pp. 1-12.

Stroop, J.R. (1935) 'Studies of interference in serial verbal reactions', *Journal of Experimental Psychology*, 18, pp. 643–62.

Szasz, T. (1972) *The Manufacture of Madness*, London: Routledge & Kegan Paul.

Tapp, J.T. (1985) 'Multisystems interventions in disease', in N. Schneiderman and J.T. Tapp (eds) *Behavioral Medicine: The Biopsychosocial Approach*, Hillsdale: Erlbaum.

Thomas, L.K. (1998) 'Multicultural aspects of attachment', http://www.bereavement.demon.co.uk/lbn/attachment/lennox.html See also Thomas, L.K. (1995) 'Psychotherapy in the context of race and culture', in S. Fernando (ed.) *Mental Health in a Multi-ethnic Society*. London: Routledge.

Tizard, B. (1979) 'Language at home and at school', in C.B. Cazden and D. Harvey (eds), *Language in Early Childhood Education*, Washington, DC: National Association for the Education of Young Children.

Tizard, B. and Hodges, J. (1978) 'The effect of early institutional rearing on the development of eight-year-old children', *Journal of Child Psychology and Psychiatry*, 19, pp. 99-118.

Tizard, B. and Rees, J. (1975) 'A comparison of the effects of adoption, restoration to the natural mother, and continued institutionalisation on the cognitive development of 4-year-old children', *Child Development*, 45, pp. 92-9.

Tronick, E.Z., Morelli, G.A. and Ivey, P.K. (1992) 'The Efe forager infant and toddler's pattern of social relationships: multiple and simultaneous', *Developmental Psychology*, 28, pp. 568-77.

Tulving, E. (1966) 'Subjective organisation and effects of repetition in multi-trial free-recall learning', *Journal of Verbal Learning and Verbal Behaviour*, 5, pp. 193-7.

Tulving, E. (1983) *Elements of Episodic Memory*, Oxford: OUP.

Tulving, E. and Osler, S. (1968) 'Effectiveness of retrieval cues in memory for words', *Journal of Verbal Learning and Verbal Behaviour*, 5, pp. 381-91.

Turner, J. (1991) *Social Influence*, Milton Keynes: Open University Press.

Tyler, S.W., Hertel, P.T., McCallum, M.C. and Ellis, H.C. (1979) 'Cognitive effort and memory', *Journal of Experimental Psychology: Human Learning and Memory*, 5 (6), pp. 607-17.

Ucros, C.G. (1989) 'Mood-state dependent memory: a meta-analysis', *Cognition and Emotion*, 3, pp. 139-67.

Underwood, B.J. (1957) 'Interference and forgetting', *Psychological Review*, 64, pp. 49-60.

Valentine, T. and Bruce, V. (1986) 'The effects of distinctiveness in recognising and classifying faces', *Perception*, 15, pp. 525-36.

Van Avermaet, E. (1996) 'Social influence in small groups', in M. Hewstone, W. Stroebe, G.M. Stevenson (eds), *Introduction to Social Psychology*, Oxford: Blackwell.

Van IJzendoorn, M.H., and Kroonenberg, P.M. (1988) 'Cross-cultural patterns of attachment: a meta-analysis of the Strange Situation', *Child Development*, 59, pp. 147-56.

Vogele, C., Jarvis, A. and Cheeseman, K. (1997) 'Anger suppression, reactivity, and hypertension risk: Gender makes a difference', *Annals of Behavioral Medicine*, 19, pp. 61-9.

Wade, T., Martin, N.G. and Tiggemann, M. (1998) 'Genetic and environmental risk factors for the weight and shape concerns characteristic of bulimia nervosa', *Psychological Medicine*, 28, pp. 761-72.

Walsh, B.T., Wilson, G.T., Loeb, K.L., Devlin, M.J., Pike, K.M., Roose, S.P., Fleiss, J. and Waternaux, C. (1997) 'Medication and psychotherapy in the treatment of bulimia nervosa', *American Journal of Psychiatry*, 154, pp. 523-31.

Wartner, U.G., Grossman, K., Fremner-Bombik, I. and Guess, G.L. (1994) 'Attachment patterns in south Germany', *Child Development*, 65, pp. 1014-27.

Waters, E. (1978) 'The reliability and stability of individual differences in infant–mother attachment', *Child Development*, 49, pp. 483-94.

Watson, J.B. and Raynor, R. (1920) 'Conditioned emotional reactions', *Journal of Experimental Psychology*, 3, pp. 1-14.

Watson, S.L., Shively, C.A., Kaplan, J.R. and Line, S.W. (1998) 'Effects of chronic social separation on cardiovascular disease risk factors in female cynomolgus monkeys', *Atherosclerosis*, 137, pp. 259-66.

Waugh, N.C. and Norman, D.A. (1965) 'Primary memory',

Psychological Review, 72, pp. 89-104.

Weaver, C.A. (1993) 'Do you need a "flash" to form a flashbulb memory?', *Journal of Experimental Psychology: General*, 122 (1), pp. 39-46.

Weg, R.B. (1983) 'Changing physiology of aging', in D.S. Woodruff and J.E. Birren (eds), *Ageing: Scientific Perspectives and Social Issues*, (2nd edn), Monterey: Brooks/Cole.

Weiss, J.M. (1972) 'Influence of psychological variables on stress-induced pathology', in J. Knight and R. Porter (eds) *Physiology, Emotion and Psychosomatic Illness*, Amsterdam: Elsevier.

Westermarck, E. (1891) *The History of Human Marriage*, London: Macmillan.

Wickelgren, W.A. (1964) 'Size of rehearsal group in short-term memory', *Journal of Experimental Psychology*, 68, pp. 413-9.

Wickens, D.D. (1970) 'Encoding categories of words: an empirical approach to meaning', *Psychological Review*, 77, pp. 1-15.

Widdowson, E.M. (1951) 'Mental contentment and physical growth', *Lancet*, 1, pp. 1316-8.

Williams, J.H. (1987) *Psychology of Women* (3rd edn), London: W.W. Norton & Co.

Williams, L.M. (1992) 'Adult memories of childhood abuse: preliminary findings from a longitudinal study', *The Advisor*, 5, pp. 19-20.

Williams, R.B. (1989) *The Trusting Heart: Great News about Type A Behavior*, New York: Timesbooks.

Willis, L., Thomas, P., Garry, P.J. and Goodwin, J.S. (1987) 'A prospective study of response to stressful life events in initially healthy elders', *Journal of Gerontology*, 42, pp. 627-30.

Wood, W., Lundgren, S., Ouellete, J.A., Busceme, S. and Blackstone, T. (1994) 'Minority influence: a meta-analytic review of social influence processes', *Psychological Bulletin*, 115, pp. 323-45.

Yarmey, A.D. (1993) 'Stereotypes and recognition: memory for faces and voices of good guys and bad guys', *Applied Cognitive Psychology*, 7, pp. 419-31.

Young, A.W. and Bruce, V. (1991) 'Perceptual categories and the computation of "grandmother"', *European Journal of Cognitive Psychology*, 3, pp. 5-49.

Zimbardo, P.G. (1974) 'On "obedience to authority"', *American Psychologist*, 29, pp. 566-7.

Zimbardo, P.G., Banks, P.G., Haney, C. and Jaffe, D. (1973) 'Pirandellian prison: the mind is a formidable jailor', *New York Times Magazine*, 8 April, pp. 38-60.

Zimbardo, P.G., McDermot, M., Jansz, J. and Metaal, N. (1995) *Psychology: A European Text*, London: Harper Collins.

Index